A Coat of Many Colors

Religion in the South

John B. Boles, Series Editor

All According to God's Plan: Southern Baptist Missions and Race, 1945–1970, Alan Scot Willis

Can Somebody Shout Amen! Inside the Tents and Tabernacles of American Revivalists, Patsy Sims

Episcopalians and Race: Civil War to Civil Rights, Gardiner H. Shattuck Jr.

A Genealogy of Dissent: Southern Baptist Protest in the Twentieth Century, David Stricklin

God's Rascal: J. Frank Norris and the Beginnings of Southern Fundamentalism, Barry Hankins

The Great Revival: Beginnings of the Bible Belt, John B. Boles

Politics and Religion in the White South, Edited by Glenn Feldman

Raccoon John Smith: Frontier Kentucky's Most Famous Preacher, Elder John Sparks

The Roots of Appalachian Christianity: The Life and Legacy of Elder Shubal Stearns, Elder John Sparks

Serving Two Masters: Moravian Brethren in Germany and North Carolina, Elisabeth W. Sommer

When Slavery Was Called Freedom: Evangelicalism, Proslavery, and the Causes of the Civil War, John Patrick Daly

William Louis Poteat: A Leader in the Progressive-Era South, Randal L. Hall

A Coat of
Many Colors

Religion and Society
along the Cape Fear River
of North Carolina

WALTER H. CONSER JR.

THE UNIVERSITY PRESS OF KENTUCKY

Publication of this volume was made possible in part by a grant
from the National Endowment for the Humanities.

Scholarly publisher for the Commonwealth,
serving Bellarmine University, Berea College, Centre College of Kentucky,
Eastern Kentucky University, The Filson Historical Society, Georgetown
College, Kentucky Historical Society, Kentucky State University, Morehead State
University, Murray State University, Northern Kentucky University, Transylvania
University, University of Kentucky, University of Louisville, and Western
Kentucky University.
All rights reserved.

Editorial and Sales Offices: The University Press of Kentucky
663 South Limestone Street, Lexington, Kentucky 40508-4008
www.kentuckypress.com

Frontispiece from the author's collection.

Map by Alex Thor, with Dick Gilbreath, at the University of Kentucky
Cartography Lab.

10 09 08 07 06   5 4 3 2 1

Library of Congress Cataloging-in-Publication Data

Conser, Walter H.
  A coat of many colors : religion and society along the Cape Fear River of North
Carolina / Walter H. Conser, Jr.
      p. cm. — (Religion in the South)
  Includes bibliographical references and index.
  ISBN-13: 978-0-8131-2405-6 (hardcover : alk. paper)
  ISBN-10: 0-8131-2405-0 (hardcover : alk. paper) 1. Cape Fear River Valley
(N.C.)—Church history. 2. Religious pluralism—North Carolina—Cape Fear River
Valley. 3. Race discrimination—Religious aspects—Christianity. I. Title. II. Series.
  BR555.N78C66 2006
  200.9756'2--dc22   2006011495

This book is printed on acid-free recycled paper meeting the requirements of the
American National Standard for Permanence in Paper for Printed Library Materials.
∞ ✪
Manufactured in the United States of America.

Member of the Association of
American University Presses

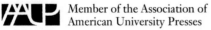

To Emily

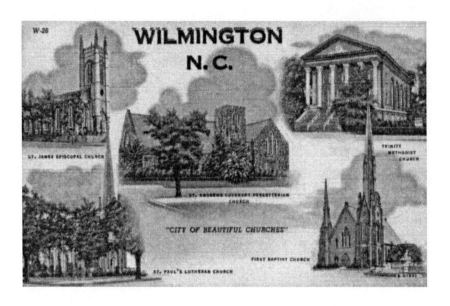

Contents

Illustrations

Acknowledgments

During the years that I worked on this book, I became indebted to many people. At my home university, my colleagues in the Department of Philosophy and Religion and the Department of History were a frequent source of encouragement. The College of Arts and Sciences awarded me a research reassignment that proved useful, and the staffs of the Special Collections and the Interlibrary Loan Service at the William Randall Library always provided excellent assistance. Tony Janson, Melton McLaurin, and Diana Pasulka read the manuscript and made many important suggestions for which I am very appreciative. Likewise, participants at conferences at the University of Wales Swansea; the Karl-Franzens Universität, Graz, Austria; and the Roosevelt Study Center, Middelburg, the Netherlands, insightfully responded to my presentations on this material. I also value the cooperation of the members and clergy of the numerous groups profiled in this volume and thank them for allowing me access to their congregations' archival materials. Similarly, I thank the Reverend Douglas Vaughan and the Session of First Presbyterian Church in Wilmington, North Carolina, for the invitation to deliver the Averette Lectures, during which discussion of some of this material occurred. Other friends, including Terry Reynolds, Beverly Tetterton, Joseph Sheppard, Ed Turberg, Janet Seapker, Adam Murray, and Bill and Betsy Simpson, gave me the benefit of their advice. Finally, my family—Walter and Eileen Conser, Janet, Megan and Jared, David and Debbie, and Emily—were always supportive as I labored on this project. I dedicate this book to Emily, my native Wilmingtonian, in celebration of her humor, warmth, and zest.

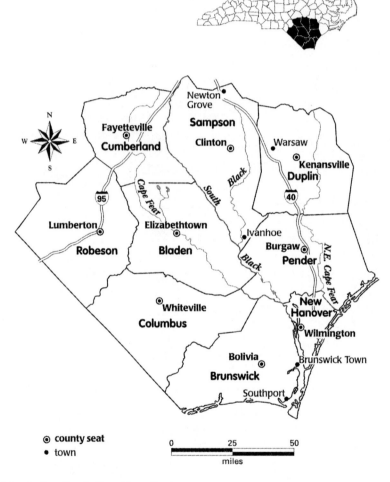

county seat
● town

0   25   50
miles

North Carolina's Cape Fear Region

Introduction

A highway traveler approaching Wilmington, North Carolina, from the west reaches a rise in the road where the city first comes into view. Within the panorama of trees, homes, and commercial buildings, one of the most striking sights is the series of steeples that punctuate the skyline. This scene should not be surprising, for there are more than 325 churches, temples, and mosques in Wilmington today. The silhouette of the city and the index of its religious organizations remind one of the prominence of religion—architecturally, socially, economically, and otherwise—in Wilmington and in the Cape Fear region, both in the past and in the present.

The Cape Fear includes the nine current counties of New Hanover, Pender, Brunswick, Columbus, Bladen, Sampson, Duplin, Robeson, and Cumberland that form the southeastern portion of North Carolina and through which the Cape Fear River and its assorted tributaries flow. Covering about 15 percent of the state's area, the Cape Fear has played and continues to play an important role in North Carolina's history. It was home initially to Native Americans whose presence dates back ten thousand years or more; European colonists moved into the Southeast in the early 1600s. Ever since its incorporation in 1739, Wilmington has served as the area's commercial and political metropolis, the center on which the periphery's products and people converged. Beyond that, from the 1840s until the 1920s and the rise of the Piedmont cities, Wilmington was the largest urban center in the state. Situated on the Cape Fear River, the harbor of Wilmington also provided the only direct access to the Atlantic Ocean among all of North Carolina's river ports.

Tethered to the political and economic fortunes of the eastern part of the state, the Cape Fear was one of the few places in North Carolina to have large-scale slave plantations; it also had one of the state's earliest and longest railroads and, as the site of blockade running and the fall of Fort Fisher, was intimately linked with the rise and defeat of the Confederate forces in the Civil War. More recently, the region's population has surged as new residents from the North flock to its beaches and suburbs, and Wilmington has been nicknamed the "Hollywood of the East" for the number of television shows and motion pictures produced there.

Against this backdrop, the story of religion in southeastern North Carolina has been largely ignored. Yet it is a fascinating history, one that can be told on at least three different levels. First, it is the story of a region with Wilmington as its symbolic center. As the metropolitan hub of the area and the largest city in the state for several decades, Wilmington attracted many immigrants who settled there and in its environs. These immigrants—whether voluntary or forced—brought their religions with them, and soon a flourishing religious life in Wilmington and throughout the region was under way. By the end of the twentieth century, religious expansion and expressions of religious diversity could be seen in all parts of the region, from Wilmington to Fayetteville, from the Lower through the Middle to the Upper Cape Fear. Wilmington, in fact, was something of a microcosm of this growth and diversity. By 2000 metropolitan Wilmington had two Jewish congregations, one of which was the oldest in the state, and two Islamic groups. A Buddhist temple and a Russian Orthodox community stood a little ways outside the city limits. The Roman Catholic presence dates back to the 1820s, and Greek Orthodox parishioners organized in the twentieth century. A multitude of Protestant faiths are evident, including Baptists and Lutherans and United Methodists, with Episcopalians, Moravians, Presbyterians, and a handful of others rounding out the roster. Religious groups that started in the United States, such as the Mormons, the Adventists, the Christian Scientists, and the Jehovah's Witnesses, also have a place here.

In a narrative that spans prehistory to the opening of the twenty-first century, it is inevitable that not every congregation in the re-

gion can be covered and that the discussion of any given congregation may not be as thorough as the store of knowledge possessed
by its members. Nevertheless, historical synthesis as represented in
this volume can illustrate patterns that congregational and denominational histories often lose. To be sure, attention will be directed
to the cadences of congregational life, the rhythms of worship, the
styles of architectural design, and the range of spiritual options that
make up the rich and detailed landscape of religion in this region.
But by addressing this terrain as a region, one can display some familiar antinomies—urban and rural, Protestant and Catholic, Christian and Jewish—and explore how these boundaries were engaged,
negotiated, and sometimes even modified. One can attend to patterns of collective identity across the region found in memory and
action. One can discern constellations of meaning found in structures such as the sacred space of burials or the civic monuments to
the Lost Cause. Finally, one can chart the persistence of issues, such
as the interaction of religion and race or religion and gender, in a
wider temporal and spatial perspective. In short, a regional examination can tell us things that exclusive attention to congregational
or denominational life may not capture.

On a second level, this history is a narrative of the American
religious experience in the South. As such, it combines themes from
the larger canvas of religion in American life and explores their
meaning in the context of this particular portion of the South. One
such theme, familiar to students of religion in America, is the move
from an establishment of religion that tolerated dissent to one of
religious liberty, albeit one that still placed specific restraints on
certain religious members of the body politic. Concomitant with
the development of religious liberty in the United States and North
Carolina was the rise of denominations as a form of the wider institution of voluntary associations. Particularly by the antebellum era,
associations devoted to moral reform had an important influence on
religious life and on the whole of American society and culture, and
this was true for the Cape Fear as well. Another theme in American
history is the religious variety (often tied to ethnicity) characteristic
of the colonial era, which was clearly found in the Cape Fear, and
its subsequent eclipse by the evangelical Protestantism of the Second Great Awakening. A third theme concerns the resurgence of
religious diversity in the late nineteenth and early twentieth centu-

ries produced by the ebb and flow of U.S. immigration policy and domestic economic opportunity. By the late twentieth century this dynamic was amplified by repercussions from the cultural polarization and the proliferation of spiritual groups associated with the baby-boom generation. Here again the experience of southeastern North Carolina, and especially Wilmington, reflected that of the nation.

That religion was significant in the region would seem self-evident to some observers. After all, this is the South, the buckle of the Bible Belt. Many commentators have noted the prevalence of religion's influence in the southern states, but they have too often depicted the region in monochromatic tones, asserting that it is powerfully Baptist and Methodist and overwhelmingly rural. Although much of the Cape Fear is rural, and Baptists and Methodists are important in its history, southeastern North Carolina provides an exception to this stereotype about southern religion. As a port city, Wilmington has always had a more urban style than its rural neighbors, and it has drawn immigrants who brought their various ethnic and religious backgrounds with them.

Yet if Wilmington and southeastern North Carolina have diverged in some areas, in terms of race, the Cape Fear has reflected the values and dilemmas of the larger South. Race has been a central factor in the religious lives of the peoples of the Cape Fear. It has shaped worship styles, architectural design, sermon topics, and personal interactions. Spatial and temporal boundaries have been drawn over (and occasionally transgressed by) race. Patterns of fellowship, images of the holy, locations of cemeteries, and the uses to which churches have been put have been molded by race, as blacks and whites in the Cape Fear fashioned their common history—both political and religious—under this prism.

The third level of this narrative is perhaps the most abstract, for the story of religion in the Cape Fear from the colonial era through the twentieth century illustrates a tension between a traditionalist and a modernist sensibility. Put another way, it discloses a turn away from the authority of hierarchy, custom, and institutions and toward self-autonomy and individual expression. The Enlightenment motif of "think for yourself" (and its corollary, "pray for yourself") contests that of the objective authority provided by bishop, church, and canon. The struggle between these sensibilities was never fully resolved; however, it was expressed in the overlay of liturgy, polity, theology, and architecture.

For example, what language should the congregation use—that of the old country (German, Hebrew, Spanish, and so forth), or the English of this new country? What liturgical styles should be employed in worship—traditional or contemporary? How far must one accommodate, or what innovations in style and practice are appropriate to the continued health of the group? Beyond these liturgical issues, the colonial opposition to the introduction of Anglican bishops (particularly strong among southern Anglican laymen) posed questions of ecclesiastical polity, but it also reflected broader sentiments about the role of any supervisory authority in this new republic. Voluntary associations, emerging powerfully in the antebellum era but characterizing the American religious experience throughout its history, were yet another example of this move toward autonomy and away from inherited structures of authority.

In its theological expression, the subjectivism found in the conversion experience of the camp meeting, in the emphasis on the democratic ethos of American versus European experience, and in the therapeutic culture of the late-twentieth-century small group movement illustrated this move away from traditional contexts of authority. Debates raged over the significance of each of these experiences; however, these conflicts between tradition and modernity simply attested to the reality of this third level in the religious life of the Cape Fear and elsewhere. Similarly, denominationalism, as the quintessential form of American religion and the religious pluralism that became increasingly common in the late twentieth century, also evidenced a distancing from legacies of established hierarchy, monarchical institutions, and legitimating custom.

In the realm of architecture, the tension between tradition and modernity is likewise visible. Here, particularly in the adoption of the many revivalist styles in nineteenth-century architecture, the tension played out in a public fashion. At one level, employment of the various revivalist modes was a local statement of progressive thinking, a recognition of broader artistic trends—in other words, an affirmation of the modern. Ironically, however, these revivalist movements in architecture traded heavily on a sentimental nostalgia that often privileged the conceptual anchors and the spiritual hopes of the traditionalist sensibility.

Consequently, although the South is often thought of as a land of conservatism in terms of politics and religion, the narrative of religion in the Cape Fear region presents unintended consequences and unresolved dilemmas as well as familiar developments. In weaving together this "coat of many colors," this study explores these regional, thematic, and conceptual levels to engage a broader set of issues relevant to the study of religion in the South and in the nation.

1

The Cape Fear and Its Indians

Although sailors make their living with attention to wind and waves, there is nothing more pleasant for transatlantic mariners than the sight of land. Such happy thoughts filled the mind of Giovanni Verrazzano as he beheld the North American coast for the first time in March 1524. Verrazzano was an Italian sailing on behalf of the French monarch Francis I, and it had taken Verrazzano and his armed and well-provisioned crew roughly fifty days to sail across the Atlantic. Though the voyage began with fair winds, within a few weeks the crew encountered a violent storm that nearly sank the ship. Their vessel was a hundred-ton royal caravel, the *Dauphine*, and Verrazzano attributed their survival to its seaworthiness, in addition to divine assistance. Shortly after setting a new westward course in the wake of the storm, Verrazzano enthusiastically announced their landfall at "a new land which had never been seen before by any man, either ancient or modern."[1]

Even if no European eyes had previously seen this land, the captain and crew soon realized that native peoples already populated it. Large bonfires on the shore, for example, were visible from onboard the *Dauphine* as it rode at anchor, and Verrazzano could see that they had been built by humans and not by the chimerical creatures that legend sometimes placed in new lands. Yet instead of going ashore, Verrazzano continued a little ways south only to turn back and anchor again in the area of his first sighting of land. This time he sent a small boat ashore to reconnoiter the land and its people. There his crewmen encountered more natives, who showed "great delight at seeing us and marveling at our clothes, appearance, and our whiteness; they showed us by various signs where we could most easily secure the boat, and offered us some of their food." The land also impressed Verrazzano, who called it a place "with many beautiful fields and plains full of great forests, some sparse and some dense; and the trees have so many colors, and are so beautiful and delightful that they defy description." Despite the amity of the Indians, this encounter with native America did not last long. Verrazzano soon called the landing party back to the ship. Like various other post-Columbian explorers, Verrazzano sought a passage to Asia and its riches. Because no such gateway was immediately apparent at this site, he needed to push on. Nevertheless, Verrazzano was sure of one thing—that his landfall had occurred at 34° north latitude—and he was glad of another—that he had not encountered any Spaniards.[2]

Over the next 150 years, other explorers would introduce North America, and specifically the Cape Fear region, to Europe. This chapter examines the complex and often conflicting perceptions of the Cape Fear that developed during this period. It also investigates the much longer presence of Native Americans in the Cape Fear region and the dynamic reality, including religious dimensions, that they represented. The Cape Fear was both exotic image and quotidian experience, a capacious land of opportunity and challenge that entices humans in the present and did so in the past.

Although some scholars scoff at Verrazzano's reckoning, most credit the relative accuracy of his calculations and the placement of his sighting of land at roughly 34° north latitude, that is, at or near the modern Cape Fear region. Yet if Verrazzano gets credit for the first European glimpse of the Cape Fear (if not on his initial landfall, then certainly when he returned from his southern detour), his was not the only sixteenth-century European encounter with what later was named the Cape Fear coast. Indeed, because the French did little to follow up on the information of this portion of Verrazzano's voyage, awareness of the Cape Fear emerged through Spanish and English explorations as well as French.

In the aftermath of Columbus's voyages into the Americas, Spanish forces quickly developed their empire in the Caribbean basin. One such venture in 1521 left Hispaniola (later the Dominican Republic) and headed for the Florida coast. Eventually, this group sailed north along the coast to 33°30' north by their own reckoning.

They then proceeded a short distance up a river they named the Jordan. The captain anchored, and the crew explored the immediate vicinity, where they encountered native peoples. Disappointed in their search for gold or other mineral wealth, they decided to leave, but not before they had enticed some seventy Indians on board. Restraining the natives, they raised anchor and set sail for home with their ill-gotten victims.[3]

Lucas Vasquez de Ayllón, justice of the supreme court in Santo Domingo and a well-connected politician and colonial entrepreneur, had helped with the arrangements for this voyage. Ayllón followed up the 1521 voyage by sending out a small expedition in 1525. Led by Pedro de Quejo, a pilot in Ayllón's employ, this group first sighted land near the present-day Savannah River and then sailed north. It is possible that they entered the Cape Fear River, but in any case, they soon left and sailed south again. By July 1525 Quejo was back in Santo Domingo with news and prizes for Ayllón.[4]

Shortly thereafter, in 1526, Ayllón set out himself to establish a Spanish colony in the area of the earlier voyages. His squadron included six ships and five hundred men, women, and children, as well as a number of Dominican friars. Upon reaching the location of the 1521 landing and sailing up the river, Ayllón's flagship ran aground and lost its cargo. Transferring to the other ships, the expedition ultimately sailed south to another location, where they broke ground for their colony of San Miguel de Gualdape. While the allusion to St. Michael the archangel is well established, the meaning of Gualdape is not known. Misfortune continued to trouble the expedition, for cold weather set in, and because word had spread about the earlier kidnapping, the native people provided no food or assistance. Many Spaniards became ill. Ayllón himself sickened and passed away on October 18, 1526, and he received a Catholic burial. Soon the remaining 150 persons abandoned the colony and returned to Santo Domingo.[5]

Franco-Spanish rivalry in the Southeast at first deterred English interest in the Carolina coast, but by the seventeenth century, that was no longer the case. Some twentieth-century scholars continue to debate whether the Rio Jordan was the Cape Fear River or whether the colony of San Miguel de Gualdape was located on that river. To late-sixteenth- and early-seventeenth-century English explorers, however, there was no doubt that the Spanish presence, wherever on the southeastern coast it might be located, posed a dangerous and jealous threat. News of the Spanish massacre of the French colonists at Fort Caroline in 1565, for example, had spread quickly to the English. In the sixteenth century Franco-Spanish antagonism was real, and Anglo-Spanish competition, symbolized by the Spanish Catholic monarch Phillip II and the English Protestant queen Elizabeth I, encompassed politics, religion, and trade. Yet with the destruction of the Spanish Armada in 1588 and changes in domestic policy and social perceptions in England, opportunities for exploration of the Carolina coastline were encouraged and slowly became a reality.[6]

On October 12, 1663, an expedition sailing out of Barbados under the command of William Hilton anchored in the Cape Fear River. Other English outposts in North America, including the settlements at Roanoke, Jamestown, and Massachusetts Bay, had been established decades before. Indeed, a year earlier, in 1662, Hilton had led another party to the same area. This group, backed by the New England Company for the Discovery of Cape Fear, hoped to purchase land from the Indians, gain title in England, and establish a colony. In his report of the 1662 voyage, Hilton described the landscape, noting the variety of trees, the verdant meadows, and the multitude of birds, fish, and deer. He suggested that the land could yield two sets of crops a year and that several towns and many farms could be accommodated in the area. Almost immediately, Hilton's description enticed a corps of New Englanders to settle on the Cape Fear. However, within months they were gone. Perhaps attacks by Indians, discouragement at the lack of economic and political support for the colony, or dissension within the group forced their departure. In any case, they abandoned the site, leaving their livestock and other supplies and renouncing the whole enterprise.[7]

Despite the failure of the New Englanders' venture, Hilton was back in the Cape Fear region in 1663. Unlike the voyage of 1662, this expedition had the support of the Lords Proprietors, the eight friends of Charles II who were given, by royal decree, the tract of land that encompassed North Carolina. Adopting the same promotional stance that he had in his first report, Hilton again wrote glowingly of the natural resources and physical beauty of the Cape Fear region. "Good tracts of land, dry, well wooded, pleasant and delightful as we have seen anywhere in the world," were matched by an "abundance of Deer and Turkies everywhere" and "a great store of Ducks." Oak trees, "all bearing Akorns very good," and especially pine trees, "tall and good for boards and masts," could be found as well. Hilton and his men traded with the local native population and enjoyed beef and pork from the cattle and hogs left by the previous New England colonists. In the conclusion of his report, Hilton took issue with the disparaging remarks from the Puritans, countering that the region possessed "as good Land, and as well Timbered, as any we have seen in any other part of the world, sufficient to accommodate thousands of our English Nation." Here in the Cape Fear was the answer to England's current problems and the bounty for a promising future.[8]

Thus, from the mid-seventeenth century and into the eighteenth, the Cape Fear entered into European consciousness under the auspices of the English. However, this awareness was an ambivalent one, in no small part due to the legacy of earlier explorations. One aspect of this ambivalence reflected the shoals, bars, and shifting sands found beneath the coastal waters and in the entrance to the river itself. This was the ensemble of grim images that gave the river its lasting name and came to encompass the adjacent region as a whole. The term *Promontorium Tremendum* (cape fear) dates back to 1526 and the map of the world by Juan Vespucci, nephew of Amerigo. In Vespucci's depiction of the Carolina coast, which is named the "new lands of Ayllón," one scholar has identified the Río de Arrecifes (river of reefs) as the historic Cape Fear River. For sixteenth- and seventeenth-century mariners, the whole coast from present-day Cape Fear through Cape Hatteras and up to the Virginia line was treacherous, and the term *Promontorium Tremendum* was applied inconsistently by mapmakers to refer to a number of different capes on a number of different maps.[9]

In 1666 a map attributed to Robert Horne was the first to use the designation "Cape Fear" for its present location. In 1672 John Ogilby published a map entitled "A New Description of Carolina by Order of the Lords Proprietors" that received wide circulation. Due to its popularity, its reaffirmation of the location of the Cape Fear as the promontory located at 33°51' north was important. In 1672 mapmaker Ogilby called the river that ran into the sea at this point the Clarendon. However, within a decade, a map printed by Joel Gascoyne fixed the name "Cape Fear" for the promontory and its river as well. By the late seventeenth century, a stable nomenclature seemed to have been established for this river and its adjacent lands.[10]

Ambivalence, however, always contains opposing energies. Another representation of the river and its region countered that of the hazardous *Promontorium Tremendum*. This was the depiction of the New World as Arcadia, an idyllic garden replete with fresh water, fertile soil, and abundant game. In his 1524 voyage Verrazzano drew on this image in the works of Virgil and sixteenth-century Italian writer Jacopo Sannazzaro when he named a portion of the southern coast Arcadia because of the grandeur of the forests.[11]

While Verrazzano was particularly impressed with the beauty of the trees, Hilton did him one better. Hilton's reports of 1662 and 1663 were designed to promote colonization of the Cape Fear region, so in his rendering, the psychological barriers and physical threats posed by the shoals and reefs were diminished, if not completely erased. Pastoral images and lists of exotic and familiar flora and fauna replaced hydrographic notations for navigating the coastal hazards. Hilton reported on oyster beds, Indian corn, and mulberry trees. Indeed, he identified more than a dozen different types of trees, including oak, cedar, walnut, and pine, and delightedly described "exceeding good land" that could be plowed without striking stones and rocks. He also surmised that tobacco would grow well here and even anticipated the successful cultivation of oranges, lemons, and pineapples.[12]

If mention of soil without rocks, board feet of timber, and crops of citrus fruits and pineapples was designed to appeal to potential colonists in New England or the Caribbean, such images were also part of a larger stylized representation of the New World. Pictorial images could match belletristic allegories from literature to form this broad narrative. Nominally a discourse of factual reporting, these representations functioned more powerfully as richly symbolic tropes that depicted a land of easy opportunity and plentiful resources. Maps are of particular interest here, for contemporary cartography not only details the physical exploration of space; it also illuminates the imaginative conceptualization of that space.

The map of the Southeast by Gerard Mercator and Jodocius Hondius in 1606 makes a clear division between the terrors of the ocean and the opportunities available on land. Mighty ships, fully rigged with billowing sails, share conceptual space with prodigious sea monsters. However, the pristine landscape is dotted with turkeys, stags, and woodlands. Native peoples, partially clad, appear at the margins and stand in as markers for primitive life. This allegorical New World lies waiting to be explored and domesticated, with untapped resources and native adversaries already displaced. The Ogilby map of 1672 continues the tradition of fantastic monsters from the deep pitted against the trim sailing vessels, in this case from England. Representations of natives show them wholly or partially naked, festooned with elaborate headdresses, and armed, albeit with primitive spears. Yet this new world of Carolina is already the arena for civilization, as tracts of land have been laid out and named, all under the jurisdiction of the Lords Proprietors. Here, pastoral Arcadia only needs the sturdy hand of the English yeoman farmer to make real this bucolic dream.[13]

Three other maps demonstrate how individuals sought to overcome the associations of *Promontorium Tremendum* and, instead, make the Carolina coast attractive. For example, the map and accompanying report attributed to Robert Horne in 1666 detailed the Cape Fear region. Sea monsters are gone, though the sailing ships remain. Particularly striking are the depictions of deer, beavers, and silkworms juxtaposed with the names of land claimants up and down the Charles (Cape Fear) River. The plotting of claims and the possession of land are further secured in another map that illustrates a solidly built fort, complete with crenellated battlements and a swallowtail flag with St. George's cross on a white field. This anonymous map, dating to the 1660s, reflects information from William Hilton's 1662 voyage to the Cape Fear. Land claims up the river are attributed to various individuals, many of whom were associated with Hilton's 1662 voyage.[14]

Although no churches appear on these maps, by the mid-seventeenth century, religion had once again received official endorsement. The results, however, were no better than before. When the Spanish Catholic Ayllón brought friars on his expedition of 1526, he probably anticipated using their services for purposes other than his own burial. Colonization of the land and Christianization of the indigenous population were already familiar themes in Spanish missionary and exploration literature. Not to be outdone, the English Protestant Lords Proprietors promised land to individuals willing to settle in Carolina. They also stipulated a hundred acres of land to the Anglican Church for each parish that it developed. Little came of these proposals, but they were a portent of future developments and an affirmation of the importance of religion in this phase of exploration and colonization.[15]

The epitome of the Arcadian vision of the Carolina coast came with the map of James Wimble published in 1738. Wimble was an early land developer and promoter of European immigration and settlement of the area. His map not only included soundings along the coast but also explicitly indicated the safe passage over the bar and up the river. Beyond that, it renamed the cape and its river "the Cape Fair." William Hilton's 1663 promotional tract had also used "Cape Fair" as the name of the river, and Wimble may have known of this earlier usage. Nevertheless, despite Wimble's energetic role in the founding of the town of Wilmington and his broader entrepreneurial efforts in developing real estate in the region, his attempt to rename the cape and its river never took hold. Thus, in the shift from Cape Fear to Cape Fair, one sees the clear attempt to remake the image of the river, to tone down the raging torrents and shifting sands of *Promontorium Tremendum* and replace them with the Arcadian representations of accessibility, fertility, and abundance. That the cape, river, and region retained the designation "Cape Fear" might appeal to the modern sensibility and its fascination with the power of the unknown. More probably, the ultimate acceptance of the name reflects the intractable reality of the shoals and reefs lying offshore and at the river's mouth and the grim toll of shipwrecks that these littoral barriers continued to take.[16]

Although Indians appear only at the conceptual margins of these maps, and the landscape seems empty, awaiting exploration and settlement by Europeans, the reality of the situation was quite another thing. In his classic study of southeastern Indians, John Swanton profiled 170 different native groups and estimated the native population by the beginning of the seventeenth century to be 171,900. More recent scholars have increased these population figures dramatically. Indians were not only on the land in appreciable numbers; they had also been there for a long time. Verrazzano may have been surprised in 1524 to see natives on the Carolina coast, but he would have been even more amazed to learn that the ancestors of these native peoples had first arrived in North Carolina sometime between 10,000 and 8000 B.C. Yet less is understood about these coastal peoples than about the Cherokees of North Carolina, for example. As James Mooney points out, the tribal name of the Cape Fear Indians is unknown, and this English name was given to them by the colonists who first lived in the Cape Fear area.[17]

Archaeologists of North Carolina employ a familiar periodization of cultural traditions for chronologically dividing this prehistoric era. These cultural traditions are the Paleo-Indian (before 8000 B.C.), Archaic (8000 to 1000 B.C.), and Woodland (1000 B.C. to A.D. 1600). These patterns of settlement and subsistence can be identified and even specified, to some degree, for the Cape Fear area. Yet in this time before history, the clues can be tantalizing and the explanations particularly tentative.[18]

When Paleo-Indians first visited the coast, they found a landscape undergoing significant changes. The Cape Fear region sits on the border of the boreal and temperate faunal zones. Deciduous forests of oak and hickory were beginning to dominate over conifers, and grasslands were increasing. Megafauna existed on the Cape Fear coast, but they would soon become extinct. Instead of relying on such game, these Paleo-Indian people probably pursued a variety of resources, including seasonally available seeds, nuts, and small mammals, as well as the occasional mastodon or giant sloth. Geological change was also apparent. The terrain of the Cape Fear lies on the Coastal Plain, that emergent portion of the seafloor over which ecosystems ranging from open sounds and chains of barrier islands to sandy and poorly drained soils developed. In 10,000 B.C. the sea stood almost ninety feet lower than it does at present. This means that the coastline at the beginning of the Paleo-Indian period was somewhere between twenty-five and forty miles farther east than it is today. By 7000 B.C., as warming trends melted glacial ice, the coastline stabilized to its current location.[19]

Not surprisingly, evidence of Paleo-Indian populations on the coast is extremely scarce. The sandy soil contains few lithic elements from which stone artifacts could be fashioned, and the rising coastline inundated settlement sites presumed to have existed. Nevertheless, the Paleo-Indian period does illustrate one important aspect of the Cape Fear throughout its prehistory: the region was a boundary area, a territory of overlapping types of flora, fauna, and native peoples. It was a zone that included the northern expression of Spanish moss and several varieties of palm trees. Fish followed the Gulf Stream as it passed the Cape Fear on its way north, and semitropical flowers and plants grew in the region as well. Yet boreal influences could be seen in the stands of hardwoods, the migration of waterfowl, and the later convergence of Siouan and Algonquian peoples. The Cape Fear region has always been less a land of sharp demarcations and more a space of blended transitions, and the Paleo-Indian period highlighted this tendency very early on.

The shift into the Archaic period was subtle but significant. Initially, archaeologists distinguished the Archaic from the Paleo-Indian period on the basis of projectile point technology and styles. Interestingly, more than twenty points from spears and arrows dating to the Archaic period have been found in present-day New Hanover County. Yet scholars now realize that other strategies for making use of resources were just as important. People in the Archaic period continued to hunt, fish, and gather wild plants and nuts. They organized in small bands, taking advantage of the increasingly stable and hospitable environment. Because their food resources did not invariably occur at the same time and place, however, Archaic peoples moved among several campsites during the course of the year. Acknowledgment of gender—that is, the social construction of sexual identity through roles, expectations, and assumptions—is appropriate here. In a subsistence economy, everyone had to work to procure enough food to survive, and traditionally, women gathered plants while men hunted game. Thus, supplying the group with wild plants, roots, berries, nuts, and seeds represented an important contribution by women to the livelihood of the group. The collection of shellfish was also an activity customarily performed by women. Thus, a form of labor often called "women's work" by later commentators was crucial to the survival of the group.[20]

One archaeological model for this nomadic foraging depicts Archaic peoples ranging over entire drainage basins, such as that of the Cape Fear River. During the winter such bands would occupy stable camps in the Piedmont, where they would hunt animals and collect other food resources. In the spring the bands would disperse and move down the river basins to the coast to take advantage of estuarine resources and ripening plant foods. Late spring and early summer could be particularly lean times, as fruiting plants were just blooming and animals could be scarce. Yet here again, the resources of the coastline—clams, oysters, and fish—could stave off starvation. Finally, in the late summer and early fall, the bands would return up the river basin to the Piedmont. Such a model of resource exploitation involves a degree of speculation; however, it underscores the reality of rivers such as the Cape Fear, which could facilitate travel and later trade from the Piedmont to the coast and vice versa. It also reminds one that these same rivers acted as barriers to east-west travel; thus the Indians of the Cape Fear region were more likely to have had contact with bands in South Carolina than with those in Virginia. And it recognizes that by the late Archaic period, because of the food resources at hand, more sedentary coastal settlements were evident, heralding the efflorescence of the Woodland period.[21]

Several important developments characterized the Woodland period generally and the Cape Fear region more specifically. While hunting, gathering, and other Archaic forms of food collection continued, agriculture was introduced. Corn, squash, and beans became obtainable, and by late in this period, a shift toward gardening was apparent, with an emphasis on the domestication of plants. Beyond that, new tools such as the shell hoe came into use. The cultivation and domestication of foods such as corn represented an important advance over foraging for wild plants. Besides expanding the strategies for land use and food collection, it also made larger and more permanent settlements possible. Women's familiarity with plants and their experience in gathering and preparing them probably meant that women played an important role in their domestication. Years of observation had taught women which species flourished, and this knowledge could be applied to the deliberate planting, cultivating, and harvesting of plants—in other words, the purposeful domestication of food. In any case, the gendered division of labor brought plants into women's domain, and both the procurement of wild plants and the cultivation of domestic plants, as well as their eventual preparation, were female duties.[22]

Another salient feature of the Woodland period was the appearance of pottery and the development of trade networks to exchange a variety of familiar and exotic items. Pottery styles have been used by archaeologists to construct chronological patterns within the Woodland period. On the basis of various cultural traits (including pottery) and physiological evidence, archaeologists divide the Coastal Plain of North Carolina into northern and southern regions. The northern section stretches from the Neuse River basin to the present-day Virginia state line, and the southern one runs from the Neuse River to the South Carolina state line. Scholars further identify the northern area as the habitat occupied by Algonquian- and Iroquoian-speaking peoples at the time of the arrival of the first English colonists. The southern tract encompassed the territory of Siouan-speaking tribes, groups that also extended westward to inhabit the hills of the Piedmont.[23]

Evidence for the emergence of trade networks can be seen in the artifacts found in Woodland cemetery sites. Mica from the Appalachian Mountains, for example, has been discovered in graves in the Cape Fear region, while shells from the coast have been found at mountain sites. Again, the Cape Fear River likely provided a conduit for trade between coastal Siouan peoples and their Siouan cousins in the Piedmont. Beyond that, Indian foot trails, roughly in the areas of the present-day roads U.S. 421, U.S. 17 North, and U.S. 17 South, skirted the area and provided access to distant points to the north, south, and west.[24]

Little is known about the Woodland native population in the Upper Cape Fear River valley. They are assumed to have been Siouan peoples, and a dozen or so groups—including the Catawba, the Cheraw, and possibly the Keyauwee—have been identified within a hundred-mile radius of the area that is now Cumberland County. In the Lower Cape Fear River valley, evidence of prehistoric Indian activity is more plentiful. Nearly five hundred sites from various periods have been identified in New Hanover County alone, but most of these are simply projectile points or other artifacts found on the surface. Moreover, because of the acidity of the sandy soil and the shallow water table, preservation of materials at these sites is often very poor.[25]

Two excavations do provide insights into southern coastal Woodland experience. The first is the Cedar Island site, found on the western side of Masonboro Sound. The location is a shell midden, or a dense refuse area composed of shellfish remains, that dates to the Middle Woodland period, with evidence of reuse during the Late Woodland era. Remains of oysters, clams, white-tailed deer, turtles, and fish have been discovered, for the site had access to the open waters and tidal marshes of the sound as well as the forests of live oak and pine trees on the upland ridge. From these faunal remains, it appears that this site was occupied from November through February and served as an encampment for hunting small animals, fishing, and harvesting shellfish. In addition to animal remains, ceramics from the Middle Woodland period and a Late Woodland platform pipe were found.[26]

The second site, Stoney Brook, is another shell midden located a half mile from the junction of Howes Creek and Middle Sound. Interestingly, the physical site is nearly identical to that of Cedar Island, with access to tidal marshes and upland ridges of live oak and pine trees. Moreover, it too dates to the Middle Woodland period and contains the remains of clams, oysters, mussels, deer, turtles, turkeys, and fish. Although no tools have survived, it is possible that these people used nets for fishing, as the remains indicate that the fish were rather small. Additional discoveries include caches of hickory nuts and ceramics and possibly a pipe bowl dating to the Middle Woodland period. Taken together, these materials suggest that this site was a seasonal village, used primarily for processing animals, shellfish, and fish. Whereas Cedar Island represented a specialized camp area where a small group procured resources over a short time, Stoney Brook was a stable central location, probably with camp structures built along the ridgeline for a large group and occupied from summer through winter to late spring.[27]

If this picture of seasonal encampment is accurate, then perhaps some pattern of yearly migratory pilgrimage to the coast continued through the Woodland period. Such a pilgrimage would redistribute the population into the resource-rich coastal zone and satisfy them for that season. But when did permanent settlements emerge on the coast? There is no clear answer for its southern portion. Ethnohistorical sources indicate that by the time of European contact, Algonquian peoples in the northern coastal area had inhabited year-round settlements for some time. Nor is it hard to imagine that by the Late Woodland period, bands along the southern coast also began to take advantage of the available terrestrial, estuarine, and marine resources and establish permanent settlements, for the southern coast, too, provided food throughout the seasons. Unfortunately, the sandy soils of the Cape Fear region do not hold the organic molds that could tell us more precisely about the age, construction, or materials of housing or other structures. We do know from the documentary accounts of William Hilton that by the historic period, the Cape Fear Indians were living in well-established villages.[28]

Thus, by the Woodland period, the native peoples of the Cape Fear had developed larger and more sedentary communities. Their adaptive exploitation of faunal resources took advantage of the riches of the environment and its reliable and varied food supply. As their numbers increased over time and their technologies became more specialized (possibly including the clearing of land for the planting of domesticated crops), the impact of these native peoples on the environment grew. And yet, in contrast to other native peoples in the Southeast, one does not find evidence of the development of hierarchical political organizations or the existence of concentrated populations living in large villages.

Native peoples in the Cape Fear encountered the imponderable aspects of life that are familiar to all people. They knew of the serendipitous and frequently inexplicable circumstances that often defined human existence. In their specific natural setting, they experienced the gentle beauty of springtime and the warmth of an early summer day. They appreciated the satisfaction of a plentiful harvest or a successful hunt. Yet they were also all too familiar with times of scarcity, when there was not enough to eat, or times of winter cold or vernal storms, when nature was harsh. Indeed, confronted without warning by the violence of those storms that we call hurricanes (a Spanish word derived from Native American linguistic roots), one might imagine the Indians' sense of awe in the presence of so mysterious and powerful a reality, a feeling that Rudolf Otto once called the numinous.[29]

And just as the natural world could seemingly be adventitious, so too could the human world. The powerful mystery of conception and birth or the coming of age of a young girl or boy could match a debilitating accident, the sudden death of a child, and even the eventual passing of an elder as occasions for spiritual reflection. In all these experiences of blessing and of tragedy, one could surmise that native peoples, like peoples in other times and places, would try to find significance in their worlds, would try to make meaningful their lived experiences of hope, grief, wonder, confusion, and surprise. Why do these events happen the way they do? What is my place in this world? What happens after my death? Challenged by the fundamental, perhaps insoluble, aspects of human experience, how did native peoples in the Cape Fear express their spiritual feelings and beliefs?

If one looks for the religious elements of prehistoric native experience, they are sometimes hard to see. The Cape Fear region, for example, has no remains of massive temples or monuments, no manuscripts of religious scriptures. Where are the spiritual values and religious experiences in the midst of all this discussion of subsistence patterns and material culture? The stereotype of Native American religious traditions in the historic era is that they respect the natural environment and its powers, that time is cyclical, and that all forms of life are interrelated. Perhaps such views can be interpolated back to the prehistoric era. Yet, in the absence of sacred stories and other texts from the Cape Fear Indians, such conjecture is too speculative. Attention to ritual experience can partially overcome these textual lacunae and provide better insights into the religious elements of their experience.

The native peoples of the Cape Fear region fit what scholar of religion Joachim Wach has called a natural religious group. They were an ethnically homogeneous group related through the bonds of kinship expressed in birth, marriage, or adoption into the group. Such natural religious groups also joined in the communal tasks of providing food, constructing shelters, defending themselves against other groups, and engaging in religious rituals. While these activities functioned to integrate the groups and reinforce social cohesion, they were amenable to change as dynamic forces altered these societies over time. Environmental transformations, political challenges, and economic failures or successes could all undermine the power of tradition and, in so doing, introduce new elements into the familiar fabric of social and ritual experience.[30]

In such societies, ritual experience became the foremost expression of religious traditions. Orthopraxis, or "correct action," took precedence over orthodoxy, or "correct belief." As one student of ritual has observed, in such homogeneous tribal societies, "religion is not something separate from community identity, ethnic customs, political institutions, and social traditions. Beliefs are rarely formulated and spelled out in these circumstances, and they do not need to be. It is the formal and informal customs and obligations—namely, ritual responsibilities like attending to the ancestors, arranging the marriage of one's children, and participating in communal festivities—that defined one as a civilized member of this type of community." Rituals can illustrate different types of ceremonies, provide clues about the structures of religious life, and, perhaps, give us insight into the purposes of these otherwise all too mute peoples.[31]

Three different types of rituals stand out as events with profound religious meaning and significance in the life of the Cape Fear Indians—rituals of feasting and fellowship, rituals of passage and transformation, and rituals of purification and communion. Each ritual expressed something important about the identity of the group and at the same time sustained and reinforced the sense of who they were and how they ought to live.

In the prehistoric counterpart to a covered-dish supper, Siouan peoples gathered for feasting and fellowship. In the Piedmont, Siouan native peoples wrapped up plant and animal foods, placed them in pits that were covered with earth, and built a fire on top. Coastal Siouans were not to be outdone. Deposits of empty shells in the middens at Cedar Island and at numerous additional locations attest to their consumption of large amounts of oysters and other shellfish. Whereas Piedmont peoples had their pit-cooked barbecue, coastal Indians had their oyster roasts, where the shells would be steamed opened or perhaps pried apart with a stone knife, the meat eaten, and the shells discarded. Indeed, it is easy to imagine an Archaic period campsite located near a stream where Indians caught fish or other freshwater resources, then cooked and consumed them. Or, somewhat later, one can imagine a group of Woodland natives sitting on the ridgetop at Stoney Brook or on the banks of a marsh under the shade of a massive live oak, feasting on steamed oysters, clams, and corn and, if the season was right, enjoying berries and nuts as well. Here, food not only satisfied bodily needs; it also fed social needs and sustained the bonds of community.[32]

Passage and transformation constituted the second set of rituals. Rites of passage centered around birth, puberty, and death—those fundamental moments of transition in the life cycle of the individual that are recognized throughout all human cultures. John Swanton suggested that Siouan peoples celebrated the birth of a child through the act of naming it. At the stage of puberty, both males and females would undergo a rigorous rite of initiation into adulthood that included isolation, continual fasting and ingestion of emetics to purify the body, and other activities to demonstrate courage and physical resilience. While Siouan females retained their birth names, Siouan males would acquire a second name, or title, once they had performed some exploit during a conflict or similar trial. In this way, the physical maturation of the individual at puberty was joined to a social construction and recognition of adulthood through these rituals of passage and transformation.[33]

Insights into the last ritual of passage, that into the next world, are provided by excavations of cemeteries. Ossuaries, or group burial sites, have been identified all along the North Carolina coast; however, distinct patterns, possibly tied to broader cultural traditions, have also been discerned. Iroquoian-speaking populations in northeastern North Carolina tended to have interments of small family groups, accompanied by marginella shells as grave goods, located within the limits of the village. Algonquian speakers in the northeastern part of the state placed their ossuaries a short distance from the edge of the village. In these cases, interment involved larger numbers of individuals, often 50 and sometimes as many as 150 individuals. These Algonquian graves often contained animal bones but few identifiable artifacts.[34]

A third pattern, found throughout southeastern North Carolina and extending into portions of coastal South Carolina and Georgia, was likewise an ossuary burial, but it differed significantly from the Iroquoian and Algonquian practices. Here, the corpses were placed in charnel houses or some other restricted area to allow the flesh to decompose. Once the flesh had decayed, the cleaned bones were removed and collected into bundles, and new corpses were placed in the mortuaries. The bundled bones were then buried at an appropriate time in ossuaries consisting of sand burial mounds. Typically, these mounds were circular in shape, from twenty-five to fifty feet in diameter and approximately three feet high. They were always located on a low sand ridge some distance from an encampment site. These mounds could contain the bones of ten to three hundred persons, and they held a variety of grave goods.[35]

Although they were often the target of relic collectors, published reports document sand burial mounds in Duplin, Robeson, Cumberland, Brunswick, and New Hanover counties. The Cold Morning site in New Hanover County, near the present-day Echo

Farms residential development, was an ossuary that dated to the Late Woodland period and contained eleven adults, four juveniles, and one fetus. The ossuary was located on a sand ridge approximately half a mile from what would have been a native encampment. The location atop a sand ridge, the skeletal measurements of the bones, and the size of the ossuary reinforce the scholarly consensus that this was a Siouan burial mound. As such, it also suggests that Algonquian incursion southward may have waned near present-day Pender or Onslow County. This transition zone of Algonquian and Siouan peoples would be consistent with the representation of the Cape Fear region as a boundary area, a territory of overlapping humans as well as other life-forms.[36]

Another major sand burial is the McLean Mound site located in Cumberland County near Fayetteville on the Upper Cape Fear River. This mound contained bundles of skeletal remains from more than three hundred persons, with both sexes represented. The mound was approximately forty-two feet in diameter and located on a sandy ridge a short distance from the probable site of an Indian encampment. Dating to the Woodland period, the mound was particularly striking for the number and variety of grave goods it contained. Beads made from shells, stone and antler projectile points, stone and clay pipes, animal bones and teeth, arrow-making and tool kits, hammerstones, celt stones, and red hematite stones were all found inside.[37]

The meaning of these materials is open to conjecture. Beads from marginella and conch shells were the most common artifacts at the site. Both types of shells could have been used as strung necklaces or other forms of adornment. Beyond that, both types of shells came from the Atlantic Ocean, more than a hundred miles downriver, attesting to the probability of trade networks between Upper and Lower Cape Fear River peoples or possibly direct journeys to the coast to procure such items. Similarly, all but one of the stone pipes were fabricated from chloritic schist, a material not available in the immediate area but found in the Piedmont and mountain regions of North Carolina. Here again, exchange networks seemed to be functioning. The presence of perforated turkey wing bones suggests the possibility of further ornaments. Projectile points, bone tools, hammerstones, ungrooved celt axes, and an arrow-making kit likely represent supplies that were thought to be needed in the next life or materials that the deceased used and would continue to use in the other world.

Findings by historians of religions have been matched by evidence from southeastern anthropologists to surmise that red ocher and animal sacrifice were auspicious elements in prehistoric burial practices. Red ocher, such as that derived from the hematite stones in the McLean Mound, has often been linked with a belief in survival after death, particularly because ocher was thought to symbolize life-giving blood. The sacrifice of animals—in the case of the McLean Mound, symbolized by the teeth of a bear and the mandible of a dog—has been associated with personal adornment, anticipation of hunting in the next world, and the continued efficacy of shamanic practices. Of course, in the absence of other evidence, one cannot be certain what they mean in the Cape Fear region; however, it does seen certain that their intentional inclusion marked these objects as important.[38]

A coastal tradition of sand burial mounds extending from the Cape Fear region southward through South Carolina to Georgia seems well established. Indeed, the prevalence of shellfish collection, seasonal village occupation, and sand burial mounds in the Late Woodland period of coastal South Carolina suggests obvious comparisons with the Cape Fear experience. Thus, these elements underscore the probability of southern influences among the people of the Cape Fear. Whatever the answer to these complicated issues of provenance and relationship may be, this coastal tradition is different from that of the Iroquoians and Algonquians to the north and from that of the Siouans of the Piedmont, where bodies buried in flexed positions and oriented to the east were the rule. Nevertheless, in burial rituals (as well as those associated with birth and puberty), the Cape Fear Indians gathered to transform the moment through ritual experience. In these observances of birth, puberty, and death, symbols were shared and common values were maintained. Whereas the naming of a child was a moment of individual recognition, the interment of many individuals in a single burial pit attested to and reinforced the cohesion and equality of the group. So too, the inclusion of grave goods or red ocher in the burial site intimated some conception of the continuation of life after death. Thus, rituals of passage and transformation were preeminently moments of intentional action that were honored by tradition, anticipated and performed with effort, and shaped by understandings that were co-operative if not always fully conscious.[39]

The third type of ritual concerned purification and communion. One example of a purification ritual involved the ingestion of a beverage made from the leaves of the yaupon plant, which grew abundantly in the Cape Fear area and was widely used by its native population. Native groups from the Piedmont and other inland areas made annual pilgrimages down the Cape Fear River in the spring to trade for supplies of the highly coveted yaupon leaves, and such trade could be lucrative for the Cape Fear Indians. John Lawson, in his early-eighteenth-century account *A New Voyage to Carolina*, stated that coastal Indians could sell the leaves to Indians in the Piedmont and mountains "at a considerable Price." From these plants the Indians brewed an elixir commonly called the "black drink" in anthropological literature. Lawson described the preparation of the drink, noting that the leaves were crushed in a mortar bowl, then either boiled or cured over a fire. Finally, the leaves were dried in the sun and would later be used to brew a tea-like beverage. In small doses, this beverage could have a calming effect and was used in conjuring ceremonies and informal gatherings. More typically, the black drink was taken in large doses in conjunction with important meetings or deliberative assemblies, where the resulting diuretic and emetic reactions were understood as acts of purification.[40]

Another example of a purification ritual was the physical isolation of females during menstruation or childbirth in structures set apart from residences and communal buildings. Although no physical evidence of such isolation huts has been found in the Cape Fear region, cross-cultural studies indicate the wide prevalence of this custom throughout the Southeast. Here, ritual separation ensured purity, encouraged a setting for reflection, and provided a procedure for ritual reincorporation back into the community at an appropriate time. Interestingly, this concern for purity extended to men too. Warriors who were about to go off on raids were likewise ritually secluded and then provided with a procedure for reincorporation into the group once they had returned from battle.[41]

The striving for purity and the desire to avoid pollution are familiar dynamics in the history of religions and have been cogently applied to the native peoples of the Southeast. Charles Hudson, for example, pointed out the "almost obsessive concern with purity and pollution" among the preliterate peoples of the Southeast, for whom achieving and maintaining purity, eliminating pollution, and restoring purity were important ceremonial purposes. To maintain purity and avoid pollution was to live in balance; it was to exist in a state of harmony with the members of the social and natural world of which one was a part. Separation from these realms of society and nature was neither a conceptual nor a technological possibility. The power of social relations and the force of the natural world were immediate, vivid, and inescapable.[42]

Within such a context, as Hudson generalized for the Southeast, "Indians lived in a world which they perceived to be for the most part orderly and predictable. . . . So long as men behaved properly and remained pure, and so long as they did not cause the forces of nature to become unbalanced, things went well in human affairs." If individuals became polluted and let balance slip away, they could expect misfortune. Conversely, if misfortune occurred, then balance had been lost and needed to be restored. In such cases, Hudson noted, southeastern Indians sought out a ritual specialist or shaman to discern the cause of the problem. Cape Fear Indians would have shared these cosmological views, and they would have looked to a shaman for assistance. Thus, in the remains found in the McLean Mound, the teeth of a bear and the mandible of a dog may well have been part of a shaman's ritual kit. Such items have been associated with shamanistic practices in other times and places and may indicate the same here. Details concerning such shamanistic rituals in the Cape Fear are lacking, but the importance of purity among Cape Fear Indians seems quite evident.[43]

Rituals of communion revolved around the smoking of the pipe. The ritual use of pipes is a familiar characteristic of the lifeways of Native Americans. Fragments of pipes and whole specimens have been found in a number of archaeological digs in North Carolina, including the Cedar Island, Stoney Brook, and McLean Mound sites in the Cape Fear region. Pipes could have a number of shapes, and those at McLean Mound included angular, platform, and detached stem pipes. All the pipes at McLean Mound were broken, or ritually "killed," as part of the burial practice, a custom widely documented among Indians of the Southeast and suggestive of the anticipated use of the pipe in the afterlife. As for the smoking material itself, anthropologists indicate that the tobacco used by native peoples in the Southeast was *Nicotiana rustica L.*, a species much stronger than that commercially produced today.[44]

One of the more puzzling aspects of the pipes from the McLean site is the designs incised on them. These designs included squares, rectangles, and triangles, as well as configurations of oblique lines, notches, and rectangles nested within each other. A pipe found at a sand burial mound in Brunswick County had an incised diamond shape filled with parallel lines. Do these designs have any special significance? On the one hand, perhaps they were simply ornamental decorations intended to enhance the beauty of the pipes. On the other hand, effigy figures, shell gorgets, and ceramic pottery have been found throughout the Southeast containing obviously symbolic markings that scholars have sought to decipher. Similarly, patterns of arcs, spirals, circles, and chevrons found on artifacts at Cahokia, the great prehistoric metropolis located near present-day St. Louis, Missouri, have been examined for their symbolic meaning and tied to motifs dealing with fertility and the Upper and Lower Worlds, themes also identified in the Southeast. Yet, given the paucity of artifacts and the absence of texts or other contextual evidence for the Cape Fear region, no final determination about these designs can be made at this point.[45]

The use of the pipe was widespread. In his observation of North Carolina Indians, John Lawson stated that both sexes smoked tobacco, "for their teeth are yellow with smoking tobacco, which both men and women are addicted to." In addition to sacred and recreational usage by ordinary members of society, shamans and ceremonial practitioners within native societies also used tobacco. Here the employment of the pipe was always a ritual event, a sacred act in which the smoke purified the participants as well as the occasion. Beyond its purifying properties, tobacco was also considered a necessary element for the proper performance of many rites of healing and divination.[46]

Scholars have suggested that early on, pipes were possessed communally and passed down from generation to generation. Obviously by the Late Woodland period in the Cape Fear region, pipes could be owned or associated with individuals and buried with their remains. In any case, during the ritual of smoking, the pipe was passed around the circle of participants, thereby uniting the group at one level while the smoke acted as a collective and individual offering rising to the sacred. Here, one had social community and religious communion united in one act. And yet rituals change as contexts change, and it is interesting that after European contact, one finds much more individualized and recreational use of the pipe among native peoples. It has also been suggested that this adaptation could mean that the pipe was no longer considered as sacred and that non-religious uses were coming into acceptance.[47]

Thus, in rituals of feasting and fellowship, passage and transformation, and purification and communion, we have a window into the mute world of those native peoples, named not by their own language but by those peoples from a distant land who occupied their ancestral homelands. In the purposes of fellowship, transformation, and purification we gain a partial insight into the religious world of the Cape Fear Indians and the ways such rituals united these peoples in the bonds of common purpose and meaning.

When one moves into the era of direct contact between natives and Europeans, one encounters the denouement of the story of the Cape Fear Indians. Initially, the easy rhythms of the Late Woodland period continued, as food remained plentiful and the cycles of seasonal and natural life persisted. Yet by the late seventeenth century, these patterns were disrupted, and conflict, disease, and disorder punctuated the lives of the natives of the Cape Fear.

As previously noted, in 1663 a group of New Englanders established a settlement in the Cape Fear region. Although the Puritans did not tarry very long, in a relatively short time, the tread of native moccasins gave way once and for all to the tramp of English boots. In his 1662 and 1663 voyages, William Hilton encountered Indians in the Cape Fear area. Going some ways up the northeast branch of the Cape Fear River during his first journey, Hilton noted that less than a hundred Indians were seen during his company's short sojourn. He further remarked that while the natives seemed friendly, the sailors had to guard against pilfering.[48]

During his second voyage, Hilton explored the northwest (main) branch of the river, remaining for three months and traveling as far as fifty miles upriver. This experience with the native population was quite different from that of his earlier visit. The center of social organization was a village that Hilton called Necoes. Although game, birds, and other animals were plentiful and easily hunted, this native group cultivated corn and even had surplus, which they sold to Hilton and his men. The domestication of plants to supplement a hunting and gathering economy was characteristic of native peoples in the Late Woodland and early contact periods, and Necoes fit this pattern. By this time, many native peoples practiced gardening and land management techniques that included felling trees to clear land for crops, but Hilton indicated that these Indians left their trees standing. In any case, the development of such agricultural subsistence strategies supported larger villages and more sedentary, less nomadic lifestyles. Beyond that, increasing reliance on agriculture encouraged greater specificity in the calculation of time, to avoid planting during a premature thaw, as well as planning ahead to produce an adequate harvest.[49]

Hilton and his men had other encounters with the native peoples. In one case, an Indian shot an arrow at Hilton and a detachment of his crew. After pursing their assailant and destroying his hut and possessions, Hilton was approached by a delegation of forty native men who sought to restore peace. As the Indians drew closer, they signaled their friendly intentions toward the Englishmen by shouting words that Hilton and his men understood to be "Bonny, Bonny." In all probability, these expressions were derived from the word *bueno* and indicated contact with the Spanish, who had been in what is now South Carolina since the 1520s. The Indians also presented two young women to the Englishmen as recompense for the attack. The two groups eventually exchanged beads and other trade goods instead, and the women remained with their tribe. In honor of the occasion, during which both parties had "concluded a firm Peace," Hilton named the (now unknown) spot Mount Bonny. A week later, Hilton met with Wattcoosa, an individual Hilton took to be the chief of the village, and purchased the river and adjacent land from him. It seems certain that the two parties did not share a common understanding of the transaction. Wattcoosa probably considered the payment as tribute or rent, while Hilton believed that he had acquired possession of the territory in perpetuity. Nevertheless, given the later history of acquisition of Indian lands by fiat and fraud, this attempt by Hilton to purchase legitimately the Indian land deserves notice.[50]

From Giovanni Verrazzano's voyage of 1524 to William Hilton's explorations in the 1660s, the process of contact between Europeans and Native Americans was a dynamic one. Transformations in the material and linguistic cultures of native people are easy to identify in the accounts of European explorers. Another trend equally apparent in this process of contact and exchange is the steady reduction in the size of the native population, which continued into the colonial era. It is estimated that the population of the Cape Fear Indians in 1600 was 1,000 persons. A census of Indians in 1715 identified a total of 206 Cape Fear Indians—76 men and 130 women and children—all of whom lived in five villages. By 1731 Hugh Meredith, a Welsh visitor to the Cape Fear region, stated, "there is not an Indian to be seen in this place . . . the small remains of them abide among the thickest of the South Carolina Inhabitants." In short, by the mid-eighteenth century, the Cape Fear Indians had moved elsewhere, died off, or become so generally scarce as to be unnoticeable.[51]

The demise of the Cape Fear Indians can be explained by several factors. European diseases, new to the native populations and against which they had no immunity, have been widely recognized for their destructive impact on native societies. Smallpox, measles, and influenza would have been just as lethal among the Cape Fear population as they were among natives in other parts of North Carolina and throughout the Southeast.

Regarding the timing of such pathological onslaughts, some scholars state that these diseases began to take their toll on an epidemic scale immediately after the arrival of the Spanish expeditions of Hernando de Soto and Juan Pardo in North America. Other scholars insist that factors such as population density and the nature of contacts between natives and Europeans shaped the reception and impact of these diseases. Ward and Davis, in their survey of North Carolina archaeology, concluded, "there is no archaeological evidence to indicate that the sixteenth-century Spanish expeditions into North Carolina had any impact on the Indians living along the presumed paths taken by de Soto and Pardo." The same cannot be said, however, for the effects of English settlement. Throughout the late 1660s, settlers from Virginia streamed into North Carolina and came into sustained contact with Piedmont and coastal native societies. Here the archaeological record abundantly demonstrates widespread disease and death. Intensified exchanges in trade and social relationships provided the basis for the decimation of native populations by disease. English settlers rather than Spanish explorers seem to have been responsible for the spread of virulent diseases among native peoples in North Carolina. John Lawson, traveling in the Piedmont region of North Carolina, described it this way: "there is not the sixth Savage living within two hundred miles of all our Settlements, as there were fifty years ago." Smallpox epidemics among the native peoples, Lawson noted, had "destroy'd whole Towns, without leaving one *Indian* alive in the Village." Although the sporadic nature of initial settlements in the Cape Fear region might have mitigated their ferocity, European diseases played a role here too, but probably not as great as elsewhere in the Southeast.[52]

A factor that is often overlooked in discussions of native societies is warfare between Indian groups, sometimes at the behest of one or another European power, and sometimes simply as a matter of territorial expansion or tribal animosity. The Tuscarora War of 1711–1715 was as much a conflict between Indian groups as one between Indians and whites. In 1711, when the Tuscarora attacked settlers on the Pamlico and Neuse rivers, the colony of North Carolina was quite vulnerable. A virtual civil war between the supporters and opponents of Edward Hyde, the deputy governor of the colony, had divided many colonists and distracted even more. Incursions by whites into traditional Indian hunting grounds, as well as the enslavement of Indians by whites, had infuriated tribal members. Politically weakened and unable to respond adequately to the attacks, North Carolina officials appealed to South Carolina and Virginia for men and assistance to retaliate against the Tuscarora. The South Carolina legislature responded by sending John Barnwell, together with a detachment of militia and a group of Indians, to North Carolina's aid. Among the Indians in Barnwell's troops were about a dozen Cape Fears. In April 1712 Barnwell negotiated a truce with the Tuscarora, brokering a treaty that in part reserved the Cape Fear area to the Cape Fear Indians and forbade the Tuscarora to enter it. Although the treaty did not hold, it is clear that the Cape Fear Indians saw this conflict as an opportunity to enhance their situation with the South Carolinians and, as importantly, to protect themselves from the Tuscarora.[53]

The Yamassee War of 1715 represented a concentrated attack on white settlers in South Carolina. The Indian groups that allied together included the Creek, Choctaw, Yamassee, Catawba, Cheraw, Waccamaw, and Cape Fear Indians. The Indian forays had drawn near to Charles Town, South Carolina, but by midsummer, the city and southern frontier were quiet. South Carolinians had repulsed the Indian attacks, but often with large numbers of casualties on both sides.

Maurice Moore, formerly of South Carolina, had gone to the aid of North Carolina in the Tuscarora War and remained there. Now, in the summer of 1715, Moore marched a detachment of whites and Tuscarora south to aid South Carolina. On his way, Moore traveled through the Cape Fear region. He had been warned that the Cape Fear Indians planned to ambush him, but with his advance information, he was able to rout them. The number of Cape Fears involved is unclear, but Moore took at least eighty prisoners with him to South Carolina. Other members of the tribe soon followed voluntarily. The Yamassee War continued into 1718, but for the Cape Fear Indians, their tribal autonomy was forfeited. Hugh Meredith noted in 1731 that Senecas and Tuscarora had "almost totally destroyed those called Cape Fear Indians." Thus, complicated patterns of intertribal relations and retaliations figured significantly in the history of the Cape Fear Indians. The dynamics of power played as significant a role as the dynamics of disease in explaining the history of the Cape Fear Indians.[54] Contexts of power and rivalries both spiritual and mundane were not confined exclusively to Native Americans. As the next chapter shows, political and religious structures developed and were sometimes divided during the history of colonial North Carolina.

2

Tensions in the Colonial Era

In his novel *The Warden*, Anthony Trollope sketches a portrait of the religious landscape of England in the early nineteenth century. Serving as cathedral and county seat for Barsetshire, Trollope's city of Barchester illustrates the complementary nature of political and ecclesiastical structures in English life. While its member of Parliament represents it politically, its resident bishop, dean, and canons administer to its spiritual needs. The story epitomizes the Anglican parish paradigm: geographically small enough to be served by its appointed clergy, who in turn provide weekly services, seasonal reminders, and sacramental celebrations for its parishioners. Mutual expectations of deference, tradition, and order suffuse the relationships of clergy and laity, and a vision of stability nurtures the life of the parish. Yet discordant elements are about to disturb this idyllic picture, taking the form of calls for ecclesiastical reform and even disestablishment.

This pattern of political and religious structures and this vision of deferential social order reach far back into English history, far enough even to help shape colonial North Carolina. Yet just as the English experience changed under the social conditions and intellectual climate of its era, so too in colonial North Carolina did the hopes for the parish paradigm and conceptions of virtual political representation break up on the social and intellectual conditions of its day. This chapter discusses the emergence of the towns of Brunswick and of Wilmington and explores the immigration of a variety of ethnic groups into the region. Not surprisingly, with these diverse immigrants came their religions and thereby an important question: what did it mean to have an established religion amidst this religious diversity? The reality of this religious mixture and the challenges it posed constituted only one of several tensions that characterized the Cape Fear region during the colonial era.

The year 1729 was a pivotal one for North Carolina and also for the Cape Fear. In that year, royal control of the colony supplanted proprietary supervision. Beyond that, the precinct of New Hanover and the parish of St. James were created. King Charles II had first established proprietary control in March 1663. In his instructions, the monarch granted the lands south of Virginia and north of Florida and extending from the Atlantic Ocean "to the west as far as the south seas" to a group of political supporters that he designated the Lords Proprietors. The king noted that he was impressed with the desire of these men to propagate the Christian faith as well as to establish a prosperous colony in these lands. At present, the king concluded, the lands were not cultivated and were inhabited only by "some barbarous people who have no knowledge of Almighty God." If the extension of the colony's boundaries south to the border of Florida and west to the southern seas was a strike against Spanish imperial claims, the reference to the potential of this fecund landscape effaced of its native population represented, as the last chapter showed, a familiar trope in depictions of the New World.[1]

In the royal charter the king instructed the Lords Proprietors to establish laws in this new colony consistent with those in England and to build churches and chapels "dedicated and consecrated according to the ecclesiastical laws" of England. However, in the aftermath of the English civil war, a spirit of religious toleration within a context of ecclesiastical establishment was now expected. The king's charter to the Proprietors recognized that some colonists might be dissenters from the established Church of England. Therefore, the Lords Proprietors, within the bounds of their own discretion, were to grant "indulgences and dispensations" to those who were conscientiously opposed to the Church of England, so long as these conscientious objectors remained obedient to civil law and did nothing to censure or undermine the dignity, liturgy, and maintenance of the established church. Thus, from the very beginning, the vision of the colony of Carolina contained a fundamental tension. Although the Church of England was to be the established church, the one that all who lived in the colony would support with their tax monies, the colony was also intended to make a monetary profit for its proprietary investors and to provide raw materials for England and a market for finished English goods. To this entrepreneurial end, it was recognized that individuals other than Anglican Church members would settle in North Carolina. To the question of how to have an established church and at the same time encourage non-Anglicans to settle in Carolina, the Lords Proprietors in faraway London proposed a policy of religious toleration. As the history of the Cape Fear region and the colony more generally would show, the policy was easier to recommend than to implement.[2]

Events moved quickly after the awarding of the royal charter, and on May 29, 1664, a group of English settlers from Barbados under the leadership of John Vassal made a landing on the Cape Fear River. Within months the area was incorporated into the county of Claredon, with Robert Sanford appointed its secretary and chief register and John Vassal named as deputy governor and surveyor general. A 1666 promotional pamphlet, designed to attract settlers to the area, claimed a population of 800 persons dispersed up and down the river but centered mostly around a village called Charles Town. In keeping with other promotional materials of the time, this pamphlet represented the Cape Fear in Arcadian terms, extolling the fertility of the land, the abundance of natural resources, and the temperate climate. The pamphlet also noted that liberty of conscience would hold in this colony and that every free individual or head of household would receive an ample grant of land from the Lords Proprietors.[3]

However, this seemingly auspicious beginning soon fell apart. Circumstances distracted the Lords Proprietors' attention from the colony as London experienced plague and fire in 1665–1666. The Proprietors also changed the system of landholding. Initially, colonists had settled on good land up and down the river according to its availability. The Lords Proprietors now decreed that landholdings should be assigned according to lot and in the order of the individual's arrival, thereby undermining established patterns of residency and land tenure. Finally, the Lords Proprietors became more interested in developing another settlement farther south near Port Royal. With disgruntled colonists leaving the region and supplies running low for any that stayed, Charles Town on the Cape Fear

River had disintegrated by 1667, bequeathing its name to a later settlement on the Ashley River in what eventually became South Carolina.[4]

South Carolina may have taken over the name of Charles Town, but it symbolically repaid the debt in 1726 when a number of men from Goose Creek, some twenty miles north of Charleston, South Carolina, migrated to the Cape Fear area. Maurice Moore, the leader of the group, was familiar with the Lower Cape Fear from his 1715 campaign against the Indians in the region. Son of James Moore, at one time the governor of South Carolina, Maurice Moore was well connected by marriage to influential persons in South Carolina and to future leaders in North Carolina. Yet by 1726, circumstances in South Carolina had become troublesome for the men of Goose Creek. In 1724 the British Parliament discontinued bounties for South Carolina's naval stores. Land to grow pine trees and slaves to produce tar, turpentine, and the like had been bought on credit in expectation of continued bounties and increasing profits. With the discontinuation of the bounties, many South Carolinians in the Goose Creek area faced bankruptcy. Additionally, political unrest between supporters and opponents of the Lords Proprietors' rule in South Carolina—disputes in which the Goose Creek men were prominent but on the losing side—motivated many to search for a new home.[5]

In 1712 the Proprietors had divided South Carolina and North Carolina but had neglected to establish a firm boundary line between the two. Not surprisingly, both claimed the Cape Fear region as their own. In 1725 George Burrington, governor of North Carolina for the Proprietors, took matters into his own hands and began issuing grants for land in the Cape Fear region. One of the major beneficiaries of Burrington's actions was Maurice Moore, who received more than seven thousand acres of land along the Cape Fear River. Other recipients included Roger Moore, Maurice's brother; Eleazer Allen and John Porter, brothers-in-law of Maurice; and Samuel Swain, Maurice's stepson. Altogether, more than nine thousand acres were granted to these men.[6]

With these extensive landholdings in place, in June 1726 Maurice Moore laid out a settlement on the western side of the Cape Fear River and called it Brunswick Town in honor of King George I of England, a member of the German House of Brunswick. The town encompassed 360 acres from Moore's ample properties and had promising aspirations. Situated on a bluff overlooking the river, its location promised easy access for trade between townspeople and the ships arriving from Europe and the Caribbean, especially after royal officials declared Brunswick an official port in 1731 with the power to clear imports and exports. Brunswick Town became the county seat of New Hanover Precinct when that precinct was created in 1729. Lots were set off for a courthouse and a jail, and officials expected court sessions and other county business and political activities to take place there. Lots were also available for purchase by private individuals, and streets were laid out as well. However, a visitor to Brunswick Town in 1731, after noting its potential for trade and governmental functions, concluded that at present it was "a poor, hungry, unprovided Place" consisting of only ten or twelve houses and "hardly worth the name of a Village."[7]

In 1731 Brunswick Town promised more than it had yet delivered, and those promises included a hefty portion of religious elements as well. In tandem with the establishment of New Hanover Precinct in 1729 had been the creation of St. James Parish. The model for parishes was the English one, in which the parish often shared the same boundaries as the precinct or borough, though occasionally a precinct might contain more than one parish. This paradigm anticipated that the parishes would be geographically compact and would have a settled population, glebe lands (i.e., lands that yielded revenues to the parish church), a vestry to supervise the parish's temporal affairs, and sufficient clergy to serve the needs of the parishioners. By 1715 North Carolina had several parishes, with the understanding that more would be added when the need arose, as in the case of St. James Parish.[8]

However, this vision of compact parishes with a settled population disintegrated on the reality of frontier conditions in North Carolina. Writing in 1704, the Reverend John Blair provided a review of his ministry in North Carolina and drew particular attention to the "mighty inconveniences in traveling." Roads were often impassable or lacking altogether. Rivers had to be forded, with the exception of one river that had a ferry, but it was owned by Quakers and was available only for their use. Ten years later, the Reverend John Urmston echoed much the same view when he lamented that it was nearly impossible "to settle a Ministry here, the people live so scattered and remote, the Parishes so large that they cannot be supplied without much labor and charge."[9]

Blair and Urmston were part of the first generation of Anglican clergy in North Carolina, and both had been sent by the Society for the Propagation of the Gospel in Foreign Parts (SPG). The SPG had been the brainchild of Thomas Bray. Dispatched to Maryland in 1700 as commissary, or representative, of the bishop of London, Bray gained firsthand knowledge of the religious situation in the North American colonies. Upon his return to England, Bray set out to establish the organization that became the SPG. The charter for the society received royal approval in 1701, and the members pressed ahead with their three objectives: the development and maintenance of an orthodox Anglican missionary clergy, spiritual work among colonial English and other non-English persons, and the raising of funds to support these aims. For this last objective the society developed a network of contributors that pledged financial support for its work.[10]

The SPG also implemented guidelines for applicants and instructions for commissioned missionaries. In their applications, would-be missionaries were required to give an account of their piety, zeal, and learning. They provided testimonials from others as to their probity and orthodoxy. However, in order to be appointed, a candidate had to be an ordained Anglican clergyman, and although the requirements for ordination were rigorous for all, they could be especially daunting for any candidate from America. Only a bishop could perform an ordination, and there was no Anglican bishop resident in America. Consequently, an American applicant had to undertake the expensive, dangerous, and protracted voyage to England and back. Such a trip could cost an aspiring candidate £100, and the passage could be lengthy—one missionary left England on December 1 and did not arrive in North Carolina until May 10. Compounding these problems were the threats of disease aboard ship, capture by pirates or national enemies, and simply being lost at sea due to violent storms or other unforeseen causes. Once in England, a preliminary step toward appointment was ordination as a deacon. This meant an examination by a bishop or his representative, often a resident chaplain, concerning the applicant's knowledge of Greek, Latin, the Bible, church history, the prayer book, creeds, and the thirty-nine articles. After diaconal ordination, the candidate faced a one-year probation period before ordination as priest was permitted. Church officials often shortened this period for American candidates, due to their distance from home and the cost of their stay in England. Additional requirements, such as another examination and payment for the certificate of ordination, also had to be met. Once a candidate could produce acceptable letters of recommendation, a certificate of ordination, and a license from the bishop of London, he was eligible for appointment by the society.[11]

Instructions for appointed clergy were likewise thorough. While waiting for their ships to disembark, missionaries should reside with respectable families, avoid taverns, and usefully pass their time by praying, preaching, and reading. During their ocean voyages they should be examples of piety and virtue for the ship's company and should continue praying and catechizing their fellow passengers. Upon arrival at their destination, the missionaries should exhibit prudence, humility, frugality, and temperance; avoid taverns and abstain from gambling; give no offense to civil government but instead observe the rules of the liturgy; preach against vice; visit their parishioners frequently; and in all things "promote the Glory of Almighty God, and the Salvation of Men, by propagating the Gospel of our Lord and Saviour."[12]

These were heady expectations, particularly since North Carolina, had been "without priest or altar" for quite some time, according to Henderson Walker, president of the council of the colony. Three of the earliest missionaries to North Carolina were colorful and controversial characters. Daniel Brett was the first Anglican missionary regularly assigned to North Carolina. Brett apparently had been sent by the Society for the Promotion of Christian Knowledge, an organization affiliated with the SPG and also founded by Thomas Bray. Brett arrived in 1701 and left sometime within the next year or so. During his short stay in the Pamlico region, he evidently infuriated many of his parishioners. William Gale, writing to his father, regretted that Brett's departure would prevent the baptism of his newborn son. However, Gale concluded that Brett's leaving "was no loss to Religion, for he was the Monster of the Age." Henderson Walker likewise condemned Brett, lamenting that the first minister sent to the area should behave so badly and provide non-Anglicans in the region with such an easy target for their criticisms.[13]

John Urmston, another missionary, was born in Lancashire, England, around 1662. After his ordination in 1695 Urmston worked as a chaplain, first in the Royal Navy and then in the Russia Company, serving in Moscow, Archangel, and the Baltic Sea. After returning to England Urmston was recommended to the SPG and departed for North Carolina under its auspices in 1710. Urmston pastored in Chowan and Perquimans precincts. During his tenure in North Carolina, he often wrote to the SPG officials in London bewailing his situation and imploring his superiors for additional salary and supplies. As early as 1711 he informed the society that he and his family "have lived many a day only on a dry crust and a draught of salt water out of the sound." In 1714 these dire straits had reached the point that he had been forced to sell the clothes off his back for food. By 1717 conditions had worsened, he wrote, because his salary was overdue. Yet he also reported that he owned a three hundred–acre plantation and occasionally employed servants. Whatever the accuracy of his complaints, Urmston, like many colonists in the New World, was ill prepared to perform the hard physical labor necessary to survive in the frontier conditions of early-eighteenth-century North Carolina. Indeed, he observed in 1711 that although his neighbors liked him, they would not do his physical labor for him because they wanted newcomers to endure the same ordeal they had experienced. Urmston concluded that if he only had servants and money he could live quite comfortably in his new situation. Urmston's hopes for a gentrified parsonage in the New World were clearly as unrealistic as his complaints were exaggerated. They were not his worst problems, however.[14]

Urmston's haughty manner and his insistence on respect for his position were often at odds with other aspects of his life. Governor Charles Eden, sometimes Urmston's ally and sometimes his foe, concluded that if Urmston was unhappy in his situation, he had only himself to blame. More moderate behavior, Eden suggested, would have helped Urmston avoid many of his difficulties. Episodes hardly in keeping with the SPG's instructions had occurred throughout Urmston's ministry. According to John Barnwell, after drinking a large quantity of alcoholic punch, Urmston and others in attendance at a 1712 meeting of the General Assembly stripped naked and began boxing with one another. Even if the story contains elements of hyperbole, Urmston's conviction for public drunkenness in

1720 is a matter of record. Finally, the circumstances surrounding his death (by which time he had left North Carolina, gone back to England, and returned to serve in Pennsylvania and Maryland) suggest further problems. In November 1731 Urmston died after falling into a fireplace. Speculation differs as to whether he fell into the fire during a drinking binge and could not pull himself out or whether he fell into the fire while dozing. In any case, Urmston's body was discovered on the hearth with his head ablaze.[15]

Scandals of a different sort characterized the North Carolina ministry of John Blacknall. Born in England around 1690, Blacknall was appointed by the SPG to be a missionary in North Carolina and was installed at St. Paul's Church in Edenton in August 1725. Brought over from England as part of the retinue of Sir Richard Everard, the proprietary governor, Blacknall soon found himself embroiled in party politics and quickly tired of his circumstances. Although the society's instructions explicitly prohibited giving offense to the civil government, Blacknall became involved in a memorable episode. One of his parishioners, a white man named Thomas Spencer, wished to marry a mulatto girl, Martha Paul. Solemnizing such unions was illegal in North Carolina, as Blacknall knew. Nevertheless, he performed the wedding, turned himself in as the guilty party, and claimed half of the £50 fine that was due to the informer in such cases. Blacknall was indicted but was never tried. Advised to leave quietly, he did just that, waiting only long enough to collect several debts owed to him before slipping away to Virginia. Blacknall's departure left the Edenton church without a priest and stood in direct contradiction of the SPG's instructions. And although it extricated Blacknall from his political entanglements, it infuriated Governor Everard.[16]

In 1728 the Reverend John LaPierre moved from his missionary station in South Carolina to the Cape Fear. Born in 1681 and raised in a French Huguenot family that departed for London in the aftermath of the revocation of the Edict of Nantes, LaPierre attended Trinity College in Dublin and received both his bachelor's and master's degrees from that institution. He was ordained in 1707 and departed the next year under SPG auspices for South Carolina. After serving the French churches at St. Denis and Santee, as well as the English parish of St. Thomas at Charleston, LaPierre moved, with the approval of South Carolina commissary Alexander Garden, to Brunswick Town in 1728. Upon his arrival, LaPierre became the first Anglican minister in the Cape Fear region.[17]

Earlier LaPierre had occasionally performed baptisms and delivered sermons in the Brunswick area. Now in late 1728 he wanted to formalize the relationship with the people of Brunswick Town. The desirability of such a relationship seemed obvious in the beginning. In their St. James Parish in South Carolina, the Goose Creek men had been known as staunch Anglicans and opponents of all dissenters. With the creation of St. James Parish, North Carolina, in 1729, land for a church was set aside together with that reserved for a jail and courthouse. Indeed, as the seat of the parish, Brunswick Town's religious importance was intended to rival its political and commercial significance.[18]

Testimonials of support from the vestry were sent in 1730 to the bishop of London, and LaPierre began his ministerial duties, baptizing, marrying, and burying as best he could under the circumstances. He overlooked the problems with his compensation, which was often in arrears and inadequate, until 1733. Then LaPierre wrote to the bishop of London requesting episcopal approval for a transfer to Craven Parish. LaPierre detailed his attempts at ministry in Brunswick Town but cited competition from an unlicensed minister and lack of vestry support as reasons for his failure. He concluded that any clergyman coming to Brunswick Town would find "a lawless place, a scattered people, no glebe, no parsonage to receive him."[19]

With LaPierre's departure in 1734, the underdevelopment of the Cape Fear area and Brunswick Town in particular was obvious. Seeking to shape the frontier by political, commercial, and religious strategies, the men and women of the Cape Fear found themselves as shaped by their world as it was by them. Land was available, but labor was scarce. Opportunities presented themselves, but resources for their fulfillment were lacking. As the Cape Fear took its first steps toward permanent settlement in the 1720s, political and commercial antagonisms with the previously settled Albermarle region began to develop. Personal animosities, even within the Cape Fear region itself, apparently began to boil over as well.

Richard Marsden, for example, was part of the second generation of SPG clergy serving in North Carolina. Like his clerical predecessors, Marsden found timely occasions as well as inveterate obstacles. Marsden, however, was never one to pass up a shot at the main chance. Born around 1675 in Yorkshire England, by 1700 Marsden had immigrated to Maryland, where he was a lay reader in a parish. He returned to England for ordination and then ministered at a church near Charleston, South Carolina. After several more trips back and forth between England and America, Marsden moved to Jamaica in 1721, where he served as chaplain to its governor. In 1724 he married a wealthy Jamaican widow. However, the fact that Marsden already had a wife back in England made this a bigamous union, a scandal that followed him throughout his later life.[20]

Marsden's subsequent career was a study in contingency. With the death of his patron in Jamaica in 1726, Marsden returned to England. His creditors there, however, instituted bankruptcy proceedings against him, so he beat a retreat and ended up in Virginia. By 1729, after mismanaging his business affairs in Virginia, he arrived in the Cape Fear, where he eventually settled down. Marsden offered his ministerial services for free, thereby competing with and displacing John LaPierre. Just how far removed the experience of Cape Fear clergy was from the English parish paradigm was still evident during Marsden's ministry. Writing to the bishop of London in 1735, Marsden averred that he not only preached at his own home without expecting compensation but even provided "the greater part of my congregation a dinner every Sunday." During the week, he often traveled sixty to seventy miles in order to preach and perform baptisms, estimating that he had baptized a total of thirteen hundred men and women. Emphasizing his commitment and dedication, Marsden requested the continued financial support of the SPG. Initially, circumstances appeared to favor Marsden, as the society agreed to divide North Carolina into northern and southern missionary districts and to appoint Marsden as an itinerant in the southern district. However, the irregularities of Marsden's past life, his continuing financial insolvency, and charges that he had preached in Virginia and North Carolina without the requisite license from the bishop of London sank his chances. The society withdrew Marsden's appointment, dismissed him from its service, and implored their "Friends in America" to be on their guard when an individual of questionable conduct and character appeared on their doorstep claiming to be appointed by the SPG.[21]

Although Richard Marsden was out of the picture, the division of North Carolina into two missionary districts remained in place. Marsden's successor, James Moir, was instructed to perform his ministerial duties both at Brunswick Town and at the village of Newton. By 1739, when Moir arrived in the Cape Fear, several important developments had taken place. First, North Carolina had become a royal colony in 1729. In his instructions to the first royal governor, George Burrington, the king had indicated that liberty of conscience would continue in the colony, although the Church of England would be the religious establishment and its churches and parishes were to be well kept and appropriately sustained for the accomplishment of their mission. Beyond that, the bishop of London had to license all schoolteachers and Anglican ministers, and the church would encourage public morality through the offices of the established faith. None of these instructions represented a departure from those of the Lords Proprietors, although the colony's governance by royal authority held out the possibility of increased activity and vigilance in colonial affairs both temporal and spiritual. Indeed, many Anglicans hoped that the spirit would be vastly improved over the rather desultory attitude and administration of the Lords Proprietors.[22]

Another major development was the founding of the town of Wilmington upriver from Brunswick. In 1733 James Wimble, mariner, cartographer, and real estate developer, drew up a map in which the town of New Carthage appeared on the Cape Fear River. Wimble was the owner of some three hundred acres adjacent to the river, and he planned for this land to become the site of a new permanent settlement. After a very brief incarnation as New Liverpool, the settlement was slightly expanded and renamed Newton (understood as New Town to differentiate it from Brunswick Town). In February 1739 the royal governor approved the act "erecting the Village called Newton, in New Hanover County, into a Town and Township by the name of Wilmington." Wilmington was now officially on the map.[23]

The establishment of Wilmington highlighted two important political processes in the Cape Fear region. The first was the rivalry that developed between Brunswick Town and Wilmington. Although Brunswick's development took place earlier, Wilmington had the advantage of active support from the royal governor, Gabriel Johnston. Shortly after he became governor in 1734, Johnston began quarreling with the Moore family and other leaders in Brunswick Town. In quick order, Johnston used his executive power to locate courts, council meetings, and the collection of customs duties in Newton. Moreover, Wilmingtonians soon completed a courthouse and a jail, and in 1741 the governor convened the General Assembly in Wilmington.[24]

The leaders of Brunswick Town could see their political prestige and economic fortunes slipping away. In 1745 the Assembly passed an act encouraging settlement in Brunswick Town. The bill noted that lots had originally been set aside for a church, courthouse, market house, and other public buildings, though little or nothing had been done toward their construction. Accordingly, lots were to be laid out again, commissioners were to administer the town, and monies were to be directed to the vestry of St. Philip's Church. Yet Brunswick Town was not to become a phoenix, rising out of the ashes. The death of Maurice Moore in 1743 took away a major player in the controversy with Governor Johnston. Moreover, an attack by Spanish warships in 1748 and a hurricane in 1761 exposed the vulnerability of Brunswick Town to military depredations and natural disasters. Politically and economically, Wilmington gained an ascendancy in the Lower Cape Fear that it never relinquished.[25]

The second political process to which the rise of Wilmington contributed was the political rivalry that developed beginning in the 1740s between the Cape Fear and Albermarle regions of the colony. The Albermarle had been the scene of some of the earliest settlements in North Carolina, as immigrants from Virginia moved south. Bath, on the Pamlico Sound, had been established in 1706, and Edenton was incorporated in 1722. With the development of these towns had come political power in the Assembly for the Albermarle area. However, during the early colonial era North Carolina was a relatively fluid society, one in which commercial contacts and political ties could place an individual within the local elite. Whether in the Albermarle or the Cape Fear, most members of this initial elite were first- or second-generation settlers in the colony. Unlike in Virginia or even South Carolina, established families, widely linked by intermarriage, emerged slowly, and obstacles to social advancement were comparatively few. Thus social mobility within traditional expectations of deference was relatively supple, and identities based on achievement vied with those based on ascription.[26]

The Cape Fear region soon became a political match for the Albermarle. The Cape Fear River, for example, provided the colony's only direct access to the Atlantic Ocean and thus represented the possible development of a lucrative overseas trade without middlemen. Beyond that, as North Carolinians sought staple commodities for this export economy, entrepreneurs in southeastern North Carolina developed trade in lumber and naval stores and eventually became some of British North America's foremost exporters of these products. Finally, although the availability of labor was a chronic problem in North Carolina, the Cape Fear valley, and especially New Hanover and Brunswick counties, had two of the highest percentages of slaves. Within all fifteen counties of eastern North Carolina, only nine individuals owned more than fifty slaves, and eight of these men lived in New Hanover and Brunswick counties. Consequently, by the middle decades of the eighteenth century, the Cape Fear region possessed a higher percentage of wealthy persons than elsewhere in the colony. The upshot was that with the establishment of Wilmington under the patronage of Governor Johnston, northern and southern interests in the colony jockeyed for power, prestige, and subsidies in a manner that made North Carolina one of the more factious colonies in the annals of early American political history.[27]

Recognition of these political processes, particularly the competition between Brunswick Town and Wilmington, helps one understand the rhythms and contexts in which the development of religious institutions along the Cape Fear during the eighteenth century took place. The establishment of St. James Parish in 1729 had raised expectations for Brunswick. Moreover, just as the commercial horizons of the Cape Fear extended beyond its coastline to the Caribbean and Great Britain, so too its religious horizons extended to London and the bishop of that city for Anglicans, and even farther for persons of other faiths. The bishop of London worked closely with the SPG in making appointments to the American colonies, which had been under his supervision and administration since 1725.

Yet reality at Brunswick Town did not match its supporters' hopes. Although authorization for the building of a church in Brunswick Town had been received in 1729, none had been constructed as late as 1745. Nor had there ever been a settled minister, as both John LaPierre and Richard Mardsen had only circulated through the region. James Murray, a well-to-do merchant recently arrived in Brunswick Town from Scotland, called Marsden one of the best preachers he had heard in America, but Marsden had always been one to curry favor among his prosperous parishioners.[28]

Slow steps toward improving Brunswick Town's religious situation began in 1741 with the establishment of St. Philip Parish on the western side of the Cape Fear River, with St. James Parish remaining on the eastern bank. In that year, James Moir was serving in both Brunswick Town and Wilmington. The vestry of St. James in Wilmington increased his salary but did not support his ministering in Brunswick Town. In 1742 a new St. James vestry reduced Moir's salary, and he moved to Brunswick Town as its minister. In 1744 Moir was provided with a small house in Brunswick that he used for church services and where he taught school as well. Yet no sooner had Moir left St. James than the Wilmingtonians wanted him to come back and perform services and baptisms for them. In Moir's view, this was simply to spite St. Philip, for he concluded that "a missionary in this river has a most difficult part to act, for by obliging one of the Towns he must of course disoblige the other, each of them opposing the other to the utmost of their power."[29]

In 1754 construction finally began on the St. Philip church. Arthur Dobbs, who arrived that year to become the new royal governor, stated that the Brunswick church was seventy-six feet long and fifty-six feet wide. Moreover, a house was ready for the parish's minister, and a glebe of three hundred acres had also been provided. Five years later, however, so little progress had been made on the church's construction that officials authorized a lottery, the proceeds from which were to go toward the completion of churches in both St. Philip and St. James parishes. Governor Dobbs proposed making the Brunswick Town church into a royal chapel upon its completion and pledged a communion plate, furniture for the communion table, a pulpit, a Bible, and copies of the Book of Common Prayer.[30]

With these incentives, construction was renewed, but a storm in 1760 collapsed the roof. Consequently, officials authorized a second lottery and distributed the proceeds, along with monies from the sale of Spanish booty from the 1748 attack on Brunswick Town, to the two parishes. In 1765 Arthur Dobbs died and was buried in the still incomplete church. His successor, William Tryon, was likewise a staunch churchman and donated money and imported window treatments for the church's completion. Finally, on May 24, 1768, the Reverend John Barnett of Brunswick Town, assisted by the Reverend John Wills of Wilmington, dedicated St. Philip Church. The interior was designed in a traditional cruciform pattern, with side and center aisles paved with brick tiles. The side walls had arched windows, and the eastern end had a fifteen-foot Palladian chancel window before which stood the altar, pulpit, and reading desk. The nave would have contained pews, probably of the box variety, with spaces reserved for the governor and his council. The exterior walls were Flemish bond brickwork with glazed headers, and the hipped roof was capped with a belfry.[31]

St. Philip Church may have been slow in its construction, but once completed, it stood as an ambitious and resolute symbol of the established church in the Lower Cape Fear region, as well as one of the most impressive churches in colonial North Carolina. With exterior walls twenty-four feet high and nearly three feet thick, glass windows imported from England, vestments for the clergy, and a communion set donated by the king for sacramental use, St. Philip's represented the union of throne and altar in a symbolically potent fashion. The fact that Governor Dobbs and Governor Tryon resided in Brunswick Town (until the latter's move to New Bern in 1770) added weight to the majesty of this church and its architectural statement of royal power.

Across and up the river, the growth of Wilmington continued in a more regular if less monumental fashion. Seizing on the advantage provided by Governor Johnston's decision to locate judicial functions in their town, Wilmingtonians erected a courthouse in June 1740. In due course they also constructed a jail, stocks, pillory, and public whipping post, and in 1774 they added a ducking stool to this penal miscellany.[32]

Town commissioners supervised municipal organization and development, except for 1760 through 1766, when aldermen and a common council had control. In a 1754 letter to the Earl of Halifax, Arthur Dobbs provided a few details concerning Wilmington. He noted that seventy families resided in the town and that a large brick church was under construction. At the foot of the main street, docks handled the river traffic from the one hundred or more ships that entered the Cape Fear River annually. Dobbs further stated that large vessels could continue some ways up the river and smaller ones could go as far as 150 miles. Peter DuBois, a visitor to the town in 1757, provided additional descriptive details. He remarked that the streets, laid out in a regular pattern, reminded him of Philadelphia. The buildings were well done, DuBois wrote, with many constructed in brick and several two or three stories high with double covered porches or piazzas.[33]

By the late 1750s, then, the salient features of the geography of Wilmington had been set out. At its core was the Market Street axis running from the river in an easterly direction through the town toward New Bern. This axis was symbolically anchored at one end by the courthouse and at the other end by the church. Just beyond the courthouse lay the wharves on the river, connecting Wilmington to the hinterland trade upriver. The river itself was a multivalent part of Wilmington, not only as a continuing source of food but also as an avenue for the colonial vessels and the eventual steamboats, blockade runners, and container cargo ships that were to shape Wilmington's economic future. Indeed, the river would commercially link Wilmington to the region's interior and to the wider world of Europe, Asia, and beyond. It would shape Wilmington as a port city and give it exposure to more cosmopolitan possibilities and more international influences than one might expect for a place of its size and location.

Moving up from the river and out from its Market Street axis, the emerging cityscape of colonial Wilmington developed in a grid system of streets that resembled Philadelphia not only in its regularity but also in its choice of names, such as Chestnut, Dock, and Market, and in the intersection of these named streets with numbered ones. In this way the orientation of early Wilmington was manifested in its architectural landmarks of judicial and spiritual space, in the regularity of its setting around its axis, and in its opening out to the world through the river and roads. Here parish and precinct overlapped for the moment, while mercantile and domestic influences pushed out from the center and expanded into the periphery.

As Dobbs noted, the church in Wilmington was still under construction in 1754. While it was being built, the courthouse doubled as a house of worship. A bequest had been given for the initial construction of this church, to be called St. James after the parish. However, much like St. Philip in Brunswick Town, construction of the Wilmington church was intermittent at best. In order to raise money, church leaders encouraged private individuals to obtain their own pews, built in proportion to the size of their subscriptions. Other individuals subsequently made gifts in their wills. Additionally, in 1751 officials levied an annual tax to last for three years and designated a percentage of the proceeds from lotteries and the sale of captured Spanish booty for the construction of St. James.[34]

By 1770 the church was finally completed. The shape of the building was square and not particularly striking. It appears to have been modeled after the St. James Church in Goose Creek, South Carolina, home of Maurice Moore and many of his family members, and reflected an architectural indebtedness to the same English sources on which the architect of the Goose Creek church drew. Of its three entrances, one faced the river, one opened onto Market Street, and the third provided access to the graveyard. Unlike St. Philip, this church in Wilmington had no belfry. Its interior followed the pattern of many Anglican churches of the day. The side and center aisles were paved with large bricks. At the front of the nave were the chancel, a reading desk, and the pulpit under a large sounding board. Beneath and to the sides of the pulpit, box pews filled the floor space and the second-floor gallery. The pews were large enough to accommodate a whole family, although some occupants would have to sit with their backs to the pulpit. Pews were not free but rather were rented annually as a source of income for the church. Additionally, the St. James vestry reserved pews for the governor and his council should they ever be in attendance. Prominent family names in the Wilmington community, such as Moore, DeRosset, Dry, and Harnett, can also be seen in a floor plan of this early church.[35]

With their classical elements, both St. Philip and St. James represent early examples of architectural revivalism, an issue discussed at greater length in chapter 3. If St. James was less architecturally imposing than St. Philip, it nonetheless made its presence known in Wilmington. The church property actually (and quite legally) protruded some thirty feet into Market Street. Other evidence of the visibility and influence of religion in Wilmington can be found. For example, in 1754 the legislature passed laws to better regulate the town of Wilmington. In its attempt to strengthen the social order, the legislature empowered the town commissioners to set the price of bread, prohibit hogs running wild in the town, purchase a fire engine, and require that chimneys be swept regularly. Turning to matters more explicitly invoking the sacred, the legislature in 1751 had already prohibited anyone from using the courthouse while religious services were taking place. Now in 1754 it noted that people walking and talking outside the building had disturbed services. Consequently, town officials directed the constables to patrol the streets during church services and to apprehend all delinquents and punish them as Sabbath breakers. Beyond that, no tavern keepers could serve or allow anyone to consume liquor in their establishments while services were under way. All offenders were to be fined and placed in the stocks. Here in this vision of good order, with its prohibition of iniquity and its encouragement of honesty, virtue, sobriety, and decorum, the lineaments of established religion in the Cape Fear region were clearly visible. Although these laws portray a civic life intended to be as regular as its municipal roads, they also tell us something about the existence and scope of the social problems, about the past experiences and present fears that necessitated their enactment.[36]

In late December 1739, George Whitefield, a well-known revivalist and Anglican priest, stopped at "New Town on Cape Fear River" and on Sunday, December 30, preached twice in the courthouse. Whitefield remarked, "there being many of the Scotch among the congregation, who lately came over to settle in North Carolina, I was led in the afternoon to make a particular application to them."[37]

Whitefield had a reputation for using any location from which to preach, nor was he reluctant about speaking to crowds of non-Anglicans. He was correct about the ethnic background of his audience, in that there were many Scots in Wilmington, including such prominent persons as James Murray, John Rutherfurd, Robert Hogg, and later Robert Schaw and Alexander Duncan. Other nationalities and religious persuasions were also represented in the nominally English and Anglican town of Wilmington. The merchant-planters Frederick Gregg, Robert Walker, and John Sampson were all from Ireland. Moses Gomez and the family of Philip David were Sephardic Jews. John Robeson, Joshua Grainger, John Sharpless, Ebenezer Bunting, and Richard Bradley were Quakers, and there was a Quaker cemetery in Wilmington. The DeRosset family was

French in background. Louis DeRosset, father of the Wilmington physician Armand DeRosset, fled to England from France in 1685 in the aftermath of the revocation of the Edict of Nantes, and Armand was born in London. The DeRossets were Huguenots, and Armand, his wife, and their children immigrated to Wilmington by 1735. Because there was no organized Huguenot congregation in Wilmington, the DeRossets eventually affiliated with the Anglican tradition, just as their countryman John LaPierre had done earlier in London and South Carolina. Significantly, James Murray and John Rutherfurd, both from Scottish Presbyterian families, also joined the St. James congregation. Add to these European groups the African slave population, largely from the western coastal region of Africa, and one has a representative sample of the ethnic and religious heterogeneity in colonial Wilmington.[38]

In this regard, Wilmington was a symbolic microcosm for the Cape Fear region as a whole. For example, in Edward Moseley's 1733 map of North Carolina, there are two areas in the southeastern portion named "Welch Settlements." The larger of the two was located on the northeast branch of the Cape Fear River in what are now Duplin and Pender counties. The first settlers to this area, often called the "Welch Tract" during the colonial era, were descended from immigrants to Pennsylvania from South Wales. With the restoration of Charles II and the strengthening of the Anglican establishment, numerous Welsh dissenters emigrated, and many established themselves in the Radnor, Goshen, and Tredyffrin townships of Pennsylvania. In October 1701 William Penn granted a 300,000-acre tract to David Evans Sr., William Davies, and William Willis. This land was located mostly in Newcastle, Delaware, with a smaller portion in contiguous Cecil County, Maryland. This site was the home of the Iron Hill Welsh Baptists, who were later responsible for missionaries in the Pee Dee region of South Carolina, and of the Welsh Pencader Presbyterian Church.[39]

David Evans Sr. was an elder in the Pencader Presbyterian Church and a magistrate in Newcastle. The Pencader church was to play an important role in the subsequent development of colonial Presbyterianism; however, in the late 1720s Evans led a small contingent to the Middle Cape Fear area. Rather than constructing compact townships, these Welsh settlers spread out on individual farmsteads along the waterways and tributaries connected to the

Cape Fear River. They transported their lumber and farm products on log rafts and flatboats down the creeks and streams that fed into the Cape Fear River and on to Wilmington and the markets of the region, the nation, and the world. During his 1730 sojourn in the Cape Fear region, Hugh Meredith visited David Evans and also mentioned his deceased countryman Thomas James. Additional Welsh family names, familiar in the region, included Bloodworth, Wells, and Jones, for Welsh immigration continued in the colonial era. Hinton James, the first student to enroll at the University of North Carolina in 1795, was born and raised in this Welsh tract.[40]

More Presbyterians came to the Middle Cape Fear. In November 1735 Arthur Dobbs, resident of Ulster and later royal governor of North Carolina, and Henry McCulloh, a London merchant, applied for a grant of sixty thousand acres along the Black River on which they planned to settle Scottish Presbyterian families from Ulster, Ireland. The term *Scots-Irish*, as historians point out, refers to those usually Lowland Scots who were moved to Ulster Plantation in Northern Ireland under James I of England as part of an English colonization plan. Thus the origin of the term reflects a political and geographical situation rather than an ethnic combination. By 1736 some of these Scots-Irish families had been established along the Black River and later went on to found Black River Chapel in 1740. Many more Scots-Irish, however, settled in the backcountry and Piedmont rather than near the coast.[41]

Other branches of Reformed Protestants also came to the Middle Cape Fear area. In 1736 Henry McCulloh and his representatives received more large grants of land for some six thousand Swiss Protestants they intended to bring over to North Carolina. In November 1736 James Murray wrote, "forty Swiss people, the beginning of six thousand contracted for," had arrived in the Cape Fear River valley. Several months later Murray stated that the Swiss families were doing well, and in 1756 he reported on a successful attempt by some Swiss to cultivate silkworms fed on wild mulberry leaves. Nevertheless, McCulloh's strategy for Swiss colonization in the Middle Cape Fear never achieved its goal. In fact, in 1754 Crown officials complained that only 854 individuals had actually settled down and that much of the grant remained unoccupied.[42]

Another contingent of Reformed Protestants arrived in the Middle Cape Fear from the Palatinate region of Germany. Originally these colonists had settled in New Bern on the Neuse River under the sponsorship of Baron Christoph von Graffenried. The Tuscarora Indian War of 1711–1715 decimated New Bern's population, however, and most survivors fled the area, at least temporarily. In 1743 Cullen Pollock evicted Palatinate and other tenants along the Neuse, and many of these dispersed Germans migrated to the Cape Fear region. By religious heritage, these Germans belonged to the Reformed tradition, and by 1740 they had organized a congregation and built a chapel in New Bern for themselves. George Kornegay, patriarch of a family in Duplin County, illustrates this pattern of settlement. Born in 1701, Kornegay came to New Bern in 1709. The Tuscarora killed the rest of his family in 1711, and George was placed under the guardianship of Jacob Miller. A founder of the 1740 Palatine Reformed Church, Kornegay soon moved west and appeared in local Duplin records by 1754. Similarly, the Teachey family, namesake for the railroad stop and town in present-day Duplin County, descend from the Palatinate colonist Daniel Tetsche, an early settler who also moved to the Middle Cape Fear.[43]

Thus, by the mid-1750s the sparse population of this region had spread up and down the Black River and both branches of the Cape Fear River and their tributaries. They settled in isolated farms and small villages such as Soracte (now Sarecta), Goshen, and Grove, and agriculture and involvement in the naval stores industry provided the residents with much of their livelihood. Religious institutions accompanied political and economic ones. The variety of ethnic backgrounds found a unifying force in a common Reformed theological heritage. As early as 1736 the Presbyterian Grove congregation met and held services, probably in a simple log church, near present-day Kenansville. Presbyterian missionary William Robinson traveled through Virginia and North Carolina in 1743 and in all likelihood visited the Grove congregation, as it was one of the oldest in the colony.[44]

In 1755–1756 Hugh McAden, a Presbyterian minister, made a missionary tour of North Carolina. On February 22, 1756, McAden delivered a sermon at David Evans's house in the Welsh tract. After staying a week and preaching again, McAden crisscrossed the area until he reached the home of William Dickson near the Grove church, where he spoke to an appreciative audience. McAden continued his journey but was not gone for long. In 1757 he returned as the first regular pastor at Grove, as well as ministering to the residents of the Welsh tract in the congregation that later became Rockfish Presbyterian Church, near present-day Wallace, North Carolina. In 1741, in the context of the Great Awakening, the Presbyterian Church in America had divided between the Old Side, who were opponents of the awakening, and the New Side, who were the awakening's supporters. As described in his son's reminiscences, McAden was a moderate New Side man who was studious, emphasized the necessity of the conversion experience, and regularly visited and exhorted his congregational members. McAden remained with the Grove church until 1767, at which time he moved to Caswell County, where he died in 1781.[45]

In addition to the Presbyterians, Missionary Baptists formed an early congregation in the Middle Cape Fear. In 1756 Samuel Newton, together with his brothers George, Jacob, and Isaac, organized a Baptist congregation. Samuel Newton served as its pastor until his death during the Revolutionary War. Originally the church was called Bull Tail Meeting House because of its proximity to Bull Tail Creek. However, the congregation later changed the name to Wells Chapel in honor of one of its pastors.[46]

The creation of Duplin County in 1749 also served as the context for the establishment of St. Gabriel Parish. John Sampson, William Houston, George Meares, and Francis Brice were among those named to the vestry. Although Presbyterians, Baptists, and others were visible in this region, it is important to remember that the established Anglican Church existed and had the full support of the royal governor. Initially, because no priest had been assigned to the parish, church officials appointed lay readers who held Sunday services at different houses throughout the county. About 1760 the Reverend William Miller was inducted as pastor of the parish. Because a church had not yet been constructed, Miller continued the tradition of meeting and preaching in different houses in the parish. At first, Miller was popular with his parishioners, but their estimate of him soon soured. Governor Dobbs certainly had a low opinion of Miller, stating that since 1754 Miller had "changed from Parish to Parish under strong suspicions of living irregularly." In December 1763 the governor and his council received a complaint about Miller from St. Gabriel Parish, and in November 1766 representatives from the parish brought further charges against their pastor.

However, the governor and council found the charges insufficiently supported and recommended to the parish vestry that Miller continue for another twelve months on a probationary basis.[47]

By the following year, though, William Miller had indeed transferred to another parish. His place at St. Gabriel was taken by the Reverend Hobart Briggs. Not much is known about Briggs. He was described as "an English man . . . Sober, Grave, not addicted to any Vice." Governor William Tryon inducted Briggs into his position in 1769 but met with opposition from the parish vestry, which wanted to keep the power of presentation and induction (basically, the ability to hire or fire the minister) under its own control.[48]

Briggs circulated through the parish, rotating among eight different houses where he held Sunday services and preached. In his first seven months he reported that he had christened 130 persons and performed sixteen marriages and ten burials. Pleased with the attention and devotion that his parishioners evidenced, Briggs noted that many were too poor to afford prayer books, so he hoped that the SPG could provide some copies. Disputes with the parish vestry, dating back to the conflict over his induction, continued. Governor Tryon sought to protect Briggs by putting him under the patronage of John Sampson. Tryon's successor as governor, Josiah Martin, also was impressed with Briggs, recommending that the SPG continue his salary and that the bishop of London support him as well. By the eve of the American Revolution, though, Briggs had disappeared from the record, possibly returning to England.[49]

Although the Middle Cape Fear had numerous and varied immigrants, perhaps the best known, most cohesive, and largest single non-English eighteenth-century group to reach the Cape Fear region were the Scots from the Highlands and Western Isles. These immigrants came to the Upper Cape Fear in several waves. James Innes (from Caithness) received his first land grant in January 1732 and at least two others soon thereafter. Hugh Campbell and William Forbes also acquired tracts of land by 1733. The land of all three men was on the Cape Fear River in the vicinity of Rockfish Creek.[50]

The royal governor, Gabriel Johnston, was a supporter of Scottish immigration. A Lowland Scot by birth and a graduate of St. Andrew's University, Johnston saw Scottish immigration as a benefit to the fledgling colony of North Carolina. In September 1739, 350

Highlanders from the county of Argyll disembarked from their ship the *Thistle* at Brunswick Town. Their leaders were Duncan Campbell, Dugald McNeil, Daniel McNeil, Neil McNeil, and Coll McAllister. The group did not stay in Brunswick Town but continued some ninety miles up the Cape Fear River to the area where Innes, Campbell, and Forbes held their lands. Whether Innes or his countrymen had communicated previously with these new Highlanders is not known. What is known is that Neil McNeil had visited the Cape Fear area in 1737 or 1738 and had returned to Argyllshire praising the opportunity for settlement it presented. Beginning a policy of incentives for further Scottish immigration that was continued by his successors, Johnston supported a subsidy of £1000 to be distributed among these Argyll families and a proposal that they be relieved of public taxes for ten years.[51]

The Argyll group was only the beginning of the Scottish Highlander immigration to the Upper Cape Fear; it would last until 1776 and the outbreak of hostilities with Great Britain. The Scottish story illustrates the familiar push and pull paradigm in American immigration history. Several sets of circumstances in Scotland—notably, changes in the organization of agriculture, decay of the clan system, and population growth—combined to encourage emigration.

In the aftermath of the failed revolution of 1745, Scottish society underwent several fundamental changes. One of the most significant concerned the transformation of the tacksmen, who were the gentry of Scotland. They were moderately well-off individuals who had been responsible for organizing the clan chief's military, but after 1746 and the abolition of clan armies, they took over land leasing for the clan chief. As improved techniques of agricultural production, shifts to large-scale sheep management, and increases in lease prices took place, land use changed, and the position of the tacksmen slowly became economically obsolete. Similarly, political changes undermined the traditional clan system and its social assumptions. For example, after the Scottish defeat at the Battle of Culloden in 1745, Highlanders were disarmed and forbidden to provide military allegiance to their clan chiefs. Highland plaids and kilts were not allowed to be worn, and justice was now administered by sheriffs rather than by clan chiefs. The result of all this, as one historian remarked, was that "the special bond between chief and clansmen was effectively broken." Finally and paradoxically, given the dislocation taking place within Scottish society, the population increased due to the availability of new crops, such as kale and potatoes, and the utilization of new medicines, such as a vaccination against smallpox. Taken together, these developments increased the Scottish population in the last half of the eighteenth century beyond what the economic and social resources seemed able to support.[52]

As these transformations took place in the Highlands, tacksmen such as Campbell, McAllister, and the McNeils, the organizers of the *Thistle* expedition, took the lead in emigration. Tacksmen who wished to head for North Carolina, for example, would advertise their intended departure, enroll interested persons, and contract for transportation. And it was not difficult to find people who wanted to emigrate. Promotional tracts, personal correspondence, and communication by word of mouth all illustrated the pull of the American colonies that complemented the push of domestic Scottish circumstances. Incentives, such as the exemption from taxes and the availability of affordable land, laid the foundation for personal recommendations. Writing in 1772, for example, Alexander Campbell described the Highlanders in the Upper Cape Fear River valley as living "as happy as princes, they have liberty & property & no Excise, no dread of their being turned out of their lands by Tyrants . . . in Short I never saw a people seemed to me to be so really happy as our Countrymen there."[53]

Other evidence of the motivations for moving to the New World can be found in the 1774 report of those "on board the Ship Bachelor of Leith bound to Wilmington in North Carolina." William Gordon, a farmer, already had two sons in Carolina who encouraged him to come over. Similarly, William McKay could not provide bread for his family in Scotland, but friends who were already in America assured him that he would be comfortable there. William Bain was a shopkeeper, but the poverty of the local residents was so great that they could not pay him. Like his shipmates, he hoped to better his condition in America. One hundred thirty-six passengers on board the *Jupiter* were bound for the port of Wilmington in 1775. Higher rents and clearances for sheep grazing had forced the farmers among them to leave, while the laborers simply could no longer find work to support their families. In all these ways the experience of dislocation, unemployment, and poverty made many in the Highlands receptive to the invitation to cross over to the Cape Fear valley.[54]

Although the records are incomplete, it is clear that Highlanders did come to the Cape Fear River valley. The mainland of Argyll, the Kintyre peninsula, and the island of Islay were the origins of many of the first emigrants. In 1767 there was a notice of fifty persons from the island of Jura in Argyll who had landed at Brunswick Town intending to go upriver. In 1771 Governor Tryon stated that sixteen hundred men, women, and children from the islands of Islay, Jura, and Gigah in Argyll had arrived in the last three years. The next year the new royal governor, Josiah Martin, reported that another thousand Scots had come; by later that same year, between six hundred and seven hundred more Highlanders had reached Cape Fear ports. Thus, although an indisputable estimate of the size of the Highland emigration is impossible, it seems reasonable that during the years of highest emigration, 1763 to 1775, some fifty thousand Scots left for North America, and something like twelve thousand came to the Cape Fear region.[55]

Whatever the size of the migration, it is clear that most of the Highlanders who came to North Carolina landed at Brunswick Town or Wilmington and then moved on to the Upper Cape Fear region. The center of the settlement was the trading village of Cross Creek, ninety miles upriver from Wilmington. The village was located at the junction of two branches of Cross Creek, a waterway that provided access to the Cape Fear River. Roads connecting the village with Orange County, the Catawba River valley, and the Dan River valley were all constructed by the late 1770s, thereby enhancing the village's position as a commercial nexus between the hinterland and Wilmington. With a gristmill, tavern, and merchant warehouses, Cross Creek had a population of seventy-five by 1765. Not surprisingly, though, with the easy availability of land and their background in agriculture, most Highlanders became farmers and resided up and down the creeks, streams, and rivers in the vicinity of the town.[56]

No more surprising than their continuation of farming was their rapid organization of religious congregations. It is noteworthy that no minister accompanied the Argyll immigrants aboard the *Thistle* in September 1739, given the prominence of religion in these Highlanders' lives. In fact, the leaders of the expedition had tried to obtain one. On February 27, 1739, Duncan Campbell and Dugald McTavish had petitioned the Presbytery of Inverary to invite the Reverend Robert Fullerton at Kilmichael of Glasserie to be the pastor of the Argyll colony in North Carolina. The petition noted that these Scots planned to settle in North America later that year. Despite the distance from their homeland, the petitioners insisted that they would forget neither Scotland nor "the Church of Scotland, whose Sons we shall always be."[57]

Dugald McTavish and three other members of the colony also encouraged Duncan Campbell to petition the Scottish Society for the Propagation of Christian Knowledge (SSPCK), a missionary organization centered in Edinburgh, for a pastor for their settlement. Neither of Campbell's efforts met with success. The presbytery tabled his petition until it could get more information about the procedures for sending a minister outside the bounds of the synod, and Fullerton's church at Glasserie strongly objected to any attempt to transfer its minister. At the SSPCK meeting of June 7, 1739, it decided to delay consideration of Campbell's petition until the Argyllshire group had settled in North America.[58]

In March 1741 the Argyll colony again requested a minister. The SSPCK recommended to the Presbytery of Inverary that a missionary with the salary of £21 be sent and asked the presbytery to forward the names of possible candidates for the position. In its June 16 meeting, the presbytery decided to wait until it had confirmation of the success of the Argyll colony before sending any names. On November 3, 1741, Duncan Campbell made another appearance before the presbytery in the hope of obtaining a pastor. He also requested that the ministerial stipend for a prospective candidate be enlarged. Campbell's presentation was successful, in that the Presbytery of Inverary agreed to find a suitable missionary for the colony on the Cape Fear River. However, by 1748 nothing had happened, so in frustration the Argyll men sent a new request for a pastor to the neighboring Presbytery of Kintyre, in which they promised any minister a yearly stipend of £50 and a manse. This presbytery replied that there was nothing it could do right now, and in any case, £50 was an insufficient salary. Finally, in 1748 seventy-seven Cape Fear Scotsmen sent a petition to the Synod of Argyll and offered £140 for a minister "authorized according to the Rules and Discipline of the Kirk of Scotland." This pledge of allegiance to the Church of Scotland echoed the words of the February 1739 petition but was no more successful than the Argyll men's earlier efforts to secure a minister from their homeland.[59]

While these negotiations with Scottish church officials were taking place, Highlanders in the Cross Creek area had been meeting informally in one another's homes for devotions, hymns, and prayers. Even into the eighteenth century, Scottish culture was still based in oral traditions. Memorization and recitation of material, whether passages from the Bible or tales from folklore, were the norm. Only a few religious resources were even available in written Gaelic. A rendition of the Westminster Shorter Catechism in Gaelic first appeared in 1651. The first fifty psalms had been translated in 1659, with the remainder obtainable for the first time in 1684. Portions of the Old and New Testaments had been sporadically accessible, but it was not until the early nineteenth century that the whole Bible was rendered into the vernacular language of the Scottish people. Even though the sacraments could not be administered without a duly installed minister, congregations could still be formed and scripture recited, hymns sung, and prayers lifted up. Thus, even when ministers and texts were no longer so rare, a broad emphasis on memorization and recitation would be characteristic of these Scottish Presbyterians for many years to come.

When Hugh McAden, traveling through North Carolina on his missionary trip, arrived in the Upper Cape Fear on Sunday, January 25, 1736, he preached to a group of Highlanders assembled at the home of one of the members. Because McAden did not speak Gaelic, he correctly surmised that few, if any, of his audience understood exactly what he had to say. He also remarked that the Highlanders were "the poorest singers I ever heard in all my life." Although it is possible that this particular Highland flock was chorally inept, it is also possible that they were singing in a style familiar in the Highlands but unfamiliar to the Pennsylvania-born McAden. In the Highland style of psalm singing, the choral leader would sing a line and then repeat it slowly with the congregation. When the people then sang the line themselves, there was time between the notes for individuals to add extra "grace notes." The result was variations being sung at the same time. Perhaps this cacophony is what McAden heard.[60]

It was not until 1758 that the Highlanders got their first regular minister. James Campbell, Highland born and Gaelic speaking,

knew Hugh McAden and responded to his report of the Highlanders' need for a clergyman who could preach in Gaelic. Campbell
had been preaching in the Pennsylvania area for four years when, in
1739, he became unsure of his faith and stopped. Shortly thereafter
he had an opportunity to talk with revivalist George Whitefield, and
Whitefield convinced him to resume his ministry. When Campbell
arrived in the Cross Creek area, the Highlanders were spread up
and down the rivers and creeks of the region, so Campbell served
three congregations, conducting two services in Gaelic and the other in English.[61]

The three churches were the Old Bluff congregation, near present-
day Wade, North Carolina; the Barbecue church, located on the
creek of that name; and the congregation that eventually became
Longstreet church. All three met initially in the homes of members. When these congregations were able to build their first meetinghouses, they were probably simple structures, square in shape
and built with logs and mud mortar. Worship services among these
Scots were equally simple. John Calvin's insistence on following
what scripture enjoined was interpreted by these Presbyterians to
forbid musical instruments. Unaccompanied singing was the form,
and the psalms, rendered into recognizable metrical tunes, were the
content. With communion celebrated only at infrequent sacramental occasions, preaching became the centerpiece of worship, with
prayers and the recitation of passages from the scriptures and catechism filling out the services.[62]

In 1771 the Highlanders finally got a minister directly from
Scotland. That individual was John McLeod, and he arrived from
the Isle of Skye on one of the many shiploads of Highlanders coming to the Cape Fear region. McLeod teamed up with Campbell,
and they served their three congregations until the American Revolution, when, in an ironic twist, the Highlanders lost both their
clergymen. The Highlanders were generally Loyalists during the
Revolution. According to local lore, Campbell, who favored the Patriot cause, was threatened by a member of one of his congregations
for his political views and decided to leave for Guilford County.
McLeod, a Tory, was captured by Patriot forces and interned as
a prisoner of war. In May 1776 the Provincial Congress released
McLeod. Shortly thereafter he left for Scotland but is presumed to
have died at sea.[63]

Writing to the SPG from Brunswick Town in April 1760, the Reverend John McDowell described the Cape Fear region as "inhabited by many sorts of people, of various nations and different opinions, customs, and manners." With the exception of African slaves, who had no choice in the matter, the many sorts of people to which McDowell alluded had come to the Cape Fear in the hope of finding better opportunities and the chance to improve their lives. They brought the manners and customs of the old country, which were sometimes adapted under the press of new circumstances, and sometimes retained. And beyond that, these people brought their religions with them. In addition to the occasional Moravian on a trading trip to or from Wachovia, Sephardic Jews, French Huguenots, English Anglicans, Welsh or Scottish Presbyterians, and an assortment of British Quakers, Missionary Baptists, and German Reformed Palatines were all part of the religious mix in the colonial Cape Fear region.[64]

In the face of all this diversity, an obvious question kept recurring: what did it mean to have an establishment of religion? At the very least, it meant a number of things, for the establishment of religion in the colony of North Carolina and the region of the Cape Fear functioned at a number of levels. Fundamentally, it meant recognition of the Christian God and worship of Him according to the rites of the Church of England. "You shall take especial care that God Almighty be devoutly and duly served," the royal instructions to Governor Burrington mandated. To this end, the Book of Common Prayer was to be read publicly each Sunday and holiday, and the sacraments were to be administered.[65]

But the establishment of religion had a wider purview than Sundays; it was codified into law in a variety of ways. One set of regulations, for example, reflected the broad perception that legal codes followed the laws of God. In this view, divine commandments were the basis of the moral order on which society was founded. Wrongdoing was sinful and, as the prologue to a 1715 law put it, if left unchecked, such malevolent behavior resulted in "the great Dishonour of the Almighty and scandal of this Province." Thus legal codes had the dual purpose of restraining and punishing evil and encouraging good behavior, beneficence, and rectitude.[66]

Many laws were passed that sought to establish the moral foundation of an orderly society. The royal instructions to Governor Burrington had called for laws "against Blasphemy, Prophaness, Adultery, Fornication, Polygamy, Incest, Prophanation of the Lord's Day, Swearing, and Drunkenness." In 1741 the colonial government passed an act "for the better Observation and Keeping of the Lord's Day, commonly called Sunday, and for the more effectual Suppression of Vice and Immorality." This legislation was a revision of a virtually identical act from 1715. In the 1741 enactment, Sunday was recognized as a day for the exercise of the "duties of religion and piety"; thus no work, sports, or games were to be carried out. The penalty for anyone doing so was a fine of ten shillings. Similarly, anyone swearing or cursing was subject to a fine ranging from two to ten shillings, depending on the circumstances, and anyone convicted of drunkenness on Sunday could be fined five shillings or put in the stocks. Persons involved in fornication or bearing illegitimate children were also subject to punishment.[67]

Although the records are not complete for the whole region, it is clear that some Wilmingtonians were punished for infractions of these laws. Abel Johnson, for example, was convicted in 1740 for "working constantly on the Lord's Day." In 1741 Jane Langdon, Catherine McDaid, and Sarah Johnston were convicted of having illegitimate children. And in 1787 and 1788 William Moore posted bond against two illegitimate children he had fathered with different mothers becoming charges of the parish. Though the evidence in the Cape Fear region is scant, a study of crime in the province of North Carolina as a whole revealed that by the mid-eighteenth century, it was less likely that personal sins would be treated as crimes. Moreover, gender played a role in prosecutions for moral misbehavior. Women accused of adultery, fornication, or bastardy had a much higher conviction rate and lower acquittal rate than did their male counterparts. Between 1663 and 1776, for instance, in North Carolina the male conviction rate for adultery was 16.1 percent, and the female rate was 29.7 percent.[68]

Although these laws probably reflected a broad moral consensus within colonial North Carolina society, other laws gave explicit sanction to the Church of England and its ministers. From King Charles II's charter of 1663 through the proprietary period and on to the royal instructions to the governors, governmental support for the Church of England was manifest. Land for parish churches in many cases was granted to, not purchased by, Anglicans. Royal governors such as Arthur Dobbs and William Tryon attended Anglican services and made gifts toward the completion of churches such as St. Philip and St. James. After 1739 Anglican missionaries received free passage on any ferry in their district, with the government paying the costs.[69]

Beyond these measures, the power of Anglican vestries to assess taxes on citizens, Anglican and non-Anglican alike, for the support of the established church was significant. Obtaining a vestry act was sometimes difficult in the colony, particularly during its early years. An act passed in 1701 created parishes, named vestry members selected by the Assembly for each parish, and authorized taxes for the building of Anglican churches and the hiring of their ministers. The Lords Proprietors disallowed this act because it did not sufficiently provide for the clergy. Another act was passed in 1715 that included most of the provisions of the 1701 legislation, and it remained in effect until 1741. Two further vestry acts were passed in 1741 and 1754, both of which sought to give the power to select the rector to the vestry. These were disallowed, as this power was reserved to the Crown and its representatives.[70]

Finally in 1764 a vestry act was passed, followed the next year by an act to enhance the support for the clergy. Unlike the acts of 1741 and 1754, this vestry act received the approval of the king, the Privy Council, and the bishop of London. Its provisions included that twelve from among the parish freeholders (owners of estates of at least fifty acres or of a town lot) should be elected as vestrymen. The minister of the parish was also included in the vestry. Once assembled, the vestry was responsible for levying an annual charge of no more than ten shillings on all taxable persons for building Anglican churches and chapels, paying the minister's salary, purchasing glebe lands and building a manse, assisting the poor, and any other charges that might arise. The sheriff was appointed collector and was empowered to seize the property of any persons who refused to pay and to auction their goods to obtain the amount of the tax. The 1765 act stipulated the amount of ministerial salaries and required that the glebe land be at least two hundred acres. It also specified the fees that the minister was to receive for such services as performing a marriage ceremony or preaching a funeral sermon. With the passage and approval of these bills, the establishment of the Anglican Church in North Carolina had legally come of age.[71]

Further evidence for the manner and meaning of a religious establishment can be seen in the provisions for dissenting Protestants. The existence of non-Anglicans among North Carolina's colonial population had been recognized as far back as the king's instructions to the Lords Proprietors. Although Roman Catholics were uniformly excluded, non-Anglican Protestants were to be accorded tolerance, or, as the royal instructions to Governor Burrington put it, "you are to permit a liberty of conscience to all persons (except papists)." Moreover, as early as 1711, toleration of dissenters was recognized in law. This gave dissenters a firmer footing than they had earlier, when the exercise of such indulgence remained a matter of caprice. Nevertheless, even after 1711, the interpretation and implementation of religious toleration for dissenters in North Carolina could often be arbitrary and oppressive.[72]

Such liberty of conscience did not extend to the refusal to pay taxes (as the provisions of the vestry acts made clear), nor were dissenters excused from other responsibilities. As Governor Tryon phrased it, he did not believe that toleration should "exempt dissenters from bearing their share of the support of the established religion." Equally important, toleration did not imply equality. From the perspective of the establishment, dissenters were not their religious peers; they were nuisances with which society and established religion had to put up.[73]

Examples abound attesting to the perceived social distance between the established religion and the dissenters. Anglican priest James Reed of New Bern surveyed his large parish and remarked of the non-Anglicans, "the Anabaptists are obstinate, illiterate, and grossly ignorant, the Methodists ignorant, censorious, and uncharitable, the Quakers rigid, but the Presbyterians are pretty moderate except here and there a bigot or rigid Calvinist." Closer to the Cape Fear, John McDowell in 1762 took pride in his Brunswick Town congregation. He noted that of the roughly two hundred families in the area, the "best in the province," including the governor, members of his council, and other leaders, belonged to his parish. In addition, another twenty families characterized as "good" worshipped at this church. The dissenters in the area, according to McDowell, amounted to a few poor families of fishermen who "call themselves new light anabaptists." Four years later McDowell's successor at St. Philip, John Barnett, disparagingly added, "new lights are very numerous in the southern parts of this parish—the most illiterate among them are teachers, even Negroes speak in their meetings."[74]

McDowell's affirmation of social hierarchy and Reed's and Barnett's pejorative statements were paralleled by remarks from the royal governors. Baptists had come to North Carolina from Virginia and had formed churches as early as 1727 and 1729. By the 1760s, as McDowell and Barnett stated, they could be found in the Brunswick region. Their presence as well as their style of ministry had come to the attention of the stalwart Anglican Arthur Dobbs, who curtly dismissed them as "strollers" and "dippers" for their particular religious practices. In 1769 Governor Tryon observed, "the Presbyterians and Quakers are the only tolerated sectaries under any order or regulation, every other are enemies to society and a scandal to common sense." Though sometimes couched within more general laments that the established church was not stronger, these harsh words, when taken together with the legislation strengthening the establishment in 1764 and 1765, provide a measure of the context and meaning of toleration for non-Anglicans in the late colonial era.[75]

Several areas of legislation illustrate the limits of toleration for dissenters in North Carolina. In 1715, for instance, Quakers were allowed to make affirmations rather than to take an oath in courts. Recognition of their religious beliefs came at a price, however, for this act also stated that no Quakers could testify in a criminal case, serve on a jury, or hold public office. This law was often reenacted, although Quakers were finally allowed to serve as witnesses by 1762.[76]

That marriages were holy unions and ought to be consecrated by a clergyman was recognized in colonial North Carolina. Yet many couples lived in common-law marriages for lack of a minister to marry them. In 1715 the colonial legislature pragmatically recognized this situation when it allowed magistrates to perform weddings. Interestingly, magistrates also performed funerals in the absence of clergy, as happened in the case of Arthur Dobbs. Dobbs was buried at St. Philip Church, and the services were performed by a local magistrate because there was no minister at Brunswick Town at the time. In 1741, however, a law was passed stipulating that only

Anglican clergymen could perform weddings; if there was no clergy available, then a magistrate could do so. All fees for the services went to the Anglican minister, unless he had refused to perform the service. Tradition states that some dissenting ministers qualified as magistrates so that they could marry fellow believers. In any case, such legislation clearly discriminated against dissenters, making dissent "burdensome and humiliating," as Stephen Weeks phrased it.[77]

In 1766 Presbyterian ministers who were settled in a specific congregation were allowed to perform marriages. This act noticeably provided no relief to non-Presbyterian dissenters, such as Baptists or Quakers. Moreover, it applied only to Presbyterian ministers called to a congregation and not to any missionary who might be traveling in the backcountry, where distance from settled communities made the need for itinerant ministers with marrying authority all the more pressing. In cases in which a Presbyterian minister presided and an Anglican minister had not refused to perform the ceremony, the fees went to the Anglican clergyman. In conclusion, it should be noted that the Crown later disallowed this concession of 1766 as destructive of the establishment of religion. Not until after the Revolution were all ministers accorded the right to perform marriages.[78]

In 1730 the royal instructions to Governor Burrington insisted that no minister should be allowed a congregation and no schoolteacher allowed to teach without an appropriate license from the bishop of London. With the subsequent growth of the dissenter population and the formation of many of their own congregations, however, dissenting clergy were allowed to take their positions if they subscribed to a test oath in which they promised not to oppose the doctrine and liturgy of the established church. In January 1759 James Campbell, for instance, took such an oath as part of the process of becoming a pastor in the Cross Creek area.[79]

The rules regarding education in North Carolina were much more obdurate. The requirement of an episcopal license for a schoolteacher dated back to the English Schism Act of 1714. Although it was repealed in England in 1718, the qualification was repeated in the royal instructions to both Arthur Dobbs and William Tryon. The upshot was that education remained under Anglican influence, if not control. In 1745 the Reverend James Moir was operating a small school out of his house in Brunswick Town, and in

1759 Governor Dobbs called for the development of schools in each county. Nothing came of Dobbs's plea, and Moir soon moved, leaving education in the Cape Fear region a matter of parents teaching their children whatever they knew, however they could. This lack of educational institutions perhaps explains the ability of James Tate, a Presbyterian minister, to open a private classical school in Wilmington in 1766. Tate's school drew students from the immediate vicinity as well as from New Bern, until he closed it at the time of the Revolution. It seems doubtful that Tate had the appropriate license. Rather, pragmatic necessity and the respect shown to Presbyterians by Anglican officials may be the reasons for allowing Tate's school to operate.[80]

A final issue defining the extent of toleration for dissenters was attendance at militia musters. A 1746 act enlisted all free men and servants between the ages of sixteen and sixty in the militia. The legislation, however, exempted ministers from the established church from enlistment or attendance at the musters. A revision of this act in 1760 extended the exemption to Presbyterian ministers called to a congregation. Preference was again given to settled Presbyterians over itinerant Presbyterian missionaries and over non-Presbyterian dissenters such as Quakers and Baptists. Anyone refusing to appear at the muster was fined from five to ten shillings. In 1770 recognition was accorded to Quakers on account of their conscientious objection to bearing arms and attending musters. The commanding officer of the militia was instructed to make a list of the Quakers in his county; these individuals were relieved of the obligation to attend the muster and were allowed to provide substitutes should hostilities break out. Although this revision extended the exemption, it kept the power of authorization in the hands of the militia establishment, against which there was no appeal if personal prejudice or malice intervened. Finally, in 1774, begrudging recognition of all dissenting ministers took place, and any dissenting clergyman regularly called to a congregation was exempted from the muster.[81]

Some historians have regarded North Carolina's colonial establishment of religion as rather weak. There was no resident Anglican bishop in the American colonies, for example. Similarly, controversies between governors and assemblies over maintenance of the Anglican Church and its clergy filled the official records. Disputes

between local ministers and their vestries likewise occurred throughout the colonial period. All this is taken as evidence of the debilita-
tion of the established church in North Carolina.[82]

A resident bishop certainly would have made it easier for those
seeking ordination. Yet the bishop of London empowered his commissaries to perform all episcopal functions except for ordination
and some related issues, and there were several commissaries in the
American colonies. Beyond that, suspicions by dissenters throughout the colonies concerning an extension of the Anglican episco-
pacy matched imperial reluctance to establish a bishop and thereby
aggravate colonial relations by adding more fuel to an already ex-
plosive situation. Significantly, even Anglican laymen in the South
often joined in the opposition to a resident bishop, preferring episcopal supervision to be looser. By the middle of the eighteenth century, the day was not far off when reconceptualizations of authority
would challenge the power of the altar as well as that of the throne.

Furthermore, it is true that assemblies and vestries could be re-
calcitrant, protective of their perceived rights and sometimes seemingly opposed to the interests of the established church. In 1711
John Urmston famously described the Assembly as composed of
"a few Churchmen, many Presbyterians, Independents, but most
anythingarians." Governors Burrington, Johnston, and Dobbs often
fenced with their assemblies, calling for increased support for the
established church. The assemblies responded by thanking the governors for their concern, which the assemblies shared, but pointed
to the cost of imperial taxes and the general poverty of the colony
as reasons for their inability to remedy the situation. And entreaties
by Anglican clergy for their salaries from local church vestries were
often met with replies of penury or ignored altogether.[83]

By the mid-1760s, however, this situation was slowly changing.
A new vestry act stipulated an oath by all vestrymen not to oppose
the established church. This was a response to situations in which
dissenters would get elected to vestries and then refuse to levy taxes
or seek to scuttle other provisions. Dissenting clergy still had to
take a test oath before assuming their pastorates. Governor Dobbs
and especially Governor Tryon were zealous churchmen, personally
engaged in and professionally committed to the maintenance and
advance of the established church in North Carolina. By the mid-
1760s, then, an established religion was a legal reality with which

dissenters had to reckon. And even if no one was executed for heresy, even if there were few trials and imprisonments in the Cape Fear region for tax refusal, one should not underestimate the power of royal authority, functioning largely within the bounds of its own discretion, putting up with one set of individuals while demonizing another group as "enemies of society and scandals to common sense."

Attention to royal prerogative and the social sources of power is important, for historians have misinterpreted the social context of religious establishment. By reading backward from the American Revolution, with its disestablishment of religion and the eventual rise of popular denominations, such as the Baptists and Methodists, in the colonial era, this misinterpretation has too glibly assumed that numbers meant power. Rather, in the colonial era, when a politics of deference and conceptions of privilege and tradition still held sway, majorities of numbers did not mean as much as they would in the new nation. Indeed, religious liberty and the denominational structures that grew up with it, if not wholly an unanticipated consequence of the struggle for political liberty, were, as seen in the next chapter, often a contentious issue for citizens of the new state of North Carolina.

3

Religious Liberty and Denominational Expansion

Fire is a fascinating element in human experience. We are drawn to it for warmth and light, and we use it to cook our food. Yet we also know better than to get too near, lest we be burned, for fire has devastating potential. Wilmingtonians in the eighteenth and nineteenth centuries were well aware of both the attractive and destructive features of fire. Prints and sketches of Wilmington from the time showed domestic scenes with families gathered around hearths and food cooking in stoves or over open flames. Commercial illustrations proudly displayed clouds of smoke rising from the smokestacks of lumber mills, turpentine distilleries, locomotive engines, and riverboats. Americans in this era understood such billows of rising smoke, and the technological power of the steam-driven piston associated with it, as icons of economic prosperity and material progress. In contrast, newspapers reports and personal correspondence during the same period often mentioned conflagrations in which whole sections of town were destroyed when sparks from residential chimneys and other sources ignited wharves laden with combustible naval stores and blazed through Wilmington.

During the 1760s and 1770s commentators noted that sparks of another sort—those of opposition to British colonial policy—were also burning in Wilmington. The decade from 1765 to 1775 was largely one of nonviolent resistance, one in which American colonists utilized boycotts, embargoes, and campaigns of nonconsumption, nonimportation, and nonexportation throughout the colonies to pressure the British government to change its policies. Wilmingtonians played an important role in North Carolina's participation in these activities. From popular demonstrations against the Stamp Act through enforcement of the Continental Congress's resolutions to the leadership of such local Patriots as William Hooper and Cornelius Harnett, men and women in the Lower Cape Fear worked on behalf of the resistance movement and continued when the goal became revolution and independence. This chapter examines the development of political and religious liberty in North Carolina, as well as the rise of that new religious organization, the denomination, in Wilmington.[1]

In 1773 Josiah Quincy Jr., a Massachusetts lawyer and political leader, dined with Hooper and spent a night with Harnett. Quincy was happy to see that Hooper, eventually one of the signers of the Declaration of Independence, was well ensconced in the Patriot fold. As for Harnett, he so impressed Quincy that he called him "the Samuel Adams of North Carolina," which was high praise coming from this Bostonian. The growth of the resistance movement in Wilmington did not please everyone as much as it did Quincy. Scotswoman Janet Schaw, witnessing the implementation of the Continental Association and the related boycotts in 1775, simply dismissed the movement's leaders and participants as "rebels." Schaw's analysis was underscored when roughly 500 Highlanders from Cross Creek, hoping to subdue this very rebellion, marched toward Wilmington but were routed in February 1776 at the Battle of Moore's Creek.[2]

While Massachusetts Loyalist Peter Oliver excoriated the dissenting clergy of New England, calling them "the Black Regiment" for their habit of preaching in black clerical gowns on behalf of the resistance movement, there is little evidence of such activity on the part of clergy in the Cape Fear region. For as long as they were in the area, Anglican clergy supported the British Crown. The Reverend Nicholas Christian, for example, was serving at St. Philip Church in Brunswick by the beginning of 1774, thereby ending a hiatus of several years in which no priest had been assigned to that parish. However, Christian left within a year, and no one replaced him. At St. James Church in Wilmington, the Reverend John Wills served from 1770 to 1777, at which point he returned to England

and settled in Somerset County. By 1778, then, neither St. Philip nor St. James had a rector. Both Christian and Wills had been closely identified with Governor Tryon and his implementation of British colonial policy. Similarly, in Duplin County, the Reverend Hobart Briggs was allied with governors Tryon and Martin, but by the eve of the Revolution, Briggs had left the scene as well. The evidence for dissenting clergy is sparse, although the stories of the two Highland ministers noted in the last chapter—Patriot James Campbell, who left the county after being threatened by one of his Tory parishioners, and Loyalist John McLeod, who was captured by Patriot forces and later released—illuminate the range of views in the Cape Fear area.[3]

The parishes of St. Philip and of St. James not only lost their clergy; their buildings suffered mutilation too. British troops under General Charles Cornwallis bivouacked in Brunswick Town in May 1776 but soon left to attack Charleston, South Carolina. This brief sojourn seems to have been enough to convince most of the population of the town to leave, for in October, a visitor stated that "at Brunswick, nearly all the houses have been deserted, from apprehension of the enemy." Nevertheless, in April 1781 British troops were back and stationed in Brunswick Town again. When travelers passed by Brunswick Town shortly after the war, they reported that the town had been torched and St. Philip Church left in ruins, with only its massive exterior walls left standing. It appears that the British troops looted and pillaged the town and church during their occupation in April 1781.[4]

British forces also occupied Wilmington. In January 1781 Major James Henry Craig and his troops entered Wilmington. Craig commandeered many buildings, including St. James Church. As a later rector described it, "the property of the Church suffered every kind of violation. The inclosure of the graveyard was removed and burnt, while the church itself was stripped of its pews and other furniture, and converted, first into a hospital for the sick, then into a Block-house for defence against the Americans, and finally into a riding school for the Dragoons of Tarleton." Although Cornwallis stayed briefly in Wilmington during April 1781, by November of that year the British troops had left, and their occupation of Wilmington was at an end. As for why the churches were harmed, one can only speculate. Perhaps the acts were military reprisals for the past history of resistance activity in the Cape Fear region. Perhaps Craig simply needed the building for his own purposes and deemed it available because no clergyman was currently assigned to the parish. In any case, the physical damage was extensive, and the detriment to the Anglican Church was even more long lasting.[5]

While these military operations were taking place, political developments were occurring that would be even more significant for religion in the Cape Fear area and the state as a whole. On November 12, 1776, representatives from all the counties as well as selected towns convened in Halifax with the charge of writing a constitution for the newly independent state of North Carolina. These delegates faced many challenges in meeting this task, and that of defining the status of religion was no less daunting. Advice on how to proceed and what to keep in mind came from many quarters. William Hooper, serving in the Continental Congress in Philadelphia, sent a long letter; New Englander John Adams provided his own "Thoughts on Government."[6]

The delegations from Mecklenburg and Orange counties received special instructions from their constituents. Due to an election dispute, the Orange County delegation was not seated until the constitution had passed its first reading; therefore, their instructions probably played little role in the constitutional deliberations. The Mecklenburg instructions, however, proved influential, as did other state constitutions, such as those from Pennsylvania, Delaware, and Virginia, that had been already drawn up.[7]

For instance, Article Nineteen of the North Carolina Declaration of Rights stated that "all men have a natural and inalienable right to worship Almighty God according to the dictates of their own conscience." The language used here was taken directly from the Pennsylvania Declaration of Rights. Article Thirty-four of the North Carolina Constitution underscored this affirmation of freedom of worship when it stated that there would be no establishment of religion in North Carolina, nor would any person be compelled to worship in a manner contrary to his or her faith or judgment. In this way, the architects of North Carolina's Constitution of 1776 proclaimed an end to the existence of the establishment of the Anglican Church. Although no reprisals or confiscations of property in the spirit of either the earlier English Reformation under Henry VIII or the later French Revolution had taken place, it is clear that the pattern of church and state relations dating back to North Carolina's beginning as a colony had come to an end.[8]

The authors of the constitution took further steps to dismantle the colonial establishment of religion. Article Thirty-one stated that no clergyman or preacher of the gospel could serve in the legislature while he continued to exercise his pastoral function. This separation between the civic and the religious institutional spheres hearkened back to similar restrictions among the Puritans of New England and others. Whatever its provenance, this regulation prevented a formal overlapping of secular and sacred authority in the legislature, as well as the potential misuse of the informal deference often given to clerical individuals. Another step taken by the representatives was to allow all ministers, not just Anglican clergy, to perform marriages. This issue had arisen repeatedly in the colonial era, and its proclamation further reduced the prerogatives previously enjoyed by the Anglican Church.[9]

Religious liberty in North Carolina had its limits, however. Article Thirty-two stated that no one could hold office or any position of public trust who denied the existence of God, the truth of the Protestant religion, or the divine authority of the Old or New Testament or who held religious views incompatible with the safety of the state. This article of the constitution provided a wide-ranging religious test for officeholding in the new state. Remarkably parallel language could be found in the instructions to the Mecklenburg delegation. These directions endorsed freedom of religion for Christians but denied officeholding to atheists, non-Trinitarians, Jews, and Roman Catholics. In his *History of North Carolina*, Samuel Ashe reported that there was no religious test in the report of the committee to the Halifax Congress, but one was inserted during the subsequent deliberations and eventually passed. According to William Foote in his *Sketches of North Carolina*, tradition correctly names David Caldwell, a Presbyterian minister representing Guilford County, as the party responsible for the introduction of the religious test.[10]

With this legislation, a religious test prohibited atheists, Roman Catholics, and Jews from holding office. Additionally, other Christians, such as Quakers and Moravians, were forbidden to serve because their pacifist principles were deemed incompatible with the safety of the state. As commentators have noted, at the base of this religious test was a consensus among the constitution's framers that disestablished the Anglican Church but still privileged Protestantism. Central here was the issue of public trust and age-old suspicions that challenged that trust in the case of those excluded from officeholding. Discrimination against Jews in the colonies, for example, had been long-standing, even if it did not take the form of bloody pogroms. Prejudices against Roman Catholics in the guise of canards about divided loyalties between national and papal authority were equally familiar in the ecclesiastical heritage of Protestantism. As for the very few atheists who might have lived in North Carolina or the much larger number of Quakers and Moravians who actually did live in the state, the same issue applied: could someone who did not believe in the existence of God or who would not take up arms in defense of himself or his neighbors be trusted? The answer in 1776 was an emphatic no.[11]

On December 18, 1776, the delegates to the Halifax Congress approved the new state constitution. The document was not subjected to a popular vote for ratification; it was just declared to be in force. The constitution for the fledgling state contained a number of structures, such as a weak executive, bicameral legislature, property qualifications for suffrage, and separation of powers, that could also be found in the constitutions of other states. Significantly, the religious test for officeholding was not unique to North Carolina either. Several other state constitutions initially maintained restrictions on political officeholding, limiting such positions either to Christians or to Protestants. North Carolina, and the new nation more generally, had moved from a religious establishment that tolerated dissenters to a situation of religious liberty. Yet, as the subsequent history of church-state relations would demonstrate, religious freedom, like other forms of freedom, was not absolute; it was subject to judicial interpretation, social experience, and the moral consensus of the majority.[12]

Another opportunity to discuss the meaning and context of religious liberty arose when the federal constitution came before the North Carolina legislature for ratification. The legislature elected delegates to a special convention that was to meet in Hillsborough and debate the issue of ratification. In this context, attention turned to Article Six of the proposed constitution, which explicitly forbade any religious tests as a qualification for public office.

Opponents of the constitution, such as Henry Abbot, feared that if there were no religious tests for federal office, "pagans, deists, and Mahometans might obtain office among us and the senators and representatives might all be pagans." David Caldwell amplified on these concerns and identified a misgiving that reverberated into the late twentieth century when he stated that the extent of religious freedom in the new nation would entice persons from throughout the world to immigrate to the United States. At some future period, Caldwell asserted, such immigration "might endanger the character of the United States." Caldwell's identification of the "character of the United States" with Protestantism was widely known at the Hillsborough convention, and his assumptions were probably shared by many others in attendance. In response, supporters of the constitution, such as James Iredell, argued that religious tests were responsible for an intolerance that produced bloodshed and war. Furthermore, such tests only impeded the scrupulous from serving, while the unscrupulous blithely fulfilled the letter of the test while ignoring its spirit. The lines of argument and the divisions over the issues reflected the earlier debate concerning the religious test in the state constitution. So too did the outcome. Fearful of the extent of federal power, and apprehensive over the lack of explicit guarantees for personal rights, opponents of the federal constitution defeated its ratification at Hillsborough. By August 4, 1788, the delegates were packing up to return to their homes. North Carolina thus joined Rhode Island as the only states rejecting ratification. However, after considerable pressure to reconsider this decision, a second constitutional convention was convened in Fayetteville in November, and this time the delegates, fearing political and economic isolation by the other states, ratified the federal constitution.[13]

With the ratification of the federal constitution completed, Americans began the task of constructing their *novus ordo seclorum*, as the Great Seal put it, their new order of the ages that would establish virtue and liberty in the new nation. It was a vision of exciting beginnings, challenging opportunities, and revolutionary changes, and it applied as much to matters of religion as it did to politics and society. On the horizon of this young republic were new forms as well as new styles of religious life—in short, a new order for American religious experience that continued some of the religious diversity familiar from the colonial era but also saw the rise of powerful new forces in the emerging republic.

Prominent among these new patterns was the institution of denominationalism, a form of church organization that would become so prevalent that it constituted, in the words of one historian, the veritable "shape" of American Protestantism and the nation's religious life in general. Intentional and purposive, rather than territorial or confessional (as in the classic European experience), the American denomination was the institutional embodiment of the legal separation of church and state in the new nation. The religious denomination enjoyed neither the privileges of establishment nor the penalties of nonconformity. Instead, the denomination was a voluntary association—one of the most familiar and prominent voluntary associations in a national culture that thrived on voluntaryism. Neither subsidized nor taxed by the federal government, the denomination as an institutional form represented a substantial change from the colonial pattern of established religion. It also represented an abiding paradox, as the tension between a legal separation of church and state uneasily coexisted with examples of a cultural establishment of religion that came more and more to reflect specific religious values and assumptions within the American nation.[14]

In the spring of 1819 Artemus Boies arrived in Wilmington. Born in Massachusetts and educated at Williams College and Princeton Theological Seminary, Boies had been called to become the pastor of First Presbyterian Church. Soon after his arrival Boies wrote a letter that described a number of features in the port town. He stated that by 1819 Wilmington contained nearly six hundred houses, most of which were constructed of brick. Continuing the pattern begun in the colonial era, the streets were laid out in a regular grid rising up from the river. However, Boies observed that the "town stands on a sandy foundation. You cannot go in any street but you have to wade thro[ugh] sand as loose as snow." Plank sidewalks raised pedestrians off the ground on a few streets, and boards bridged the creeks that crisscrossed parts of town and pooled in lagoons or ran down to the river. Most roads, however, were as Boies described them: muddy and sometimes impassible quagmires after rainstorms, and otherwise dusty and grimy thoroughfares. And once the sun went down, circumstances deteriorated. Candles were used in domestic and commercial situations to provide light, while big lamps filled with whale oil were placed at the intersections of a few streets to illuminate the wayfarer's path.[15]

Boies also noted that three churches were operating in Wilmington at the time: his Presbyterian congregation, a Methodist congregation, and the St. James Episcopal congregation. Presbyterian institutional development in North Carolina had proceeded slowly during the colonial era, in part due to immigration patterns, in part due to the establishment of the Anglican Church. As noted in the last chapter, colonial Presbyterians in the Middle Cape Fear formed the Grove, Black River, and Rockfish congregations, while their counterparts in the Upper Cape Fear organized the Old Bluff, Barbecue, and Longstreet churches.

In 1813 the Presbytery of Fayetteville and the Synod of North Carolina were organized, and the Presbyterian congregation in Fayetteville (the former Cross Creek community, renamed in 1783 for the Marquis de Lafayette) built a church in 1815. Presbyterian ministers had preached in Wilmington as early as 1756, and in 1785 a bill was presented to the General Assembly for the incorporation of a Presbyterian church and the appointment of trustees to receive funds for the church. Development of the church proceeded slowly, however, and it was not until 1817 that the Presbyterian congregation took steps toward its formal affiliation as part of the Fayetteville Presbytery.[16]

The cornerstone for this Presbyterian church in Wilmington was laid in May 1818, and the building was dedicated a year later. In November 1819 a catastrophic fire destroyed nearly three hundred buildings in Wilmington, including the new First Presbyterian Church. A newspaper account noted that this was the third major fire in Wilmington in the last twenty years and estimated the loss of property at between $600,000 and $700,000. Adam Empie, the rector of St. James Episcopal Church, offered the Presbyterians temporary use of space at his church to hold their Sunday services. By 1821 a new Presbyterian church in a current architectural style had been completed and was in use.[17]

During the eighteenth century, colonial emulation of English aristocratic tastes in art and architecture had grown, and architects such as Inigo Jones and Christopher Wren exerted their influences directly in the metropolis of London and, by extension, in the provinces as well. Wren's prestige was especially visible in domestic architecture and in the building of churches. After the Great Fire of 1666 destroyed much of London, Wren proposed a plan for re-building the parish churches. Not all his ideas were adopted in the reconstruction of London, but his influence on colonial ecclesiasti-cal architecture was powerful. Bruton Parish Church in Williams-burg, as well as Old North Church and Old South Meetinghouse in Boston, owed their architectural designs to Christopher Wren. Although none of the churches in the colonial Cape Fear region was built in the Wren style, the disposition to recognize and adopt broader architectural trends was evident even then—for example, in the incorporation of a Palladian window in St. Philip Church in Brunswick—and it would continue to characterize the region in later years.[18]

By the late eighteenth century, architectural pattern books such as Andrea Palladio's *Four Books of Architecture*, Colen Campbell's *Vitruvius Brittanicus*, and William Adam's *Vitruvius Scotius* had gone through several editions and were known in North America. The most popular example of this genre was James Gibbs's *A Book of Architecture*. If these volumes were added to the various carpenter's handbooks, as many as fifty-one different books existed by 1760 to assist the American builder in the construction of a home, a public building, or a church. In this context, the impact of James Gibbs was especially noticeable. In his construction of St. Martin-in-the-Fields (1726), with its pedimented and colonnaded portico and tiered steeple, and through the dissemination of such plans in his *Book of Architecture*, a style that Americans would call the Federal style in church architecture came into being.[19]

In his *Book of Architecture*, Gibbs not only provided plans and sec-tion drawings for St. Martin but also supplied six alternative designs for the steeples, each of which contained a variation on the tiered steeple idea. Direct adaptation of Gibbs's designs or mere use of one of his specific elements could be found in many churches, with St. Michael Church in Charleston, South Carolina, Christ Church in Philadelphia, and First Baptist Meetinghouse in Providence, Rhode Island, among the most notable. Evidence for the further impact of Gibbs can be seen in the work of Asher Benjamin, especially in his First Congregational Church in New Haven, Connecticut (1812–1814) and in his own architectural handbook, *The American Builder's*

Companion. Here Benjamin not only provided plans for churches but also gave practical advice on basic matters of construction.[20]

Western architectural history from the late eighteenth century up to the introduction of art nouveau in the late nineteenth century is well known for its parade of fashionable and resuscitated styles: Federal, Greek Revival, Gothic Revival, Moorish Revival, Romanesque Revival, and more. With parallel developments in literature, painting, and music, revivalism seemed to have become an aesthetic principle unto itself. How did this happen? Briefly put, revivalism in architecture used the deliberate quotation of the past in a building's style in order to evoke associations with that earlier era. Such quotations could be very eclectic; they could also be rather artificial at times.

Nevertheless, these quotations traded on evocations of a specific past: Greek classicism, medieval solemnity, and the like. As a sensibility whose roots resided in the Romantic antagonism to the present, this revivalist impulse developed an affinity for some aspect of the past, contrasting this pristine previous era with the irresolute present and extolling the earlier period's superiority. Such a veneration for the past led to new interest in archaeological investigation; however, even this took place within a wider cultural context of sentimental nostalgia. Such a nostalgia longed for an idealized past. It often invoked tradition and hierarchy, not innovation and self-expression, as canons of authority. The antiquarian of any age was preferable to the modern; the ancient was always better than the present. Working at visceral as well as conceptual levels, this nostalgic element in revivalism again contrasted a golden past with the decrepit present and thereby stood as an aesthetic critique of contemporary society. It also provided a foundation for much work in nineteenth-century architecture.[21]

Thus, by the beginning of the nineteenth century, a well-developed and widely available architectural vocabulary existed in the United States. It was a vocabulary that had its roots in England, but it had been transformed to meet the needs, wishes, and realities of its patrons in the newly independent United States of America. It is into this context that the 1821 Presbyterian church needs to be placed. Although the building no longer exists, an etching and interior description provide a good idea of its Federal style appearance. The name *Federal style* drew its inspiration from the late-eighteenth-

and early-nineteenth-century mercantile and shipping world of New England; it was used so widely in the construction of New England meetinghouses and churches that it became virtually synonymous with that region. Indeed, because of those powerful connections, the Federal style became one of the most familiar modes of ecclesiastical American architecture, dominating the landscape for many years and continuing to influence it thereafter. Consequently, it was still an attractive style in which to build when, in 1820, the Presbyterians undertook to rebuild their church.

The exterior presented a familiar portico and steeple adjoined to the rectangular body of the church. Fronted by four columns, the portico stood two stories high, above which lay the cornice and a triangular tympanum enclosed within the pediment. The steeple rose in two stages and was topped by a tall spire that in turn was capped by a weather vane. Made of brick, the church also had a set of arched windows. Exterior double doors opened into the narthex, which led up the stairs to the gallery or into the sanctuary. The interior of the church contained box pews measuring about five feet square. As was still the custom of the time, church officials rented the pews to raise revenue for the church. At least one box pew was reserved for strangers, and slips pews were set apart for blacks, whether free or slave. The interior was painted white and accented by scarlet curtains and green venetian blinds. Although the architect is not known, the building style clearly adopted some of the elements that had been introduced by Gibbs and continued by Benjamin. Regardless of the specific provenance, this church represented a distinguished architectural statement and was an important testimony to the resilience of its congregation.[22]

What would be the style of worship services in the new church built in 1821? In general, a Scottish accent could still be heard among these Cape Fear Presbyterians. The influence of the diaspora from Scotland might have been greater in the Middle and especially the Upper Cape Fear regions; nevertheless, styles of worship and patterns of piety from the old country persisted in Wilmington too. Thus, as one observer wrote, you might enter a Scottish Presbyterian church "at any time after the congregation had assembled, and you would not hear a whisper, or see anyone looking around to scrutinize the dress of their neighbor. They all sat with bowed heads . . . such was the reverence of those old Scotchmen for the house of God."[23]

Yet as is the case with many diasporic events, time and changing cultural conditions influenced the rhythms and content of the experience. For example, in the aftermath of the First Great Awakening of the 1740s, many Presbyterians debated the use of Isaac Watts's hymns as supplements to or replacements for the singing of the psalms that had traditionally been part of Presbyterian worship. John Calvin had sanctioned the use of only those practices that were a part of scripture, and by this time, *The Whole Psalms of David in English Metre*, edited by Francis Rous, was widely available and used among American Presbyterians. Even though Watts's hymns were clearly products of human composition rather than divine inspiration, as the scriptural psalms were regarded, their appeal to the "religious affections" provided an imprimatur in the post-Awakening context that helped justify them, although it could not trump the invocation of Calvin's authority. Whether the Presbyterians of Wilmington sang the psalms, Watts's hymns, or a combination of both, the whole congregation carried it out. Typically, there would be no organs or other instruments for accompaniment. Due to the relative scarcity of hymnbooks, precentors would read two lines of a song at a time, which the congregation would then repeat, until they had sung all the stanzas. Eventually, as hymnals and choirs became more prevalent, the pattern of precentor-led singing was discontinued.[24]

Three other features—prayer, preaching, and communion—played significant roles in Presbyterian worship. In 1787 American Presbyterians composed a *Directory of Worship* that provided some measure of uniformity and consistent expectation for their public worship. In private prayer the worshipper was expected to kneel, while in public prayer, which could easily last twenty or thirty minutes, the approved posture was to stand. Although the directory did not bind a minister to a specific style and content of prayer, elements of adoration, thanksgiving, confession, and forgiveness were generally expected. Similarly, no one stipulated the style and content of sermons, although tradition among many southern Presbyterians favored delivery of the sermon without notes. An appeal to emotion and an informal style of delivery in the pulpit had become more acceptable in the post–First Awakening context; however, as a graduate of Princeton Theological Seminary, with its Old School reputation, it is probable that Artemus Boies preached in a conservative fashion. In any case, it was typical for sermons to last for one to two hours, although if more than one service was to take place on the same day, the sermon would be shortened. The content of the sermon focused on the exegesis and application of biblical texts. Seminary-trained and schooled in Hebrew and Greek, to enable them to read the scriptures in their original languages, Presbyterian ministers were expected to explicate the major themes of Christian theology when preaching to their congregations.[25]

Communion was a feature of Presbyterian worship that illustrated both the persistence of Scottish traditions and their slow transformation over time. The focus here was the sacramental season, a celebration that, in Scotland, typically lasted for several days and involved fasting, prayer, and a series of sermons, with communion as the culmination. Communion was not available to everyone. The communion table was actually "fenced off" so that only those who had previously satisfied the session of the church in terms of the probity of their behavior and had been given a communion "token" were allowed access to the table and its elements.[26]

One historian observed that some fifty years after the height of Scottish immigration to North America, "much of the religious culture of the Old World had been recreated in America." Particularly in the rural reaches of the Middle and Upper Cape Fear regions, this pattern of multiday meetings focused on prayer, penitence, and communion remained a fixture among Presbyterians. These occasions combined the festivity of fellowship with the ecstasy of purification through rituals of self-examination and the public confession and absolution of sin. They were paralleled by quarterly meetings in other denominations, especially the Methodists, and thus contributed to the development of the camp meeting revivalism that played such a prominent role in the beginning of the Second Great Awakening.[27]

Among rural Presbyterians, the sacramental season most often coincided with the agricultural rhythms of harvesting and planting. In the more urban atmosphere of First Presbyterian Church in Wilmington, communion was observed on a quarterly basis, more in keeping with the calendar than with the seasons. Sermons would still be delivered over the course of several days; the examination of prospective participants, the distribution of tokens, and the fencing off of the communion table would still take place.

However, the physical proximity of church to residence, as well as the less intense spiritual and material preparation needed for a journey that lasted a few city blocks rather than several weeks, separated the rural and urban experiences in terms of their atmosphere, if not their consequences.[28]

The 1821 First Presbyterian Church in Wilmington shared with the 1822 First Presbyterian Church in New Bern the distinction of being two of the earliest examples of the Federal style of church architecture in the state. Indeed, the Federal style church and its later revivals became iconic emblems of religious architecture in the United States. However, the Federal style was not the only architectural style in Wilmington and the Cape Fear area. The Methodist church (the second one Artemus Boies referred to in his letter) provided a stunning example of Greek Revival architecture.

Begun as a reform impulse in the Church of England, and shaped by the experiences of John and Charles Wesley in the Holy Club at Oxford and elsewhere, British Methodism was a revival movement whose signature was emotional worship, itinerant preaching, and lay leadership. These same dynamics survived the transatlantic crossing to North American soil, and by December 1784 the foundation of the Methodist Episcopal Church in the United States was laid in Baltimore. Thomas Coke and Francis Asbury were designated superintendents for this fledgling denomination.

John Wesley had only reluctantly given his blessing to the organization of a distinct American Methodist Church. In reality, however, several developments, including the expansion of Methodist missionary efforts and Wesley's outspoken criticism of the American Revolution, had already moved American Methodism toward a break by the time of the Christmas Conference of 1784. Certainly the stream of preachers coming to America either at Wesley's direct behest or with his tacit approval served as catalysts for the Methodist organization. Wesley's friend and coworker in revivalism George Whitefield, for example, barnstormed up and down the Atlantic seaboard several times. In December 1739 Whitefield halted long enough to preach in Wilmington, the first of several stops he made over the years in the Cape Fear area. Another English visitor was lay preacher Joseph Pilmore, who was commissioned by Wesley in 1769 to serve in America. Pilmore preached in Wilmington and Brunswick Town in January 1773 and again in March during his tour of the southern colonies. The efforts of Whitefield and Pilmore and others like them were significant not only for the number of new congregations they established but also for the connections they supplied between like-minded spiritual seekers throughout the colonies. Beyond that, their urgent message to forsake sin and find assurance in the transforming experience of trusting in Jesus energized many, and these recent recruits redefined themselves within a new world of fellowship, commitment, and expectation. Finally, the fact that Pilmore was simply a lay preacher and not an ordained clergyman signaled the prominent role that such laypersons would play in spreading the Methodist tradition in its early years.[29]

If Joseph Pilmore brought Wesleyan Methodism to Wilmington, the honor of establishing the first Methodist congregation belonged to William Meredith. In 1784 Beverly Allen and James Hinton were sent to circulate through the Cape Fear area and serve the eighty Methodists there. They both moved the following year, however, leaving the Cape Fear Methodists bereft of effective leadership and with their numbers disintegrating. The few remaining were subsumed into the Bladen Circuit by 1786.[30]

It was not until 1797 that William Meredith, who had previously served as a missionary in the Caribbean and had been briefly affiliated with William Hammett, arrived in Wilmington. Meredith's reasons for settling in Wilmington are unclear, but his ministry was both striking and characteristic. Almost immediately his preaching drew a small group of followers composed primarily of free blacks and slaves living in the city. Methodism had been growing slowly in North Carolina in the post-Revolutionary era, with an estimated membership of 9,362 whites and 1,810 blacks in 1795. Preaching to slaves in the late 1700s and early 1800s was not unlawful, but Meredith's activities did draw official suspicion, and a law prohibiting the holding of meetings with blacks after sunset was passed. In response, Meredith arose before sunrise and met with his people, but he was arrested and jailed for disturbing the peace. Undeterred, Meredith continued to preach through the barred window of his cell, drawing such a large crowd that the authorities finally released him. Thereafter, Meredith raised enough money to build a small meetinghouse, which tradition places at the corner of Walnut and Second streets in Wilmington. There Meredith continued to preach and to minister to his congregation, still composed predominantly of black Wilmingtonians.[31]

There is even more drama in Meredith's story, for shortly thereafter arsonists burned down his meetinghouse, and another temporary tabernacle was erected in its place. Within a few months, after a major fire swept through Wilmington, Meredith was quoted as saying, "as they [Wilmingtonians] loved fire so well, God has given them enough of it." A final biographical episode in Meredith's life—perhaps ironic, given his prominent role in the founding of Methodism in Wilmington—is that he was never formally admitted into the Methodist Episcopal Church. Meredith applied for admission to the South Carolina conference, in which Wilmington was located, in 1798 but was refused. However, the conference guaranteed that if he maintained his good behavior and gave the title of his meetinghouse to the Methodist Episcopal Church, he would be admitted the next year. Because Meredith was not present at the next annual meeting of the conference, and it could not be ascertained whether the title had been transferred to the denomination, Meredith's admission was again delayed. Before the next annual conference took place, Meredith had passed away, but his will bequeathed his property to Francis Asbury for the Methodist Episcopal Church.[32]

Certainly one of the most salient features of Meredith's congregation was its overwhelmingly black membership. Historians have noted that American Methodism in the South often contained a biracial constituency; however, the predominance of blacks in Meredith's following in a town such as Wilmington was notable. Interestingly, this preponderance continued for a number of years. In 1800, for example, there were 48 whites in the Wilmington district and 231 blacks. By 1812 the number of white Methodists was 94 and the number of black Methodists had increased to 704. Throughout its early years, blacks supported Methodism. As William Capers, onetime Wilmington pastor and later Methodist bishop, described the situation in Wilmington, "the negro church, or meetinghouse, was a common appellative for this Methodist church."[33]

The growth of Methodism among black Wilmingtonians stemmed in part from its early opposition to slavery. In 1780, for instance, the minutes of the annual conference stated that slavery was "contrary to the laws of God, man, and nature, and hurtful to society, contrary to the dictates of consciences and pure religion." The minutes further called on all friends of religion to set free any slaves they might own. Effective leadership and charismatic preaching by William Meredith probably also played a role, as blacks found in him a welcoming and supportive friend; in his message of spiritual transformation, they found a temporary inversion of the otherwise obvious restrictions that confined their lives. Finally, the previous visits by Pilmore, Allen, and Hinton may have laid a foundation on which Meredith was able to build.[34]

Although the racial composition of Meredith's congregation was striking, in broader terms, his ministry and the development of Methodism in Wilmington demonstrated many traits held in common with the wider traditions of early American Methodism. For example, all accounts of Meredith's initial experience in Wilmington emphasize his success as a preacher. From atop tree stumps, from his jail cell window, and finally from his little chapel, Meredith reached out and captured his audience. But Meredith's homiletics were not the learned and modulated phrases of his Princeton-trained Presbyterian colleague Artemus Boies. Instead, Meredith, like others of his Methodist brethren, preached vernacular sermons, hewn with only a smattering of biblical learning and more noteworthy for the earnestness of their emotional appeal than for the depth of their theological concepts. Nor did early-nineteenth-century Methodists feel any shame in their lack of familiarity with current biblical scholarship, theological literature, or intellectual traditions. Wilmington pastor Joseph Travis, for instance, recounted how Francis Asbury had once rebuked him for studying Greek rather than concentrating exclusively on saving souls. The priorities of Methodism were clear in Asbury's mind, and the things and comforts of this world were decidedly secondary.[35]

Beyond its oral expression in everyday language, Methodism was a powerful expression of emotion. It was, as one historian phrased it, "a hot boiling religion." William Capers captured the reigning ethos of Methodism in his appraisal that Methodists were enthusiasts who preached a message of justification by faith for all persons. This proclamation was particularly appealing to persons "politically powerless and socially demeaned," as historian Donald G. Mathews put it. Capers made the same point when he wrote that Methodists were "exceedingly humble" and "the poorer of the people."[36]

Methodism, in other words, found a ready audience among persons marginalized by a society that valued gentry sensibilities, economic position, and the panache of social connections. These social outsiders discovered in Methodism an experience of fellowship and community that equipped them, even challenged them, to begin a new life. Moreover, as Mathews pointed out, Methodist leaders multivalently represented this social location quite well, generally being literate but little educated, often laypersons who spoke to people like themselves, and in the same language.[37]

This vernacular and emotional register found many forms of expression, from simple hymn sings to the camp meeting experience of physical release, which some viewed as expressions of divinely inspired *ekstasis* and all agreed broke the bounds of decorum in a paroxysm of excitement. Capers described a camp meeting in 1802 that occurred south of the Cape Fear region:

> Persons who were not before known to be at all religious, or under any particular concern about it, would suddenly fall to the ground, and become strangely convulsed with what was called the jerks; the head and neck, and sometimes the body also, moving backwards and forwards with spasmodic violence, and so rapidly that the plaited hair of a woman's head might be heard to crack. . . . In other cases, persons falling down would appear senseless, and almost lifeless, for hours together; lying motionless at full length on the ground, and almost as pale as corpses. And then there was the jumping exercise, which sometimes approximated dancing; in which several persons might be seen standing perfectly erect, and springing upward without seeming to bend a joint in their bodies.[38]

Rural camp meetings and town revivals became familiar features of religion among Cape Fear Methodists. Providing opportunities for religious revitalization and social fellowship, these gatherings during the Second Great Awakening (1800–1830) contributed to the growth of Methodism in the area. Moreover, even if such convulsive experiences as the jerks occurred only occasionally, Capers assumed that they fit well within the range of emotional expressions acceptable in Methodist worship.[39]

Yet just as camp meetings could bring disorder to the human

body, the Methodists were criticized (sometimes to the point of burning down their churches) for bringing disorder to the societal body. Their attacks on slavery were the most obvious examples of their potential for social upheaval, and many Methodist missionaries acknowledged the suspicions that their mere presence, let alone their calls for action, precipitated among southern planters. Beyond the slavery issue, Methodists extolled a lifestyle that stood in stark contrast to that of the elite in southern society. Expectations for the clergy modeled the example that all Methodists were to emulate. Methodist clergy, for instance, were encouraged to rise every morning at four. Such an early start was necessary because, as Capers noted, in one of his first appointments he visited roughly six hundred souls dispersed over twenty-four locations on a circuit of about three hundred miles during the course of each month. Methodist preachers were also discouraged from marrying. Nevertheless, once Capers did marry, he was appointed to the church in Wilmington, where his annual salary was never more than $200, even though his housing expenses totaled $300. Finally, preachers were enjoined to discourage what was called "superfluity in dress" and to disown any who distilled grain into liquor. Clearly, the watchwords of the people called Methodist were simplicity, holiness, and, most of all, discipline.[40]

Besides unsettling conventions of race and social manners, Methodists also showed signs of inverting familiar patterns of gender. Whereas most American Christian denominations followed the Pauline injunction that women should keep silent in church and should not exercise authority over men, historians have identified a limited number of female Methodist preachers. To be sure, the Methodist Church hierarchy did not officially recognize these female preachers. Nevertheless, these women responded to the need for preachers as Methodism expanded into frontier territories, and they validated their activities by reference to female prophetesses in the Bible and other biblical texts (besides Pauline ones) and, most of all, by the authority of the spirit in their own lives. In addition to the issue of female preaching, Methodists were well known for encouraging women, as well as men or even children, to testify about their religious experiences, to exhort fellow believers as to the necessity of conversion, and to extol the virtues of a holy life. There is no evidence of female preachers among the early Methodists of the

Cape Fear region, nor do local records provide the names of specific female exhorters. However, the practice of telling fellow communicants about one's own religious experience was so widely accepted and practiced within early southern Methodism that it likely occurred in Wilmington as it did elsewhere.[41]

In all these ways, early-nineteenth-century Methodism joined the antinomianism of emotion and spirit to the structure of the bishop and the conference. Enrolled in classes, love feasts, and night watches; encouraged to lead holy lives, and examined quarterly as to their success in so doing; and, finally, embraced in worship services that proclaimed the abundance of grace freely given to all, Methodists preached a message of volitional sacrifice that challenged them at many levels. Their aspirations for redemption were derived from John Wesley; however, their method was not the regulation of society but rather (at least in early Methodism) the recruitment of the individual through the radicalizing experience of committing oneself to a new life in a community of other equally dedicated and zealous believers.

After arsonists burned down William Meredith's first meetinghouse, a second one was built on Front Street. In January 1806, while visiting Wilmington, Francis Asbury noted that this simple wooden chapel measured sixty-six by thirty-six feet and had a gallery all around it. About his 1813 congregation, William Capers said, "much the greater number were negroes, the whites were very poor, or barely able to support themselves with decency." However in 1816 a new meetinghouse was built to replace the older building. This third meetinghouse lasted until April 30, 1843, when another major fire engulfed it.[42]

By the time a new Methodist church was erected in 1844, it was clear that Wilmington Methodism had experienced a sea change. Black Wilmingtonians, both slave and free, continued to worship there, but the social location of many of the white members was different. No longer simply the "very poor" of Capers's day, the Front Street Methodist congregation now boasted such well-known persons as physician and plantation owner Dr. John D. Bellamy, shipbuilder James Cassidey, and businessman Henry Nutt, among others. By the 1840s, then, Methodism in Wilmington had become respectable, leaving behind the rambunctious and hyperkinetic frenzies of the camp meeting for a measure of refinement in the pulpit and the pew. In this transformation, Wilmington Methodists again paralleled wider developments within antebellum Methodism as they sought and achieved social mobility and gentrification.[43]

Refinement is a social sensibility, an aspiration to live in a particular style characterized by graceful manners, speech, posture, and dress. Historians trace its roots back to the Renaissance courtiers but also point to the cult of gentility that emerged in early-eighteenth-century Britain as a powerful expression of this desire. The great merchants and planters in the American colonies copied the manor houses and styles of dress championed in the elite circles of London, albeit on a reduced scale. Moving forward to the nineteenth century, scholars find this same set of social impulses filtering down into the American middle class. No longer simply the monopoly of the elite, now small merchants, successful artisans, minor government officials, and well-off farmers sought to live life gracefully, to adorn their lives with objects and tokens that indicated their owner's taste and reflected their success in the world.[44]

The clearest symbol of this new era in Wilmington Methodism was the 1844 church itself. The building was constructed in the Greek Revival style, one of the leading architectural modes of the day. Greek Revival was a wide-ranging movement in early- to mid-nineteenth-century Western architecture. From Berlin to London, from Edinburgh to Washington, D.C., its popularity drew on its associations with classicism in liberal arts education, new archaeological discoveries in Athens and on the Peloponnesian peninsula, and sympathy for the Greek independence movement. Not surprisingly, architects and builders responded to and furthered these interests as they became familiar with the Greek version of Doric, Ionic, and Corinthian orders through such volumes as James Stuart and Nicholas Revett's *Antiquities of Athens* or John Haviland's *The Builder's Assistant.*[45]

Greek Revival architecture, to the extent that it invoked references to the democracy of ancient Greece, resonated nicely with the populist background of Methodism and its spiritual enfranchisement of all. However, Greek Revival architecture was also considered tasteful and relatively frugal. As Virginian writer George Tucker stated, "all the most civilized nations of the earth unite in considering the Grecian architecture as the standard of excellence." Ithiel Town, a prominent architect, similarly praised "Grecian Architec-

Front Street Methodist Church (Courtesy of Grace Street Methodist Church)

ture, which from its simplicity, elegance, and grandeur, is evidently gaining the confidence and admiration of all who possess a true and classic taste, throughout the civilized world." Grecian architecture, he concluded, is "very fortunately at the same time, a much more permanent and economical style for general use in both public and private buildings." The choice of Greek Revival architecture, then, could both validate continuity with their heritage and acknowledge the growing regard of Wilmington Methodists for refinement, respectability, and dignity.[46]

The primary element used in the Greek Revival style was the temple form, a rectangular shape that obviously fit well with preceding ecclesiastical architecture in America. In their own ways, both Federal and Greek Revival architectural styles had roots in and quoted elements from classicism. Moreover, by the 1820s, Greek Revival was being employed in North Carolina, most notably in the remodeling of the capitol building in Raleigh. Thus, by 1844 and the construction of Front Street Methodist Church, Greek Revival designs had the attraction of regional familiarity and the cachet of national architectural prestige. John C. Wood and his brother, Robert Barclay Wood, built the church. The Woods had constructed several other structures in town and were well known for their successful use of brick and stone materials. Front Street Methodist Church had a traditional Doric portico fronting its rectangular temple frame. The one-story portico included fluted columns, a standard entablature with a frieze containing triglyphs and metopes, and a triangular pediment. When first constructed at a cost of $7,100, its frontal appearance invoked the Athenian Parthenon, although the later addition of a cupola disrupted its classical symmetry. Francis Asbury once estimated that one-quarter of Wilmington's population worshipped at the Methodist church. By 1844, with the completion of their new building, Wilmington Methodists had the largest church in town. Moreover, with their division of Wilmington into wards—a move that paralleled the political organization of many cities into political precincts—the Methodists' penchant for discipline and efficiency was now coupled with an icon of genteel respectability.[47]

If architecture signaled respectability and refinement on the part of Wilmington Methodists, their affiliation with the southern Methodist Church indicated their acceptance of the norms of the broader regional culture. Whereas eighteenth- and early-nineteenth-century southern Methodists had distanced themselves from the dominant culture by abstaining from alcohol and fancy dress, practicing a range of emotional expressions in worship, and permitting testimonies from females, mid-nineteenth-century Methodists embraced the norms of their region and sought a comfortable place in it. Beginning in the 1840s, and surely by the 1850s, slavery became the dominant issue for religious bodies as well as political ones in America. Thus, when the Methodist Episcopal Church South was formed at a May 1845 meeting in Louisville, Kentucky, and shortly thereafter Front Street Methodist Church added "South" to its name, a compelling statement of community and regional identification was being made.[48]

Methodism also took root in the Upper Cape Fear valley. The preacher was Henry Evans, a free black cobbler who had paused in Fayetteville around 1780 on his way to Charleston, South Carolina, and decided to stay. After mending shoes during the week, Evans preached on Sundays. His ministry was so successful, particularly among blacks, that town authorities initially forbade him to speak within town limits for fear of his disturbing the peace. Unfazed,

Evans moved to the nearby sand hills and other remote locations and continued his preaching. Some white slave owners began to attend, and eventually the ban against Evans was revoked and a rough wooden tabernacle was erected for him and his congregation. More and more whites came to hear him, and soon the building had to be enlarged. In 1805 his congregation joined the Methodist Episcopal Church, and in 1808, after Evans had retired for health reasons, a white pastor was assigned to replace him. By 1812 the membership of the Fayetteville Circuit contained 130 whites and 162 blacks, and by 1834, with the construction of a Methodist church on Hay Street in Fayetteville, Methodism in the Upper Cape Fear was well established.[49]

The third church operating when Artemus Boies arrived in Wilmington in 1819 was the oldest: St. James Episcopal Church. In the aftermath of the American Revolution, with religious disestablishment and the exodus of most of its clergy to either Canada or Great Britain, the Anglican Church in America had suffered a great fall. Yet by 1789, with the adoption of a constitution and a set of canons under American bishops, the pieces were being put back together, and Anglicanism in America was reorganized as the Protestant Episcopal Church. John Wills, the last rector to be sent under the auspices of the Society for the Propagation of the Gospel (SPG), left St. James in 1777, but by 1795 a new vestry had been established. Solomon Halling, a physician by training who had been ordained a priest in 1792, accepted the call to become the rector for St. James.[50]

In 1809 Halling left for another parish, and St. James was without a rector until 1811, when Adam Empie assumed the post. The first decade of the nineteenth century was a time of desuetude for the Episcopal Church in North Carolina. Bishop Charles Pettigrew never even visited New Bern or Wilmington. There were only five priests in the whole state, and the congregation of St. James had dwindled to twenty-one communicants; most of these were women, along with a handful of their husbands who had been baptized but refused to become full members. Parish records indicate that by 1814, when Adam Empie left the congregation for the first time, the number of communicants had risen to 102.[51]

In 1837 a visitor to Wilmington attended services at St. James and confided to his diary that although he had enjoyed the organ and sermon, he had mistaken the church building for "a dutch barn" and "thought it some old remnant of former times that was left to stand tenantless and moulder of itself for the good it had done." The vestry of St. James seconded this harsh view, and at a parish meeting in October 1837 the decision was made to demolish the old church and replace it with a brand new building. On March 25, 1839, the wrecking crew began to tear down the 1770 building. In April the cornerstone was laid, accompanied by remarks from the rector, Robert Brent Drane. On March 29, 1840, Bishop Levi Sill- man Ives consecrated the new church.[52]

Whereas First Presbyterian chose the Federal style and Front Street Methodist the Greek Revival, St. James picked the Gothic Revival for its new edifice. As such, this church was the first com- plete example of the Gothic Revival style in the state of North Carolina. Although New Bern's Christ Episcopal Church (1824) contained Gothic elements, St. James went much further in utiliz- ing the Gothic Revival inventory. The exterior of St. James featured pointed arches, lancet windows, buttresses, and a crenellated central tower with pinnacles and further crenellations running the length

St. James Episcopal Church (*Ballou's Pictorial*, February 24, 1855, in author's collection)

of the roofline. The interior contained hammer beam trusses, votive candles, and an eastern-end apse. All this marked St. James as unmistakably Gothic Revival in style.

Interest in the Gothic Revival style had emerged in Great Britain as early as the mid-eighteenth century in such disparate ways as Horace Walpole's house, Strawberry Hill, and Batty Langley's pattern book on Gothic architecture. Even more powerful an incentive was the construction of new churches undertaken in England as a result of the Church Building Act of 1818. Of the 214 churches erected, 174 were constructed in some variety of Gothic Revival. To its admirers, Gothic exemplified the mystery and majesty of the Christian Middle Ages. Its spires sublimely pointed to the heavens rather than to the pagan connotations invoked by the Greek Revival style. Thus, when the new St. James's cornerstone was laid in April 1839, Reverend Drane complimented the vestry, indicating that the Gothic style was especially well suited to sacred uses and associations. "The experiences of ages," Drane said, "had proved that it [Gothic architecture] was better calculated than any other to fill men with awe and reverence, to repress the tumult of unreflecting gaiety, and to render the mind sedate and solemn."[53]

Although no conclusive answers are available in parish documents, one can speculate on the choice of Gothic Revival by the vestry of St. James. Of course, the early Gothic Revival style in America had its roots in the English Gothic, and American Episcopalianism was heavily indebted to its English heritage. Beyond that, Drane ardently admired the style, and perhaps during his education at Harvard University he had seen the Federal Street Church finished by Charles Bulfinch in 1809, with its Gothic pinnacles, spires, and other architectural quotations. Bishop Ives, another friend of the Gothic, had served in New York City from 1827 until he became bishop of North Carolina in 1831, and he may have been familiar with the second Trinity Church on Wall Street or St. Patrick's Cathedral on Mott Street, both of which were impressive examples of early Gothic Revival architecture in America.

A third powerful example of Gothic Revival, and one widely emulated, was Trinity Church in New Haven, Connecticut. Ithiel Town, that eclectically successful purveyor of Greek as well as Gothic style, completed the building in 1817. Town himself claimed that compared with other styles, the Gothic was more appropriate and "better suited to the solemn purposes of religious worship." Whatever dismay Town's remarks might have caused clients for whom he had built churches in the Greek Revival mode, his design for Trinity Church was stunning for its time. The building is basically rectangular, with an attached tower on the front. Characteristically, lancet windows and pointed arches decorate the exterior; its tower is topped with pinnacles, and crenellations run along the rooflines and between the pinnacles. Moreover, the design immediately found imitators. St. Luke's Church in Rochester, finished in 1825, and St. Paul's Church in Troy, New York, completed in 1828, both utilized a central tower attached to the rectangular body of the church, and crenellations were employed along the rooflines and between the pinnacles crowning the towers. Consequently, whether it was the distant inspiration of St. Luke's Chelsea, one of the best known churches from the parliamentary church building program, or one closer to home, such as Trinity Church on New Haven Green, there was ample architectural precedence for the St. James vestry and its architect to choose Gothic Revival in 1839.[54]

In one area—the social location of its parishioners—the new St. James showed little evidence of change. If the Methodists sought respectability and upward social mobility, the men and women associated with St. James knew that they already had it. Names such as Moore, Waddell, and DeRosset still shaped the social ambience at St. James. And the box pews, rented annually to families or individuals, continued to demonstrate social prominence through spatial location and proximity to the pulpit.

The architect chosen by the St. James vestry was Thomas U. Walter, a professional designer with a national reputation. By the time of this commission, he was best known for his design of the Girard College for Orphans, a monument to American Greek Revival style. Walter was also an organizer and played an instrumental role in the founding of the American Institution of Architects, for which he later served as president. Moreover, like Ithiel Town, Thomas Walter was successful in a number of architectural modes, designing more than two hundred projects by the early 1840s in the Greek, Gothic, and even Egyptian Revival forms. Not all those projects were executed, and some were constructed under the supervision of other individuals; however, there was no doubt as to Walter's architectural expertise and his awareness of the current architectural scene in America. In the view of many, the highlight of his career was his appointment as the designer and architect of the new wings and dome of the U.S. Capitol building, the new Treasury Building, the central room of the Old Library of Congress, and assorted other federal buildings in Washington, D.C.[55]

The decision to engage Walter's services was a bold one for the St. James vestry in 1839. A more typical arrangement was to employ a local artisan who then hired laborers to carry out the actual construction. Significantly, in Wilmington this corps of carpenters, masons, and plasterers was often composed of free blacks or slaves who were permitted to contract out their labor. If the vestry challenged convention by going outside for its design architect, it tripled the offense when it contracted John Norris, a New Yorker, as the supervising architect and the Wood brothers, John and Robert, both recent arrivals originally from Nantucket, as mason and builder. In any case, by the mid-1840s Wilmingtonians could take pride in their beautiful examples of Federal, Greek Revival, and Gothic Revival architecture. Wilmington's ecclesiastical architecture, though not avant-garde in its design, would often show a self-confidence and maturity that might be considered surprising for a city of its size and location.[56]

Giovanni Verrazzano or one of his crew may have offered up the earliest Catholic prayer in the Cape Fear region when they made landfall in 1524. Roughly three hundred years later in May 1821, the young bishop of Charleston, John England, visited the northern portion of his diocese and stopped in Wilmington. Upon his arrival, England assembled the local Catholics, noting that they consisted of twenty men (no women or children) who hailed from Portugal, Ireland, France, and Cuba. England noted that a Father Burke had spent two weeks in Wilmington in 1796, and an unnamed Jesuit had passed through the town in 1807; otherwise, no priest had ever settled in the city or the region. Not surprisingly, since there was no one to administer the sacraments, many of these Catholics had worshipped with local Episcopalians, Methodists, and Presbyterians.[57]

Bishop England spent six days in Wilmington, celebrating the Mass, baptizing children and women, and preaching. Since no Catholic church existed in Wilmington, England offered Mass in the private home where he was staying. Interestingly, the pastor and trustees of the Presbyterian church invited England to speak in their church in the evenings. England accepted the invitation and found himself addressing large and curious groups on the nature of the Catholic religion. He had to turn down a similar offer from the rector of St. James Episcopal. From Wilmington, England traveled on to Fayetteville, where he administered the sacraments and spoke in the evenings, this time in the Episcopal church.[58]

After a stop in Baltimore, England began his return trip to Charleston, during which he rested again in Wilmington. The bishop continued this pattern of occasional visits to the Cape Fear region throughout his tenure. England understood that, without a resident priest, his flock needed someone to administer the sacraments, and he hoped eventually to organize a formal congregation. Because there was no priest available for assignment to Wilmington, England appointed several laymen to read the Mass prayers on Sundays for the assembled Catholics. He also established a local branch of the book society to provide catechism and instructional materials, and he began a subscription fund for the building of a Catholic church.[59]

England recognized that the state of Catholicism in North Carolina was at a low point. Given the dearth of congregations, priests, and churches, many individuals had "nearly lost all idea of Catholicity." In addition to his energetic organizational efforts throughout his diocese, Bishop England brought a particular understanding of Catholicism that was well suited for its time, a style of administration and public ministry that resulted in significant successes by the time of his death. England, in the estimation of one historian, was a powerful advocate of "republican Catholicism," a sustained effort to adapt Catholicism to the environment of the early American republic. To this end, England developed a written constitution for the diocese that called for the election of parish lay trustees and annual conventions of clergy and laity to discuss issues facing the church. The bishop's goal was for the laity to be "empowered to cooperate but not dominate." In an effort to avoid what England considered the excesses of trusteeism in other dioceses, he insisted that all church property be vested in the diocesan bishop. Beyond that, England abolished pew rentals in his diocese, considering the practice divisive for the congregation and providing those without pews an easy excuse to not attend services. Finally, England's preaching style, particularly in public settings, was irenic, open-minded, and reasonable. For instance, after speaking in the Presbyterian church in Wilmington in 1821 to a cross section of largely Protestant townspeople, England concluded, with a justifiable sense of accomplishment, that "there was created in Wilmington a spirit of enquiry and the prejudices which were very general against Catholicity were removed." Reaching out to a wider audience that went beyond his coreligionists, England struck a tone in keeping with the best aspirations of this early republican era.[60]

England's episcopal initiatives, however, were not universally well received, particularly by those conservatives within the Roman Catholic Church who denounced his efforts as "democratic" and "liberal." Such words, in the aftermath of the French Revolution and by the heyday of the Continental Restoration, were anathema to many Europeans. One of England's most prominent critics was Ambrose Marechal. Born in France and ordained in 1792, Marechal taught at St. Mary's Seminary in Baltimore, a school administered by his religious order, the Sulpicians. In 1817 Marechal was appointed archbishop of Baltimore, which made him England's ecclesiastical superior. Marechal cherished the authority of the clergy and criticized England's diocesan constitution and its active role for the laity. Molded by the revolutionary and anticlerical experience of France, Marechal was intensely suspicious of anything that smacked of ecclesiastical reform, as well as extremely defensive about the place of the Catholic Church within the wider culture, particularly the American culture with its conspicuous Protestant influences.[61]

Beyond issues of culture and polity, Marechal's understanding of Catholicism was miles apart from England's. The latter blended the traditional hierarchy of Catholicism with the democratic aspirations of his time. England's Enlightenment piety was private and tolerant; his devotional life focused on Mass, prayers, and charity; and his churches plain and without much decoration. By contrast, Marechal deplored the lack of statuary, altar pictures, and devotional ornaments he found in the Baltimore cathedral. Moreover, as a Sulpician, Marechal emphasized the sacrament of penance, with its assumption of the ubiquity of sin and the necessity for the priest to transmit the pardon of forgiveness. Finally, Marechal was an exponent of "devotional Catholicism" rather than the "republican Catholicism" of England. Within this style of devotional Catholicism, attendance at the Latin Mass was supplemented with vernacular language devotions, often taking place in public settings; each had a specific focus, such as the Sacred Heart of Jesus, the Immaculate Conception of Mary, or a devotion connected with a particular person, such as St. Patrick or St. Anthony. By the 1840s, as a result of support by persons such as Marechal and Bishop Benedict Flaget, as well as the influx of European immigrants familiar with these ritual practices, devotional Catholicism had become a widespread and distinctive feature of the American Catholic experience.[62]

In 1842 John England died, and Ignatius Aloysius Reynolds succeeded him as bishop of Charleston. Born in Kentucky and trained by the Sulpicians, Reynolds was the protégé of Ambrose Marechal. Reynolds's allegiance to the worldview of his mentor was revealed in a controversy over a new translation of the Bible undertaken by Francis P. Kenrick, bishop of Philadelphia. When Kenrick translated a passage in the Gospel of Matthew as "repent," in order to emphasize a change of heart by the believer, Reynolds vehemently insisted on "penance," with its connotation of human weakness and clerical forgiveness as the only possible translation. Reynolds's views on diocesan politics were equally clear, in that he never once assembled the conventions of clergy and laity that had been so central during England's administration.[63]

If Ignatius Reynolds's ascension to bishop of the Diocese of Charleston represented the triumph of baroque devotional Catholicism over its enlightened republican counterpart, it also witnessed an important event in the life of Cape Fear Catholics. On January 1, 1845, Bishop Reynolds officially formed the Roman Catholic parish of St. Thomas the Apostle in Wilmington. The Reverend Thomas Murphy was appointed pastor of the congregation. The Irish-born Murphy had completed his training for the priesthood in Charleston. After his ordination in 1836 he was stationed in Fayetteville for a time before his eventual assignment to Wilmington. The Wilmington congregation numbered around forty, with Irish working-class immigrants predominating, although persons such as Dr. William Berry, Bernard Baxter, and Catherine Ann McKay Fulton often served as patrons for the congregation. The parishioners met at first in a rented space, but plans were soon under way to complete Bishop England's dream of a Catholic church in Wilmington. In November 1845 Berry, Baxter, and Fulton purchased a site for a church on Dock Street between Second and Third streets and gave it to Reynolds. Murphy received donations toward the church's construction, and on May 28, 1846, Bishop Reynolds officiated at the laying of the cornerstone.[64]

With the consecration of St. Thomas the Apostle Church on July 18, 1847, Wilmington had another Gothic Revival church. The original context for Gothic architecture had been the construction of medieval Roman Catholic cathedrals, so it was natural that the Gothic Revival style appealed to nineteenth-century Catholics as well. And although the biblical St. Thomas is often remembered for his doubts, there seemed to be little uncertainty in the construction of this church. Father Murphy superintended the project, while Robert B. Wood served as architect and builder. The inspiration for the architectural style drew on Thomas U. Walter's design of St. James Episcopal, which Wood had completed just a few years earlier. Crenellations shape the roofline, although a central gable with lancet windows replaces the tower found on the Episcopal church. The result is a building that conveys an architectural message of solidity and impregnability and makes a bold assertion of identity and presence by the antebellum Catholics of Wilmington.[65]

No consideration of denominational expansion would be complete without a discussion of the Baptists. Baptists had come down from Virginia into North Carolina probably as early as the 1690s; however, the first Baptist church in the colony was the Chowan Church, begun in 1727 by Paul Palmer. Two years later Palmer helped found the Shiloh Church in Camden County, thus securing a Baptist foothold in North Carolina. Evidence for Baptists in the Cape Fear region during the early eighteenth century is sparse but significant. In 1759 the vestry of St. James Church in Wilmington noted that "an Enthusiastic sect who call themselves anabaptists" existed within the parish. Similarly, in 1762 Anglican minister John McDowell wrote that a few poor families of fishermen, who called themselves "new light anabaptists," had settled at Lockwood's Folly south of Brunswick Town.[66]

These fishermen and their families had come from Cape May, New Jersey. Initially they were without a minister, but Ezekiel Hunter, pastor of the New River Baptist congregation in Onslow County, organized them into a church in 1772. Hunter was a Separate Baptist, a part of the Baptist tradition in America whose roots derived from secession out of New England Congregationalism. The group's first leader in North Carolina was Shubal Stearns, who, together with his brother-in-law David Marshall, founded the Sandy Creek Church near Guilford, North Carolina, in 1755. With their allegiance to the "new lights," or supporters of the First Great Awakening of the 1740s, Separate Baptists cultivated an evangelical style of religion that emphasized the necessity of a testifiable conversion experience prior to baptism and entrance into a congregation. They were also widely known for employing an affective style in their services—what the St. James vestry derogatorily called "enthusiastic"—with weeping, screams, and physical convulsions commonplace. Finally, the Separate Baptists were Arminian in their theological orientation, stressing the free will of the individual to accept salvation and to persevere or desist in that acceptance.[67]

Further insights into the social background and religious assumptions of the Separate Baptists can be gleaned from other observers. For example, in 1766 the Anglican priest John Barnett reported that Separate Baptists were numerous south of Brunswick Town. He noted, in a disparaging tone, that "the most illiterate among them are their teachers, even Negroes speak in their meetings." Barnett's revulsion was underscored by another commentator who remarked that the Separate Baptists allowed women to pray in public and permitted "every ignorant man to preach that chose."[68]

Like their early Methodist counterparts, these Separate Baptists came from the margins of society and represented a counterculture of sorts to the aspirations and activities of the elite of the region. Fisherfolk, laborers, small farmers, and slaves, these Separate Baptists stood outside the wealth and power of society. To the amazement of the members of the established order of colonial society, illiterate persons, black or white, inspired only by the spirit were their teachers and leaders. And like the early Methodists, women were allowed to pray (and perhaps even to testify) in public. These Separate Baptists were pietistic primitivists, baptizing only adults, living a life of self-control and simplicity, and disciplining or even excommunicating those members who did not. All this (and more) was authorized by their interpretation of the experience of the early Christian church and their desire to imitate the life and spirit of that experience. Their attempt to restore apostolic practice and traditions convinced these Baptists of the authority of their particular practices and sustained them in the face of controversy and opposition.[69]

Baptist beginnings in Wilmington can be traced back to the early nineteenth century. A Baptist church was organized by October 1808 with a membership of twenty persons. When it assembled the congregation must have been loosely organized, for neither William Capers in 1813 nor Artemus Boies in 1819 mentioned a Baptist church in the town. However, T. E. Hyde's 1826 map of Wilmington indicates the presence of a Baptist church on Front Street between Ann and Nun streets. The building was a small, two-story frame house located on a bluff that overlooked the river; it is still known as Baptist Hill. The church belonged to the Cape Fear Association of Baptist Churches. First formed in 1805, the Cape Fear Association had fourteen churches in 1826 and 1,563 members spread over eight counties on both sides of the river. The Cape Fear Association was a Regular Baptist rather than a Separate Baptist group. The Regular Baptists were more tinctured by Calvinism than were the Separates. The Regulars emphasized the selection of persons by God in the process of salvation, and once chosen, they persevered in faith according to God's predestined plan. For their part, the Separates complained that the Regulars were too lax in admitting individuals who could not testify sufficiently about a conversion experience. Another characteristic of the Regulars was their support for missionary activities. Some Baptists, but not Separates, objected to missions as having insufficient biblical sanction. Regular Baptists, however, did not agree with this interpretation, and the minutes of the Cape Fear Association offer repeated evidence of their support for missions.[70]

Due to its large size, the Cape Fear Association subdivided in late 1826 into the Goshen and Cape Fear associations, with Wilmington becoming part of the Goshen Association. In 1833 the Wilmington congregation reorganized. The reasons for the reorganization are not known, although other Baptist churches at this time undertook similar moves in response to controversies over the work of the Baptist State Convention and the appropriateness of mission activities.[71]

Still located on Front Street, the congregation was generally known as the Front Street Baptist Church. With both the Presbyterians and the Methodists just a few blocks north of the Baptists, Front Street became something of a church row. Wilmington itself had matured organizationally by the 1840s. Besides being the most populous town in the state, Wilmington was also a regional trading center. A railroad between Wilmington and Raleigh, claimed by its supporters to be the longest in the world at that time, was completed in 1840. Steamship traffic plied the Cape Fear River in increasing volume, adding to the commerce already produced by the many sailing ships loading and unloading at its docks. Political clubs and newspapers, along with doctors, lawyers, and teachers, grew in number and helped shape the style and timbre of Wilmington society. Finally, civic landmarks complemented the ecclesiastical and domestic architecture of the city. These included the elegant three-story Greek Revival customs house; the newly built market house, with its vendors' stalls; and the Bank of Cape Fear, renovated after a major downtown fire in 1840. Taken together, all this symbolized the distance that Wilmington had come politically, socially, and religiously from its origins in the colonial era. And as the next chapter demonstrates, that distance was the foundation for a new stage in the religious life of the Cape Fear region.

4

Bonds of Association

In his well-known study *Democracy in America*, Alexis de Tocqueville sketched a portrait of early-nineteenth-century America. Like many other European visitors, Tocqueville discussed at length the institutional conditions he encountered. The Frenchman was intrigued by the political situation of the American republic, but what surprised him most of all was the vital importance of religion in the fabric of the nation. Tocqueville found that religious groups were quite varied and had a noticeable influence on everyday life. Separation of church and state was widely supported, which meant that churches were simply voluntary associations, neither subsidized nor penalized by the federal government. Religious institutions were supported by the private donations of money, time, and effort that fueled all such associations, of which there were many. "Americans of all ages, all conditions, and all dispositions constantly form associations," Tocqueville wrote. Besides political groups, there were "associations of a thousand other kinds, religious, moral, serious, futile, general or restricted, enormous or diminutive. The American makes associations to give entertainments, to found seminaries, to build inns, to construct churches, to diffuse books, to send missionaries to the antipodes."

Tocqueville's remarks were insightful, and this chapter applies his observations about the prevalence and influence of voluntaryism to the Cape Fear. Religious organizations proliferated in the area during the antebellum years, as did other types of voluntary associations. Likewise, the continuing influence of evangelicalism, and especially the Revival of 1858, must be assessed. Also explored here is a topic that Tocqueville slighted: the religious experience and background of black slaves in the region. As another European commentator, Philip Schaff, stated, slavery was the Achilles' heel of American society. In that remark he recognized the perduring influence of slavery on the past and future of American society, and not the least on its religious life.[1]

By the 1840s and 1850s churches had proliferated across the religious landscape of the Cape Fear region, following the pattern of denominational expansion and architectural style exemplified in Wilmington. As discussed in the last chapter, Episcopalians, Presbyterians, Methodists, and Roman Catholics had all established congregations in the Port City. The Baptists were there too, and in keeping with their denominational heritage, they had fissiparously developed another congregation, the Orange Street Baptist Church, around 1844 in a dispute over the ministerial leadership of Front Street Baptist. In the northern reaches of New Hanover County, Hopewell Presbyterian Church (1800), Moore's Creek Presbyterian (1788), Maple Hill Baptist, and Riley's Creek Baptist, both in existence by 1826, as well as the Methodist Wesleyan Chapel founded in 1824, anchored religious life in these sparsely settled farming areas.[2]

In Brunswick County the Methodists were active. By 1799 there was a Methodist chapel in Shallotte, and Francis Asbury preached in it that February and again in January 1802. Other Methodist congregations met in the homes of members at Lockwood's Folly and Town Creek. Trinity Methodist Church in Smithville (Southport) was founded in 1812 and was given its present name in 1851. Two campgrounds, one in Shallotte and the other near Town Creek, were established and served as popular sites for Methodist revival meetings. In addition to the Methodists, according to the 1850 federal census there were eight Baptist churches in the county, including the Shallotte First Baptist Church and the descendants of the "new light anabaptists" of Lockwood's Folly discussed in the previous chapter. Although the original St. Philip Anglican Church in Brunswick Town had long since been abandoned, a new St. Philip Episcopal Church in Smithville was first organized by 1851 as a mission of the Diocese of North Carolina. By 1853 this Greek Revival church had twenty-three members.[3]

In the rural expanses of the Middle Cape Fear (Columbus, Bladen, Robeson, Duplin, and Sampson counties), Baptist and Methodists successfully expanded their numbers, while Presbyterians continued to draw on their earlier Scottish presence in the area. Of the 105 Middle Cape Fear churches captured in the 1850 census, 51 percent were Baptist, 28 percent were Methodist, and 16 percent were Presbyterian. Baptist congregations included Hickory Grove (1834) and White Oak (1858) in Bladen County. Columbus County had Macedonia (1806) and Tabor City (1840), both of which began in log churches; Pleasant Hill (1848), which first met in a schoolhouse; and Whiteville (1853), which had monthly meetings led by traveling Baptist preachers. In Duplin County Baptists were present at Nahunga (1803), Kenansville (1837), Wallace (1844), Magnolia (1852), and Warsaw (1856); in Robeson County they gathered at Saddle Tree (1788), Lumber Bridge (1835), and Lumberton (1855). Finally, in Sampson County, Brown (1816), Salemburg (1842), Piney Green (1848), and Clinton (1856) were all established Baptist congregations. These churches were rather small at first. Although eventually replaced by frame buildings, many, such as Macedonia and Tabor City, were initially built from trees felled at or near the site.[4]

Methodists were also visible in the antebellum Middle Cape Fear. Elizabethtown, for example, was visited by Francis Asbury during the late eighteenth century; however, it was not until 1834 that Trinity Methodist Church was established. About 1848 the original building was replaced by an unadorned two-story frame structure with a single entrance on the gable front of the sanctuary. The interior contained a gallery for slaves on three sides. Carver's Creek Methodist Church (near present-day Carvers) originated in 1746 as a Quaker meetinghouse and became a Methodist church under the influence of Asbury around 1800. In 1859 the church was rebuilt in the Greek Revival style with a pedimented portico and columns. A gallery for slaves ran along one end and down two sides of the interior. There was a separate entrance to the gallery at the front of the building, just inside the narthex. A third Methodist institution in Bladen County was the Greek Revival chapel constructed about 1845 by Anna Purdie on her plantation and used for family worship. Other Methodist churches—some simply framed, others built along Greek Revival lines—were found at Whiteville (1845), Magnolia (1854), Kenansville (1858), Olivet (1800), Lumberton (1803), Roseboro (1829), and Clinton (1851).[5]

The Presbyterians also experienced growth. Brown Marsh Church in Bladen County could trace its origins to 1786. In 1828 Thomas Sheridan, a free black carpenter, replaced the log structure in which this congregation had been meeting with a modest frame church that had one entrance on the gable end and another on the long side. Inside, plain benches faced a raised pulpit that dominated the interior space and proclaimed the centrality of preaching for this congregation. The organization of the South River Church, also in Bladen County, dates to 1796, although a congregation may have met there informally even before the American Revolution. By 1850 this group had constructed a Greek Revival church. The earliest Presbyterian church in Columbus County was in Whiteville, founded in 1856; Rockfish Presbyterian, in neighboring Duplin County, dates back to 1756. Grove Presbyterian Church, in present-day Kenansville, is even older, tracing its roots to 1736 and the early Scots-Irish settlers in that area. In 1855 a new church was erected in the stock Greek Revival style, with the increasingly familiar slave gallery, although here it was at the back of the church rather than ringing the sides and end. In Robeson County the Philadelphus Presbyterian Church was in existence by 1795. In 1859 Gilbert Higley, a carpenter originally from Connecticut, built a new church for this congregation that combined the vertical proportions of the New England meetinghouse with a recessed portico, columns, and other elements of the Greek Revival style. Similarly, Centre Presbyterian Church in Maxton, first founded in 1797, rebuilt its church in 1850 in the Greek Revival fashion with a recessed portico and interior gallery. As late as 1801 preaching continued in both Gaelic and English, and by 1852 its membership topped 350, making it one of the largest churches in the area.[6]

Finally, in Sampson County the Black River congregation in present-day Ivanhoe met informally as early as 1740. In 1859 a Greek Revival building, replacing an earlier structure, was completed. A pedimented portico with Doric columns fronted the temple form, while separate outside entrances led to the interior slave gallery. Inside, straight-back pews without cushions stood atop heart-of-pine floors. Certainly among these Middle Cape Fear Presbyterians—and, to a large extent, among the Baptists and Methodists as well—the shape of the rural country church was identified with this Greek Revival temple form, complete with pediment, columns, and portico. Variations in design were possible, of course, but the familiarity of this architectural form and the ease with which it was employed in the building of rural churches made it a dominant feature of the religious landscape in the Middle Cape Fear and elsewhere.[7]

The Upper Cape Fear included Fayetteville and Cumberland County. Fayetteville's population had risen to over forty-six hun-

Black River Presbyterian Church, Sampson County (Photo by author)

dred persons by 1850, with blacks, both slave and free, accounting for 45 percent of the total. Cotton was an important money crop in the county. Side-wheel and stern-wheel steamers plied the Cape Fear River as far as Fayetteville, making trade and transportation on the river, together with the development of railroads and plank roads, important features of the commercial economy of the Upper Cape Fear.

On the religious landscape, Baptists, Methodists, and Presbyterians were plentiful; however, in Fayetteville, Episcopalians and Roman Catholics could also be found. Further examples of the Greek Revival country church included the Old Bluff (1758) and Big Rockfish (1844) Presbyterian churches. Together with Longstreet Presbyterian Church (in present-day Hoke County) and Barbecue Presbyterian Church (in Harnett County), Old Bluff was an early Highland Scots congregation. In 1858 the Old Bluff congregation dedicated a new building in the prevailing Greek Revival mode. Its temple form was fronted by a recessed portico, columns, and pediment. Through skilled drill work, the suggestion of triglyphs and dentils appeared on the frieze and pediment. Two exterior doors provided separate entrances to the gallery that overlooked the sanctuary on three sides. The Big Rockfish Church constructed its own Greek Revival building in 1855, although there the carpentry was more restrained.[8]

Fires were a threat in Fayetteville as well as in Wilmington, and in 1831 Fayetteville suffered a conflagration that marked a milestone in that city's history. A contemporary account reported that well over six hundred buildings were destroyed, with losses estimated at $1 million to $1.5 million. Among the buildings destroyed was the First Presbyterian Church organized in 1800. Henry Rowland, its pastor, traveled to northern cities, where he collected $7,000 toward rebuilding the church. Robert Donaldson, a wealthy New York businessman and former Fayetteville resident, prevailed upon A. J. Davis to draw the architectural plans for the new church. Davis was the partner of Ithiel Town and a well-known architect in his own right. The new building, constructed from brick on the walls of the previous structure, followed the Federal style of architecture and had a prominent steeple. It was dedicated on August 12, 1832.[9]

True to their itinerant heritage, Methodists could also be found in the Upper Cape Fear. The Fayetteville Methodist Circuit was first organized in 1807 and by 1842 had changed its name to the Cumberland Circuit as its boundaries changed. A number of camp-grounds, initially established as sites for revival meetings, eventually developed into formal congregations. Bethany Methodist Church, north of the town of Stedman and established as a church in 1848, illustrated this pattern. Camp Ground Methodist Church simply retained the name of its earlier heritage, organizing formally as a congregation by 1841; by 1860 it had constructed a Greek Revival structure with a pedimented front and paired entrances. In addition to campground-based assemblies, other churches were established, such as Cokesbury Methodist, founded in 1853 in Stedman. Finally, in Fayetteville itself, Methodism took hold after late-eighteenth- and early-nineteenth-century visits by Francis Asbury, but it was bolstered by the successful ministry of Henry Evans, a free black cobbler. Evans's work eventually led to the establishment of the Hay Street Methodist Church. Even though it escaped destruction in the 1831 fire, these Methodists decided to build another church in 1832. In 1835 they dedicated the new building, an edifice described by the local paper as "large and handsome."[10]

Cape Fear Baptist Church, founded in 1785 and located on the Cape Fear River some twenty miles south of Fayetteville, was re-built in the Greek Revival style in 1859. This congregation, together with the Cedar Creek Baptist Church formed in 1800, belonged to the Cape Fear Baptist Association. Other Cumberland County Baptist churches established in the antebellum years included Concord (1842), Lebanon (1850), Magnolia (1852), and Suggs Grove (1855). First Baptist Church in Fayetteville was begun in 1837. James Mc-Daniel served as its first pastor, as well as presiding for nineteen years as president of the Baptist state convention. The congregation met in a wooden frame church located on Old Street.[11]

St. John's Episcopal Church can trace its formation to 1817. Bethel Judd was the church's inaugural rector, and its first building was consecrated in 1819. Unfortunately, this church, described by Bishop Richard Moore as the "equal, perhaps in point of elegance, to any in the state," was destroyed in the 1831 fire. When servic-es were resumed in 1832, the edifice had been redesigned in the Gothic Revival mode. The local paper praised the building as "a singularly happy effort" and "bold and striking"; it complimented the architect, William Drummond (who would soon begin work on the new state capitol in Raleigh), for introducing "into our Southern country a style of architecture to which we have been hitherto unaccustomed." Although Greek Revival churches were more numerous, the example of St. John's displayed the power of the Gothic Revival style, particularly among those congregations that, by virtue of historical tradition or social aspiration, sought to send a different message in this populist era.[12]

In addition to Wilmington, Fayetteville was one of the only other Cape Fear communities to have a viable Roman Catholic Church during this period. In 1812 the Reverend J. P. Clorivière stopped in Fayetteville while traveling through North Carolina and collected twenty fellow Catholics for Mass. In July 1821 Bishop John England visited the Catholics in Fayetteville during his tour of North Carolina. England celebrated Mass and heard confessions but confided in his diary that he "found the Catholics [in Fayetteville] to be very few, very negligent, and poorly instructed."[13]

The prospects for Fayetteville Catholics soon improved. In 1829 a converted warehouse served as a small chapel for the group. When this structure was destroyed in the fire of 1831, the Catholic community built St. Patrick's Church, a substantial wooden frame structure with paired windows and entrances on the gable side. A steeple topped the building, while pointed windows across the front and down the sides provided visual unity. St Patrick's was also the site in 1829 and 1831 of the conventions of North Carolina Catholics, a diocesan assembly initiated by Bishop England.

Thus, although some degree of denominational variety existed in Fayetteville, the larger picture of religion in the Upper Cape Fear was similar to that in both the Middle and Lower Cape Fear regions. Baptists and Methodists still dominated. According to the 1850 census, these two groups accounted for 78 percent of the churches in Cumberland County; Presbyterians had 12 percent, and Episcopalians and Roman Catholics the remainder.[14]

The prevailing religious ethos among the antebellum churches of the Cape Fear was evangelicalism. From the days of George Whitefield's preaching tours in the region to the enthusiasm associated with the Second Great Awakening (1800–1830), evangelicalism had been sweeping through the Cape Fear. The core of this evangelical impulse was the belief in the necessity of a conversion experience (usually occurring at a revival meeting) that was so real, so strong, and so dramatic as to provide the individual with a virtual spiritual rebirth. This natal event was one that the individual should be able to testify about to anyone who would listen. That these conversions often took place at revival meetings, and that these revival meetings had become popular among Baptists, Methodists, and even Presbyterians, made them all the more familiar and comprehensible.

Bonds of expectations and common understandings of symbols and phrases developed among those who had been affected in this manner. For evangelicals, the world quickly became divided between those who had and had not been converted, but this posed little problem in the evangelical perspective. Revival preachers never tired of reminding their listeners that the gates of heaven were wide open, and all were invited to answer the altar call. In camp meetings in the countryside, as well as revivals taking place in towns such as Wilmington, emotion was at a premium, and theological agendas and scholarly exegesis at a minimum. The evangelical spirit was, above all else, practical, intent on achieving as many conversions as possible. Although he never preached anywhere in the Cape Fear region, Charles Grandison Finney's statement that "the end of ministry is the salvation of the soul" was a sentiment that would have resonated with many.[15]

One implication of the pervasiveness of evangelicalism was a complicating of religious identity. Previous constructions expressed in terms of national heritage and denominational affiliation—Scots Presbyterians, Welsh Methodists, English Episcopalians—gave way to an emphasis on religious experience that also tended to downplay denominational self-consciousness. Thus the ethnic identifications that were so pronounced during colonial times and into the national period became blended and more passive factors in the antebellum era. Although annual celebrations of the old country and its traditions might still take place in churches, use of the home language (such as Gaelic worship services) died off. "Born-again Christian" became the emblem of this evangelical and often nondenominational experience. And although denominational churches still existed, mutual cooperation between pastors and congregations who regarded themselves as spiritual brothers and sisters in an evangelical faith also expanded.

It may seem paradoxical, therefore, that the Methodist and Baptist denominations surged in numbers and popularity during this period. Of the Cape Fear churches enumerated in the 1850 census, more than 80 percent were Baptist and Methodist. These denominations demanded less theological training than the Presbyterians; embraced flexibility, spreading out wherever there was a spiritual need; and preached an Arminian theology that, in its emphasis on free will rather than divine election, resonated with the regional and even national mood of confidence in the self-made individual. Thus, Methodists and Baptists grew to be the largest denominations in the Cape Fear, just as they became the largest religious groups in the South as a whole.

The focus of the revival meeting was always on the individual—alone, solitary, and without the mediations of ecclesiastical institutions or priestly offices. "What must I do to be saved?" was the challenge issued by the revivalists to all in their audiences. And yet, joined to this call for personal transformation was an equally strident insistence on action in society. As Finney consistently reiterated, involvement of the individual in Christian moral reform was always the sign of a true conversion. Just as the conversion experience transformed the identity of the sinner, involvement not only in the life of the local church but also in the plethora of antebellum moral reform associations marked the expected commitment of the convert.

During the Second Great Awakening and its aftermath, as populations expanded and new settlements proliferated, the evangelical nexus of conversion and commitment located revitalized believers and first-time converts into congregations. It enlisted these same souls in the benevolent empire of temperance, mission, and Bible societies, into that network of voluntary associations that Tocqueville commented on and that were transforming the social and religious landscape of America.

Evidence of the range of associations can be found in the financial assistance provided by two Wilmington congregations. Front Street Baptist gave money to Baptist home missions and educational groups, as well as relief to the poor. The Presbyterians made contributions to support the Foreign Mission Society, the Domestic Mission Society, the Colonization Society, the Bible Society, the Seamen's Relief Society, and Union Theological Seminary in Virginia.[16]

Such societies existed at the national level, and they also had local chapters. Associations to produce and distribute copies of the Bible free of charge were a prominent example of this trend. In 1813 the North Carolina Bible Society was organized; in 1817 an auxiliary branch was formed in Fayetteville, and in 1819 the Bible Society of Wilmington was founded. Dedicated to "enlightening, reforming, and evangelizing the world," the members of the Wilmington society pledged their money and time. Cognizant, moreover, of the battles over the interpretation of the Bible, the society promised to produce the scriptures "in the common version, without note or comment." Their efforts continued through the 1850s, although reorganizations took place and supplementary groups were developed.[17]

Whereas the Bible societies saw their efforts as part of the reforming spirit of the day, another reform impulse, the temperance movement, took a different slant on moral questions. This desire to change the behavior of Americans, whether Citizen writ large or Wilmingtonians on the local level, was a familiar theme. When he first arrived in Wilmington, Presbyterian pastor Artemus Boies informed his brother that "the people are very friendly, the society cultivated and enlightened. But fashion and gaiety are far far too much the character of the southern cities. Professing Christians think they may go to the Balls and the theatre without sin and so they do. In rooting out this erroneous impression, I anticipate much difficulty and trial." Boies, however, did not shut down any Wilmington theaters, and in 1844 the Baptists were still admonishing several members for attending them.[18]

Boies's agenda and the efforts of the Baptists exemplified the larger evangelical strategy for moral reformation in America. In his *Lectures on Revivals of Religion*, Charles Grandison Finney chastised those who had squandered their time "in vain amusements or foolish conversation, reading novels or doing nothing," and he railed against drinking, smoking, and attending the theater. To the evangelical, distance from the things of the world was necessary, and self-examination, repentance, and personal transformation were the evangelical means to that end. The scale of sin was typically individualistic, and the tone was moralistic; however, in the aftermath of the Second Great Awakening, it was a rhetoric for reform that continued to be powerful in the South and the nation as well.[19]

Efforts to restrict the production and consumption of alcohol were part of the larger evangelical effort to reshape and reform the lives of Americans in the name of religion. The founding in 1826 of the American Temperance Society gave a national focus to the movement and a basis for the establishment of local affiliates. By 1832 thirty-one societies in North Carolina, including several in and near Fayetteville, had been organized. By 1833 Wilmington had a temperance society that met variously in the town's Baptist, Presbyterian, and Methodist churches through the 1850s. Yet antebellum southern society always remained powerfully ambivalent about temperance. Although Presbyterian synods, Baptist associations, Methodist quarterly meetings, and Episcopal diocesan conferences had all denounced drunkenness, efforts to restrict or prohibit the production and consumption of alcohol by law rather than by moral suasion and personal admonition were considered by many southerners an invasion of private individual rights. Moreover, for churches to lobby on behalf of the legal enforcement of prohibition or temperance was, in the view of these same southerners, to engage in politics, which was outside the proper orbit of religious institutions.[20]

Being a port city, Wilmington gave rise to another prominent association that sought to assist sailors who had disembarked from one ship and were waiting to sail out on another. The Seamen's Friend Society was formed in 1844 to improve the social, religious, and moral condition of sailors and to save them from what one pamphlet called the "insidious snares and seductive vices" with which the city tempted them. The sailor's character, stated this fund-raising pamphlet, was too often marked by "recklessness, intemperance, debauchery, and bold impiety." Removed from the "restraining influences of domestic and social life," forced to fraternize with their profligate "friends of the forecastle" and always subject to the "despotism of the deck," they ended up in "abodes of obscenity" while waiting for their next ship. Their need was for "hospitals for their bodies" and "sanctuaries for their souls," and to this end, the rector of St. James and other clergy and laymen in Wilmington joined the society and encouraged others to do likewise.[21]

The gendered language of this pamphlet is significant, particularly in its antithesis between the debauchery of ship life and the safe maternal haven of domestic life. In another context, the

Reverend Thomas Hunt, a temperance organizer and early pastor of First Presbyterian Church, noted that "the influential portion of Wilmington was a free-living, generous, and hospitable class." In order to succeed in his temperance efforts, Hunt concluded, "I had to appeal to the ladies." Here again a feminine sphere of mothers and wives, of domesticity and piety, was counterpoised to the masculine world of business, politics, and demon rum.[22]

In colonial North Carolina, prescriptive religious literature and civil law both recognized the subordination of women to men. In the everyday demands of frontier life, common efforts sometimes provided for functional equality in certain areas. "Many of the Women are very handy in Canoes, and will manage them with great Dexterity and Skill," observed John Lawson. "They are ready to help their Husbands in any servile Work, as Planting, when the Season of the Weather requires Expedition." By the antebellum era, much of the Cape Fear remained rural and had changed little from Lawson's description. In the pockets of commercial development and manufacturing such as Wilmington and Fayetteville, town life separated the workplace from the home and disconnected the masculine and feminine spheres.[23]

Scholars have demonstrated how prescriptive religious literature of the antebellum era ascribed to women the features of natural religiosity and purity, domesticity, and submissiveness to men. Gender conventions were powerful in the South; however, religious life provided circumstances by which white elite and middle-class women could circumvent these conventions and enter into public life. To be sure, this was an unintended consequence, for pastors, etiquette writers, and religious editors rarely, if ever, explicitly promoted women's involvement in the public sphere.[24]

Nonetheless, since women were considered to be naturally religious, pure, and innocent, it was acceptable for them to be involved in religious organizations, particularly those that emphasized women's roles as maternal safeguards of society. Thus women sometimes formed their own sister societies, such as the female auxiliary to the Seamen's Relief Society. More expressive of female autonomy were the groups organized and run by women themselves. The Universal Female Benevolent Society, organized in Fayetteville, dedicated itself to "promot[ing] the cause of religion" and relieving "the wants of the poor who are aged, infirm, or sick." It was joined in its relief efforts by the Female Orphan Asylum Society and the Sewing Society of St. John's Church, whose focus was indigent children.[25]

In Wilmington a Ladies Foreign Missionary Society was begun in 1832 at the Presbyterian church. Twelve years earlier the Episcopalians at St. James had started a Female Missionary and Common Prayer Book Society, and in 1821 the Ladies Working Society was organized at St. James. The rector applauded their efforts "in manufacturing various articles, the net proceeds of which are devoted to missionary and other charitable uses." By the 1840s this group had helped finance a charity school, purchased a lot and built a hall for expansion of the church, financed the construction of a wall enclosing the church property, and contributed money to build a study for the rector.[26]

Sunday schools were another area of female involvement. There were Sunday schools in North Carolina by the early nineteenth century, and by the 1830s the Episcopal, Methodist, Presbyterian, and Baptist churches in Wilmington had all organized their own. In December 1836 the Baptists and Presbyterians joined the members of the Methodist Sunday school at their church for a common service. This cooperative exercise was repeated in 1837.[27]

For elite and middle-class white women, the significance of this involvement in religious organizations was enormous. At the very least, going to these meetings and attending church services got them out of the house. In a culture that believed that women were domestic and that their proper place was at home, and in a household economy where a woman's day might begin before daybreak and extend well into the night, many housewives (especially rural women) could spend all their time attending to the chores of hearth and family. But because women were thought to be naturally religious, they could attend these public meetings without compromising their respectability. And once at the meetings and engaged in the benevolent and meaningful activities of the various societies, women quite unintentionally found sources of empowerment. In missionary societies they learned geography and developed global interests. In all such societies women developed networks of contacts and friends. Beyond that, they exercised practical skills such as public speaking, setting agendas and running meetings, and raising and spending their own money. To be sure, the activities of such organizations and societies were presented as complementing rather than usurping the prerogatives of the male clergy and lay leaders; female submissiveness was not challenged. Although at least half the teachers in the Baptist, Presbyterian, and Methodist Sunday schools were women, all the superintendents were men. Women were not ordinarily allowed formal authority in church institutions, but avenues for exercising extracongregational influence existed and were explored.[28]

The gendered bonds of association that women developed through their participation in female benevolent societies were paralleled by white middle-class Wilmington men in fraternal associations such as the Masons and the Odd Fellows. The International Order of Odd Fellows originated in Great Britain in the late eighteenth century and organized its first American lodge in Baltimore in 1819. Mutual aid was an important aspect of the fraternity, as members in difficult circumstances could appeal to the others for assistance, and all brothers were promised a decent funeral. Social purposes were evident too, as Odd Fellows' meetings were known for their consumption of beer and spirits and for their singing and revelry.[29]

The Odd Fellows had their origins in the English working class and its culture. However, by the 1830s, the American membership had shifted to skilled tradesmen, lawyers, and merchants. With this change came a transformation in the lodge's reputation. Weekly assessments replaced charity donations, rambunctious members were disciplined or expelled, and by 1860 alcohol had been banned in all lodges. The Wilmington lodge emerged in the midst of this sea change. First established in 1842, the Wilmington Odd Fellows often assembled at churches. Although they continued to meet for celebrations and ritual ceremonies, the Odd Fellows also began a school in Wilmington in 1843.[30]

Masons traditionally trace their pedigree back to Solomon's temple and the ancient world, but the historical origins of Freemasonry date to early-eighteenth-century England. Masons first organized in Wilmington with the chartering of St. John's Lodge #1 in 1755. In early America, Masons often met for purposes of eating and drinking in members' homes. This seems to have been the case in Wilmington too, for early meetings reportedly took place at the home of William Hooper, some eight miles south of Wilmington. This area became known as Masonboro owing to the number of Masons reputed to live there.[31]

If William Hooper supplied the hospitality, Cornelius Harnett
Jr. provided the emblem for Wilmington Freemasonry in the late
eighteenth century. Harnett served as grand master of the St. John's
Lodge and was deputy grand master of North America for the Masonic Order. Masonry in this era espoused the virtues of the Enlightenment and the ideology of republicanism. At one level the Masons
epitomized a politics built on fraternal equality and voluntary connections rather than on bloodlines, inherited status, or residence.
They invoked a classical heritage of balance, architectural proportions, and simple clarity that was in line with the rhetoric of national leaders such as George Washington, John Adams, and Thomas
Jefferson. Moreover, as the young American nation grew, it had to
redefine its politics from the colonial pattern of ascribed identity
and deference to local elites to a new style of politics extended over
time and space. Because candidates for political office were often
not well known, the bonds of Masonic brotherhood could prove
useful and powerful. Significantly, between 1776 and 1836, eighteen
of the governors of North Carolina were Masons.[32]

Cornelius Harnett was an Anglican vestryman and was buried in
St. James's graveyard, but his epitaph captured his religious views.
The inscription read: "Slave to no sect. No private path he trod; but
looked through nature, up to Nature's God." Harnett's words evoke
the spirit of Deism, the form of Enlightenment religion that accepted the existence of the deity and, for Thomas Jefferson at least,
the existence of future rewards and punishments. For the Deists,
however, this god was the God of Nature, the supreme architect
and builder of creation who had devised a self-regulating universe
in much the way that a craftsman might make a perfect timepiece
that never needed to be wound or a celestial mason might construct
a perfect temple that never needed to be repaired. The match between this rational religion and Masonry—with its heritage of architecture, its symbols of compass and ruler, and its rhetoric of virtue,
truth, and brotherhood—was close and compelling.

In June 1804 the brothers of St. John's #1 laid the cornerstone
for their new lodge on Orange Street between First and Second
streets. Joseph and Benjamin Jacobs of Hingham, Massachusetts,
designed the lodge. One of its meeting rooms contained a painted
overmantel with the inscription, "Holiness to the Lord." Over the
inscription was an all-seeing eye, and beneath it was a landscape

with a rising sun flanked by shields and Masonic symbols. Wilmington Masons met in this building from 1805 until 1825, when it was sold. From 1825 to 1841 they assembled in a building on Front Street. Freemasonry, however, was not confined to Wilmington. Phoenix Lodge #8 in Fayetteville was chartered in 1793, and Harrell's Masonic Lodge in Sampson County was constructed in 1841 in a Greek Revival building with a schoolroom on the ground floor and the meetings rooms above.[33]

On December 27, 1841, the Wilmington Masons laid the cornerstone for another new lodge, located on Market Street between Front and Second. A year later the lodge was completed, and dedication ceremonies took place. The main speaker, the Reverend William M. Green of Chapel Hill, discussed the life of St. John the Evangelist and "closed with a tribute to Christianity, of which Masonry claims to be the humble handmaid." The invocation of Christianity and the positioning of Masonry as its handmaid might well have taken place among late-eighteenth-century Masons; however, its meanings would surely have been understood differently. Masonry underwent a profound crisis in the 1830s in the aftermath of a celebrated murder trial involving New York Masons and the subsequent development of anti-Masonic groups.[34]

As they sought to rebuild their organization and remake their identity, the tone and ethos of Masonry changed. No longer simply an eating and drinking club that engaged in secret handshakes between courses, Masons in the 1830s and 1840s embraced the middle-class virtues of sobriety, self-restraint, and personal moral reform. In so doing, Masons displayed congruence with the evangelical impulse directed toward these same ends. However, Masonry had an ambivalent relationship with antebellum Christianity. Papal proscriptions had forbidden Catholics to join the Masons, and many evangelical Protestants were likewise deeply suspicious of the group. Nevertheless, other Protestant churches hosted Masonic meetings, and their clergy delivered invocations, addresses, and benedictions at their meetings.[35]

Finally, fraternal associations such as the Masons or Odd Fellows, in the perceptive words of one historian, provided American men with "a middle-class institution parallel to evangelical Protestantism." Beyond a functional similarity, both evangelical Protestantism and fraternal ritualism "depended upon an agency outside of the individual to generate a personal transformation; both depicted man as inherently deficient; and both evoked grim visions of death and hell to precipitate an emotional response that could lead men to an unknowable and distant God." In the Masons, one had a fraternal association that was open to those men who pledged loyalty to the organization and its members, faithfulness to virtue and truth; in return, they were promised acceptance into a ritualized world of meaning and brotherly love. Membership in a lodge did not necessarily preclude membership in many churches. However, for a large group of men, in ways not yet fully understood but attested to by their membership numbers, the camaraderie, civic service, and ritual organization of the lodge paralleled, if not eclipsed, the institutional church as a sphere of meaning and association.[36]

Whereas the bonds of voluntary associations were meaningful for white men and women, the bonds of involuntary servitude posed different realities for blacks. The Cape Fear region had sizable black populations, and the counties of Brunswick and New Hanover had some of the largest slave plantations in North Carolina. In the demographic snapshot provided by the 1850 census, the population of Brunswick County was 49 percent black, and that of New Hanover County was 53 percent black. These numbers were significantly higher than the 36 percent figure for the state as a whole. The black population consisted of slaves and free blacks. Generally, free blacks were a very small percentage of the total population in the Cape Fear. Interestingly, rural Robeson County had the largest free black population in the region and one of the largest in the state, while Wilmington had the largest free black urban population within the Cape Fear.[37]

The majority of these free blacks worked as unskilled laborers on rural farms or turpentine plantations or as fishermen or stevedores on the Cape Fear River. Economic diversity and commercial life in Wilmington offered further opportunities for some free blacks as boat pilots, artisans, and mechanics. Cabinet makers, carpenters, masons, and plasterers all found work as the construction market periodically boomed in antebellum Wilmington. The wealthiest free black in the state, a carpenter by the name of James D. Sampson, resided in Wilmington. While the average wealth of North Carolina free blacks in 1860 was $34, Sampson was worth $36,000.[38]

Slave life in the Cape Fear was also divided between rural farms and urban towns. In the Lower Cape Fear, plantations had dotted the river and its tributaries since colonial times. With names such as Pleasant Hill, the Hermitage, Sans Souci, Belevedere, Lilliput, Clarendon, and Orton, the Lower Cape Fear region was one of the few in North Carolina to develop the agricultural bases and social customs associated with the plantations of Tidewater Virginia or Low Country South Carolina; Cape Fear plantation life never reached the level of development of its counterparts in those states, however. From the colonial era onward, the Lower Cape Fear was known for its concentration of slaves working on multiacre plantations and producing naval stores, turpentine, and rice.[39]

Slave life on these plantations was harsh and often isolated. Thomas Jones remembered that his Cape Fear master gave clothes to his slaves every year. Each adult slave received a pair of shoes and a hat, plus one blanket and five yards of cotton material from which to make other articles. Weekly food rations consisted of a peck of raw corn that the slaves would grind and fashion into loaves to cook. Plantation slaves might spend their whole lives nominally confined to the plantation itself. Another Cape Fear slave, William Robinson, remembered occasions when slaves would slip off the plantation without the owner's permission to attend "frolics" or social gatherings of slaves elsewhere. Robinson told of these slaves being whipped by the master upon their return to the plantation, although other accounts indicated that the masters allowed participation in these social occasions.[40]

Slaves also lived in towns such as Wilmington. In these situations they might live in quarters attached to the master's town house or in the town house itself. Thomas Jones's story illustrates the diversity—economic and social—that life in a town could represent for a slave. After his plantation owner died, Jones was sold to Owen Holmes of Wilmington. Jones's contract with Holmes stipulated that he would work as a dockhand on the river and reimburse his master a certain amount of money. Beyond that, Jones was allowed to rent space in Wilmington for a residence. This situation was significant but not unique. Slaves sometimes paid their masters a set fee, leaving open the possibility of earning additional monies or saving any that was not paid to the master. Similarly, although most slaves lived under the close supervision of their masters, some in Wilmington and other towns experienced the relative autonomy of private quarters. Slaves in Wilmington also enjoyed some leisure time during which they could fraternize with others or hire themselves out part-time for extra money. Many slaves had vegetable gardens that they used to supplement their meals, or they sold the produce for cash. Even during the late colonial period, Janet Schaw during a visit to Wilmington commented on the slaves' resourcefulness in augmenting their diets with what they grew in their gardens. Thus blacks were a visible and important part of antebellum Wilmington. They provided most of the labor for the agricultural and commercial enterprises that drove the regional economy. As skilled artisans they constructed and enhanced such private dwellings as the Bellamy Mansion and such public buildings as Thalian Hall. Their lives were entwined with the very fabric of antebellum Wilmington.[41]

Black religious experience in the antebellum era followed the rhythms of rural or town life and explored the opportunities to be found there. Slaves on plantations and farms sometimes received no training in Christianity and had no opportunities to worship. During the colonial era, attempts to convert and baptize slaves were episodic in the Cape Fear region. Richard Marsden conceded to baptizing "some negro slaves"; in 1767 John Barnett claimed that twelve adult slaves and eighteen of their children had been baptized by him the previous year. Yet even these missionary efforts faced opposition. Planters were more interested in the productive capacity of slaves rather than the state of their souls. Moreover, some slaves had been told that Christian baptism would set them free, and this view increased the planters' reluctance to allow missionaries to preach to their slaves.[42]

By the antebellum era the attitude regarding slaves' conversion to Christianity had generally changed, although some masters still objected. Thomas Jones, for instance, reported that his master refused to let his slaves have anything to do with Christianity. According to Jones, his master said that heaven and hell did not exist and that "Christians were all hypocrites." Other masters continued to harbor suspicions about the implications of Christian baptism and membership in a church. Nevertheless, in the aftermath of the Second Great Awakening, many whites not only experienced their own conversions but also came to believe that Christianity supported slavery. In their view, the Bible endorsed slavery in several scriptural incidents, and a message of obedience to one's master was found in other passages. Furthermore, in the wake of slave revolts that had been promoted in part by reference to biblical images of exodus and liberation, slave owners wanted to control the biblical message that their slaves would hear.[43]

In this cultural context, many slaves were exposed to Christianity on the plantation grounds. John D. Bellamy Jr. recalled that a Wesleyan Methodist preacher by the name of Morgan C. Turrentine came to Dr. John Bellamy Sr.'s Grovely Plantation in Brunswick County, where, on alternate Sundays, he would preach to the slaves as well as perform marriages and baptize children. The young Bellamy also attended these services and noted that "there was no shouting, no emotional outbreaks at these services. I can truly say I have never seen a more attentive religious audience than that comprised of the slaves nor have I heard more stirring music than their native spirituals."[44]

Although Turrentine's services took place in the slave quarters, there were other sites where the religion of the masters was preached. Foremost among these were the rural country churches, with their galleries for the slaves. As discussed earlier, many congregations in the Upper and Middle Cape Fear had built Greek Revival churches with slave galleries in their interiors and separate entrances on their sides. Surviving churches provide architectural evidence of the existence of slave galleries, as do the recollections of ex-slaves, who spoke of regularly attending the churches of their white masters. Finally, black exhorters were also used to preach to the slaves. John Bellamy remembered that on those Sundays when the Reverend Turrentine was not scheduled to preach, the slaves "frequently had their own preachers, and it was at such times that services became quite emotional, having the mournings and shoutings that so often occur at camp meetings."[45]

Whether the services took place in a local church or in the slave quarters, and whether they were performed by a trusted white minister or a black exhorter, white masters exerted control over the situation. The message that the masters wanted preached was not "proclaim liberty unto the captives" but rather "obey those in authority." Given the multiplicity of messages in the Bible, southern slave owners wished to restrict slaves' access to the scriptures. Thus, some slaves indicated that the possession of any book, including the

Bible, was prohibited; others stated that learning to read or write was the real reason for any punishment. For example, once Thomas Jones of Wilmington finally obtained a spelling primer, he went to great lengths to conceal its existence from his master, for fear of being whipped. The slave owners' concern about slave literacy was also expressed in the 1831 legislation prohibiting free blacks in North Carolina from teaching slaves to read or write and in the corresponding 1830 legislation prohibiting slaves themselves from learning these same skills. Not surprisingly, in this restrictive context, any religious instruction of slaves was confined to oral recitation and memorization.[46]

The religion of the masters was not the only form of religion to which the rural slaves were exposed. William Robinson remembered that during his days as a slave in the Cape Fear, slaves were often taken to the master's church. There the preacher's message would always be obedience to their masters, which "was not what our people wanted to hear." Later at night, after the whites had retired, the slaves would congregate at a distance in the swamps and hold their own religious meetings with preaching, songs, and prayers. Cooking utensils, pots, and kettles were turned so as to catch and muffle the sounds. As Robinson noted, it was not uncommon for slaves to be whipped on Monday morning if they had been discovered participating in these clandestine religious services. Slaves, therefore, took other measures to secure their safety, posting watchmen to sound an alarm at the approach of strangers and stringing taut grapevines across roads high enough to knock slave patrollers off their horses.[47]

The tenor of the slaves' meetings was different from that in the masters' churches. Preaching often highlighted God's deliverance of His people from bondage, as in the story of Moses and the liberation of the Hebrew slaves. Singing and praying were also important expressions of the slaves' religious experience. Even John Bellamy Jr. was impressed with the emotional outpourings, the "mournings and shoutings," that he witnessed. Without any whites present, not even a young boy, the slaves took advantage of the opportunity for uninhibited religious expressions. The documentary sources for the Cape Fear only suggest the emotional tenor and ecstatic fervor of the slaves' meetings, but the words of their songs convey a profound picture of their religious world. For example, the stanza of one spiritual proclaimed, "when we all meet in heaven, there is no parting there," conveying insight into the fragility and uncertainty of the slave world. William Robinson remembered another spiritual that invoked God's involvement in Daniel's escape from the lion's den and the Hebrews' escape from Egypt and concluded with the rhetorical question, "And why not deliver me?" Other North Carolina slaves told of singing "Swing Low, Sweet Chariot," with its invocation of a band of angels coming to carry one home to a sweeter and better reward in heaven. Even songs sung in the fields that were used to notify slaves of an upcoming meeting could contain religious messages. As Robinson recollected, one such song contained these words:

You may hinder me here
But you cannot there,
God sits in heaven
And answers prayer,
There is a meeting tonight.[48]

Slaves who lived in towns had different religious contexts from those in rural areas, but often some of the same structures. For example, many urban slaves attended the churches of their white masters. One ex-slave from Wilmington put it this way, "We went to church regular. All our people marched behind our owners, and sat up in the gallery of the white folks' church." Front Street Methodist Church had such galleries, and it also had a large black membership. When Francis Asbury visited the church in 1803 he reported that the congregation had "about eight hundred and seventy-five Africans and a few whites in fellowship." By the 1860s the gap between the numbers of whites and blacks had closed, although blacks still predominated. When whites and blacks met together, blacks occupied the galleries. For other occasions, such as class meetings and the like, black and white Methodists met separately. As one observer of the Wilmington scene described it, "they hold all their official meetings, love-feasts, class meetings, prayer meetings, etc. separate. They have, indeed, two organizations, as nigh as can be, in the same church, under the superintendence of the same pastor."[49]

St. James Episcopal Church also had black members. Church records for the years 1839 to 1852 list slave and free black baptisms, marriages, and funerals. By 1833 a black congregation of roughly three hundred members used the church facilities on Sunday evenings. Calls for catechizing slaves are found in diocesan pronouncements, and it is probable that Bishop Ives's catechism for slave children was also used. Among the Presbyterians, twenty-one of the eighty-four members of the 1851 congregation were black. In 1847 the interior of the church had been remodeled, with the box pews replaced by slip pews; specific ones were used by the black members of the church. The Presbyterians also organized a Sunday school for blacks.[50]

Catholic bishop John England provided instructions to blacks during his tour of the state. Blacks and whites worshipped at the same services; England had abolished rented pews, but the two groups probably sat in separate locations. The Roman Catholic congregation in Wilmington had a few black members, the best known being Maria Anna Jones, a slave of Catherine McKoy Fulton. The Baptist congregation on Front Street included many slaves. Church records indicate that blacks joined the church often, and in January 1845 the church's pastor, the Reverend A. J. Battle, began to lead separate services for black members on Sunday afternoons. In May of that year, two black deacons were selected to work with the black congregation under the watchful eye of the pastor and white members.[51]

Here then was the religion of the masters on the plantations and in the towns. The master's message of submission to those in authority was the dominant theme preached; the threat of punishment both on earth and in the hereafter for any who refused was always implied. The varied sites of this religious experience—from segregated Sabbaths through supervised class meetings to secret meetings in the swamps—allowed different kinds of religious expression. However, as seen in the multivalence of the spirituals, what appeared on the surface was often not the only meaning available.

The spirituals contained themes of resignation, an aching desire to go to heaven and be rewarded for a lifetime of endurance and struggle, pain and suffering. But there was another side as well—the theme of liberty and freedom. It took as its paradigm the liberation of the Hebrews and their exodus from Egypt. William Robinson's recollection of Daniel's escape from the lions and the Israelites' flight from Egypt provides examples of this theme in the slaves' spirituals.

Another well-known instance is the song "Go Down Moses," with its explicit call for liberation from slavery. Harriet Tubman invoked this same Mosaic image in describing her work as a conductor on the Underground Railroad. Although the activities of the Underground Railroad are better documented in the Piedmont of North Carolina, Robinson praised the efforts of two Cape Fear Quakers, Mr. Fuller and Mr. Elliott, for their work in assisting Cape Fear slaves to freedom. Robinson wrote that "one man would haul the slaves at night to the end of his station and get back home before daylight, undiscovered, then they [the slaves] would be conveyed the next night in the wagons from that station to the next, and so on until they reached Canada." Robinson also described how his brother, James, escaped to the North. "He went to an underground railroad station twelve miles from Wilmington," Robinson stated. After air holes were strategically placed, his brother "was put in a box, this box was enclosed in another box, and the second box in a third box, and sent by express to New York." That Canada was the ultimate destination, rather than simply north of the Mason-Dixon Line, was the result of the passage of the Fugitive Slave Act in 1850. Thus, in 1853 and 1854, when two ships from Wilmington sailed into Boston harbor with slaves aboard, the slaves who escaped and made their way ashore had to travel on to Canada, lest they be apprehended and returned to their owners.[52]

Slave resistance and rebelliousness could take forms other than flight to Canada. Intentional slowdowns and misunderstandings of work orders, destruction of property, and even assaults on whites were all methods that the slaves employed. Beyond these, slaves escaped from their masters in a variety of ways and for different purposes and periods of time. William Robinson described two times in his youth when he ran away from his master but remained nearby so as to receive food and assistance from family members. Though this truancy might be short-lived and was often a response to a specific action by the master, other forms of running away evolved into Maroon communities that might last for longer periods and involve a number of persons. Robinson encountered one such community during one of his flights. The marshes and swamps adjacent to the Cape Fear River, along with the Great Dismal Swamp in northeastern North Carolina, were widely believed to harbor runaway slaves. Although such communities relied on stealth and evasion of whites for their success, over the long term, facility in English, familiarity with white society, and proficiency at some skills were the trademarks of those who successfully escaped to freedom.[53]

Representing an escalation in violence, both in the actions undertaken by slaves and in the response by whites, were slave insurrections. Two of the better-known examples of this type of slave resistance were the revolts by Denmark Vesey in Charleston, South Carolina, in 1822 and by Nat Turner in Virginia in 1831. Both Vesey and Turner recruited their followers at slave prayer meetings, invoking biblical imagery of the Lord's deliverance from oppression. The Cape Fear region experienced no revolts on the scale of those led by Vesey or Turner. Nor would it be accurate to suggest that all uprisings, resistance, and noncooperation by slaves in this region were inspired by the Bible or religious sources. Nevertheless, the Cape Fear did witness active resistance by slaves and violent reprisals by whites.

For example, in 1767 the New Hanover County Court received a report that twenty armed slaves were at large in the region. In response, officials authorized the sheriff to deputize thirty armed men and to capture the runaways or kill any that resisted. In 1775 Janet Schaw stated that many Wilmingtonians expected their slaves to revolt and defect to the British if hostilities broke out with the Crown. Subsequently, when a group of armed blacks was discovered in a nearby woods, a curfew was imposed on all blacks in Wilmington. Suspicions continued among whites in postwar Wilmington, and in 1785 free blacks in both Wilmington and Fayetteville had to register with town authorities, pay a fee, and wear a piece of cloth on which was written the word "FREE." Fears abounded that slave revolts might spread to North Carolina from the examples taking place in Haiti and Santo Domingo. In the summer of 1795 runaways raided a plantation in the Wilmington vicinity, killing one man and wounding another. In retaliation, a posse apprehended and killed five slaves. The dead included one man reputed to be the "General of the Swamps," the leader of a large Maroon community in the nearby marshes.[54]

Fear of slave insurrections grew in the early nineteenth century, as did reprisals against blacks. In 1802 whites in the northeastern section of the state discovered evidence of a well-planned slave revolt patterned, they believed, after the Haitian revolution and Gabriel Prosser's 1800 conspiracy; it had apparently been organized by black preachers at religious meetings of the slaves. A number of slaves were arrested and executed. News of this plot brought increased restrictions for slaves and stepped-up use of slave patrols, especially in the coastal and southeastern counties of the state.[55]

Publication of David Walker's *Appeal to the Coloured Citizens of the World* in 1829 sparked renewed anxiety among southern whites. Born in Wilmington in 1785 or 1796 (accounts differ) of a free mother and a slave father, Walker was a free black who lived much of his adult life in Boston. However, before moving to Boston, Walker sojourned during the early 1820s in Charleston, South Carolina, and participated in its black religious life. Such involvement would have brought Walker into the orbit of Denmark Vesey, and one scholar has concluded that even if Walker was not directly acquainted with Vesey, he probably knew of Vesey's planned uprising in 1822. Vesey's influence might be perceptible, but Walker's pamphlet was more than simply a call to arms. Rather, its message was that American slavery was a moral monstrosity. Blacks should refuse to submit to it any longer, and whites should work for its immediate and total abolition if they wished to escape the coming wrath of God. Slaves in revolt, violently throwing off their chains, was a possibility from which Walker did not shrink. He hoped that such a crisis could be avoided and that blacks in America would be afforded the economic and political opportunities of other citizens, so that they might obtain an education and improve themselves as white Americans were doing.[56]

Concern mounted among southern whites once it was discovered that Walker's *Appeal to the Coloured Citizens* was circulating among slaves. In August 1830 James F. McRee, magistrate of police in Wilmington, informed Governor John Owen that a free black in Wilmington had provided the town commissioners with a copy of the pamphlet that had been given to him. Upon further investigation, it was concluded that Jacob Cowan, a Wilmington slave who operated a tavern there, had received two hundred copies of the pamphlet with instructions to distribute them in Wilmington, Fayetteville, and New Bern. Cowan denied following these directions, but copies had also appeared elsewhere in North Carolina. In response to this information, the North Carolina legislature enacted restrictions on both slaves and free blacks in the state. Walker's *Ap-*

peal to the Coloured Citizens was banned, and possession of it was punishable by imprisonment or even death. The powers of slave patrols were increased, and the penalties for harboring runaways were strengthened. Free blacks could no longer marry slaves, and the conditions for manumission were further restricted. Finally, slaves could not be taught to read or write, and they were forbidden to possess any book or pamphlet.[57]

Anxiety over possible slave conspiracies deepened in the aftermath of the Nat Turner uprising. Rumors flashed throughout North Carolina alleging mayhem, destruction, and revenge carried out by slaves. Two weeks after the Turner uprising, officials uncovered a plot to revolt among slaves in Duplin and Sampson counties. Under torture, several slaves confessed to the conspiracy and implicated up to eight thousand blacks in those counties. The uprising had supposedly been planned for October 1831. After dispatching selected local families and seizing their horses and goods, the slaves planned to march to Wilmington, where they expected to be met by two thousand other slaves and free blacks. From Wilmington the plan was to continue first to Kenansville and then to Fayetteville, freeing slaves and consolidating control. Such charges fueled white frenzy. On September 12, 1831, reports of a Spartacus-like slave army approaching Wilmington motivated many to seek the safety of the militia post. When no attack took place and no slave army could be found, white Wilmingtonians forcefully interrogated resident blacks. The resulting confessions indicated that as many as four thousand slaves had supposedly planned to raid Wilmington in early October.[58]

It is entirely likely that slaves in southeastern North Carolina had heard of Turner's rebellion, and it is even possible that some slaves spoke of insurrection among themselves. Equally probable, however, is that many slaves confessed to what their masters wished to hear in order to end their painful interrogations. Reprisals by slave owners for slave resistance ranging from insubordination to insurrection were swift and backed up by the force of law. Slaves who ran away could expect whippings and other punishments if they returned to their masters. Runaway slaves that were suspected of committing crimes could be outlawed, a process whereby anyone who sighted them could kill them with no legal repercussions. Although return of the slave alive was usually the goal, some owners preferred that particularly obstinate slaves be killed, because they would be compensated for the death of an outlawed slave. J. W. Bradley of New Hanover County, for instance, offered a reward of ten dollars for the return of his slave alive, and fifty if he were brought back dead. For some slaves, the thought of a return to servitude or to further punishment was unbearable. One runaway in New Hanover County, upon being outlawed and recaptured, "jumped into the river and drowned himself."[59]

Only a few additional laws were passed by the North Carolina legislature in response to the Turner episode. Many in the legislature, including the governor, recognized that there were enough laws on the books; what was needed was stricter enforcement. An exception in this context was the passage of a law prohibiting free blacks from preaching. Given Turner's and Vesey's connections with black religious communities, as well as the role of free blacks in both these episodes, further restrictions on black religious life went into effect.[60]

In this way, antebellum laws restricting the lives of slaves and free blacks became tighter and tighter, while their opportunities for religious instruction or fellowship became even more closely supervised. Nevertheless, the simple, visible existence of the free black population challenged the ideological and social underpinnings of the slave system, and blacks in North Carolina continued to experience spheres of limited autonomy counterpoised by contexts of restriction. Preaching from the Bible could mandate submission to those in authority, but it could also privilege the prophet's call to proclaim liberty unto the captives. The duality of resignation and resistance found in the spirituals matched the complexity of the lived experience of servitude and rebellion. Thus, whether it took the form of a secret nighttime meeting in the brush, the joyful singing of a spiritual whose words proclaimed liberty in a code language known only to its singers, or the quiet meditation on a biblical passage memorized by one unable to read, the slaves' religious expression was profound.

Scholars have long recognized the importance of Christianity in the religious life of the slaves. Historians have also acknowledged the role of African religious traditions, and in this context, the Cape Fear provides an interesting case study. Most slaves coming to North Carolina did not arrive directly from Africa; rather, they came overland from Virginia and South Carolina. Because of this reality, it is difficult to pinpoint the specific African background of the North Carolina slave population, other than to say that they came from West Africa. Still, some scholars have argued that, particularly during the colonial period (when slaveholders had less interest in promoting Christianity), African influences, including traditional African religious practices, continued to play a significant role among southern slaves.[61]

Ritual ceremonies, festival observances, and recognition of an African cosmology characterized slaves in North Carolina. This African cosmology included the exhibition of proper ritual respect to those beings who affected one's life; a recognition of the power of humans to shape their own lives; a holistic understanding that accented communal rather than individual fulfillment; an awareness of the continuity among past, present, and future; and a consciousness of the power to heal contingent on maintaining harmony with other persons.[62]

Although documentary evidence for this cosmology is scarce, particularly in the Cape Fear region, other evidence dealing with festivals and rituals is more plentiful. Jonkonnu was an Afro-Caribbean festival that emerged in North Carolina sometime before 1824. It took place annually around Christmas, often lasting until New Year's Day or until the Yule log burned out. Troupes of male dancers in a variety of costumes would visit shops and residences in locations such as Wilmington and perform in the expectation of receiving a small donation. The costumes worn by dancers closely resembled those worn in the Senegambia region of Africa. In that African context, the costumes connoted conceptions of power. Interestingly, North Carolina is thought to be the only state where this festival flourished. Combining elements of social license and ritual inversion, the Jonkonnu festival opened up a social space in the lives of the slaves. Decreased workloads, increased mobility, and anticipated (even demanded) gifts for the dancers were all time-honored expectations that the slaves shared with the white community. This event also demonstrated the reality of religious syncretism by the nineteenth century, when the Christian Christmas and the West African harvest and fertility celebrations were combined.[63]

Just as the Jonkonnu celebration reflected African roots in its costumes and dance, rituals associated with birth, puberty, and death likewise disclosed an African heritage. The birth of a child was celebrated with a naming ceremony. Although Anglo-American names dominated among North Carolina slaves, during the colonial era, perhaps as many as 20 percent of the slaves had African names. Particularly in the period before the influence of the Second Great Awakening, biblical names were scarce. Given the opposition of many slave owners to mission work among the slaves, this absence is not surprising. Consequently, one finds many names based on the day on which the child was born or his or her birth position in the family. Both these naming traditions were also African practices. Similarly, marriage ceremonies among slaves could have an African flavor, particularly the nuptial ritual in which the bride and groom jumped over a broomstick held knee high and were thereby recognized as husband and wife. William Robinson remembered slave weddings in which feasts of raccoon, opossum, and sweet potatoes were prepared. Residual African influences can also be seen in the tradition of adorning burial sites with grave goods such as seashells, particular types of pebbles, even broken glassware, plates, or cups that were associated with or belonged to the deceased. Dancing and drumming—sometimes ecstatically, other times solemnly—could also be found in slave funerals, echoing remembered African contexts.[64]

In addition to the continuation of traditional religions, another dimension of the African experience in the slaves' spiritual world was the presence of Islam. The Muslim religion had reached North Africa as early as 660 and had penetrated into sub-Saharan Africa by the eighth century. By the beginning of the eleventh century, Islam had arrived on the banks of the Senegal River and soon spread east toward Lake Chad and northern Nigeria. Documentary evidence is only slowly becoming available, but it seems likely that at least some slaves taken from their West African homelands would have been Muslim. One scholar tentatively estimated that 15 to 20 percent of all slaves brought to the New World were Muslims; another historian suggested that about thirty thousand slaves (or 10 percent of all West Africans introduced into the United States between 1711 and 1808) were Muslims.[65]

A fascinating example of antebellum Muslim presence, and one that is especially well documented, occurred in the Cape Fear region. It involved an individual named Omar Ibn Said, born in 1770 in Futa Toro on the Senegal River and educated for twenty-five years before he began teaching and engaging in trade. In 1807, after being captured in a war and sold into slavery, Ibn Said arrived in Charleston, South Carolina. He was purchased first by one master and then, upon that master's death, sold off to another Charlestonian. Ibn Said eventually ran away and ended up in Fayetteville, North Carolina, where he was captured and jailed. At this point, James Owen, a Bladen County planter and brother of future governor John Owen, bought Ibn Said and brought him to his plantation. James Owen belonged to the Presbyterian church in Fayetteville, and in December 1821 Ibn Said was baptized and joined that church. In 1835 Owen and his family, including Ibn Said, moved to Wilmington and transferred their membership to First Presbyterian Church. Ibn Said remained in Wilmington until his death in 1864.[66]

Information about Ibn Said's life is available through a short autobiography he wrote in Arabic in 1831, as well as reminiscences by those who knew him, such as Matthew Grier, the pastor of First Presbyterian Church in Wilmington. These sources, as well as the subsequent work of scholars such as Allan D. Austin, provide biographical details and sketch out the religious context of Ibn Said's life. Educated in the Qur'an, Ibn Said followed traditional Muslim practices before his enslavement: praying five times a day, acknowledging the profession of faith ("There is no God but Allah and Muhammad is the Prophet of God"), giving alms, and fasting from sunrise to sunset during the month of Ramadan. He had also made the pilgrimage to Mecca. Based on descriptions of his appearance in North Carolina, as well as a surviving daguerreotype, Ibn Said wore a white turban, signifying a level of accomplishment in Qur'anic study and identifying the wearer as a marabout, an individual learned in Muslim religious affairs.[67]

Ibn Said's Christian baptism raises interesting questions about his religious experience. The Qur'anic requirements for believers could be revised to accommodate those in extraordinary circumstances. Prayers could be said privately, and an exemption from fasting could be permitted if one was engaged in the type of strenuous work typically expected of slaves. Obligations to give alms could also be adapted to the reality of the slave existence. There is little evidence concerning Ibn Said's daily life after his enslavement. Matthew Grier reported that when James Owen first acquired Ibn Said, he was a "staunch Mohammedan" and fasted during Ramadan. By the time of his baptism, he had become a Christian, Grier stated, in "all outward signs." Ibn Said's autobiography begins with the quotation of sura 67 from the Qur'an, but it also states, "I open my heart, as to a great light, to receive the true way, the way of the Lord Jesus the Messiah." Similarly, another manuscript from around 1840 begins with the Muslim invocation, "In the name of God the Merciful, the compassionate. May God have mercy on the Prophet Mohammed." This statement is then followed by the Lord's Prayer. Some have hailed Ibn Said as a convert to Christianity, while others have been more skeptical. It seems clear that Ibn Said conformed, at least in his outward activities, to the life of a Christian, although it seems just as likely that he did not totally abandon his Muslim background.

Africa, then, continued to reside in the antebellum South. Through Muslim and traditional religious rituals and beliefs, African spirituality and practices (even when attenuated) provided threads in the religious fabric of Cape Fear religion.[68]

Upon his return to Fayetteville and his home church in April 1858, the Reverend James McDaniel wrote of a recent visit to Wilmington. So hoarse from continuous preaching that he could no longer talk, McDaniel described the afternoon before his departure from Wilmington. On that day McDaniel, together with two other local Baptist preachers, had gathered with a large number of persons and proceeded down to the Cape Fear River, where the ministers had baptized the new believers. McDaniel concluded that a "great work" was going on in Wilmington.[69]

The "great work" to which McDaniel referred was the Revival of 1858. Surprisingly, as a religious episode, the revival has been studied primarily as a northern phenomenon. One historian writing in 1979 stated that its revivals were "confined to Northern cities," and another scholar wrote that its events "appeared most visibly in the North where systems of communication and commerce were more highly developed than in the South." This assessment would have come as a surprise to Wilmingtonians in the spring of 1858, for Wilmington newspapers were carrying accounts of religious meetings among Presbyterians, Methodists, and Baptists that were larger than normal in numbers and attended by persons not often seen at such religious gatherings.[70]

The Wilmington experience began in the early spring of 1858 when John Latta, an elder at First Presbyterian Church, returned from a synodal meeting in Greensboro. With pastor Matthew Grier away on church business, Latta and others organized a series of daily prayer meetings. These initial gatherings soon grew into a regular series of Sabbath services, midday prayer meetings, and interdenominational or "union" convocations. By March 1858, John Lamb Prichard, the pastor of Front Street Baptist Church, wrote that prayer meetings attended by "Christians of all denominations" were being held at his church at sunrise. "All Christians, and citizens, strangers and seamen" were cordially invited to attend. Charles Deems, pastor at Front Street Methodist Church, confirmed Prichard's observations. In April Deems remarked that prayer meetings at noon were well attended at Front Street Methodist and that many persons had joined his church.[71]

Several aspects of this Revival of 1858 are striking. First, although the revival began in the urban North, it expanded to the towns and cities of the South and Midwest and even had a parallel movement in Great Britain. Newspaper accounts described religious meetings not only in New York, Boston, and Philadelphia but also Cincinnati, St. Louis, Mobile, Raleigh, and Wilmington.[72]

Second, while women had played conspicuous roles in previous revivals, men were more visible in the 1858 episode. Grier stated that in 1852 the majority of the eighty-four members of his church were women. The men, he said, "were working hard at turpentine, and at sawing logs, and at buying and selling, and getting gain, and they had little time and not much heart for active work in the church." Those men who were active, such as John Latta, exercised wide influence in the congregation. By 1858 Grier noted that the membership of First Presbyterian had risen to 170, and men formed a much larger percentage of the congregation. In fact, several prominent businessmen in the community had publicly declared their faith and joined the church during the revivals. Beyond that, the meetings also reached out to incorporate blacks. Because blacks were not able to attend meetings during the day, separate services in the evenings were held for them.[73]

The Revival of 1858 is often called the "businessmen's revival," in part because it occurred in the aftermath of the economic panic of 1857 and in part because of the noontime prayer meetings that businessmen often led and in which they so visibly participated. These midday prayer meetings were marked by their appeal to union or interdenominational participation. Reaching across Protestant denominational lines to unite members of various churches, this revival invoked the theme of Christian unity. Revival organizers emphasized that no controversial points (such as the slavery question) would be discussed or become the focus of prayers. Instead, these would be orderly, businesslike meetings, reaching beyond denominational and political differences toward what the organizers believed was a deeper, common piety available to all Christians.

Recognition of these characteristics reminds one of the comforting and consoling appeal of such a religious revival in the aftermath of the economic devastation of 1857. It also reminds one of the power of such a call to unity in the context of the sectional, political, and denominational disunity that seemed to be the order of the day. Wilmingtonians in 1858 were all too aware of the schisms within the Presbyterian, Methodist, and Baptist denominations that divided them into northern and southern branches; of the violence in "Bleeding Kansas"; and of the controversy over the *Dred Scott* decision. Perhaps these Protestant churches that had modeled secession could now maintain unity. Perhaps, as one historian put it, a baptism of Christian unity could offer the means to avert a "baptism of blood."[74]

The Revival of 1858 did not prevent the Civil War from occurring; nor did it supply the spiritual unity that could mend denominational differences. However, in many respects it did provide an apt close to the turbulent antebellum era in the Cape Fear. Befitting that period's reform emphasis, missionary projects were undertaken that formed the basis for several new churches in Wilmington. Beyond that, out of a prayer meeting in April 1858 came "plans for active Christian usefulness" among young men. This became the foundation for a local chapter of the Young Men's Christian Association (YMCA), a group that sought to sustain the spiritual improvement of young men without reference to denominational affiliation. This goal fit smoothly into the tenor of the 1858 revival in Wilmington and elsewhere. Finally, in its quest for conversions and its use of interdenominational overtures, the revival reflected its compatibility with evangelicalism and the voluntary structures that shaped religious life in the American nation. That blacks were involved in the revival, though still in a second-class capacity, demon-strated the power of the message that attracted them and the limits of the cultural captivity in which the southern church lived. Yet, as the next chapter shows, the multivalence of that religious message and the evocative power of cultural memory could give rise to com-munities of religious identity—some revitalized, and others created anew.

5

Mystic Chords of Memory

In the history of religions, sacred space has taken many forms. Natural locations such as mountains, mesas, and rivers; human edifices such as temples or cathedrals; consecrated sites such as churchyards and memorials have all served as sacred contexts for religious believers. Consequently, whether hallowed by human intention and interaction or simply perceived by the faithful to manifest the holy, landscapes can become holy places. And these holy places often contain monuments (the word originally meant "brings to mind")—objects that invoke memories among their onlookers. Beyond that, if memory connects to objects, then, as this chapter demonstrates, memory can also help define physical space and construct human communities.

In any inventory of sacred space, locations where the dead are disposed of have a central role. The mosaic that makes up burial practices consists of many separate pieces. To begin with, the shape and placement of burials in America have changed over time. During the struggles of early settlement, isolated graves were dug wherever the colonists happened to be. This tradition evolved into burials on private family land, a pattern widespread throughout the rural portion of this region and one that continues in the present. Colonial and antebellum plantations in the area, such as Orton in Brunswick County, Rocky Run in New Hanover, or Jonathan Evans in Cumberland County, all have their familial graveyards on site.[1]

Where towns such as Brunswick or Wilmington grew up, denser populations allowed for larger, multiple-family graveyards. These locations were often churchyards, though occasionally burials took place within the church itself. For example, at St. Philip's churchyard in Brunswick Town, several burials surround the church, and twelve floor graves have been placed within the church. In the eighteenth century, grave monuments were often ledger, box tomb, or head- and footstone in style and constructed from wood, slate, or sandstone. Mary Quince (d. 1765) and Mary Jane Dry (d. 1793) were both buried at St. Philip's churchyard in box tombs, while Rebecca McGuire (d. 1766) reposes under a ledger. Alternatively, vaulted graves for Henry Toomer and the family of Charles Jewkes, dating from 1786, can be found at St. James's churchyard in Wilmington. Although slate was used to identify these burials at St. Philip and St. James, wooden markers were more common. In the Lower Cape Fear, where stone markers would have to be imported due to the lack of native stone, the possession of a gravestone was a sign of status during these early years. Consequently, wooden markers were widely used, even though the humid summers and hurricane seasons could take their toll, rotting or smashing the markers and erasing the visibility of the deceased.[2]

Although some stones were imported from England, most prepared gravestones came from eastern commercial centers such as Boston, Providence, or New York City. Occasionally the stonecutters would sign their work; otherwise, the carver's distinctive pattern and style would indicate its provenance. Reflecting a Christian heritage that emphasized memento mori ("remember that you must die"), skulls, crossbones, and skeletons were the dominant symbols carved into the stones. A fascinating exception occurs within the yard of the Highland Scots Longstreet Presbyterian Church. The churchyard is enclosed by rubble walls constructed from fieldstones cleared from the site, and many of the markers are made of local sandstone that reflect the conventional styles. However, the gravestone of Laulin McNeil, dated 1733, is carved in the shape of a shield. The tradition of a shield shape continues the Scottish custom of placing the shield of a deceased warrior into his grave as a memorial, and it was a fitting testimony to the continuing influence of the Scottish homeland among these Presbyterians.[3]

During the nineteenth century several changes took place in the burial practices of Americans. One of the most important was the rise of the rural cemetery, located on the outskirts of town. A major impetus for the development of rural cemeteries was dissatisfaction with in-town graveyards. Examples of ill-kept and overgrown churchyards were available for all to see; more horrific were the stories of overcrowded church burial chambers actually bursting at the seams, as happened in Paris in 1790 and New York City in 1822. Visions of bones sticking out from the ground were trumped by tales of noxious gas exuding from crypts and coffins, poisoning the air and sickening any who came into extended contact with it. Combined with these dismal reports was the demand for city land for commercial development. One might think that any buried bodies would be removed if the property was bought and used for other purposes. However, city newspapers regularly recounted anecdotes in which corpses were desecrated or burial sites simply covered over.[4]

In Wilmington the graveyard of St. James Church was not the town's only burial spot. A small graveyard on North Fifth Avenue dated back to the eighteenth century. A municipal burial ground was located on Fourth and Dock streets. These sites were matched by ones connected with the Baptist Meetinghouse, Front Street Methodist Church, Lebanon Chapel, and eventually St. Thomas Catholic Church. Finally, there were potter's fields (so-called after the verse in Matthew 27:7) for the indigent, and tradition holds that there was also a graveyard on the south side of Market Street, east of Fifth, where criminals who had been executed at the adjacent Gallows Hill were interred.[5]

By the 1840s conditions were changing in Wilmington, as they were elsewhere. In 1841 the vestry of St. James offered sites for families to build vault tombs; however, a prohibition on further interments within the city limits was expected to be enacted soon. In August 1844 the vestry resolved that due to overcrowding in the churchyard, all further burials would be restricted to current members of the congregation or to those with a family member already buried there.[6]

In 1852 a group of Wilmington civic leaders led by Armand J. DeRosset III met to consider the problem of graveyards in the city. Their answer was to develop a new burial ground, eventually named Oakdale Cemetery, on the edge of the north side of town. Oakdale was to be modeled on the well-known example of Mount Auburn Cemetery in Massachusetts. Mount Auburn, which had opened in 1831, was the American prototype of the rural cemetery and had been fashioned in part after the Père Lachaise, the famous garden cemetery in Paris.[7]

The rural cemetery represented a conceptual and organizational departure from previous practices. Situated some distance from the commercial center of town, the rural cemetery provided a spacious setting that was landscaped in an orderly fashion and designed to evoke emotional associations with nature. Its curving pathways were deliberately intended to counteract the symmetry of the city, and its trees, plants, and other horticulture sought to display a balance between nature and civilization. Supervised by a board of directors rather than a church vestry or parish council, these sites were privately incorporated under the law. Finally, in the choice of the word *cemetery* (from the Greek for "sleeping chamber"), these organizations denoted a shift in the presentation and understanding of the burial space.[8]

Oakdale Cemetery provides an excellent illustration of the rural cemetery, and it was the first in the state of North Carolina. Originally sixty-five acres in size, Oakdale promised generations of Wilmingtonians an expansive space for burial of the dead. Nor was Wilmington alone in the adoption of the rural cemetery model. Besides Mount Auburn, other prominent rural cemeteries included Laurel Hill (1836) in Philadelphia, Greenwood (1838) in Baltimore, Hollywood (1847) in Richmond, and Oakland (1850) in Atlanta. Here again, antebellum Wilmington reached for refinement, seeking to express a higher degree of gracefulness, taste, and gentility rather than simply to provide for the functional disposal of the dead. Consequently, when Oakdale's board of directors, men well known in the community and active in their churches, opened the lots for purchase in 1854, and the city prohibited any further burials within the town limits the following year, Oakdale's future looked promising.[9]

Rural cemeteries such as Oakdale were designed, in the apt words of one scholar, as "didactic landscapes." Commentators on Oakdale inevitably praised the sturdy trees draped wreathlike with Spanish moss; the dark, winding stream; and the stands of dogwoods, azaleas, and camellias, all of which provided a striking setting for this garden of graves. Nature, so powerfully evident but always subdued in funereal fashion, provoked and enhanced contemplation among the cemetery's visitors. Moreover, a wide array of symbols now adorned the graves. The obelisk, associated with Egyptian funeral architecture, was supplemented with the lamb (innocence), oak (stability), lily (resurrection), and weeping willow and urn (bereaved memory). Crosses and Bibles could also be found. These symbols expanded the eighteenth-century inventory of carved images from the familiar skulls and crossbones. This enlarged iconographic repertoire both underscored the sacredness of the space and indicated significant changes from earlier representations of death.[10]

Oakdale, with its crescent and circular pathways and its serpentine roads throughout the grounds, intentionally sought to remove its visitors from the congestion of urban space and place them within an island of repose. Guests and residents alike were encouraged to come to Oakdale, where "Affection resorts to commune with Memory and to shed tears with Sorrow." Just as rural cemeteries were designed and landscaped to allow communion with nature—an encounter that, by the Romantic era, had been enveloped with transcendental associations and spiritual significance—so too were they chalices of memory.[11]

Cemeteries were the arena for personal sorrow and affectionate remembrance, and they were also the depository of collective memory for the community. For example, in a sad irony, the first

Oakdale Cemetery (Postcard in author's collection)

person buried in Oakdale was the six-year-old daughter of Armand DeRosset, president of the cemetery's board of directors. Deaths of young children were still an all-too-common occurrence in nineteenth-century America. However, by this time, Romantic theology, funeral iconography, and linguistic custom had softened the presentation of death, especially that of youngsters. The dead were merely sleeping a painless sleep, recumbent among family and friends until, in the Christian tradition, at least, they were awakened by the millennial Second Coming of Christ.[12]

Every burial at Oakdale contained a context of personal sorrow and personal memories, but by the 1850s, structural changes had occurred to better serve the clients of cemeteries. In keeping with the shift to a more hopeful and sentimental presentation, lighter-colored stones, such as marble, supplanted the darker slates or granites in the construction of grave monuments. Quarries in Pennsylvania, Vermont, New York, and Georgia were the major suppliers of marble to the Cape Fear region. Traditionally, cabinetmakers such as Matthew Lawton of Wilmington also served as undertakers, fashioning coffins, and as monument agents, ordering stone for markers. Lawton worked with C. T. Duncomb, a marble cutter in Norwalk, Connecticut. In contrast, Apollos Sweetland itinerated as a marble cutter from his base in Fayetteville through Virginia, North Carolina, and South Carolina from 1818 to 1827. Fayetteville was also the location of the workshop of George Lauder. Born in Scotland in 1810, Lauder came to North Carolina in the 1830s to work on the state capitol. Lauder's style of stonecutting was distinctive, and he was prolific, filling graveyards in the Upper Cape Fear and producing thousands of markers for graves from the coast to the Piedmont during his long career. Adept at high-relief carving and capable of cutting Scottish thistles, biblical tableaux, and a variety of other symbols, Lauder developed a successful business and illustrated the economic and entrepreneurial aspects associated with the development of sacred space.[13]

In December 1868 Lauder completed a ten-foot obelisk, commissioned by a group of Fayetteville women, to commemorate the Confederate dead. This monument, located in Cross Creek Cemetery, was the first Confederate monument in North Carolina and serves as a fitting reminder of the capacity of cemeteries to act as locations for the memory of the public community as well as the private individual. Early on at Oakdale, for example, sections were purchased by the Masons and Odd Fellows. Later, another area was reserved for Methodists from the Front Street Church, and in 1855 a portion was dedicated as the Hebrew Cemetery. In this manner, individual identity was joined with fraternal or religious identity into a public memorial. Two events were publicly remembered in Oakdale: the yellow fever epidemic of 1862 and the Civil War. In both cases, special burial arrangements recalled the past and honored the sacrifices that had been made.[14]

Nineteenth-century Americans often called yellow fever the "scourge of the South," owing to the prevalence of the disease in this region. Wilmingtonians were familiar with it, suffering outbreaks on a regular basis and a severe attack in 1819. In August 1862 the blockade runner *Kate* arrived in Wilmington from Nassau in the Bahamas. Prior to Nassau, the *Kate* had been in Havana, where it had been exposed to yellow fever by the ship the *Flying Cloud*. The *Flying Cloud* had also infected a British ship headed for Bermuda, where a similar yellow fever epidemic occurred in the fall of 1862. When the *Kate* docked in Wilmington, it already had sick crewmen aboard, but in their desire for the food and supplies the *Kate* carried, officials allowed the ship to forgo the normal quarantine procedures. The death of one of the crew on August 8, however, turned out to be the beginning of an epidemic. Between August 8 and November 14, 1862, nearly four hundred people who had died from yellow fever were buried in Oakdale Cemetery alone. Although the final figures are not known, one estimate indicates that around fifteen hundred people were infected. Once infected, yellow fever mortality rates could reach 40 percent, or at least six hundred deaths from yellow fever in Wilmington.[15]

Thucydides' description of plague-filled Athens as "death raging within the city and destruction without" would have fit Wilmington in late 1862. John Bellamy Jr. recollected standing on the porch of his family's new mansion on Market Street "watching wagon-loads of corpses go by to Oakdale Cemetery." Another witness poignantly remembered that "the streets were empty, save the rolling sound of hearses or physicians' vehicles. The dogs howled from hunger, and the very birds of the air had deserted the city. Death and pestilence had possession of every place. Want and misery were everywhere discernible."[16]

Perhaps as much as 50 percent of the town's population evacuated to other locations; those who stayed coped as best they could. One theory concerning the origin of yellow fever was that it was transmitted through impurities in the air, so some residents burned barrels of rosin, trying to disinfect the atmosphere. Another theory, however, was that the disease was contagious, so sanitation and quarantine measures were also strictly enforced. As the unseasonably warm fall wore on, a few churches closed their doors, the telegraph service stopped, and most stores suspended operation. Food became scarce, and a free soup kitchen was set up. Relief efforts took many forms. Jewish Wilmingtonians took up a collection, and Roman Catholic nuns belonging to the Sisters of Mercy came from Charleston to tend the sick. Robert Drane, rector of St. James Episcopal; John Prichard, pastor of First Baptist; and Thomas Murphy, priest at St. Thomas the Apostle, all remained to minister to the ill and bereaved. Each of these men fell victim to the disease.[17]

In November frost finally broke the grip of the pestilence, and Wilmington, its material and spiritual resources severely taxed, began the process of recovery. A five-acre section was reserved in Oakdale for the yellow fever victims. It is distinctive for its open character and few markers, reflecting the haste of many of the burials during the epidemic's height. But even though the specific identities of these persons have been effaced, the power of the space, together with a simple explanatory tablet to commemorate the event, is evident and striking.

As deaths from the yellow fever epidemic abated, other losses from the ongoing Civil War were continuing. For example, of the 15,301 Confederate soldiers wounded or killed at the Battle of Gettysburg in 1863, 4,033 were North Carolinians. Nearly one in five of the total white population of the state served in the Confederate armed forces, and many Cape Fear families experienced the loss of loved ones. By 1864 Union forces were marching toward the Cape Fear, and in December 1864 a Union fleet assembled off Fort Fisher, south of Wilmington, and landed a force of 3,000 Union soldiers on Christmas Day. After a brief skirmish, these soldiers retreated. However, on January 12, 1865, a larger Union armada began shelling the fort, and after fierce hand-to-hand fighting, the Union forces took Fort Fisher. Wilmington was occupied on February 22, 1865.

On April 9, 1865, at Appomattox Court House, General Robert E. Lee surrendered to General Ulysses S. Grant.[18]

The war had divided families and congregations; it had even caused two pastors to leave town. Matthew Grier, the pastor of First Presbyterian, departed Wilmington for Philadelphia in June 1861 because he favored the North and his congregation did not. A similar development occurred at St. John Episcopal Church, a new congregation begun as a missionary extension of St. James. The church, constructed in an English Gothic parish church style, opened for services in April 1860 with Jonathan Wainwright as the rector. He served until August 1861, when he transferred to the Diocese of Connecticut because of his endorsement of the Northern cause. John Prichard of First Baptist supported the hope of one indivisible union, but when North Carolina seceded in May 1861 Prichard threw his lot in with his fellow North Carolinians. Finally, if the onset of hostilities was painful, so too was the aftermath of Wilmington's fall to Federal troops. Alfred Watson, rector of St. James, did not offer prayers for the president of the United States as the Union military officials had expected. Upon learning this, General Joseph R. Hawley, the Union commander, seized the church and ordered the pews and furnishings torn out and the building turned into a military hospital. A Lutheran church that had just begun construction was occupied by Federal soldiers who camped in the churchyard and used pews and desks for fuel, while stabling their horses in the church. Other congregations lost items to looters. For some Wilmingtonians, Federal occupation would spawn as many memories as the war itself.[19]

On May 10, 1872, the Ladies Memorial Association of Wilmington unveiled a monument in Oakdale inscribed "To the Confederate Dead." Atop the granite pedestal stood a bronze statue of a Confederate soldier in full dress uniform at parade rest with his rifle. Medallions of Robert E. Lee and Thomas "Stonewall" Jackson were fixed to the pedestal, and the plot was ringed with decorative wrought iron fencing. Beneath the monument, in a lot donated by the Oakdale Cemetery Corporation in 1867, lie the remains of 367 unknown Confederate soldiers, most of whom died in local hospitals at the end of the war. Just as with the yellow fever epidemic, the Civil War confronted Wilmington with unprecedented numbers of dead. Thus, the monument to the Confederate dead celebrated their individual sacrifices of the past, while seeking to instill that same dedication and valor in present and future generations.[20]

The statue of the Confederate solider, knapsack on his back, standing at rest with his rifle, became an iconic image not only in Wilmington but also throughout the South. Sometimes located in the square before the county courthouse, on the lawn of the university, or atop a knoll in the cemetery, this monument came to symbolize the "Lost Cause" in the postwar South. Complete with rituals, organizations, and beliefs, the Lost Cause became a civil religion in the South, a cultural expression and functional equivalent of more familiar religious patterns. The faith of the Lost Cause sought to explain the meaning of the Southern defeat in the war and to give instruction for the South's future development. As a supplement to, if not a surrogate for, traditional southern Christianity, the Lost Cause was a potent impulse among southern whites.[21]

Eulogizing the fallen soldiers at the Oakdale Confederate monument, one writer promised that they would never be forgotten "until the Southern heart had ceased to thrill at the recollection of our glorious past." To that panegyrical end, white Wilmingtonians joined commemorative associations and celebrated Confederate Memorial Day or the birthday of Robert E. Lee. For example, in 1894 the Ladies Memorial Association became the Cape Fear chapter of the United Daughters of the Confederacy. Three years later, these women organized the local branch of the Children of the Confederacy. In 1895 the Sons of Confederate Veterans established a unit in Wilmington. Well before these organizations were formed, many residents of Wilmington observed Confederate Memorial Day on May 10, the birthday of Stonewall Jackson, by placing flowers on Confederate graves and, after its construction, on the Confederate monument at Oakdale. These commemorative activities grew, and by May 10, 1871, the Ladies Memorial Association had organized a parade led by Confederate officers and with disabled Confederate veterans, some with peg legs and others in carriages, given a special place of honor. The entourage made its way from a temporary downtown encampment out to Oakdale Cemetery, where speeches were delivered and women decorated the graves.[22]

Wilmingtonians also dedicated other monuments to the Confederate dead and to specific leaders. Although Monument Avenue in Richmond is well known for its large statuary, two monuments in Wilmington illustrate the same desire to remember the past and shape the future. In October 1909 the cornerstone was laid, and on April 20, 1911, the George Davis statue on Market Street was unveiled. Davis was born in New Hanover County and spent most of his life in Wilmington. He represented North Carolina first in the Confederate Provincial Congress and then in the Confederate Senate. From July 1864 to April 1865 he served as attorney general of the Confederate States of America.[23]

Sculpted by Francis H. Packer, a nationally known artist, the statue depicted Davis in an expressive pose, with his right hand extended as if he were delivering a speech. Packer also worked on the Wilmington monument dedicated in 1924 to "The Soldiers of the Confederacy." In this work, Packer collaborated with Henry Bacon, the architect of the Lincoln Memorial and a native of Wilmington. The sculpture presented a bare-headed Confederate soldier standing guard over a fallen comrade. The inscription states in part, "Confederates, blend your recollections, Let Memory weave its bright reflections." Here too, memory in a public context and monuments as evocative reminders were on display. And in this display, in which the motif of sacrifice played such a dominant role, white Christian southerners recollected that, like the crucified Christ, their aspirations would live on, even though they had been defeated; in short, the sacrifices of the Lost Cause had not been in vain.[24]

Cemeteries mark boundaries between the living and the dead. More mundanely, cemeteries often illustrate social boundaries of race, class, and religion as well. For instance, in 1860 the Wilmington town commissioners bought fifteen acres of land adjacent to Oakdale as a black burying ground. In 1871 the Pine Forest Cemetery Company finally received the deed to the property from the city. Handsome gravestones mark many individual plots at Pine Forest, and a number of prominent leaders of Wilmington's black community, such as John E. Taylor, deputy collector of customs; Dr. James F. Shober, the first black physician in the area; James B. Dudley, a prominent educator; Robert R. Taylor, a well-known architect; and Frederick Sadgwar, a skilled craftsman, are buried there.[25]

Beginning in 1867 the Wilmington National Cemetery began interring the bodies of Federal servicemen. Initially, 1,035 Union soldiers who had been buried at Oakdale were transferred to the National Cemetery. In addition, some of the 1,500 Federal soldiers

The Soldiers of the Confederacy Memorial (Photo by author)

who had died from disease, especially typhus, in Wilmington between February 26 and June 30, 1865, were buried there. Finally, the cemetery also received the remains of 557 members of the U.S. Colored Troops who had died in the attacks on Fort Fisher and Wilmington. Most headstones in this cemetery are government issued, emphasizing uniformity and military camaraderie. Significantly, however, the black soldiers were placed in a separate section, removed from their white brothers in arms.[26]

Distinctions of class as well as race come into play in Wilmington cemeteries. At its opening, lots at Oakdale were auctioned off for a minimum of fifty dollars per lot, with most going for nearly one hundred dollars. An area was set aside, however, where burials cost only five dollars per adult and three dollars per child. Although five dollars was no mean amount in the 1850s, these burials were limited in number, and the area had little of the dignity of the rest of the cemetery. Consequently, in 1876 Bellvue Cemetery was opened on fifteen and a half acres adjacent to Pine Forest Cemetery. The charter of Bellvue noted that burials in cemeteries such as Oakdale incurred "expense too great for men of moderate means to sustain"; therefore, an alternative was needed. Far simpler than Oakdale in design and execution, Bellvue contained stands of oak, cypress, and magnolia trees that shaded the graves.[27]

Two other burial sites date back to the mid-nineteenth century. Pine Tree Burying Ground, located between Queen and Wooster streets, probably was used to bury victims of the yellow fever epidemic. Oak Grove Cemetery on South Seventeenth Street was used by the county as early as the 1870s to bury the destitute. Although many of these persons were black Wilmingtonians, records indicate that black and white working-class folks bought plots here too. Thus, the edge of the boundaries might be a bit blurred, but separation by race and class was evident in Wilmington in death as in life. Significantly, with burials of Roman Catholics, Protestants, and Jews in Oakdale, religion was not as visible a means of demarcation as were class and race.[28]

The final chapter in the history of the development of the modern cemetery concerns the emergence of memorial lawn park cemeteries in the twentieth century. Whereas the initial appeal of the rural cemetery was its separation from congested urban space, by the twentieth century, many rural cemeteries found themselves encircled by cities. Furthermore, while advocates of the rural cemetery had encouraged visitors to commune with nature in the cemetery's environs, there were more and more complaints about city residents having picnics, playing games, and even arranging assignations on the cemetery grounds. As early as 1869 a newspaper article informed Wilmingtonians that two policemen would be posted at the gate to Oakdale on Sunday "to protect the sacred place from unwarrantable and disorderly intrusion." Whether these efforts were entirely successful or not, a later notice announced that bicycle riding in Oakdale was no longer allowed.[29]

The twentieth-century memorial park represented a further change from its colonial antecedents and its rural cemetery predecessors. Instead of picturesque natural settings, forested with obelisks and ornate markers, the memorial park was an open meadow. Particularly in its early years, this type of cemetery removed the reminders of individual deaths by eliminating fencing around lots, leveling grave mounds, discouraging the use of gravestones, and reducing the inscriptions on those stones that were allowed. In so doing, the directors of the memorial park cemetery enacted predetermined plans for the land that curtailed the expression of individual preferences. Whereas the rural cemetery invited individual families to embellish their lots within the confines of refinement and good taste, the memorial park took a larger measure of control over the landscaping, maintaining, and perpetuating of the cemetery. Offering services that now included embalming, cremation, chapel ceremonies, and grief counseling, the memorial park distanced families from direct encounters with death as it broadened and professionalized its services.[30]

The ambience of the memorial park was different too. Its open vistas rejected the somber religious statuary of the Victorian era and shifted the atmosphere. Selected monumental sculpture replaced the variety of shapes and symbols found in rural cemeteries. Bronze markers, flush to the ground, gave the cemetery a more unified, less cluttered appearance, and they did not impede the lawn mower's efficient manicure of the grounds. Taken together, these pieces of the memorial park provided, in the words of a 1950 memorial park guide, "a constant source of inspiration," an "unswerving faith in eternal life—a serene confidence that death is not the end, but the beginning."[31]

Originally sixty-five acres when it opened in 1948 in Wilmington, Greenlawn Memorial Park nicely displayed this latest stage in the evolution of burial space. Owned by a corporation that was listed on a stock exchange, Greenlawn attempted to offer all necessary services from pre-need contracts through perpetual care of the grave. Its flat grave markers provided privacy for the lot holders, while its monumental statue of Moses (dismantled in 2001) and its life-size depiction of Jesus on the way to Golgotha infused religious associations into the totality of the grounds.[32]

The sacred space of churchyards and cemeteries, then, is a historically complex and socially constructed terrain. Repositories in the material culture of grief and hope, private recollections and public memory, they can open a fascinating perspective onto other realms of religious significance among the residents of the Cape Fear.

Memory can shape a metaphorical past as well as fashion an anticipated future. As Albert J. Raboteau observed, in appropriating the story of Exodus as their own story, blacks first in slavery and then in freedom "envisioned a future radically different from their present." Exodus "symbolized their common history and common destiny." As discussed in the last chapter, blacks were members or attendees at Presbyterian, Episcopal, Methodist, Baptist, and Roman Catholic churches in Wilmington. One of the largest cohorts was located at Front Street Methodist Church, and there one of the most dramatic episodes in the immediate postwar era took place.[33]

The scene opened at dawn on a Sunday morning in late February 1865. Just a few days earlier the Confederate stronghold, Fort Fisher, had finally fallen to Union forces, and now these same forces, including soldiers from the U.S. Colored Troops, had occupied Wilmington. It was the regular practice of the black members of Front Street Methodist Church to hold a prayer meeting at sunrise on Sunday, so they assembled according to their tradition. When Front Street's pastor, the Reverend L. S. Burkhead, arrived at the church, he found that one of the black class leaders had begun the service and was reading from the ninth psalm, with its description of righteous judgment rebuking the wicked, vanquishing the enemies, and rooting out evil. At that point, rather than turning over the pulpit to Burkhead, the class leader introduced the Reverend William H. Hunter, a former slave from North Carolina and now a Methodist minister and army chaplain in the Fourth U.S. Colored Troops. Hunter rose and congratulated the congregation on their newly acquired freedom. "A few short years ago, I left North Carolina a slave; I now return as a man," Hunter proclaimed. "Thank God the armies of the Lord and of Gideon have triumphed and the Rebels have been driven in confusion and scattered like chaff before the wind." Hunter's remarks electrified his audience, and joyfulness and excitement poured out. Even Burkhead conceded that "to these colored people this was their great jubilee. They had just crossed the Red Sea dry-shod."[34]

Chaplain Hunter's influence would be more than oratorical. On the orders of the Union military commanders, the services at Front Street Methodist were soon divided between Burkhead, who held forth in the morning, and Hunter, who preached the afternoon service. Beyond that, Hunter was instrumental in the exodus of 642 black members of Front Street Church in order to form the first African Methodist Episcopal (AME) church in Wilmington. Hunter fully realized the significance of the move, often invoking Psalms 98, which states, "O sing to the Lord a new song, for he has done marvelous things. His right hand and his holy arm have gotten him victory." For the newly freed blacks of Wilmington, this was indeed a time of new songs, marvelous things, and glorious victories in their religious lives.[35]

Although some two hundred black members and two hundred white members remained at Front Street Church, the departure of more than six hundred blacks was significant. Their exit came after efforts to depose the white pastor and acquire the property of Front Street Church failed. The new African Methodist Episcopal church, which took the name St. Stephen, was formally organized in May 1865. In March 1867 the trustees of the congregation purchased land for a church just a few blocks away from Front Street Methodist Church. On April 4, 1867, during the annual meeting of the South Carolina Conference of the AME Church, the cornerstone was laid for a new wooden frame church.[36]

Once the congregation was formed, Chaplain Hunter left. The Reverend James Hanby, upon appointment by Bishop Daniel Payne, took over leadership of the congregation. A succession of pastors followed Hanby, and by 1879, the membership of St. Stephen had reached fifteen hundred. In need of more room, the congregation decided to tear down the frame structure and build a new church on the same site.[37]

The result, finally completed in 1888, was a magnificent brick church in a late Gothic style, with a prominent gable and an imposing spire-topped bell tower anchoring the corner. The interior was equally striking, with gas light fixtures reflecting off chandeliers and illuminating the dark wood of the sanctuary. The church was constructed by its members. Lewis Hollingsworth designed the plans for the building, Daniel Lee supplied the bricks, and other church members provided the carpentry and masonry. Church women helped too, providing meals for the workers; some even carried bricks in their aprons to the construction site.[38]

St. Stephen
African Methodist
Episcopal Church
(Photo by author)

The Methodists may have been distinctive for the size of their black congregation, but they were not alone in witnessing an expression of black autonomy. The Episcopalians also developed a new black congregation. During the Revival of 1858, Thomas Atkinson, Episcopal bishop of North Carolina and a resident of Wilmington, sought to create a new congregation where the pews would be free (instead of rented or purchased) and strangers would be welcomed. Atkinson realized that there were only limited accommodations for blacks in the St. James and St. John churches. Consequently, he supported the establishment of a new congregation, St. Paul's Episcopal Church, which was designed as a racially mixed congregation with free seating, although blacks were expected to sit in the upstairs gallery.[39]

On June 5, 1858, St. Paul's Episcopal Church, located at Orange and Fourth streets, opened with a black choir and a Sunday school for black children. Because it was illegal in North Carolina to teach blacks to read, the Sunday school focused on the oral recitation of the church catechism, together with the singing of hymns. Initially, Bishop Atkinson served as priest for the congregation. However, due to the pressures of his other duties, alternative arrangements soon became necessary, and various individuals officiated at the church from 1859 to July 1862, when services at St. Paul's were suspended due to the yellow fever epidemic. At the time of its closure, the congregation consisted of thirty-four white members and sixteen blacks.[40]

In 1866 St. Paul's reopened as a mission for blacks, with a total of thirty-nine members drawn from the old St. Paul's congregation and the two other Episcopal churches in town. In the autumn of 1869, the charge of this all-black congregation was given to the Reverend Charles O. Brady. Brady came to Wilmington from the Diocese of Connecticut and was the first black minister to be admitted to the Diocese of North Carolina.[41]

With the arrival of Brady, the congregation sought its own identity. Church members adopted the new name of St. Mark's, and they purchased a lot and broke ground for their new church on March 6, 1871. Contributions for the new building came from northerners as well as from members of the St. Mark's congregation. William Ralph Emerson and Carl Fehmer, two accomplished Boston architects, drew up the plans for the church. Best known as a residential designer, Emerson is credited with shaping the popular Shingle style in American architecture. The plans for St. Mark's Episcopal Church—an English Gothic building with a steeply pitched roof and octagonal bell tower—were one of Emerson's few southern projects.[42]

It is probable that Alfred Howe, a member of the St. Mark's congregation and a successful contractor and builder in Wilmington, supervised the construction of the church, which, upon its completion, the local paper praised as "one of the neatest edifices of its kind in the state." By December 1871 worship services had begun at St. Mark's for the approximately sixty members of the congregation. St. Mark's has the distinction of being the first Episcopal church built by and for blacks in North Carolina.[43]

A different story is found in the Presbyterian experience. In the context of the Revival of 1858, members of the First Presbyterian Church raised money to purchase a lot and build a new Presbyterian mission church in Wilmington. On November 21, 1858, fourteen members of First Presbyterian Church transferred to this new church, which was simply called Second Presbyterian Church. The Reverend Martin McQueen was the first pastor of this congregation, which met in a handsome board-and-batten church that combined elements of Carpenter Gothic and Italianate designs. The decorative exterior woodwork, the portico entrance, and the scalloped cupola were originally set off by stands of live oak trees.[44]

Due to the disruption of the yellow fever outbreak and the Civil War, the congregation closed the building and returned to First Presbyterian for services. In October 1866 the property was authorized to be sold to a group of black Presbyterians in the city. These individuals, in connection with the Freedmen's Committee of the General Assembly of the Presbyterian Church USA (Northern), organized the First Colored Presbyterian Church of Wilmington on April 21, 1867. It had been established initially as a mission congregation by the Reverend Peter Hodges in 1866, but William T. Carr became pastor for the thirty-three members in 1867, at the time of its formal organization.[45]

The fact that northern Presbyterians helped organize a black church in Wilmington was not unique. As early as 1865 the northern church recognized that ministers and teachers would be needed in the South. The Northern Presbyterian General Assembly es-

St. Mark's Episcopal Church (Photo by author)

Chestnut Street Presbyterian Church (Photo by author)

tablished a committee on freedmen, which noted that ex-slaves in the South were "no longer willing to be controlled by their former masters." They needed a separate existence, "independent of the churches where white people both hold the property and choose the session." Northern Presbyterians, therefore, could either assist in the formation of new black Presbyterian congregations or watch as blacks left for those denominations that allowed them to express their religious autonomy. By 1875 the missionary efforts of the Northern Presbyterian Church had produced more than forty black congregations with nearly four thousand members in North Carolina.[46]

In this work the Wilmington church, renamed Chestnut Street Presbyterian Church for the avenue on which it stood, played a visible role. In 1873 Daniel J. Sanders became pastor. He was also the editor of the *Africo-American Presbyterian*, a paper that he produced from the church. Sanders left the congregation in 1883 and was later selected as president of the Biddle Memorial Institute (subsequently named Johnson C. Smith University) in Charlotte, North Carolina, but the Chestnut Street congregation continued to be a leader in the black community of Wilmington.[47]

Whether it was the walkout from the Methodists, the start-up of the Episcopalians, or the buyout by the Presbyterians, black religious institutions commenced, black clergy and laity assumed leadership roles, and the hopes of the black community germinated. As these fledgling churches matured, they fostered space for individual blacks—a public space that rarely existed anywhere else in the increasingly restrictive confines of the developing Jim Crow South. This public dimension of the black church included an array of secular services—schools, libraries, insurance companies—as well as familiar religious functions. Churches also served as the focal point for rallies, meetings, parades, and lectures. Whereas whites celebrated Confederate Memorial Day, blacks commemorated Emancipation Day. And because Wilmington blacks could have no statue to black abolitionist David Walker to parallel that of George Davis, churches became the backbone of the black community and the arena where memories were shaped, displayed, and recalled.[48]

If the beginnings of these three faith communities represent stories of exodus and emancipation, of singing unto the Lord a new song, they are only part of the tale. Three other groups—Baptist, African Methodist Episcopal Zion, and Congregationalist—also built up congregations in this era. Black Baptists in Wilmington began a new chapter in their religious life in this period. The pastor of First Baptist Church held separate services on Sunday afternoon as early as 1845 for the black parishioners. In 1864 the Baptists allowed the black members to hold their own worship services and to employ their own preacher. In November 1864 these congregants requested and received permission to leave First Baptist Church and form their own congregation, First African Baptist Church. Although several other Baptist churches released their black members after the conclusion of the Civil War, it was striking that this departure occurred while the war was still under way and the slavery system, at least legally, was still intact. This African Baptist congregation first met in a building by the Cape Fear River, but in 1869 it moved to Fifth and Red Cross streets and adopted the name First Baptist Negro Church. A year previously, in 1868, Ebenezer Baptist Church had been formed through a secession from First African Baptist. By 1869, then, Wilmington had two black Baptist churches.[49]

The organization of an African Methodist Episcopal Zion congregation in Wilmington was closely tied to the work of James Walker Hood, a missionary and later bishop in the AME Zion Church. In 1865 the New England Conference of the AME Zion Church sent Hood to North Carolina. Following the Federal army's advances, Hood went first to New Bern, then Edenton, and finally Wilmington. In Wilmington he contacted thirteen blacks who attended Fifth Street Methodist Episcopal South Church and convinced them to organize their own congregation under AME Zion auspices. This church began on Easter morning 1865 as Christian Chapel AME Zion Church of Wilmington, with George W. Price as its first pastor. In December 1877 fire destroyed the chapel, and it took until 1882 for the new church, named St. Luke AME Zion Church, to be completed by the members of the congregation. With its powerful massing, large gable front, and monumental tower in contrasting stone, St. Luke was an attractive example of Victorian Gothic architecture.[50]

Hood also played an instrumental role in the introduction of black Masonry to North Carolina. In 1866 the Giblem Lodge was organized in Wilmington, and Hood oversaw the establishment of lodges in Raleigh and Fayetteville in 1867. The three-story, stuccoed-brick, Greek Revival lodge hall in Wilmington was finished in 1873. The hall hosted the state's first black Agricultural and Mechanical Fair in 1875 and later the city's first library for blacks. In addition to black Masons, there was an association of black members of the Grand Order of Odd Fellows in Wilmington, who built their own hall by the 1880s. Like their white counterparts, these black fraternal organizations were connected with their religious communities. Many black ministers, as illustrated by Hood, were also members of these groups. Beyond that, these fraternal organizations promoted temperance, hard work, and frugality as Christian virtues in and of themselves and as methods for blacks to advance in American society.[51]

Emancipation also brought new opportunities for black women. Marriages could now be solemnized, children raised without fear of separation, and church freely attended. The role of black women in the southern church was as important as that of white women. Black women participated as members, fund-raisers, and teachers. They gathered for fellowship and supported mission programs, particularly those that focused on Africa. Finally, black women were involved in benevolent activities dealing with education and, later in the nineteenth century, anti-lynching laws. Gender conventions for black women—particularly those in the middle class, but all black women by extension—paralleled many of the same expectations that white women experienced. Purity, subordination to men, and a religious nature were the characteristics attributed to and enjoined on these women. Working outside their homes was an economic necessity for most black women. However, their extensive involvement in their religious communities gave them a context for public recognition and a venue for challenging racist misrepresentations of black life. This "politics of respectability," as one scholar called it, challenged both women and men to model Christian virtues, and by doing so they hoped to earn the respect of their fellow citizens and to lift up the black race within the wider American society.[52]

Just as Hood came from the North to organize an AME Zion congregation, agents of the American Missionary Association (AMA) came south to provide relief and organize educational and religious institutions. Often following in the wake of Union forces, newly freed slaves congregated in towns such as Wilmington. An estimated ten thousand to twelve thousand refugees entered Wilmington after its fall to Union forces in late February 1865. Hunger and sickness were widespread, and many adults died, leaving orphans. In 1866 the AMA established an orphanage in Wilmington and one in Atlanta. James J. Gregory of Marblehead, Massachusetts, donated the money to establish the Wilmington orphanage, which operated for six years.[53]

In 1868 the AMA purchased land and built a wooden meetinghouse for religious services. Initially named Christ Congregational Church, in the 1880s it was renamed Gregory Congregational Church in honor of another donation by James Gregory. This gift funded the construction of a Gothic Revival brick church adorned with a tall steeple. Additionally, Gregory gave the church a bell inscribed "The North to the South, in Sympathy and Love."[54]

An observer on the scene in North Carolina remarked in 1867, "the school stands next in importance in the freedmen's estimation to the church and the preaching of the gospel, and the teacher to the preacher." This was certainly the case in Wilmington. One black soldier reported that on March 11, 1865, just days after Wilmington's surrender, seven hundred black children assembled in the basement of a Wilmington church to enroll in school. The AMA opened schools in Wilmington in April 1865; in 1866 the Williston Free School (renamed in 1884 the Gregory Institute) was established under AMA auspices. Additionally, the Presbyterian Church, the Episcopal Church, and the National Freedmen's Relief Association operated schools in local churches in Wilmington. Finally, Sabbathday schools were organized in four black congregations—St. Stephen AME and St. Luke AME Zion, as well as the black Presbyterian and Baptist congregations. Although these efforts to develop schools were significant in the history of education in the Reconstruction South, they are also important as expressions of the desire for freedom and autonomy that characterized the development of black religious organizations. Access to education opened up opportunities for the newly freed blacks, empowering them and enabling them to make their way in the promised land of freedom.[55]

The fact that so many of these schools developed in conjunction with the new black churches was significant. Amidst the violence and intimidation symbolized by the activities of the Ku Klux Klan, North Carolina society by 1872 had reversed many of the political gains that blacks had made in the initial phases of Reconstruction.

"Trouble and destitution, as well as hatred and revenge, await our poor people in these Southern States," one black soldier presciently stated in 1865. Soon restrictions on black participation in politics and economic development were matched by the institutionalization of segregated schools and public places. E. Franklin Frazier's observation that the black church became a "refuge in a hostile white world" would hold true for Wilmington and much of North Carolina.[56]

The broad patterns of religious development in Wilmington were paralleled in the Middle and Upper Cape Fear regions. Duplin County provides a representative picture of black religious organization in the rural expanses of the Middle Cape Fear. Black Baptist churches predominated, with nineteen congregations formed between 1865 and 1885. First Baptist Church in Kenansville was begun in 1866. Originally known as First Colored Missionary Baptist Church, it was the first church in the area organized for black Baptists. Once land was purchased for a building, a simple wooden frame house of worship was erected with hardwood floors, handmade pews, an old piano, and two cast-iron heaters. First Baptist Church of Warsaw was initially called Bear Swamp Church when it was organized in 1867. The congregation met in a brush arbor and sat on benches fashioned from mill scraps. In 1871 land was donated to the congregation, and in 1882 a church was constructed. Keathern Baptist Church grew out of the Wells Chapel Baptist Church in 1868. The white members of Wells Chapel decided to build a new sanctuary, and they gave the old building to the black members, who formed their own congregation. Later, the blacks moved the building to Harrells in Sampson County and renamed the church Keathern Baptist.[57]

Donations also played a role in the establishment of other churches. In 1876 J. T. Newberry purchased a tract of land and presented it for the building of St. James AME Zion Church in Magnolia. Members of this rural church walked or rode in mule-drawn carts to church services, as was typical in this period. In 1878 James Wells of Rockfish gave land for the establishment of Rockfish AME Church in Teachey. A church was soon constructed, and it shared its pastor with AME congregations in Magnolia and Rose Hill. As noted previously, agents of the AMA set up schools in Wilmington. No schools, however, were established for newly liberated blacks in

Duplin County, due to the intimidation and violence by the local whites who opposed them.[58]

In the decade following the end of the Civil War, Fayetteville blacks founded AME Zion, Presbyterian, and Episcopal congregations. Methodism in antebellum Fayetteville was divided between the Hay Street Church, which served whites, and the Evans Chapel (named for Henry Evans, who was buried in it), which had a black congregation. In 1867 James Walker Hood persuaded the members of the Evans Chapel to join him in the AME Zion tradition, and for three years Hood served as pastor of the Evans Chapel. In 1893 the congregation replaced its wooden church with an impressive Gothic Revival structure with matching corner towers symmetrically joined to a two-story gable front. The nucleus of the Haymont Presbyterian Church began as an all-black Sunday school class that met in First Presbyterian Church. In 1874 the Haymont church was organized through the efforts of First Presbyterian's pastor and the Reverend F. L. Montgomery, who became an early leader in the new church. Finally, in 1873 the Reverend Joseph Huske, rector of St. John Episcopal Church, assisted the black members of his congregation in establishing their own church. In 1896 Eva Cochran, a New Yorker who wintered in Cumberland County, provided the funds for the construction of an impressive Gothic Revival building that contained elements of the Shingle style. The stained glass windows in the sanctuary were prepared by the Tiffany firm of New York.[59]

Fayetteville, like Wilmington, saw the development of education under the direction of the AMA. Efforts began in 1865, and by 1866 there were three schools with two teachers and 263 pupils. One of these schools was led by the Fayetteville-born brothers Robert and Cicero Harris. Located in Evans Chapel, the Harris school was renamed in 1867 the Howard School, for General O. O. Howard, superintendent of the Freedmen's Bureau. It continued into the twentieth century, eventually evolving into Fayetteville State University.[60]

Throughout the Cape Fear, then, hard work matched philanthropy, agency on the part of blacks was coupled with assistance on the part of some whites, and courage challenged violence in the formation of black religious institutions. Beyond the boundaries of the Cape Fear, religious reconstruction throughout North Carolina indicated the attractiveness of independent congregations for newly freed blacks, despite many obstacles. By 1864, for instance, the AME Zion denomination had established the North Carolina Conference, with more than 6,500 members and 12 ministers. By the end of the 1860s the African Methodist Church had formed its own North Carolina Conference, with more than 7,000 laypersons and 50 clergy. In 1867 black Baptists formed a statewide general association that was renamed the Baptist Educational and Missionary Convention of North Carolina in 1869. By 1882 this convention had 95,000 members in 800 churches with 450 ministers. Presbyterians, Episcopalians, and Congregationalists had smaller numbers, but these too pointed to the desirability of religious autonomy among blacks. In 1875 there were 4,000 black North Carolinian Presbyterians, while the Episcopal Diocese of North Carolina could claim 363 black communicants and 2 priests. The Congregationalists never had more than 8 small churches in the state, most of which had white leadership. For black North Carolinians in the Cape Fear and elsewhere, emancipation and exodus were linked together in this great jubilee of freedom. However, as in the biblical story, the future in the promised land would often be full of conflict and challenges.[61]

When at the Jewish Passover seder a young child asks, "Why is this night different from all others?" the question provides an opportunity for an adult to recount the story of the exodus from Egypt, to remember the connection between past and present, and to reinforce the power of memory in Jewish religious life.

Jewish history in the United States divides into three large sections, and this same simple periodization applies to the Cape Fear region. Jewish settlement in North America began in 1654 in New Amsterdam. With the accumulation of a larger community, the Shearith Israel synagogue was dedicated in New York City in 1730. Coming to the New World from Holland, England, and the Caribbean, the Shearith Israel congregation was Sephardic (from Obadiah 20) in background. The Sephardic tradition, with its specific liturgical order, Passover requirements, and familiarity with secular philosophy, came originally from the Iberian Peninsula and the engagement of Jews with Muslim and Christian cultures.[62]

The Shearith Israel congregation was matched by other early

Sephardic groups, including Touro synagogue in Newport, Rhode Island (1763), and Beth Elohim in Charleston, South Carolina (1794). Evidence for Sephardic Jews in Wilmington exists nearly coterminous with the founding of the town. Philip David appears in the New Hanover County Court minutes in September 1738, and Moses Gomez in June 1740. Other Jewish families that became established in eighteenth- and nineteenth-century Wilmington include those of Aaron Lazarus, Jacob Levy, and Aaron Rivera. These residents of Wilmington were economically successful. Gomez had servants, and Lazarus was a partner in a major Wilmington export house, a director of the Bank of the Cape Fear, and the first director of the Wilmington and Weldon Railroad. Philip David and his son, David, were both prosperous carpenters, while Jacob Levy was an accomplished auctioneer.[63]

Religious and social prospects were bleaker for these early Jews of Wilmington. Estimates suggest that the Jewish population in the South during the colonial period ranged between three hundred and five hundred persons, but no more than twenty-five Jews lived in Wilmington during this time. With these small numbers, it was unlikely that they could form a minyan, the traditional quorum of ten adult males needed for public prayer services, let alone a self-standing congregation. Instead, prayer services took place in the home, and those who were affluent enough traveled to Charleston for High Holy Day services. Similarly, without consecrated burial grounds in Wilmington, those who could afford to sent deceased family members to cemeteries in Charleston or in the North for proper burial.[64]

Finally, without a congregation or other social structures to reinforce the ethos and rituals of Judaism, it was difficult for these Wilmington Jews to preserve a distinct Jewish identity. Aaron Lazarus, for example, contributed money to St. James Episcopal and was a trustee of the church. Lazarus was quoted as saying, "I can worship Jehovah in any of his temples," a sentiment that reflected his ecumenical tastes. Jacob Levy was also a trustee of St. James. Aaron Rivera married a Christian woman, and his funeral was held in St. James. The small size of the initial Jewish population in Wilmington put pressure on its members and made assimilation with the Christian majority a matter of convenience as much as of volitional association.[65]

After waning in numbers in the late eighteenth century, the Jewish community of Wilmington experienced a renascence in the mid-nineteenth century. Immigrants from Europe fueled this recovery and marked the second period in American Jewish history. These Europeans immigrants, who were Ashkenazic Jews (after Genesis 10:3 and Jeremiah 51:27), came in two separate waves and originated in two different areas.

The first cohort came principally from the German-speaking lands of central Europe, and their immigration spanned 1820 to 1888. The second group left eastern Europe, generally Poland and Russia, and arrived in America between 1880 and 1925. Parallel patterns occurred in the Cape Fear region. Groups of immigrants originally from Bavaria reached Wilmington in the 1840s and 1850s. Encouraged by the post-Enlightenment moves toward emancipation of the Jews, but disenchanted by the failure of the Revolution of 1848 to achieve greater freedom in their lands, these Jews were drawn to the United States by its promise of civil equality and economic opportunity. Coming to the South, many Jewish men found work as itinerant peddlers. As a port town with good connections to railroads, Wilmington was an ideal base of operations for these entrepreneurs.[66]

Religious developments kept pace with economic ones among this growing assemblage of German Jews. In 1853 a charitable organization taking the name True Brothers Society was founded in Wilmington with the goal of establishing a Jewish cemetery. On March 6, 1855, Rabbi Isaac Lesser of Philadelphia dedicated the Hebrew Cemetery within the Oakdale Cemetery grounds. Twenty Jews and at least two hundred other friendly and curious residents of the town attended Lesser's dedicatory remarks. Wilmington Jews now had a cemetery, but they still needed to organize a congregation. Rabbi Lesser, a strong advocate of Orthodox Judaism, assisted the Wilmingtonians in their goal of formal organization. Services continued to be held in homes, but in 1860 this Jewish community advertised for a person to serve as cantor, ritual butcher, and circumciser for the congregation. E. M. Myers answered the advertisement in September 1867. Myers, a cantor rather than a rabbi, consecrated a brick building, formerly used by the congregation of First Presbyterian Church, as a synagogue for the Wilmington Hebrew Congregation. Services began later that month.[67]

The development of Judaism in Wilmington would have a rocky course, however. Within a year, the new Jewish congregation had disbanded due to disputes over modes of worship, and religious services resumed in members' homes. Although Rabbi Lesser had promoted the Orthodox brand of Judaism, the next Jewish congregation in Wilmington would be of the Reform tradition. Reform Judaism was familiar to Wilmington Jews from their German backgrounds, as well as from Reform congregations in Charleston, Baltimore, and Cincinnati. In 1872 Rabbi Isaac Mayer Wise, one of the leaders of Reform Judaism in America, applauded efforts to organize a Reform congregation in Wilmington, noting that Abram Weill and Solomon Bear were instrumental in this cause. Fund-raising appeals were under way, and the local newspaper encouraged Wilmingtonians to "meet with a hearty and generous response" this call for help.[68]

Several features distinguished Reform Judaism from its Orthodox counterpart. Reform services were carried out in the vernacular language rather than chiefly in Hebrew, as was the custom among the Orthodox. Strict dietary laws and the requirement for daily minyans were relaxed in the Reform tradition, and families could sit together rather than segregating females and young children from adult males. Organ music was allowed, and sermons delivered by the rabbi assumed a much larger role in Reform services than they did in Orthodox ones. In all these ways, the Reform tradition sought to eliminate what it regarded as superfluous and antiquated accretions in Judaism, so as to concentrate on its ethical and religious essence. Beyond that, Reform leaders such as Wise wanted to demonstrate the compatibility of Judaism with American society, and to that end, the renovation of services, the abolition of certain obligations, and the transformation of attitudes out of the ghetto and into the American democratic context were a price gladly paid.

On May 12, 1876, the Temple of Israel was dedicated. Three aspects were striking about this congregation and its new house of worship. First was the role of the women of the congregation in the financing of the building. As early as 1867, a women's auxiliary group, called the Harmony Club, assisted the Wilmington Hebrew Congregation. By 1872 this association, renamed the Ladies Concordia Society, devoted itself "to promote the cause of Judaism and to aid by our funds the maintenance of the temple of worship in

our midst." Paralleling Christian women's organizations, this society emphasized that it was only supplementing the work of the
all-male building committee. Nevertheless, the Concordia Society
purchased a Pilcher Tracker organ, a Torah, and a parsonage for
the rabbi, as well as providing funds to maintain the temple in good
repair. To achieve these ends, the society sponsored fund-raising
concerts and dances, in addition to organizing Purim festivals for
the children and annual dress balls for the adults. In these and other
ways, the Ladies Concordia Society played an instrumental part in
the life of the temple.[69]

While fund-raising efforts were going on behind the scenes,
on a prominent corner of downtown Wilmington the Temple of
Israel was under construction. Some observers might have known
that this was going to be the first Jewish temple built in the state of
North Carolina; any onlooker could see that the architectural style
was different from that of the surrounding buildings, especially the
churches. The temple was built in a Moorish Revival style, an architectural design characterized by frontal towers with bulbous domes
or a central dome, horseshoe arches, and patterned elements used
as decoration. In an era that traded heavily on associations evoked
through artistic representations, the Moorish Revival style elicit-
ed the exotic character of the Orient and followed Greek, Gothic,
and even Egyptian Revival styles of architecture. Moreover, because
Gothic Revival was so closely bound up with the nineteenth-century
Christian architectural tradition, Moorish Revival provided a fashionable alternative for use in Jewish sacred spaces.

Antecedent examples of Moorish Revival could be found in the
Alhambra (1758) built in London's Kew Gardens or in the Royal
Pavilion (1815) constructed in Brighton, England. In the United
States, residential usages by P. T. Barnum's Iranistan (1848) or
Frederick Church's Olana (1874) were matched by the World's Fair
Crystal Palace in New York City in 1853–1854. All these examples
were secular uses of Moorish elements, illustrating that it was a
well-established historical architectural form by the middle of the
nineteenth century.[70]

It was in Jewish religious architecture that Moorish Revival
found its greatest application. Within European architectural circles,
the first synagogue to use Moorish elements was the one designed
by Gottfried Semper in 1838–1840 for the Dresden congregation.

In short order, many prominent European congregations commissioned Moorish Revival buildings, such as the Leipzig synagogue (1855) by Otto Simonson, a student of Semper. It also included synagogues in Vienna (1858) and the Dohány Street synagogue in Budapest (1859), both designed by Ludwig von Förster. In 1861 Ernst Zwirner's Cologne synagogue was dedicated, and in 1866 the Berlin synagogue on Orangienburgerstrasse by Eduard Knoblauch was completed. Moorish Revival styles were incorporated in Edward Salomon's Manchester, England, synagogue in 1874 and in the same year for the one in Liverpool, England, designed by W. & G. Audsley. Two further examples, Otto Wagner's S. Rumbach Street synagogue (1875) in Budapest and the Tempio Maggiore constructed in Florence by Falcini, Michele, and Treves in 1882, round out this European sampling of the style.[71]

The first American synagogue to contain Moorish elements, such as the bulbous domes on its twin towers, was that of the Keneseth Israel congregation completed in 1864 in Philadelphia. The Plum Street synagogue, designed in 1866 by James Key Wilson in Cincinnati for the congregation of Isaac Mayer Wise, had thirteen domes and two minarets; Temple Emanu-El, dedicated in San Francisco the same year, had fewer domes but was unmistakably in the same style. Between 1868 and 1872, two important New York City synagogues, Emanu-El and Central, and Rodeph Shalom synagogue in Philadelphia were constructed in the Moorish mode. Five other buildings—B'nai Jeshurun (1885), Khal Adeth Jeshurun (1886), and Zichron Ephraim (1889) in New York City, together with B'nai Jehudah (1885) in Kansas City, Missouri, and B'nai Israel (1891) in Salt Lake City, Utah—give a sense of the range and attractiveness of Moorish Revival architecture in nineteenth-century American Judaism.[72]

The cornerstone for the Temple of Israel in Wilmington was laid on July 15, 1875, with Marcus Jastrow, rabbi of the prestigious Rodeph Shalom congregation, providing the keynote speech. On May 12, 1876, the temple was finished and dedicated, with Samuel Mendelsohn, the newly elected rabbi of the Wilmington congregation, presiding. The architectural design of the temple was resplendent. A gable end faced the street and was flanked by twin towers that were capped with gilded onion domes. Horseshoe arches decorated both the gable and the frontal towers. A crescent moon stood

Market St. at 4th St., looking West, Wilmington, N. C.

Temple of Israel (Postcard in author's collection)

over the entrance and beneath a round arch, suggesting an association with medieval Spain and its trio of Christian, Jewish, and Islamic cultural influences.

In the interior, the orientation of space moved from the entrance in an eastwardly direction toward the raised platform (bimah) from which readings took place and the ark in which the Torah scrolls were kept. The Tablets of the Law, containing the Ten Commandments, and a symbolic eternal light were also visible. Early on, synagogue space was more rectangular than longitudinal, for Jewish liturgy had no choirs or clergy that processed and recessed up and down an aisle. By the nineteenth century the orientation was still east (toward Jerusalem), but the demands of congregational size and the need for clear sight lines sometimes dictated a more longitudinal interior shape. Worshippers in the temple sat in pews that were initially rented or sold. Since this was a Reform congregation, women were not segregated from men, and families were encouraged to sit together. With the sermon and readings in the vernacular, and with women now seated on the main floor, female participation in the services markedly increased.[73]

The members of the Temple of Israel took up the responsibilities of congregational life using the prayer book of Isaac Mayer

Wise in their new house of worship. Tradition has credited Alexander Strausz, a Hungarian immigrant and onetime architectural partner in the Cape Fear Building Company, as the one responsible for the Moorish design. However, during its fiftieth anniversary, temple president Marcus Jacobi stated that Samuel Sloan was the architect, and Sloan's offices were in Philadelphia. The Philadelphia location becomes important, for local historian James Sprunt, in his *Chronicles of the Cape Fear River*, first published in 1916, wrote that the plans for the temple had been "drawn in Philadelphia." Sloan was a nationally recognized architect and was well known in Wilmington for his plans for First Baptist Church (1859), First Presbyterian Church (1859), and the Bank of New Hanover (1873). Sloan was also familiar with Moorish Revival architecture, having sketched an "oriental villa" for his 1853 publication *Model Architect*. The plan showed an octagonal building capped with an onion dome. In 1859 Haller Nutt, a wealthy Mississippian, commissioned Sloan to produce drawings for a residence, named Longwood, based on Sloan's oriental villa. Due to the disruption of the Civil War, the project was never completed; nevertheless, it demonstrated Sloan's thorough familiarity with the Moorish Revival style. However the credit is divided between Strausz and Sloan, the Temple of Israel is unique in the inventory of religious architecture of Wilmington. It even caused Isaac Mayer Wise to proclaim, "for simple elegance this temple is unsurpassed in the United States."[74]

In addition to the involvement of women and the choice of architectural style, a third noteworthy feature of the founding of the Temple of Israel was the superb credentials of its first rabbi, Samuel Mendelsohn. Born in Russia in 1850, Mendelsohn was educated in Berlin, Germany, and in Philadelphia. After a three-year stint as rabbi for a Norfolk, Virginia, congregation, Mendelsohn came to the temple in February 1876 and remained rabbi of the congregation for forty-six years. Mendelsohn accepted the call to Wilmington at the urging of Marcus Jastrow, his former teacher and lifelong mentor. Personal accounts of Mendelsohn depict him as a scholarly individual, and during his tenure as rabbi, he gave several public lectures on topics ranging from the history of the Jews to the evolution of theology to issues in practical philosophy. He was also known for his publications on biblical materials and a volume entitled *Criminal Jurisprudence of the Ancient Hebrews*.[75]

Mendelsohn's concern with jurisprudence found expression in his inaugural address to the temple congregation on May 13, 1876. Taking the text of Ezekiel 44:23–24, with its charge to teach the people the difference between the holy and the profane, the clean and the unclean, Mendelsohn expressed his excitement about his new position and asked for the solicitude of the members of the congregation. In this same address Mendelsohn paid tribute to his parents and teachers for their role in preparing him for the rabbinate. He alluded to the "great moral and spiritual truths" of the Torah and the Talmud, truths that were gifts from the patriarchs and prophets of old and that guided Jews in the present as well. In this exegetical exercise, Mendelsohn invoked the founding events of the Hebrew people, and he called on the power of the past to shape the present and future of this congregation. Links of association and lineage in memory had a forceful impact on this Jewish community, just as they had among blacks in Wilmington. Allusions to many of the same charter events—bondage, liberation, and a promised land of opportunity—formed the discourse of their pasts and helped them both imagine their futures.[76]

As rabbi for over forty years, Mendelsohn was well respected in Wilmington as a voice of instruction and goodwill to the Christian majority. For instance, when Front Street Methodist Church burned in 1886, the temple congregants proposed that their building be used as a substitute. The Methodists accepted the offer and met in the temple for two years until their new church was ready. While Mendelsohn provided the spiritual leadership for the congregation, members such as Frederick Rheinstein, David Kahnweiler, brothers Sigmund and Bernhard Solomon, and Joseph Sternberger, among others, became prominent merchants in Wilmington. Men from the temple were inducted into the Masons, Odd Fellows, and B'nai Brith, and they shared cultural ties with other Germans living in Wilmington. Finally, the congregation was not only well respected in Wilmington, with personal ties to Wise in Cincinnati and Jastrow in Philadelphia; it was also well connected with the top echelon of the Reform movement in American Judaism. It was no surprise, then, that when Mendelsohn died in 1922, a local newspaper eulogized him as a "beloved rabbi" and one of Wilmington's "foremost citizens and scholars."[77]

Beginning in the 1880s another phase of Jewish immigration to the United States began, and with it another segment of the Jewish experience in the Cape Fear. These were Jews from eastern Europe and Russia who, in response to economic turmoil, persecution, and political unrest, left their homelands for America. Most of these immigrants settled in the urban centers of the Northeast and Midwest; however, by the 1890s some were coming to the South and to Wilmington.[78]

Although this eastern European group shared a broad religious heritage with the German Jews and had the same initial hopes of economic success and civil peace that motivated their coreligionists, there were intramural differences between the two groups. Historic animosities between Germans and Slavs simmered beneath distinctions in religious temperament, linguistic tradition, and economic opportunity. Whereas the Germans were Reformed, the Russians and Poles were staunchly Orthodox and had little understanding of and even less sympathy for the religious modifications the Reform congregation had undertaken. As if keeping kosher in the land of pork barbecue was not hard enough, Yiddish was the language of the eastern Europeans—a language that no one else in Wilmington spoke. By contrast, the German Jews built bridges to other German-speaking residents of Wilmington, particularly with the Lutheran congregation in the city. Similarly, by the time of the second generation, German Jews and German Christians could reminisce nostalgically, if selectively, about the fatherland, whereas for the Russian and Polish Jews, the wounds that had caused their recent emigration were too fresh for such indulgences. Finally, the economic opportunities in the late 1800s were not as promising as they had been in the 1840s and 1850s, when the bulk of German Jews were getting established. The German Jews wondered how the appearance of these new immigrants on the scene would affect their continued acceptance in the wider community. Still, German Jews in Wilmington made no effort to block the admission of the new immigrants, and they closed ranks with their fellow Jews if questions came from Gentile outsiders, preferring to keep the friction of dispute within the religious family.

Many eastern European Jews in Wilmington settled near Fourth and Walnut streets, creating a semblance of their former lives in this New World. Because their religious services still took place in individual homes, on January 6, 1898, ten men met to form the B'nai

Israel Society, whose purpose was to build a house of worship and to start a cemetery.[79]

In February the society purchased land for its own cemetery. Orthodox minyans were held in rented space on Market Street until 1913, when the cornerstone for a new synagogue was laid on Walnut Street. In attendance at this ceremony were the mayor of Wilmington, Rabbi Mendelsohn, and the pastor of First Presbyterian Church, among others. The patterned brick face of this building incorporated the Star of David (a symbol first used in American synagogue architecture in 1845) into its masonry. This was an Orthodox congregation, so women sat in the balcony, and services were conducted almost exclusively in Hebrew. Family names such as Schwartz, Kaminsky, Horowitz, Kosch, and Abramowitz signify the east European background of B'nai Israel, the second Jewish congregation in Wilmington.[80]

The third large period of Jewish history in the United States and the Cape Fear region occurred after World War II. Recognition of the European Holocaust and the emergence of the new state of Israel, migration to the area by Jews from both inside and outside the United States, and the growth and leadership provided by the Wilmington congregations characterized this era. Beginning in 1925, after the passage of restrictive immigration legislation by the U.S. Congress, Jewish immigration virtually ceased, and the Jewish population in the South stabilized. An 1878 survey of Jews in North Carolina found 200 in Wilmington and 52 in Fayetteville; by 1937 these numbers increased to 315 in Wilmington and 133 in Fayetteville. Although these two cities contained the largest Jewish populations in southeastern North Carolina (Fayetteville's Beth Israel synagogue opened in 1922), there were other Jews in rural areas of the Cape Fear region. Rural Jews tried to carpool to towns and synagogues, particularly for special services, and in the 1940s rabbis such as Mordecai Thurman visited Jewish families in areas outside of Wilmington. In 1954 the North Carolina Association of Jewish Men and Women, together with I. D. Blumenthal of Charlotte, sponsored the Circuit Riding Rabbi Project and recruited Rabbi Harold Friedman to drive a twelve-hundred-mile route. Friedman met Jewish families living near Whiteville, Wallace, Burgaw, and points west and north as well, where he held classes and services. His visits provided opportunities for rural Jewish families to escape their religious isolation and to enjoy fellowship and spiritual nurture with other Jews. In the mid-1950s Rabbi Reuben Kesner succeeded Rabbi Friedman and continued the itinerant work until the 1980s.[81]

In the 1950s the B'nai Israel congregation of Wilmington made two important decisions. First, they changed from an Orthodox to a Conservative synagogue. The Conservative movement in American Judaism was an attempt to find a middle ground between what was perceived by some as the overly innovative tendencies of the Reform tradition and the excessively rigid strictures of the Orthodox. For example, in B'nai Israel, substantial portions of worship services were conducted in Hebrew, kosher food restrictions were more fully observed, and in 1955 the first female teenager celebrated her bat mitzvah.[82]

The second major change was the determination in 1953 to leave downtown Wilmington and build a new synagogue in the suburbs. The size of the Wilmington congregation had outgrown the available space, so, in keeping with many national trends, the new synagogue was designed by Hartman Architects of Baltimore in a more contemporary style, with an emphasis on functionality. With families sitting together, it was no longer necessary to build a separate gallery for women. Although women were more visible, their traditional support for the congregation continued when members of the Sisterhood of B'nai Israel furnished a kosher kitchen, organized fund-raisers, and eventually served on the board of directors. Fayetteville's experience once again paralleled Wilmington's when the Beth Israel congregation switched from Orthodox to Conservative and in 1957 broke ground for a new synagogue.[83]

Eli N. Evans has written insightfully about contemporary southern Judaism and especially about the isolation of rural Jews, for whom "the lonely days were Sundays." Jews in modern Wilmington have institutionally integrated in the society, providing civic leadership, business success, and philanthropic charity. Incidences of anti-Semitism have been infrequent in the region and are condemned by public officials. For instance, when swastikas were painted on the Temple of Israel's doors in 1938, the mayor of Wilmington personally supervised their removal. When the entrance to B'nai Israel synagogue was bombed in the early 1970s and the roof set on fire in May 1995, church and civic leaders in Wilmington condemned the acts and donated supplies for repair.[84]

Pressures on Jewish religious identity are perennial in a region such as the Cape Fear, with its historically Christian traditions. Nevertheless, in line with national demographic trends indicating the transfer of population from the Snow Belt to the Sun Belt, the estimated Jewish population has grown, particularly in the Lower Cape Fear, with its beaches and expanding economy. Drawing principally on retirees from the Northeast and professionals attracted to business, medical, and educational opportunities, the Lower Cape Fear Jewish population has doubled in recent years. Similar regional migrations can be seen at the national level. The three cities with the largest concentrations of Jews in 1877 were New York City, Philadelphia, and Chicago; in 1998 they were New York City, Los Angeles, and Miami–Fort Lauderdale.[85]

By 1898 Solomon Fishblate, member of the Temple of Israel, well-known merchant, and prominent Democratic politician, had served on the board of aldermen for many years and as mayor of Wilmington for three terms. Fishblate's political career was a symbol of the harmony between the Christian and Jewish communities and the lack of religious rancor in Wilmington. It was all the more significant because North Carolina had allowed Jews' full participation in the political process only since 1868. November 1898, however, would become a flash point in Wilmington's history because of the race riot that occurred.

In the summer of 1897, one of the state's few black newspapers had praised the accomplishments of blacks in Wilmington. By that year, blacks slightly outnumbered whites in Wilmington's population. Blacks held some public offices, such as on the board of aldermen, in several federal positions, and in the legal system. A black middle class had quietly begun to emerge, and black economic progress was visible as black shopkeepers, artisans, and professionals grew in numbers throughout the city. Black social life, often centered in the churches, prospered too.[86]

At the state level, black political power had been enhanced by the development of a coalition of Populists and Republicans who sought to overturn the established power of the Democratic Party. In so doing, this coalition (called the Fusionists) reached out to black voters, and their accomplishments included electoral success in 1894 and a gubernatorial victory in 1896. In response, Democratic Party leaders determined to make race a major issue in the 1898 election and stumped throughout the length and breadth of the state calling for an end to "negro domination" and the reassertion of "white supremacy." Vigilante groups of poor whites, called Red Shirts, demonstrated in many cities, including Wilmington, brandishing firearms and threatening those who opposed them. Mass meetings of Democratic supporters occurred, such as the one in Wilmington in October 1898 in which Alfred Moore Waddell spoke. Shouting that he would never "surrender to a ragged rabble of negroes led by a handful of white cowards," Waddell pledged resistance to the political status quo, even "if we have to choke the current of the Cape Fear with [black] carcasses."[87]

Adding to the tension, Alexander Manly, editor of Wilmington's black newspaper the *Daily Record*, had published an editorial in August 1898 in which he defended blacks against charges of sexual marauding and protested the scapegoating of black males. Democratic politicians used Manly's editorial as further evidence of black insubordination, and newspaper editorials and barbershop conversations called for his lynching.[88]

In this context of violence and intimidation, the November 8 election in Wilmington took place quietly, with no incidents, little black voter participation, and ultimately a Democratic victory. The quiet did not last long, for on the morning of November 10, Alfred Moore Waddell led a mob of two thousand men, most of whom were armed, into a black neighborhood, and they torched the building from which Manly's newspaper was published. Although few blacks had guns, shots were fired as the violence of the riot escalated. Later that day, the mayor and the board of aldermen—lame ducks after the election, but still officially in office—were forced to resign in a coup d'etat that placed Waddell in the mayor's seat.[89]

The repercussions from the riot were alarming. Firsthand witnesses and newspaper accounts reported that large numbers of blacks fled their homes for refuge in nearby woods and swamps. This diaspora disrupted the black community, decimating congregations, derailing economic progress, and deterring political involvement. The exact number of black fatalities is unknown. Coroner David Jacobs impaneled fourteen inquests but recognized that other victims had been secretly buried.[90]

Alexander Manly, who also taught Sunday school at Chestnut

Presbyterian Church, had escaped from Wilmington before the election. Several white and black leaders were placed on northbound trains and banished from town; other departed to save their lives. The Reverend J. Allen Kirk reported that white rioters, suspecting that black churches were being used as armories and assembly points for black counterattacks, had trained cannons on a number of black churches, only to discover that they were empty. Kirk was the pastor of Central Baptist Church and a leader in the Ministerial Union, an association of black clergy in Wilmington. The union had spoken out in support of Manly's editorial and assisted Manly in finding a location for his press. Kirk fled Wilmington for his safety. The *Raleigh News and Observer* stated that J. T. Lee, pastor of St. Stephen African Methodist Episcopal Church, also left after being accused of inciting the riot. In addition, the Reverend I. J. Bell was banished. Although the riot was about race and politics, the white leaders recognized the power of the black clergy, exiling some and intimidating those who remained.[91]

White clergymen played a visible role, interpreting the meaning of the riot for their congregations as well as for distant parties. The Reverend Peyton Hoge, pastor of First Presbyterian Church, shouldered his Winchester rifle as he took his turn patrolling the streets the night of the riot. The following Sunday he preached to his congregation, "since we last met in these walls we have taken a city. . . . It has been redeemed for civilization, redeemed for law and order, redeemed for decency and respectability. . . . For these things let us give God glory." The Reverend J. W. Kramer of the Brooklyn Baptist Church stated that "in the riot the negro was the aggressor. I believe that the whites were doing God's services, as the results have been felt in business, in politics, and in the church." The Reverend Milton Barber of St. Paul's Episcopal Church likewise saw divine providence working out its purposes in the actions of the whites; however, he cautioned, "if we allow anything to divert us from carrying out the good intentions which prompted us in this redemptive crusade, we may reasonably expect God's visitation upon us." Finally, the Reverend Calvin Blackwell at First Baptist Church told his congregation that "God and the white-robed angels fought against the devil and his black-robed angels and God prevailed and banished the black leader and his deceived ones and there was peace in Heaven." Characterizing the violence that took place during the riots as "purification," Blackwell stated in an interview "that a few negroes were shot was a mere incident. You can't make an omelet without breaking a few eggs. The primary purpose was not to kill but to educate."[92]

Political redemption, social purification, and paternalistic education became the watchwords for the white supremacist movement in North Carolina and for its interpretation of the riot of 1898. Waddell's October 1898 speech in which he had threatened to fill the Cape Fear River with black bodies also acknowledged the power of memory in the current struggle. Waddell insisted that the "shameful memory" of "negro domination" must be expunged in order for a proper society to prosper in Wilmington. A hundred years later, other Wilmingtonians tried not to forget but rather to revive historical memory when they commemorated the riot of 1898 through activities designed to "honor the memory, heal the wound, restore the hope." Unleashing the pain and the authority of stifled stories and suppressed experiences, participants in the public forums, lecture series, interracial dialogues, and community development projects of the 1898 Centennial Foundation reexamined the events of November 1898 in Wilmington. In reopening this chapter of the city's history, black and white residents—none of whom actually participated in the events of 1898—recognized the potency of personal and collective memory as they committed themselves to reexamine their common heritage. Such an effort pitted memory against countermemory, tradition against revision, ancestor against ancestor in an attempt to grapple with the legacy of racial segregation. In its own way, the struggle represented a crossing over from bondage and an entrance into a future of hopeful expectations.[93]

6

Religion and the New South

In 1912 a Wilmington Chamber of Commerce brochure proclaimed the city the "gateway" of North Carolina and extolled its "delightful" climate and "luxuriant crops." The account rated the port as "the best and safest along the Atlantic Coast" and Wilmington's residences as "unequaled in the South." Three years later, another tract praised the Port City as "a garden spot," "a land of flowers and rare botanical growth, inhabited by a generous and hospitable people." In this throwback to the promotional literature of the 1600s, Arcadian images of fertility and possibility trumped any mention of poverty, disease, or backwardness. These twentieth-century writers positioned Wilmington and its environs in the prosperous and progressive ranks of the New South, a place where old problems had been put to rest and everyone looked forward to the future.[1]

These modern-day boosters more than matched their seventeenth-century predecessors in their praise for the fecundity of the land, insisting that "no man of ordinary intelligence who is willing to work can fail to make a good living on as little as ten acres of land." Yet the Chamber of Commerce was more than a real estate association or a farmers' cooperative. Change was in the air, and these promoters had in mind commercial and industrial development as much as agricultural. In 1916 the population of Wilmington was 29,892, up from its 1860 total of 9,552, making it still the largest city in the state. Growth was taking place not only in population but also in trade; manufacturing of fertilizer, cotton products, and naval stores, as well as wholesale merchandising of peanuts, corn, vegetables, and fruit, diversified and strengthened the local and regional economy.[2]

Change and growth were also visible on the religious landscape. On the eve of the Civil War, Thomas Fanning Wood, a Wilmington surgeon, noted that there were twelve churches in the town. By 1916 the number had risen to fifty-four congregations. Over 60 percent of the membership belonged to Baptists and Methodists, although Presbyterians, Episcopalians, Roman Catholics, and Jews were noticeably present. New groups, including Lutherans and the Church of Christ, Scientist, added greater variety to the religious mix of the city, and new houses of worship enriched the inventory of ecclesiastical architecture in the Port City as well. As this chapter will show, growth among congregations, diversification among denominations, and outreach to new populations, both locally and internationally, characterized Cape Fear religion during these years.[3]

Wilmington made a striking architectural statement when the congregations of both First Baptist and First Presbyterian hired prominent architect Samuel Sloan to design new churches for them. By January 1858 discussions were under way in the Baptist congregation about a move to a larger location, and in May 1859 the congregation approved the construction of a new church on the corner of Market Street and Fifth Avenue. Sloan's plan for the church was Early English Gothic, with double towers of unequal height anchoring two corners of the building. Lancet windows and pointed arch door entrances contributed to the verticality of the structure, which one scholar thought "epitomizes the affluence of pre–Civil War Wilmington." By the fall of 1859 construction was under way; however, work stopped in July 1861 due to the scarcity of supplies and the shortage of workmen occasioned by the demands of the Civil War. It was not until May 1, 1870, that the Baptist church was completed and worship services were held in the new facility.[4]

On April 13, 1859, the Presbyterian church on Front Street burned to the ground. Members organized pledges for the construction of a new building, and the congregation made the decision to move from the immediate vicinity of the docks and the river to a location on Third Street, two blocks away from St. James Episcopal Church. Although Front Street had once been a "church row" occupied by prominent Baptist, Presbyterian, and Methodist congregations, by the mid and late nineteenth century, congregations were relocating and establishing new spatial identities in proximity to each other and in connection with changing residential patterns in the city itself. After the ashes had cooled, the Presbyterians looked no further than their Baptist neighbors for an architect for their new church. Samuel Sloan's plans for the Baptist sanctuary impressed the leaders of the Presbyterian congregation, and they commissioned him to draft renderings for them. Sloan's design for the Presbyterians continued the Gothic Revival style but focused the structure on one central spire, tall enough to be seen easily from the Cape Fear River and even farther away. James Walker provided local supervision for the project, and on April 28, 1861 the congregation dedicated the church with a celebratory worship service.[5]

Like Thomas U. Walter, Samuel Sloan was a nationally recognized architect with close ties to Philadelphia. Sloan designed a variety of buildings, including hospitals and churches as well as prominent residences for the mercantile elite of Philadelphia. The Wilmington commission came at a propitious time for Sloan, as the economic panic of 1857 had stalled the architecture and construction industries in the Northeast. In addition to First Baptist and First Presbyterian churches, Sloan provided designs for the Bank of New Hanover in Wilmington, Memorial Hall at the University of North Carolina at Chapel Hill, the Western Insane Asylum at Morgantown, and the governor's mansion in Raleigh.[6]

In 1860 Baptist pastor John Lamb Prichard observed that he had preached recently to an assembly of sailors comprising at least six nationalities, including Norwegians, Swedes, and Prussians. The Scandinavian and northern European presence was discernible in Wilmington well before the 1860s. Written records attest to German settlers in Wilmington in 1840, though oral traditions claim that isolated Norwegian and Swedish sailors passed through Wilmington even earlier.[7]

By 1852 there was a militia company of German volunteers in Wilmington with fifty-seven persons enrolled. When knowledge of this militia company reached the Lutheran Synod of North Carolina centered in the Piedmont, synodal officials raised the question: if there are a sufficient number of Germans in Wilmington to form a military company, are there enough Germans interested in forming a Lutheran congregation? Accordingly, in 1858 the Reverend Joseph A. Linn and the Reverend Gotthardt D. Bernheim traveled to

Wilmington and, to their delight, found that between four hundred and five hundred Germans lived in Wilmington, many of whom were Lutherans. Soon thereafter, on May 30, 1858, Bernheim and Linn met in the Presbyterian church, which had been made available for them, to explore the formation of a Lutheran church in Wilmington. The next day fifty-eight persons enrolled as members of St. Paul's Evangelical Lutheran Church.[8]

St. Paul's fell under the supervision of the Missionary Society of the Synod of North Carolina, and this body sought a permanent minister who could preach in German as well as English. The Reverend John Mengert of Evansville, Indiana, was their choice. Born in Bremen and educated at the University of Bonn, Mengert had served previously as a missionary in India. He arrived in Wilmington on December 23, 1858, and immediately began his pastoral duties. As there was no church building yet, Mengert and the church council made arrangements to rent space from St. James Episcopal Church. By April 1859, when the North Carolina Synod received the congregation into connection, there were seventy-two members.[9]

The congregation moved swiftly to find suitable land for a permanent sanctuary, and on September 6, 1859, they laid the cornerstone for a new church on the north side of the intersection of Market and Sixth streets. Hanke Vollers, a member of the congregation and owner of a local construction company, submitted plans for a church in the Gothic Revival style. Work began on the structure and had progressed to the point of finished walls and a slate roof when construction was halted; demands for men and material for the Confederate army, the outbreak of yellow fever, and the resignation of Mengert had drained resources and energy from the project. It was not until 1869 that the Lutheran church was completed. Preserving Vollers's basic design but supervised and finished by Wilmington architect James F. Post, the building contained a pedimented facade and center tower capped with a spire and cross finial. The Ladies Society purchased many items for the interior, which featured varnished yellow pine from the region contrasted by red cushions and carpeting.[10]

In 1907–1908 Henry E. Bonitz, a church member and prominent local architect, designed the addition of a transept for the church. Stained glass windows were also planned, but for this project the congregation went out of town to the well-known firm of Frank Ellsworth Weeder Stained Glass Studios in Philadelphia. Between 1908 and 1921 fourteen windows were installed in the sanctuary.[11]

Stained glass has figured prominently in religious architecture since the Middle Ages. At its simplest, the piece contains a collection of colored segments of glass that are painted with a design and then fired in a kiln, fusing the painted details with the surface of the colored glass. Finally, the individual sections are joined together and set into the window opening. As such, stained glass windows have improved church interiors and often instructed the faithful in sacred history and biblical stories. Yet stained glass has always contained a symbolic element for the religious believer that goes far beyond any didactic function. As one scholar put it, light streaming into a sanctuary is "palpably present, yet immaterial," it is "an intimation of the world of the spirit." Moreover, in biblical texts, light has been associated with knowledge and power, with spiritual awakening and the goodness of creation.[12]

The early windows in St. James Episcopal were nonfigural, perhaps reflecting the sentiment of John Henry Hopkins, Episcopal bishop of Vermont and the author of *Essay on Gothic Architecture* (1826). Hopkins harbored deep suspicions regarding depictions of human figures, believing that they led to idolatry; he preferred quotations from biblical texts. In contrast to those views, the Frank Weeder Studios designed St. Paul's windows based on well-known paintings by major artists. Furthermore, the designs were fabricated in opalescent glass, a style made famous in the work of John La Farge and Louis Comfort Tiffany. Opalescent glass windows have a milky, iridescent appearance that is produced by mixing various molten glasses and later exposing the result to metallic fumes during the cooling stages. Joining two or more layers of glass together creates shading and depth.[13]

By the late nineteenth and early twentieth centuries, reproductions, prints, and engravings of religious art as well as illustrated books such as Gustav Dore's *The Holy Bible Containing the Old and New Testaments* or J. James Tissot's *The Life of Our Saviour Jesus Christ* had produced a pictorial vocabulary and a popular recognition from which creators of stained glass could work. Thus the windows at St. Paul's included copies of "Gethsemane" and "Jesus in the Temple" by the prominent German painter Heinrich Hofmann, in addition to "Jesus, the Light of the World" by the influential English artist William Holman Hunt. Each window was donated by an individual sponsor or family in the church, thereby reminding one of the need to bring together architect, artist, and patron. The cost of such magnificent pieces of art was considerable, and many congregations made do with plain glass in sanctuary windows until the finances were available and the next majestic creation of glass and paint was installed.[14]

As St. Paul's congregation grew, other developments in the German American and Lutheran communities were taking place. As noted in the last chapter, many members of the Temple of Israel and St. Paul's came from Germany originally and socialized together occasionally. Actually, though, most of the Jews hailed from Bavaria, while the first Lutherans emigrated from Hannover and northern Germany. Historically, these two regions had shared as much as Texas and Massachusetts had in American history, and suspicions still lingered. Yet in the context of Wilmington, old differences were often overlooked in the hope of a prosperous future. Thus, Germans in Wilmington formed a Germania Lodge and in 1871 celebrated the German victory in the Franco-Prussian War and the unification of the German states into a nation.

As one participant in the 1871 festival stated, "all classes of German citizens, Israelites and Gentiles, Protestants and Roman Catholics joined heartily" in this celebration. Ethnic, class, and religious identity blended momentarily in this gala occasion. The local paper reported the event in detail, noting the 225 persons in the official parade; the worship service led by the pastor of St. Paul's, with participation by Methodist and Presbyterian clergy; and the concluding banquet attended by nearly 300 and culminating with formal toasts to the old fatherland, their adopted country, and the city of Wilmington.[15]

In addition to noting the presence of Germans from several religious communities, this account also observed that sermons, speeches, and toasts were delivered in both German and English. This bilingual situation nominally pertained at St. Paul's. In 1870, for example, the congregation decided that communion services should be conducted eight times a year, four in German and four in English. Yet the German language predominated, as minutes of congregational and council meetings were kept in German, sermons were usually delivered in German, and hymns were often sung in German.[16]

Here was the context for the development of a second Lutheran congregation in Wilmington: St. Matthew's English Evangelical Lutheran Church. Many of the ten members that formed the original congregation on March 21, 1892, came from St. Paul's, which led to a distance between the two groups, especially at first. Though located in the northern portion of the city, the church's identity was more linguistic than locational. Fully faithful to the Lutheran tradition, this congregation was culturally more comfortable with English than was the congregation of St. Paul's. Ironically, the first pastor at St. Matthew's was Gotthardt D. Bernheim, the initial organizer and later pastor of St. Paul's. Bernheim served at St. Matthew's until 1899. After the first church burned, the congregation moved to Seventeenth Street and constructed a new building in 1942.[17]

Important developments, architectural and otherwise, were also occurring among the Methodists. On Sunday, February 21, 1886, that venerable Greek Revival jewel, the Front Street Methodist Church, burned in a fire that destroyed most of the northwestern section of Wilmington. Ground was broken for a new church in a new location at Fourth and Mulberry streets, several blocks away from the wharves, on November 24, 1886. In May 1887 the congregation voted to change its name to Grace Methodist Episcopal Church, South, and on December 7, 1890, the service of dedication took place.[18]

The architectural style chosen for Grace Methodists was Romanesque Revival. Associated nationally with the work of Henry Hobson Richardson and his followers, Romanesque Revival was widely used in American public buildings and churches during the late nineteenth century. Typical of this style, Grace Methodist had several small towers with steep roofs overshadowed by a large and imposing steeple. Dark red brick walls, rounded arch entrances, heavy porches, and an irregular silhouette emphasized a sense of massiveness in its exterior. Inside the sanctuary a curved altar, ringed by plush green kneeling cushions and illuminated by crystal chandeliers, focused the attention of worshippers. The new Grace Methodist stood as a stunning example of Victorian taste and sensibility in Wilmington and the Cape Fear.[19]

Grace Methodist Church (Postcard in author's collection)

In 1847 A. M. Chreitzberg, pastor of Front Street Methodist, began a mission in the working-class neighborhood known as Dry Pond in the southern section of Wilmington. For two years the congregation met in private homes. Then in 1849 Miles Coston donated a site on Fifth Street (later changed to Fifth Avenue), and a one-room frame house of worship was erected. It was remodeled several times until 1889, when construction of a new church began; this new building was dedicated on September 26, 1890. Many said that Fifth Avenue Methodist had the largest seating capacity (1,150 worshippers) among churches in the state at the time.[20]

Fifth Avenue Methodist's architectural vocabulary expressed several of the elements associated with the late-nineteenth-century Gothic Revival style, sometimes called High Victorian Gothic. A steeply pitched gable fronted the dark red brick sanctuary building, which was flanked on two sides by massive recessed towers of unequal height. Benjamin D. Price of Philadelphia was the architect. He was also the chief architect for the Methodist Church and, beginning in 1877, prepared annual catalogs of church plans that were issued by the Department of Architecture of the Board of Church Extension of the Methodist Episcopal Church. Soon the Methodist Episcopal Church, South began to issue a version of the same catalog, reviewed and revised each year by Price. His catalogs were used throughout the nation in the late Victorian era.[21]

Price's designs also provided detailed plans for church interiors, and Fifth Avenue Methodist's was noteworthy in at least three respects. First, the interior space was finished in dark mahogany and offset by deep red carpet in a color combination familiar to the Victorian era. Brass chandeliers contained both gas jets and electrical lights, and the distinctive stained glass windows allowed further illumination. Designed by E. V. Richards, a local craftsman, the windows' nonfigural patterns contained more golds, greens, yellows, oranges, and lavenders rather than the cobalt blues and ruby reds that predominated in stained glass of the era. Striking also were two large circular windows containing hexagrams. The six angles and sides may have symbolized the biblical six days of creation; however, many observers would have identified it as the Star of David.[22]

A second striking feature of the interior was the double slanted aisles that curved around the projecting altar. This arrangement exemplified the transformation of the chancel area into a more

Fifth Avenue Methodist Church (Postcard in author's collection)

theater-like space in the nineteenth century. Fifth Avenue Methodist illustrated the auditorium sanctuary, with pews curving around a semicircular pulpit platform that projected out farther into the congregational space than the more traditional chancel separated from the nave by steps, aisles, and railings. With the pew rows sloped toward the chancel, sight lines were clearer, and the connection to the preacher and the message of the sermon all the more intimate and enhanced.[23]

The auditorium-style sanctuary may have appeared to imitate the theater in its use of space, but there was no question that the Methodist Church still distanced itself from many worldly things. The *Directory of Fifth Street Methodist Church* (1888) not only listed the names of members but also clearly indicated the grounds for expulsion from membership. Citing the old Methodists adage "a desire to flee from the wrath to come, and to be saved from sin" as the basis for admission to membership, the directory specified the sins to be avoided, which included working, buying, or selling on the Sabbath; playing games of any kind or participating in recreational activities on the Sabbath; drinking spirituous liquors; displaying extravagance in dress; and singing songs or reading books that did not tend to the knowledge or love of God. Should anyone persist in these activities, they would be admonished, tolerated "for a season," and then expelled from membership. Architecturally engaged with the world, these Methodists did not conform to the world but rather sought to transform it through lives of personal holiness and spiritual discipline.[24]

The third noteworthy aspect of its interior, in conjunction with the auditorium-style sanctuary, was Fifth Avenue Methodist's Akron-plan Sunday school. Although Sunday schools dated back to the late eighteenth and early nineteenth centuries, their popularity as adjuncts to worship and venues for instruction had grown tremendously by the late nineteenth century. The question, however, was where to locate them. Sanctuaries were often considered inappropriate locations for regular Sunday school activities, which would demean the sanctity of liturgical space; in addition, the fixed pews did not provide a conducive educational environment for the children. Thus, alternatives were sought. Rooms adjacent to the sanctuary or in the basement were often tried. Lewis Miller, an entrepreneur who served as Sunday school superintendent for thirty-five years at

First Methodist Church in Akron, Ohio, developed the Akron-plan Sunday school, which was later modified by George W. Kramer, an architect who specialized in church design.[25]

As initiated by Miller and refined by Kramer, the Akron plan placed the Sunday school adjacent to the sanctuary but separated from it by a movable partition. Normally, the partition remained in place, and the Sunday school classes could group as appropriate in their area and then, upon dismissal, move to the sanctuary for worship. On the occasion of a major event, the partition could be removed, allowing the sanctuary to increase (often double) its seating capacity. This was the plan at Fifth Avenue Methodist, where an assembly space adjacent to the sanctuary and separated by roll-up doors could be opened to extend the sanctuary. Moreover, seats in the Sunday school had backs that could be reversed to face the altar once the partition door was rolled up.[26]

Auditorium sanctuaries, with their fashionable style and large scale, expressed, as one scholar noted, "the ambitions and aspirations of upscale Methodists in late-Victorian America." Certainly for Fifth Avenue (which had outgrown its working-class origins) and for Grace Methodist (which had its own variation on the Akron plan), architectural design and spatial innovations captured the confidence of these congregations and the hopes they had for the future and themselves.[27]

As a port town, Wilmington served as a stopover for innumerable seamen from all over the globe as they made port calls and finished or began another voyage. In 1880 Fifth Avenue Methodist became the center of a fascinating story regarding one such sailor. The tale involves Charlie Han Soong, born in the Kwantung Province of China in the village of Wench'ang. Charlie Soong left China and arrived in Boston in 1878, intending to work in the store of a relative. A year later Soong stowed away on a U.S. government revenue cutter. After the vessel left port, he was discovered and brought to the ship's captain, Eric Gabrielson, who enrolled Soong in the crew and kept an eye out for him. When Gabrielson was transferred to Wilmington in 1880, Soong hitched aboard the next ship bound for that city and followed his friend. The two were reunited, and Soong again became a member of Gabrielson's crew. The captain, a God-fearing, longtime Methodist, introduced Soong to Colonel Roger

Moore, a member of Front Street Methodist Church, and Moore invited Soong to attend church with him, first at Front Street and then the following week at Fifth Avenue Methodist. There, Soong met the Reverend Thomas Page Ricaud, who began giving him private instruction and, on November 7, 1880, baptized Soong.[28]

Soon after his baptism, plans were afoot to get Soong enrolled in school and prepared for a life as a Methodist missionary in his homeland of China. Julian Carr of Durham, North Carolina, pledged financial support. After taking classes at Trinity College (later renamed Duke University) and at Vanderbilt University, Soong returned to China in 1886. Although he was affiliated with the Methodist Church for the rest of his life, Soong's work as a missionary was short-lived. Instead of preaching, he opened a printing shop that specialized in producing inexpensive editions of the Bible in Chinese.[29]

In 1894 Soong met Sun Yat-sen and became involved in Sun's revolutionary plans to overthrow the Manchu government. Initially using his printing shop as a cover to produce Sun's tracts and manifestos, Soong eventually became a member of Sun's inner circle of advisers and his financial organizer. Charlie Soong had married in 1887, and his family's fortunes would become intimately tied to those of China in the aftermath of the fall of the Manchus. One daughter, Ai-ling, married financier and government official H. H. Kung; another daughter, Ching-ling, married Sun Yat-sen; a third daughter, May-ling, married Chiang Kai-shek. The eldest son, T. V. Soong, received his degree in economics at Harvard University and served as minister of finance and foreign minister for the Kuomintang Party. Called the "J. P. Morgan of China," T. V. Soong was reputed to be the richest man in the world in the late 1940s. Charlie Soong's other two sons also went into banking and finance and achieved success. Fifth Avenue Methodist continues to cherish the memory of Charlie Soong. Interestingly, another connection between that congregation and China appeared in the person of the Reverend Lily Chou, a Shanghai-born Methodist minister who became the first female senior pastor of Fifth Avenue in June 2002. Chou's uncle was the chaplain for Chiang Kai-shek's family.[30]

Other Wilmington congregations also shared in the China connection. For example, Augustus Foster Lyde was born in Wilmington in 1813 and baptized that year at St. James Episcopal Church. In

1831 he entered the Episcopal General Seminary in New York City to begin his studies for the priesthood. While at the seminary, Lyde became caught up in the antebellum enthusiasm for foreign missions. In 1833 he proposed the establishment of an Episcopal mission to China and volunteered to go. In 1834 the executive board of the Episcopal Missionary Society authorized a mission to China. Lyde graduated from General Seminary that year and received his ordination as a deacon. However, his health was in decline, and he was unable to fulfill his missionary wish. Instead, Henry Lockwood, Lyde's friend and classmate, was the first Episcopal clergyman appointed to work in China. Lyde died later that year but is often referred to as the "real founder of the Chinese Mission of the Protestant Episcopal Church."[31]

First Presbyterian Church in Wilmington had a sustained relationship with Christian missions in China. In 1897 the Jiangyin mission station, first begun in 1895 a short way up the Yangzi River from Shanghai, incorporated the staff from the nearby Wuxi mission into its facility. Among those who moved from Wuxi to Jiangyin were three Presbyterian ministers, R. A. Haden, James McGuiness, and Lacy Little, in addition to a medical missionary, Dr. George Worth, and his wife, Emma. George Worth had been born in Wilmington in 1867 and became interested in a future as a medical missionary while attending evangelism meetings at the YMCA during his college days at Chapel Hill. After George finished his medical studies and married Emma Chadbourn, a friend since childhood and a fellow member of First Presbyterian, the Worths left for China in 1895.[32]

By 1927, after decades of work by the missionaries, and just before the Chinese nationalist backlash threatened its future, the Jiangyin mission station had achieved some notable successes. The missionary compound included a hospital, a training school for nurses, separate high schools for girls and boys, a Bible school for women, and a school for needy children. Its staff incorporated five ordained and nine unordained male Chinese helpers, six female Bible teachers, and thirteen foreign missionaries. The Christian church membership numbered nearly one thousand, supplemented by thirteen centers of evangelistic work in the countryside. As this summary shows, medical, educational, and evangelistic purposes were all pursued at Jiangyin. Each of these dimensions experienced challenges and degrees of suspicion among the resident Chinese. Western-style education, for example, ran up against the centuries-old tradition of Confucian training, and Western medical practices were little understood and often associated with the black-market sale of body parts and worse. Finally, preaching the Christian gospel and seeking converts among the Chinese confronted the practices of filial devotion, traditional Chinese religion, and Buddhism and thus were seen as spiritually misguided and socially disruptive.[33]

The year 1927 probably represented the high point of the Jiangyin mission's experience, for in the next decades, nationalist reaction, the Sino-Japanese war, and the political turmoil between Chinese Nationalists and Chinese Communists enervated the mission. Finally, in 1951, after fifty-six years of work, the Jiangyin mission closed.[34]

In its rich experience, the Jiangyin mission illustrated two salient dimensions of American missionary history. First, with its emphasis on educational, medical, and evangelistic work, the missionaries at Jiangyin took a comprehensive approach to mission work. In the context of late-nineteenth- and early-twentieth-century American missions, this approach reflected the so-called progressive, modernist, or social gospel attitude. This understanding of missions recognized the power of economic and social conditions in human lives and sought to reconstruct native societies in Western modes. Thus, evangelical work could take place in a stand-alone context, but more often it was integrated into the Western education and medicine that the mission station offered. Teaching, healing, and preaching went hand in hand at Jiangyin and, coincidentally, converged at least in part with some secular Chinese reformers who wished to adapt "modern" Western models to the Chinese political, economic, and social situation. The conclusion of one historian that "the Protestant missionary movement in twentieth-century China was most successful when it proved itself useful in secular ways" has been repeated by historians of other missionary enterprises, although the debate continued in American missionary circles during the twentieth century.[35]

A second significant feature of the Jiangyin mission was its relationship with First Presbyterian Church in Wilmington. Baptized, confirmed, and married in that church, George Worth was a familiar sight in the congregation. Many of the members rejoiced when

George and Emma went off to China, which, for Americans, represented the most prominent location among foreign missions in the late 1800s. George Worth cultivated his relationship with First Presbyterian throughout his career as a medical missionary. He and his family members kept up a regular correspondence, informing the congregation of recent news, of needs that the mission had, and of their successes in the mission field. When the Worths returned home on furlough, they always provided "lantern slide shows" for the congregation, and in 1936 Dr. Worth showed stereopticon pictures and movies of Jiangyin. In 1903, during one such furlough, Worth made an appeal to the Woman's Auxiliary of the Wilmington Presbytery, challenging it to assume financial responsibility for the development of medical work at Jiangyin, including a new hospital. The Woman's Auxiliary raised the $4,000 needed for the hospital's construction and, during the succeeding years, continued to support the medical work at Jiangyin. As noted in chapter 4, women's involvement in such church-related pursuits was one of the few approved venues for female activity outside the home, and it provided women (particularly elite women) with opportunities to develop their organizational skills and expand their worlds outside the domestic sphere.[36]

Another aspect of the special relationship between Jiangyin and First Presbyterian was the virtual adoption of the mission station by the congregation, and especially by one of its prominent members, James Sprunt. A wealthy Wilmington merchant and an elder in First Presbyterian Church, Sprunt took a particular interest in the educational initiatives undertaken at Jiangyin. In 1909 Sprunt donated $10,000 for the Jiangyin mission to build schools for boys and girls and also pledged further contributions. In April 1910, when the schools were completed, they were named James Sprunt Male Academy and Luola Murchison Sprunt Academy for the patron and his wife. Between 1902 and 1951 the Woman's Auxiliary and members of First Presbyterian Church (with Sprunt making hefty contributions from 1909 through 1938) contributed $566,688 toward the support of the Jiangyin mission and its staff.[37]

This special relationship between the "home church" and its "spiritual daughter" sometimes caused friction with denomination-level church officials. Sprunt made it clear that his donations were for the Jiangyin mission and not for a general mission fund.

If he thought that funds were being diverted from Jiangyin or that denomination-level officials were failing in some regard, one could be sure that a letter of concern would quickly leave Sprunt's pen. Thus, although a connection such as that between Jiangyin and First Presbyterian could relieve denomination-level agencies of the need to support a given mission, it also put these missions outside the direct control of the denomination.[38]

Issues of financial support and denominational supervision were pressing for another Cape Fear missionary to China, the Reverend David Herring. Herring grew up in Pender County, and his family had been associated for generations with the Wells Chapel Baptist congregation. Under the auspices of the Southern Baptists, Herring was in China with his family by the early 1880s. Located first in Shantung Province, he also worked at Chengchow in Honan Province during his forty years of missionary service.

In several respects, Herring's missionary experience provides a counterpoint to that of the Worths at Jiangyin. Herring chafed under denominational control, much preferring that specific churches take up the challenge of financial support for missions and bypass denominational agencies altogether. Herring also advocated that missionaries wear Chinese clothes, at least in the interior parts of the country, away from the large cities. Photographs of Herring and his family show him with a shaved forehead and queue, wearing a skullcap and long Chinese robes. (Significantly, there are also photographs of George Worth and his family in similar apparel.) Herring's choice of dress and his independent spirit did not sit well with his superiors, and in 1884 Herring resigned from the Southern Baptist Board of Foreign Missions and continued to work in China in an independent gospel mission supported by specific American congregations. In 1902, however, Herring sought reinstatement with the Southern Baptists and agreed to dispense with Chinese-style clothing.[39]

In one respect, the approaches of Herring and Worth were quite different, for Herring insisted that his mission station carry out only evangelistic preaching, with no attempt at educational or medical endeavors. Herring stated that his work as a missionary was to preach the gospel, pure and simple, and that there was neither justification nor need to expand into social reform. Herring, like the Worths and many other Christian missionaries in China, could

speak the dialect of his local area. He respected Chinese intellectual and educational traditions, even after the abolition in 1905 of
the traditional examination system based on Confucian teachings,
and saw no need to attempt to replace them with Western models.
In this regard, Herring represented the more conservative side of
American missionary experience, with its single-minded emphasis
on preaching and conversion to the exclusion of other social purposes. Nonetheless, although American missionary work in China
and elsewhere has been criticized for its involvement in imperialism and its perpetuation of orientalist stereotypes, the conclusion of
historian Lawrence Kessler seems, on balance, to be accurate. Missionaries, Kessler wrote, "were the most knowledgeable and perceptive of foreign observers in China." Stationed in the interior as
well as in the cities, competent if not fluent in local languages, and
resident for much longer periods than the diplomats, merchants,
and military officers that otherwise filled out the ranks of foreign
observers in the Middle Kingdom during these years, missionaries had an intimate, realistic perspective on Chinese life, and they
shared that perspective with home congregations and others, thus
providing most of the firsthand knowledge that their fellow citizens
had of China.[40]

The Cape Fear connection to China was not confined to Protestants. Thomas F. Price was the first North Carolinian to be ordained
to the Roman Catholic priesthood. That would have been historical
distinction enough; however, Price was also the cofounder of the
Catholic Foreign Missionary Society of America, popularly known
as the Maryknoll Fathers. Born in Wilmington in 1860 and baptized
at St. Thomas Catholic Church on Dock Street, Price was the son
of a prominent Wilmington journalist. After completing his education, Price was ordained at St. Thomas in 1886. He served parishes
in New Bern and Raleigh and became well known as the editor of
the apologetic magazine *Truth*. Active in domestic missions in the
South, Price called for the establishment of an American foreign
missionary seminary in conjunction with Catholic University of
America. This suggestion led to plans for the Catholic Foreign Mission Society of America, which received papal endorsement in June
1911. With this groundwork laid, Price worked to raise money for
the seminary and for foreign missionaries. In 1918 the first group
of missionaries departed for their assignment at Yeungkong near

Canton. Price was a member of this initial delegation, but he died in a Hong Kong hospital on September 12, 1919. Although his physical presence in China was short-lived, through his fund-raising for foreign missions and his role in the founding of the Maryknoll organization, Price played a significant role in Catholic missions in China and was a source of pride for his fellow Catholics in Wilmington.[41]

Wilmington Catholics also took pride in other developments in their religious life. For example, James Gibbons, successively bishop, archbishop, and cardinal and arguably the most prominent American Catholic in the late nineteenth century, lived in Wilmington from 1868 to 1872. Mentored by Archbishop Martin Spalding, for whom he served as secretary, Gibbons was consecrated in 1868 as bishop, with the duties of administrating the Vicariate Apostolic of North Carolina. A vicariate apostolic is a region that is in need of financial and organizational assistance in order to become independent enough to qualify for diocesan status. As a mission area, North Carolina was under the jurisdiction of the Congregation for the Propagation of the Faith in Rome; however, Gibbons was responsible for the day-to-day administration of the vicariate.[42]

During Gibbons's installation at St. Thomas in Wilmington, an official referred to North Carolina as a "state, which in a religious sense, may be called a desert." Though perhaps not charitable, the remark was accurate regarding the status of Catholicism in North Carolina. There were only two priests for the whole state, and the Catholic population was no more than seven hundred persons. Gibbons himself admitted, "everything had to be started; missions inaugurated, schools established, priests to be had, conversions to be made." During his residence in Wilmington, Bishop Gibbons lived with St. Thomas's pastor, Father Mark Gross, in a small building adjacent to St. Thomas Church, sharing meals and pastoral duties.[43]

As Gibbons acknowledged, many tasks needed attention, and he set out immediately to strengthen the fortunes of Catholicism in the Carolinas. Priests were slowly enlisted into the vicariate, and Gibbons traveled throughout the state preaching to assemblies of Catholic and non-Catholic audiences. Much like his predecessor John England, Gibbons was successful as a public speaker, and several of these presentations eventually ended up in Gibbons's famous apologetic volume *The Faith of Our Fathers.*

In two areas, schools and converts, Gibbons left his mark on the Cape Fear region. Gibbons was a firm supporter of Catholic schools and believed that, whenever possible, Catholic parents should send their children to parochial schools. Immediately upon his arrival in Wilmington, he wrote to church officials in Ireland to request that members of the Order of the Sisters of Mercy be sent to establish Catholic schools in his vicariate. Gibbons's overtures were unsuccessful, and he eventually turned to the Sisters of Our Lady of Mercy of Charleston, South Carolina, for recruits. The Charleston Sisters of Mercy were already familiar with Wilmington, having assisted in 1862 with the sick and dying during the yellow fever epidemic. Now, after their arrival in September 1869, the sisters would remain a presence in Wilmington for over a hundred years.[44]

Within a decade of their appearance, the Sisters of Mercy had opened three schools: the Academy of the Incarnation (1869) for white girls; St. Peter's Parochial School (1871), a tuition-free school for black girls; and St. Joseph's Male Academy (1876) for white boys. In 1871 these three small schools merged and eventually became St. Mary's School. Throughout the nineteenth century the issue of religious education had been a controversial one in America. In Massachusetts, for example, combatants in the 1830s and 1840s had taken sides over proposals for nondenominational versus sectarian religious instruction in the public schools. Even such supposedly nondenominational instruction still reflected Protestant values and Protestant scriptures, a fact that became all the more glaring as the size of the Catholic population in America grew. Requests to eliminate religious education or to balance Catholic and Protestant views in the public schools often went unheeded; thus, parochial schools became increasingly attractive to Catholic families.

In addition to educational growth in Wilmington, Gibbons played an important role in the religious formation of Catholicism in Sampson County. The story concerns Dr. John Monk, a physician in the village of Newton Grove who attended the local Methodist church. In January 1871 Monk received a shipment of medical supplies. The materials were wrapped for packing purposes in a recent issue of the *New York Herald*. One of the newspaper articles, recounting the dedication of a Catholic church in New York City, contained the verbatim sermon of Archbishop John McClosky on the topic of the unity of the church. Struck by the sermon, Monk dashed off a letter addressed "To Any Catholic Priest, Wilmington, N.C." and requested information about Catholic doctrines and practices. Bishop Gibbons wrote back to Monk, answering specific questions and recommending a number of books for further information and reflection. The correspondence between Monk and Gibbons continued, and on October 27, 1871, Monk and his family traveled to Wilmington, where they met Gibbons for the first time. Later that day, Gibbons baptized the physician, his wife, and two daughters at St. Thomas.[45]

Dr. Monk's family became a center of convert Catholicism. In March 1872 Gibbons visited Newton Grove and promised that the priest at St. Thomas in Wilmington would make the eighty-mile journey to Newton Grove once a month and spend a week there. On August 11, 1874, Gibbons consecrated St. Mark Church in Newton Grove, and over the next twenty years this Roman Catholic outpost in the rural Cape Fear added a parochial school and grew to some three hundred persons, comprising converts and their families. As Gibbons later joked, this physician-convert was "the Monk who fathered three hundred children."[46]

Further developments in the early twentieth century would have dramatic significance for Catholicism in Wilmington. After Gibbons's appointment as archbishop in 1878, there was an administrative interlude in the Vicariate of North Carolina until the naming of Father Leo Haid as vicar in 1887. Haid envisioned a revitalized vicariate that would be crowned by three jewels. He anticipated that Wilmington, as the largest city in the state, would one day become the seat of a diocese, and he hoped the same for Asheville in the west and Belmont Abbey in the Piedmont. Father Christopher Dennen, pastor of St. Thomas in Wilmington, shared Haid's dream, and on October 21, 1909, Haid laid the cornerstone for a new church in Wilmington. On April 28, 1912, Cardinal Gibbons returned to Wilmington and dedicated it as St. Mary Pro-Cathedral.[47]

Built in the Spanish Baroque style with twin towers, a broad gabled entrance, and a domed roof, St. Mary was a stunning addition to the inventory of ecclesiastical architecture in Wilmington. Modeled in part on St. Lawrence Catholic Church in Asheville, North Carolina, St. Mary was constructed of brick, terra-cotta, and tiles. The stained glass windows were completed by Franz Meyer of Munich, Germany, and depicted scenes such as the Nativity and Adoration by the Magi, the Resurrection, and the blessing of Augustine by Gregory the Great.

This magnificent building, suffused with a sense of imperial grandeur and striking beauty, was built without the use of steel or wood beams and even without nails. Instead, the builders, Rafael Guastavino Sr. and his son, Rafael Guastavino Jr., employed their

St. Mary Roman Catholic Church (Postcard in author's collection)

own system of brick and tile construction that utilized these masonry materials for both structural and decorative purposes. The Guastavino system, as their process was known, used portland cement to bond tiles together so strongly that the tiles would usually break before the mortar would separate. As a result, masons constructed domes and vaults by supporting themselves on just completed work and leaning over the edge to extend the masonry below and in front of them. Other advantages of the Guastavino system included the lighter weight of tile versus stone vaults and the tiles' resistance to the spread of fire.[48]

Guastavino Sr. was born in Valencia, Spain, in 1842 and immigrated to America with his son in 1881. Before his departure for America, Guastavino had completed a series of buildings in Barcelona that were illustrative of his vaulting system and also had an influence on a number of Spanish architects, such as Antonio Gaudí. During their careers, the Guastavinos were involved in the construction of more than a thousand structures, including some two hundred churches, cathedrals, and chapels in the United States. As builder-designers, the Guastavinos collaborated with several prominent American architects, including McKim, Mead, and White; Richard Morris Hunt; Ralph Adams Cram; Cass Gilbert; and Bertram Goodhue. Some of the best-known projects on which the Guastavinos worked included the Cathedral Church of St. John, the New York University Library, the Smithsonian Museum, the Bank of Montreal, Madison Square Presbyterian Church, Columbia University Chapel, the Chapel at West Point, and the Great Hall at Ellis Island. At the height of their business, between 1905 and 1930, the Guastavinos participated in the construction of thirty to sixty new buildings a year. Guastavino Sr. came to North Carolina in the mid-1890s to work on the Biltmore House in Asheville. Enjoying the region, he built a house in Asheville, where he died in 1908. At that point, his son took over the company's projects, including the completion of St. Mary in Wilmington. Guastavino Jr. died in 1950 in Bay Shore, Long Island. When the Guastavino Company closed in 1962, due to rising labor costs and the increased use of concrete, their system of cohesive construction had left its mark on American architecture.[49]

With the dedication of St. Mary Church in 1912 and its assumption of the status of procathedral (or seat of the vicar apostolic

of North Carolina) from St. Thomas the Apostle Church, a signal
event took place: the segregation of those two Wilmington parishes.
Upon the completion of St. Mary, Father Dennen of the St. Thomas parish took over parochial duties at St. Mary, and Father Thomas
Hayden assumed responsibility for St. Thomas. In 1914 Dennen
requested that the parishes of St. Mary and St. Thomas be divided
along racial lines. He argued that members of integrated congregations were not respected in the South and that the mingling of
black and white Catholics thwarted all the efforts of Wilmington
Catholics to be accepted within southern society. Additionally, Dennen stated, in a line of reasoning often advanced by others in the
Catholic hierarchy (and among southern Protestants as well), blacks
were not happy with the integrated arrangements and resented the
greater attention paid to the white parishioners. Bishop Haid agreed
with Dennen's proposal and had it enacted.[50]

The segregation of the parishes also meant the segregation of
schools. In 1916 the priests of the Society of St. Joseph of the Sacred
Heart, known as the Josephite fathers, took charge of St. Thomas
Church, including its school. By that point, white children attended
the school attached to St. Mary, while black children went to the
one at St. Thomas. Moreover, Josephite priests and members of the
Franciscan sisters from Mill Hill, an English missionary community, staffed the spiritual and educational institutions in St. Thomas
parish. Another religious order, the Sisters of Blessed Sacrament
for Indian and Colored People, was represented by the financial offerings of Mother Mary Katherine Drexel, founder of the order.
Rather than sell St. Thomas to raise funds for the construction of
St. Mary, Drexel provided a grant of $12,000 for the purchase of
St. Thomas Church, on the condition that it be made available for
black Catholics in Wilmington. Although she did not intend for St.
Thomas to become a segregated parish, she unwittingly provided
the funds that led to that development.[51]

In 1925 church officials suppressed the Vicariate of North Carolina and established the Diocese of Raleigh, encompassing the whole
state. There were 51 priests (including both diocesan and members
of religious orders), 127 women religious, and approximately 6,000
Catholic parishioners in North Carolina at the time. Raleigh was
chosen as the seat of the diocese, although its Sacred Heart Church
thereby became the smallest cathedral in the nation. Of the sixty-

four parish and mission churches in the state, twenty-four had resident priests. Catholicism had advanced since the day of Gibbons's installation in Wilmington. Architectural landmarks, such as St. Mary Church, had imprinted the religious landscape. However, the issue of race—sometimes erupting, as in the race riot of 1898, and other times smoldering, as in the segregation of parishes—haunted Catholics as it did Protestants in the Port City.[52]

The central drama of Catholic religious life is the Mass, celebrated by a priest and offered daily, although most laypersons attend once a week. The rhythms of Catholic life extend out beyond the Mass, however. Whereas Protestants reduced the number of sacraments, some groups limiting them to only baptism and communion, Catholicism's sacramental system encompasses the believer from cradle to grave. Baptism, confirmation, matrimony, extreme unction, holy orders, confession, and communion nurture believers throughout their entire life, enveloping the individual in a web of sacred actions and sacred times that structure his or her religious life. Less focused than Protestant evangelicalism on a decisive spiritual rebirth of conversion, Catholicism allows for revivals and ecstatic transformations but puts them within the context of this larger pattern of liturgical and sacramental resources.

Such a sacramental system is augmented by annual schedules of festivals, saints' days, and devotional practices, such as that of the Forty Hours. In the last, for a period of forty hours, interspersed with sermons and chants, faithful believers pray before the altar on which the sacraments are exposed. During one such observance in Wilmington, Bishop Haid presided over the large number in attendance. According to a front-page article in the local paper, the services were "elaborate and impressive," and Haid's sermons were "eloquent and scholarly."[53]

Other elements distinguished Catholics from Protestants in their lived experience of each other. For example, the sight of Sisters of Mercy on their way to tend to yellow fever victims or to teach their students would have been noteworthy in the predominantly Protestant town of Wilmington. None of the sisters living in Wilmington were members of contemplative orders. Instead, they were visibly committed to service, though just as visibly attired in such a way as to set them apart from others. The Sisters of Mercy wore full-length, long-sleeved black wool tunics, tied at the waist by a cincture from which a rosary dangled, and topped by a complete headpiece composed of wimple and veil that encircled their faces and covered their necks and hair. If their outerwear showed an indifference to the heat and humidity of Wilmington, their daily lives and their teaching styles demonstrated an inner devotion and discipline that were every bit as resolute.

Catholic education was well known for its religious formation as well as its academic expectations. In fact, Catholic education during the Jim Crow era of segregation probably provided some of the best schools available for blacks at the time. Compassion often went hand in hand with service, but this did not mean that the sisters were unwilling to use a paddle or a ruler to correct an unruly student. Such rigor was negligible, however, in comparison to the standards the sisters demanded of themselves. Poverty, chastity, and obedience were the formal vows of the Sisters of Mercy, while humility and subservience to the priest were expected as well. In addition to their teaching obligations, the sisters often performed such menial tasks as doing the priests' laundry and mending their clothes. And yet, these religious orders provided women with an opportunity for service in the religious life that was not available to Protestant women. Purity of purpose was wedded to an intensity of commitment and freedom from distractions or sexual expectations that at least some Protestant women envied and most women religious cherished.

The example of the women religious was compatible with many of the gender conventions in the wider American culture and set a standard for Catholic laywomen as well. These nuns and sisters were self-evidently religious and pure, and they were demonstrably subservient to men, features ascribed to women (as discussed in chapter 4). By extension, Catholic laywomen were considered naturally religious and were expected to be faithful in their marriages and guardians of the home and all that it represented. In a 1930 radio address on the Catholic Truth Hour, Mrs. Frances Slattery acknowledged that while a Catholic woman lived "under the influence of her husband," still she "rules the Christian home." Mrs. Slattery went on to insist that the "protection" of family morals and the "preservation of their spiritual ideas" belong to women, for in the end, the "great moral issues . . . should be the special concern of women."[54]

In their purity and domesticity, Catholic women were regarded as the maternal safeguards of American society. Consequently, just like their Protestant counterparts, Catholic women became involved in religious organizations, particularly those that emphasized charity, convalescence, and education. At St. Thomas in Wilmington, women joined the Blessed Virgin Sodality and made monthly visits to the sick of the parish. Additionally, this association raised funds to assist with some of the financial obligations of the church. At St. Mary, Court #1036 of the Catholic Daughters of the Americas was formed to promote unity and charity and to help meet the needs of the parish.[55]

Although such associations provided women with opportunities for fellowship and benevolence, they were also contexts in which women developed organizational skills, raised money, and increased their social awareness, and they did these things outside the direct supervision of the priest or other male authorities. Consequently, for Catholic as well as for Protestant women, religion provided the basis for many gender conventions, but it also paradoxically provided contexts for the circumvention of those very conventions. Finally, it should be noted that although these gender conventions were generalized for all women, in reality, they were more easily applied to elite and middle-class women, who had the requisite leisure time or could at least stay at home. For Catholic immigrant and rural women, these preconditions were rarely available. Yet even in these contexts, the normative power of gender conventions was often apparent.[56]

If the sphere of women was domestic and moral, then the sphere of men was public and commercial. Participation by Catholic men in Masonry had been prohibited by the pope in 1738. Consequently, religious fraternal organizations developed, such as the Knights of St. John at St. Thomas Church and the Knights of Columbus at St. Mary Church. In both cases, camaraderie, patriotism, and assistance in times of need were the hallmarks of these groups, and they served to forge bonds of association and elements of Catholic identity in Wilmington as elsewhere.[57]

In 1886 the *Wilmington Morning Star* proudly announced that the first electric street lamps were being put into operation in the city. Technology continued to change the face of Wilmington's townscape as electricity replaced oil lamps and the streets were finally beginning to be paved. As late as 1897, one observer lamented that

Wilmington's streets "were barely fordable drifts of black sandy loam." However, cobblestones, then bricks, and eventually asphalt covered the city's streets. To be sure, paving produced runoff floods after rainstorms, and faulty wiring resulted in fires, just as open flames had. Nevertheless, Wilmington embraced these changes.[58]

Already by the 1890s, residential expansion in the northern part of the city was under way, and new churches as well as new homes were being built. Brooklyn Baptist Church, named for the neighborhood in which it was located, started as a mission of First Baptist Church in 1886. The following year it moved to Fourth and Brunswick streets. The name of the church was changed to Calvary Baptist by 1936. St. Andrews Presbyterian Church completed a new church at Fourth and Campbell streets in 1889. Adolphus G. Bauer, earlier an assistant to Samuel Sloan in the design of the governor's mansion in Raleigh, was the architect of this Gothic Revival house of worship.[59]

Another sign of the changing times was the introduction of the trolley system. These transportation lines and the streetcar suburbs they facilitated became prominent elements of early-twentieth-century Wilmington. With the formation of the Wilmington Street Railway Company in 1887, the streetcar era had begun. Horse-drawn cars gave way by 1898 to electric ones, and construction of a number of city routes took place. Formed in 1907, Tidewater Power Company ran lines north and south on Front Street and east from Princess Street to Seventeenth Street and eventually all the way to Wrightsville Beach. The swaying trolley cars were a familiar sight in downtown Wilmington and were a popular means of transportation out to the beach and to Lumina Pavilion. However, in 1939 the trolleys were discontinued, replaced by public bus service and private automobiles.[60]

As an urban entity dating back to the eighteenth century, Wilmington had a compact downtown core around which suburban neighborhoods formed. Powered by the streetcar (and later private automobiles), these suburbs offered, as one scholar put it, rural associations "within convenient commuting distance to the city." Developers touted suburban neighborhoods as areas free of the noise and congestion of the downtown, replete with residential lots planned for single-family dwellings and landscaped with native plants, thereby evoking picturesque, naturalistic settings in which to raise families.[61]

The development of planned suburbs first emerged in North Carolina between 1900 and 1930, particularly under the influence of the City Beautiful movement. This social vision was inspired nationally by the Chicago World Exposition of 1893 and continued into the 1920s. In metropolitan centers such as Chicago, Denver, Kansas City, and Washington, D.C., its advocates established urban planning, public transportation, and impressive architecture as its signature elements. In its southern expression, the City Beautiful movement emphasized a bucolic vision that developed quiet residential neighborhoods adjacent to the transportation lines necessary for commuting to work. Together with neighborhood residences went neighborhood churches and schools. Consequently, while engineers and construction workers expanded vertically and introduced the first skyscrapers into the Wilmington skyline—the nine-story Atlantic Trust and Banking Building in 1910–1911 and the eleven-story Murchison Building in 1913–1914—land developers moved horizontally and offered real estate lots in areas such as Carolina Place, Carolina Heights, Winoca Terrace, and Delgado Village.[62]

Carolina Place was the first residential suburban development in Wilmington and New Hanover County. In February 1906 sixty-eight acres of former farm- and pastureland were auctioned off. American Suburban Corporation of Norfolk, Virginia, placed the winning bid and announced its intention to develop the land into individual lots with streets, landscaping, and water and sewer connections. Trolley lines would also be constructed for this area, which lay southeast of Market Street. American Suburban Corporation had built similar projects in Norfolk and Richmond, Virginia; Jacksonville, Florida; and Greensboro, North Carolina. Here in Wilmington the plan was to design affordable housing for working families of moderate means. Deed restrictions prevented the sale of liquor on any property for twenty years and prohibited the sale of any lots to blacks.[63]

The proposed lots sold quickly, and one of the earliest and largest purchases was an entire city block bought by Mary Bridgers. Miss Bridgers was the daughter of Rufus B. Bridgers, president of the Wilmington and Weldon Railroad, the predecessor of the Atlantic Coast Line Railroad. Miss Bridgers planned to build a residence as well as a Christian Science church, as she was a local leader of that denomination. This church, completed in 1907, was one of the earliest Christian Science churches in North Carolina. Its style was Classical Revival, with Doric columns beneath a traditional frieze and pediment. The Christian Science congregation worshipped in this building until 1923, when it sold the structure to Temple Baptist Church and moved into a new structure located on Chestnut Street.[64]

The Chestnut Street Christian Science Church was located in the Carolina Heights suburb, a subdivision of roughly thirty-two acres on the north side of Market Street across from Carolina Place. The force behind the Carolina Heights projects was again Mary Bridgers, who purchased the land in 1907. Miss Bridgers worked with T. W. Wood and residential architect Burrett Stephens in the initial planning of Carolina Heights. The lots there were larger and the intended clientele wealthier than in Carolina Place. Property covenants similar to those in Carolina Place were enacted in Carolina Heights.[65]

In October 1910, while inspecting a construction site, Miss Bridgers sustained severe injuries in an accident and died a month later at the age of thirty-nine. Because of her religious beliefs, she had received no medical attention. Instead, members of the local Christian Science community prayed for her healing. The circumstances surrounding her death and the prominence of her family in the region reminded Wilmingtonians of other connections between the Port City and Christian Science.[66]

In January 1844 newlyweds Mary Baker Glover and her husband, George, arrived in Wilmington from Boston. After a short trip to Charleston, the Glovers were back in Wilmington by February and took up residence in Hanover House, a recently opened boardinghouse in the downtown area. The Glovers attended the nearby St. James Episcopal Church, and Mr. Glover was active in the local Masons as well as pursuing business interests in the construction industry. Friends described the couple as happy and popular. Although Mrs. Glover's health was said to be delicate, she was considered witty, charming, and dainty. This idyllic beginning to their marriage soon took a bad turn, however, as George Glover's business interests collapsed and he contracted yellow fever. Although his wife sat by his bed praying for his recovery, Glover died on June 27, 1844, and was buried in St. James graveyard with full Masonic honors. By August his widow was back in New England.[67]

Mary Baker Glover later married Asa Eddy, and she is better known historically as Mary Baker Eddy, the founder of Christian Science and its organizational leader until her own death in 1910. As described by Mrs. Eddy in *Science and Health, with Key to the Scriptures*, first published in 1875 and subsequently revised, the true nature of creation and reality is spiritual rather than material. The healing of sin and disease takes place by yielding to the actions of the divine mind, by experiencing the presence of God directly.[68]

Eddy's views were part of a larger movement in late-nineteenth-century American religion that one historian called "harmonial religions," for their desire to align the individual in harmony with the cosmos and the infinite. Mary Baker Eddy, however, distinguished herself from the Unity School of Christianity of Charles and Myrtle Fillmore or Ernest Holmes's International Association of Religious Science Churches (although followers of the Fillmores and Holmes both established organizations in Wilmington by the late twentieth century). Fending off critics and riding out internal disputes, Mrs. Eddy began the Church of Christ, Scientist and watched it prosper not only in New England and America but internationally as well.[69]

In Wilmington, Christian Scientists established a reading room, the first in the state, in 1895. The initial Christian Scientist church, completed in 1907, sat on the corner of the city block purchased by Miss Bridgers. In 1923 the congregation moved several blocks north to a new house of worship on Chestnut Street. This substantial brick building continued the Classical Revival style of the congregation's earlier edifice. The architectural idiom of the Classical Revival found wide support within early-twentieth-century Christian Science circles, replacing, as one historian put it, "the emotionalism of the gothic" with "the rationalism of the classic." Under the influence of architect Solon Spencer Beman, ready-to-order architectural plans designed in Classical Revival forms became easily available and widely used.[70]

Though not designed by Beman himself, Wilmington's Christian Science church of 1923, with its temple form, colonnaded portico, Corinthian capitals, frieze, and pediment, clearly fit into the larger national architectural pattern. The interior of this building also exemplified a familiar design. Beneath a shallow domed ceiling, the congregation sat in a crème-colored sanctuary. Windows that

First Church of Christ, Scientist (Postcard in author's collection)

were partially colored but without human figures allowed plenty of light into the interior space. At the front, framed quotations from Jesus and from Mary Baker Eddy flanked large letters stating, "God Is Love." The simplicity of the worship space matched other elements of Sunday worship services. Readers, usually male and female and elected by the congregation, replaced ordained clergy and recited selections from Mrs. Eddy's writings and from the Bible. They also led the congregation in hymns and silent prayers. Congregational meetings on Wednesday evenings focused on testimonies by members regarding the benefits of Christian Science. With their subdued and solemn Sunday service offset by the more spirited Wednesday testimonials, Christian Science practitioners in Wilmington shaped a life of moderation and spirituality that matched the cool exterior and warm interior of their architecture.

The third suburban development in Wilmington was Winoca Terrace (*Winoca* being an acronym for Wilmington, North Carolina). Located to the west of Carolina Heights, this subdivision targeted buyers between the working class of Carolina Place and the upper and upper middle class of Carolina Heights. It offered its clientele large lots, water and sewer connections, and proximity to the all-important trolley lines. Landscaped at the street level with azaleas, palms, and crape myrtles and eventually canopied overhead with Spanish moss–draped oak trees, Winoca Terrace promised a sylvan oasis within the city limits of Wilmington. Rather than hosting the establishment of a new denomination, Winoca Terrace became home to the expansion of several denominations already quite familiar in Wilmington's religious history.[71]

St. Paul Episcopal Church, originally located on Orange and Fourth streets, moved in 1914, at the request of the bishop, to a location acquired two years earlier adjacent to Winoca Terrace. Constructed in a multigabled brick veneered style, the new church contained stained glass windows from the Fourth Street church. In 1958 the Wilmington architectural firm of Lynch and Foard supervised extensive renovations on the church.[72]

In 1917 the cornerstone for the new Presbyterian Church of the Covenant was laid near Winoca Terrace at Fifteenth and Market streets. Kenneth M. Murchison of New York and James F. Gause of Wilmington were the architects for this church, built in a Gothic Revival style. James and W. H. Sprunt underwrote many of the costs, and their Scottish heritage is symbolized in a prominent stained glass window commemorating the signing in blood of the Solemn League and Covenant in old Greyfriars Churchyard, Edinburgh, on February 28, 1638. Additionally, ginkgo trees brought from China and donated by the Presbyterian missionaries George and Emma Worth decorated the exterior landscape. In 1944 the congregation of St. Andrews Presbyterian Church merged with Church of the Covenant to form St. Andrews–Covenant Presbyterian Church, using the facilities of Church of the Covenant.[73]

The third church constructed in this suburban neighborhood was Trinity Methodist Church. Begun as a Sunday school mission in 1889, this group evolved into the Market Street Methodist Mission later that year. In 1891 the church organized as the Market Street Methodist Episcopal Church, South, and James W. Craig, a former riverboat pilot who had served on blockade runners, was the first assigned preacher. Craig once quipped that whereas he previously guided ships to their havens, he now guided his fellow men to their eternal rest. By 1916, as the city grew, this congregation decided to move and purchased a lot at Fourteenth and Market streets. In 1922 the congregation celebrated the first services in the church, by now renamed Trinity Methodist. The church, designed by Wilmington architect Leslie N. Boney Sr., presented a monumental portico entrance supported by Corinthian columns. The large sanctuary contained eight magnificent stained glass windows fabricated by the Pittsburgh Plate Glass Company and installed by 1935. With affinities to the Tiffany style of stained glass, these windows contained a variety of Christian symbols in addition to depictions of familiar scenes, such as William Holman Hunt's "Jesus, the Light of the World."[74]

In addition to Carolina Place, Carolina Heights, and Winoca Terrace, the planned community of Delgado Mills Village was developed. By January 1900 this village consisted of more than one hundred houses for some five hundred people employed at the Delgado Cotton Mills located south of Carolina Place. Heat for the mill workers' uninsulated houses came from stoves or fireplaces; outhouses were common until the mid-1930s, when toilets were first installed. Three churches ministered to the people of the mill village. In 1905 First Presbyterian Church established a Delgado mission that was later taken over by the Church of the Covenant. Subsequently, Delgado Presbyterian Church became an independent congregation. In 1913 a Baptist mission from First Baptist Church started; this was the origin of Gibson Avenue Baptist Church. Additionally, a short-lived Episcopal mission, St. Luke, served this area.[75]

With the development of suburbs such as Carolina Heights, Carolina Place, and Winoca Terrace, Wilmington matured as a city. Wilmington was no longer the "walking city" of the eighteenth and nineteenth centuries, with its hodgepodge of commercial, civic, and residential spaces scrambled together. It had become a modern city with the vertical elevation of multistory buildings and the horizontal expansion through speculative land development of residential subdivisions. Transportation—in the form of elevators, in the one case, and trolleys, in the other—made possible these urban transformations. In the modern city, space was more clearly defined, with less overlap between residential and commercial functions. Southern patterns of urbanization diverged from their northern counterparts in scale and capitalization, population density, and architectural grandeur. Nevertheless, these new cities were signature elements for the boosters of the New South, public confirmations of a new day in Dixie.

Wilmington's early suburbs were predominantly residential areas, domestic garden spots separated from the bustle of the downtown and available for the white middle and upper classes. With the exception of schools, churches were one of the few public spaces represented in these residential suburbs. The planting of congregations on Wilmington's east side established a denominational presence in these neighborhoods. Recognition of the spiritual needs of the residents of these new tracts matched an awareness of the potential for growth in these subdivisions. Programs were established; some were familiar, such as Sunday school, while others were innovative, such as affiliation with the YMCA or the Boys' Brigade. Finally, by establishing fresh congregational identities in such spatial proximity to one another, these new suburban congregations found opportunities for interdenominational cooperation. By the second decade of the twentieth century, Wilmington had diversified and matured its townscape and, putting behind the devastation of the Civil War, had once again become the economic, political, and religious metropolis of the Cape Fear region. Moreover, as the next chapter shows, by the end of the twentieth century, the religious heterogeneity of the region would increase, and its journey toward religious pluralism would be well under way.

7

Pluralism in the Port City and Beyond

Among the many proponents of reform in the New South, one of the most single-minded was Hugh MacRae. A Wilmington entrepreneur, mining engineer, and land developer, MacRae believed that a significant obstacle to progress in the South was the lack of a dependable labor force. Economic modernization had no chance of success without reliable workers; efficiency was unattainable and regional growth impossible without a proper foundation. MacRae's vision, Jeffersonian in its roots and expansive in its outlook, was to construct model farm communities in the Cape Fear region. He believed that such examples could revitalize the agricultural basis of the southern economy. He hoped that successful farming of the available southern land would produce profits for farm owners and act as a magnet for further investment of capital and labor in the southern economy. So MacRae bought large tracts of land, invested significant amounts of money, recruited numerous immigrants from Europe, and achieved commendations for his efforts. Unintentionally, these new European settlers also contributed to the religious and ethnic diversity of the region and thus symbolized the pluralism that characterized the Cape Fear during the remainder of the twentieth century.

MacRae envisioned bringing industrious families from Europe to live in his planned communities. Given free transportation from Europe to North Carolina and the opportunity to purchase farmland

at reasonable prices, many took up MacRae's offer. This resettle-
ment option was not open to blacks, and after one failed experiment
with single men, it was tailored to families contacted by MacRae's
agents in Europe. On units of ten acres, the settlers intensively cultivated crops and trucked them to the nearby rail stations of the
Atlantic Coast Line Railroad for shipment to the North. Beginning
in 1905 and continuing into the 1940s, MacRae and his agents in the
Carolina Trucking Development Company organized six communities within a fifty-mile radius of Wilmington.[1]

One of the earliest of these social experiments was St. Helena,
a community named for the mother of Emperor Constantine and
located near Burgaw, about twenty miles north of Wilmington. In
1905 the first group of families arrived from Italy. MacRae claimed
that they came from a village where no serious crime had occurred
in over four hundred years. These were the type of people that Mac-
Rae wanted to bring to America. By 1908 approximately 150 Italians
lived in St. Helena, eventually to be joined by Hungarian, Russian,
and Polish families.[2]

MacRae set aside a section of St. Helena for the establishment
of a church. Although he was an Episcopalian himself and closely
supervised all other aspects of the communities, MacRae did not
dictate in the matter of religious preference. Consequently, in 1908
three brothers from St. Helena plus carpenters from Wilmington
erected St. Joseph Roman Catholic Church. Initially, Father James
Gallagher of St. Mary Church in Wilmington traveled to St. Helena to offer the Mass. The first full-time pastor, appointed in 1909,
was Father Umberto Donati; he was succeeded in 1911 by Father
Charles Kneusels. Under Kneusels's leadership the cornerstone for
a parochial school was laid in 1921. This school continued in use
until 1950, when it closed and transferred its operations to St. Stanislaus Church in Castle Hayne. Meanwhile, beginning in 1935, the
Conventual Franciscan Friars of the Immaculate Conception Province took over the administration and pastoral duties of St. Joseph
Church. The Franciscan Sisters of Syracuse, New York, assisted the
friars in teaching at St. Joseph's School. In September 1934 a fire
destroyed the church, and for the next twenty-one years the congregation worshipped in the school building. In 1955 a new St. Joseph
Roman Catholic Church, still served by Franciscan friars, was built
and opened for worship.[3]

Roman Catholics were not the only ones to build a church in St. Helena. In 1932 Russian families in St. Helena constructed the Sts. Peter and Paul Russian Orthodox Church, which for many years was the only Russian Orthodox church in the state. The Reverend John G. Boruch served as priest for the parish. Born in Russia in 1877, Boruch came to the United States in 1897 after completing his education. As was permitted in the Russian Orthodox Church, Boruch married, and he and his wife had four children. Fifteen families formed the charter members of Sts. Peter and Paul, gathering each week for services in Church Slavonic. Father Boruch served this parish until his death in 1969. In that year the Reverend Igor B. Bensen of Raleigh agreed to visit St. Helena on the second Sunday of each month to hold services. Job transfers of younger members and the passing of older ones took a toll on Sts. Peter and Paul. In 1996 Father Nicholas Kowal celebrated Christmas and New Year according to the Orthodox calendar for an assembly of about a dozen members.[4]

Though the size of the congregation dwindled, the church itself made an eye-catching architectural statement in a region more accustomed to Greek Revival frame churches. Designed by Olga Boruch, daughter of the parish priest, and built by J. T. Carroll of Wilmington with the assistance of members of the church, Sts. Peter and Paul reflected its Russian heritage. It was adorned in several places with the traditional three-bar Russian Orthodox cross, but the most striking exterior feature was the golden bulbous dome mounted atop a tall octagonal drum and capped by a large Russian cross. Although the rectangular brick exterior was otherwise simple, with rounded side windows and a small rose window over the entrance, the interior of the church was brightly decorated. A center aisle led from the narthex to the main altar, behind which was the wall of icons (iconostasis). Additional images, stands of candles, banners, and small side altars filled out the chancel space, providing a rich visual context for the worshipper. Scholars debate the details but agree in tracing this pattern of ecclesiastical architecture back to examples in Kievan Russia. Specific features, such as the bulbous dome, reflected Byzantine craftsmen and their influences, as well as accommodations to the climate. In winter, snow and ice would slide off the dome's sides rather accumulate on a flat or hemispherical surface. These domes became a universal feature of Russia's church architecture. Their ubiquity, in the words of Tamara Rice, "transformed the Russian skyline, giving it an elevation which nature failed to provide in that universally flat countryside." The silhouette of Sts. Peter and Paul played a similar role in the level expanses of Pender County.[5]

The Russian Orthodox Church traces its presence in North America back to 1794 and the arrival in Kodiak, Alaska, of several missionaries. The 1867 sale of Alaska to the United States and the transfer of the episcopal see from Sitka to San Francisco in 1872 shifted the locus of the Russian church in North America. Immigration during the nineteenth century slowly increased Russian Orthodoxy; however, the outbreak of the Russian Revolution in 1917 complicated relations between Russian Orthodox in the United States and the patriarch in the Soviet Union. By 1970 the Moscow patriarch granted autocephaly, or administrative self-governance, to the newly renamed Orthodox Church in America (OCA). The OCA founded new missions churches, including several in North Carolina. Beginning in 1979 another Russian Orthodox congregation met in Raleigh, and by the year 2000 four other congregations had been established. One of those, St. Nicholas Mission, began in Fayetteville in 1994.[6]

Another MacRae community, Marathon, brought additional ethnic and religious variety to the Cape Fear region. Founded in 1905, this settlement was initially populated by single Greek men. The Greeks soon left, however, convincing MacRae to colonize only with families, and his agents replaced the Greeks with Polish immigrants. The Poles were successful at farming and eventually organized their own church. In 1914 construction of St. Stanislaus Kostka Roman Catholic Church began on land donated by the Hugh MacRae Development Company. Named for the son of Polish nobility who had been born in 1550 and canonized in 1726, this parish was initially a mission of St. Mary in Wilmington; in 1935 it came under the administration of the same Franciscans who had charge of St. Joseph's parish in St. Helena. In 1950 the parish purchased a decommissioned army building from the Camp David base in Holly Ridge, dismantled it, trucked it to their site in Castle Hayne, and reassembled it. This building served as a church, parish hall, and school and was the location of annual festivals celebrating Polish heritage with food, costumed dancers, and music. In 1997 the parish

Sts. Peter and Paul Russian Orthodox Church (Photo by author)

demolished the old army building and constructed a new house of worship that was large enough to accommodate the growing congregation and to host the popular Polish festival.[7]

Although the original Greek settlers did not stay in Marathon, other Greeks and their families made their homes in Wilmington and became part of the growing Greek Orthodox community. Historians acknowledge a 1768 Greek colony in New Smyrna, in present-day Florida, but they cite the communities in Galveston, Texas, and New Orleans, developed in the 1860s, as the locations of the earliest Greek Orthodox churches in the United States. By 1922 several institutional developments had expanded the Greek Orthodox presence. By that year, with a population of approximately half a million and with 141 churches throughout the country, the Greek Orthodox tradition had become a visible reality in America.[8]

In September 1921 Meletios Metaxakis, metropolitan of Athens, established the Greek Orthodox Archdiocese of North and South America. The next year, upon Meletios's election as the ecumenical patriarch of Constantinople, the American archdiocese became a province of the church of Constantinople, and Meletios named Alexander Demoglou as archbishop. In 1930 Athenagoras Spyrou succeeded Alexander and served until 1948 and his own election as ecumenical patriarch. Michael Konstantinides, previously the metropolitan of Corinth, became the new archbishop of the American diocese in 1949 and offered prayers at the inauguration of President Dwight Eisenhower, the first time a Greek Orthodox prelate had done so. With the death of Archbishop Michael in 1959, the ecumenical patriarch named Iakovos Coucouzes as his successor. When Archbishop Iakovos retired in 1996 at the age of eighty-five, Spyridon Yorgi, born in Ohio, succeeded him, becoming the first American-born archbishop in the Greek Orthodox Church. Spyridon's tenure experienced several controversies, however, and he resigned in 1999. Demetrios Trakatellis, who had spent many years in America and had taught at the Orthodox Holy Cross Seminary in Massachusetts and at Harvard University, where he had also done graduate studies, became the new archbishop in 1999. From its establishment as an archdiocese through the election of American-born or American-educated prelates, the Greek Orthodox Church matured institutionally during the twentieth century.[9]

Although Greek sailors undoubtedly visited the Port City earlier, a nucleus of Greek families existed in Wilmington by the end of the first decade of the twentieth century. Many of these families came from the Greek island of Icaria, located in the Aegean Sea near the coast of Turkey. A Wilmington chapter of the Pan Hellenic Union, formed in 1910, reached out to all Greeks living in the city. The informal camaraderie and assistance provided by this society paralleled the official services offered by the Greek Consul for North and South Carolina, whose offices were in Wilmington. Although the consulate eventually reorganized and moved to Atlanta, efforts at mutual aid and fellowship continued at the Greek Social Center located on North Front Street.[10]

Campaigns to establish a Greek Orthodox parish also occurred. Priests from Charleston, South Carolina, and Norfolk, Virginia, occasionally came to Wilmington and conducted services. Usually these took place in the parish house of St. John Episcopal Church. In 1917 the local paper noted the cordial relations between the Greek Orthodox Church and the Episcopal Church, reporting that "Greek services will be held in a local Episcopal church. The services will, of course, be conducted in the Greek language."[11]

In 1945, after a decade of sporadic efforts, the Greek community in Wilmington raised the funds and constructed its own house of worship, St. Nicholas Greek Orthodox Church. The Reverend Efthemios Papazisis was the first priest assigned to St. Nicholas. Born and educated in Greece, Papazisis had served other Greek congregations in South Carolina and New York before coming to Wilmington. Located at Second and Orange streets, St. Nicholas's architecture included a wide gable entrance flanked by two rectangular towers. Whereas the exterior of the church was simple and massive, the interior was ornate and colorful. Center and side aisles shaped the nave, and the chancel contained a resplendent iconostasis that, when combined with the fragrance of the incense used during worship services, moved the believer into a sensual space far removed from the outside world. Growing in size and developing organizations such as the American Hellenic Educational and Progressive Association for men, the Ladies Philoptochos Society, and the Greek Orthodox Youth Association, the congregation remained at this location until 1980, when it moved into the former facilities of the Grace Baptist Church on South College Road. Transforming the comparatively austere setting of the Baptist church into the rounded domes and iconography of an Orthodox one involved the installation of an iconostasis and six tiers of icons on the walls, as well as iconography on the ceilings, in the chancel, and in the rear of the church. Renovation of the facade and the construction of exterior Greek domes with crosses was also planned. Equally visible to Wilmingtonians was the popular Greek festival begun in 1993, which introduced Greek folkways, food, and religion to many non-Greeks in the region. Tours of the church and explanations of the Greek Orthodox faith matched samples of moussaka, spanakopita, and baklava in affirming Orthodoxy's place in Wilmington's diverse religious landscape.[12]

Parallel developments took place in Fayetteville. In 1908 three Greek brothers set up a café, and over the succeeding decades, another half dozen restaurants began under Greek ownership. Father George Stephanis often made the trip from Raleigh to serve the Fayetteville Greek community. By 1956 a Hellenic Community Center had been constructed, and the Reverend Kallinikos Hatzilambrou was assigned to the Fayetteville community. Services continued to be held in the Hellenic Center until 1964, when ground was broken for a new church building. In June 1984 Archbishop Iakovos consecrated the Sts. Constantine and Helen Greek Orthodox Church.[13]

The community of Castle Hayne has already been mentioned in conjunction with St. Stanislaus Catholic Church. A settlement at Castle Hayne dated back to the colonial era, but in 1905 Hugh MacRae brought immigrants from the Netherlands, Hungary, and Poland to begin another of his farming experiments. With its large Dutch population, modern-day Castle Hayne became well known for its successful horticulture industry. In 1926 William H. Sprunt, a member of St. Andrews Presbyterian Church, donated funds for the erection of a Presbyterian chapel in Castle Hayne. Named for the Reverend A. D. McClure, a previous pastor of St. Andrews, this church was dedicated in October 1926 and began offering services. The chapel remained a mission of St. Andrews until 1957, when McClure Memorial Presbyterian Church became an autonomous congregation.[14]

A small colony, the fourth started by MacRae, began in 1906 in Columbus County. Its people came from Germany and Hungary, and they settled on MacRae land originally called Brinkly. With the influx of Germans, they adopted the name of New Berlin.

By 1917, with tensions over German foreign policy increasing, the town changed its name to Pershing. However, according to one account, a conductor on one of the trains serving the area always mispronounced the name as Perishing. This so aggravated the town's inhabitants that they changed the name again, this time to Delco, after the Delco lighting system.[15]

Defensiveness and attempts to deflect suspicion were widespread among German Americans in these years. What one historian called a "Furor Teutonicus" engulfed German Americans in their daily pursuits, their commercial relations, their recreational activities, and their religious lives as well. One example symbolized the situation in Wilmington. In April 1917 St. Paul's Evangelical Lutheran Church, a body that cherished its German heritage and had used German in its worship services since its founding, abolished the use of German.[16]

Before its name changed to Delco, New Berlin had two major religious communities. The first was a German Baptist congregation formed in 1910 and called the New Berlin Baptist Church. It later changed its name to the First Baptist Church of Delco but remained located on Kaiser Road. Other Baptist churches emerged in this portion of the Cape Fear during the remainder of the twentieth century. The second community was the St. Elizabeth of Hungary Roman Catholic Church, established in 1914. Several Hungarian families had moved to New Berlin, as they had in MacRae's other settlements. Their presence was often inconspicuous, however, so the St. Elizabeth church became important as a visible witness to their existence in the Cape Fear region and their part in the success of MacRae's experiments. Unfortunately, a fire in 1969 destroyed the church, and the remainder of the congregation affiliated with Christ the King Roman Catholic Church in Riegelwood.[17]

Columbus County was also the site of another MacRae settlement. Named Artesia, it was the only one of the six experiments to fail outright. Very few farms were ever sold, and no foreign immigrants settled on its land. Nor was it incorporated into another settlement, as Castle Hayne eventually assimilated the population and institutions of Marathon. Instead, weeds overgrew the land, and the colony became a distant memory and a scholarly footnote.[18]

Van Eeden, the last of MacRae's farming colonies, became a historical statement of a different sort. Named for Frederik van Eeden, a Dutch man of letters, this colony began in 1912 with Dutch families who tried truck farming and then dairy work but finally abandoned the colony for more dependable employment in the cities. The land reverted to the MacRae Corporation, and that seemed to be the end of the story. However, by 1939 Alvin Johnson, a friend of Hugh MacRae and director since 1922 of the New School for Social Research in New York City, had become increasingly concerned about the plight of Jews under the Nazis. He had already recruited several Jewish scholars for the faculty of the New School. Now, he formed a corporation with MacRae's support that bought 150 acres of farmland at Van Eeden. Johnson's plan was to relocate central European Jews onto this farmland in Pender County and thereby lessen the annihilation that he feared was in the offing. A study of the Van Eeden colony documented the lives of eleven families who lived there. Coming from professional backgrounds in education, medicine, architecture, finance, and accounting, these refugees faced tremendous obstacles as they sought to begin new lives by raising their chickens, goats, and cattle or tending their gardens of lettuce, spinach, radishes, and strawberries. Occasional trips to Wilmington provided welcome opportunities for shopping, for attending services at the Temple of Israel, and for enjoying something closer to the urban culture from which most of them came. With the end of the war, the Van Eeden settlers left, and in 1949 Johnson's corporation liquidated its assets and sold off any remaining property. Although the Van Eeden experiment never rescued the hundred of thousands of Jews that Johnson and MacRae had hoped, it offers yet another testimony to the unexpected richness of the history of this Cape Fear region and the range of the human spirit.[19]

The MacRae colonization project provides an emblem for religious life in the Cape Fear region during the twentieth century. With Italian, Polish, and Hungarian Roman Catholics, Russian and Greek Orthodox, Dutch Calvinists, German Baptists, and central European Jews, it demonstrates the existence of religious diversity. When these immigrants came to this New World, they brought their religions with them, as had so many in the past, and they established new congregations—some of which continued, and some of which were short-lived. Adjustments in lifestyle were often demanded by the new environment, and congregational debates over language, music, polity, and liturgy contributed to broader discussions of identity in this new place. Pride in heritage continued, even if it periodically submerged only to resurface later in festivals that combined folkways and religion, food and patron saints, for private and public affirmation. Respected by their Protestant neighbors for their hard work and occasional commercial success, the MacRae colonies were never intended as an experiment in religious pluralism. However unintentionally, this experiment demonstrated the religious paradigm for America emerging in the late twentieth century and beyond.

Whereas the MacRae experiment represented change in the religious culture, one must not forget the continuity that characterized everyday religious life. The rounds of pastoral service and the cadences of congregational life persisted: the rhythms of marrying and burying, of baptizing and blessing, of preaching and praying, of confessing, singing, and partaking, of grieving, sharing, and believing. Through music, word, and sacrament, through visiting the sick, teaching Sabbath schools, or witnessing the bar mitzvah, confirmation, or first communion of a young adult, religious believers throughout the Cape Fear carried out their lives in their holy communities and gave evidence of their belief in the sacred amidst the mundane.

Change and continuity molded the region's religious life. However, the sources of innovation came not only from the dynamics of communal experimentation but also from broader events occurring in American society. Four social forces impacted religion in the Cape Far in the last two-thirds of the twentieth century: technological improvements, the domestic impact of World War II, the civil rights and feminist movements, and modifications in the immigration experience. Taken together, these four factors transformed religious life and culture in the region, shaping its outward demeanor and inner spirit.

Although all these forces brought visible changes, none were as immediately discernible as the transformations introduced by technology. Developments in four areas—power generation, sanitation, transportation, and climate control—demonstrate the considerable effect of technology on religion. As noted in the last chapter, in 1886 the first electric street lamps were operating in Wilmington; later, when Wilmington's first suburbs appeared, electrically powered streetcars accompanied them. Keeping up in fashion, congregations replaced their oil lamps with electrical ones, muting the interior ambience from the flickers of candles and the smell of natural fuels to the steady, odorless illumination of electrical current. A parallel metamorphosis took place in the countryside after 1935 and the creation of the Rural Electrification Administration, which provided electricity in the middle and upper portions of the Cape Fear as it did throughout rural areas in the state. By the end of the century, power lines ran the length and breadth of southeastern North Carolina. And if electricity ultimately provided the current for spotlights on steeples and the incandescence for message boards, holiday ornaments, and pulpits, the telephone lines that eventually accompanied their electrical counterparts ushered in the reality of the electronic age and its access to the Internet through telephone modems.

Connection to the Internet changed modes of communication for churches, temples, and mosques, just as it did for secular institutions. From Web searches for any possible topic through e-mail notifications of virtual meetings and beyond, information delivery, popular culture, and religious life were fundamentally changed by these technological revolutions.

Cable, telephone, and electrical wiring eventually went beneath the ground, where they joined other underground conduits—sewers. Sanitation and, more broadly, public health issues are not often connected to religious life. Nevertheless, from the everyday experience of the comfort of parishioners assembled for worship and other activities through the more attention-grabbing headlines about services canceled due to contagious disease, technology played a part here too, and one that has had an influence on the lived experience of religion.

Mid-nineteenth-century sanitation facilities in Wilmington were simple—chamber pots in some bedrooms and privies in the backyard, with connections to a nearby stream or collection basin. At the end of the century, there was a small privately owned sewer system to which 547 buildings (possibly including a few churches) were connected, but 4,256 outhouses still existed in Wilmington. In 1910 there was a city-owned sewer system, but its inadequacy was attested to by the quip of one resident that "you could smell Wilmington in Burgaw."[20]

That resident was Dr. Charles T. Nesbitt, a physician who arrived in Wilmington in 1906 and in 1911 became the chief health officer for the city. During his six years as superintendent of health, Nesbitt agitated for a municipal water system, improved sewerage, and the eradication of conditions that produced malaria and typhoid fever. In these efforts he achieved some success, as the average death rate in Wilmington dropped from 29.43 per thousand in 1911 to 13.6 in 1916. Similarly, by 1914 nearly two hundred buildings in downtown Wilmington had installed indoor flush toilets, and within several decades, outdoor privies had become extinct in the downtown, though not in the region as a whole.[21]

Achievements such as the installation of indoor plumbing and the reduction of death from contagious diseases made the influenza pandemic of 1918–1920 all the more poignant to those who suffered through it. From the spring of 1918 through the autumn of 1920, 700 million were infected worldwide, with the number of dead estimated at between 20 million and 40 million persons. In the United States three waves of influenza during those years claimed more than 500,000 lives—an astonishing figure compared with the 53,402 total combat deaths of U.S. armed forces personnel in World War I. Of the 13,644 North Carolinians who died during the influenza pandemic, 233 were from New Hanover County. Given the speed with which the disease spread and the continuing deployment of many physicians overseas in the aftermath of the European conflict, local medical staffs and hospitals were quickly overtaxed. Public officials encouraged hygienic precautions such as muffling sneezes and coughs, washing hands and eating utensils, and avoiding public meetings. To this end, the New Hanover County Board of Health voted on September 27, 1918, to close all theaters, pool halls, and churches. On that Sunday, September 30, every Wilmington church suspended its services. Other counties took similar steps. For two and a half weeks the ban on public gatherings remained in place, being revoked on October 18. Some Wilmingtonians remembered the yellow fever outbreak, when churches closed, families withdrew from one another, and prayers were offered to the bereaved. The development of influenza vaccines in the 1940s provided immunization against selected strains of the virus and prevented a repetition of this event for the rest of the century.[22]

The third example of technological influence, transportation, impacted religious life in the Cape Fear as it did throughout the nation. Americans' love affair with the automobile is well known, particularly in the second half of the century, when engineering improvements and the availability of financing brought cars within the reach of more and more Americans. Wilmingtonians followed this national pattern, replacing horse-drawn streetcars with electric trolleys for reasons of efficiency and sanitation. However, in 1939 the trolleys made their last run to the accompaniment of a brass band and 150 onlookers, and modern bus transportation began. By the 1960s, in the wake of urban renewal in downtown Wilmington, several churches had moved out to the ever-growing number of suburban developments. Often public transportation did not serve these tracts, or in some years, the buses did not run on Sundays. Churches responded by including parking lots in their physical plans and advertising free parking for all who wished to worship. Residential proximity to one's house of worship became rarer then previously. Indeed, the mobility made possible by the private automobile gave parishioners greater choice in finding their own "spiritual homes," that is, a congregation whose style, theology, and social background made a comfortable fit.[23]

As the need for adequate parking entered into the purview of congregational sessions, building and grounds committees, and parish councils, the centrality of the automobile in American family life became clear in other ways as well. As noted earlier, in 1954 Rabbi Harold Friedman headed the Circuit Riding Rabbi Project, visiting Jewish families outside Wilmington. Roman Catholics began a Trailer Apostolate or Motor Mission in 1949, driving chapel trailers to rural portions of the region and the state. As fully equipped as a mobile home, though considerably more cramped, these motorized vehicles adapted new technologies to age-old purposes. In 1969 the Reverend John Todd began offering worship services at a drive-in theater in Wilmington as an outreach ministry of First Presbyterian Church. Proclaiming "no offering will be taken" and "come as you are" (a variation of the line used by the Reverend Robert Schuller when he began his Southern California ministry in 1955), Todd and his counterparts coupled mobility with informality in these modern American religious settings.[24]

The final technological innovation, climate control, may have been one of the most far-reaching for the region, as well as for its religious life. It was customary for some downtown Wilmington churches to suspend services in the summer, while others curtailed their activities. Those Wilmingtonians who could afford to do so left the city for cooler (and supposedly healthier) locales during the "dog days" of the long, hot summers. Any who remained sought shade from the sun and reduced all unnecessary activity in the face of the stifling humidity. Rocking chairs under covered porches, pitchers of tea, and hand-held palm fans were standard features of Cape Fear life in the summer. At worship services the ubiquitous church fan replaced the palm variety, and giving gentlemen permission to remove their jackets simply recognized the vicissitudes of the region's climate.

Electric fans, first available in 1882, could circulate air, but they did little to reduce the humidity. By 1922 Willis Haviland Carrier, "air-conditioning's Edison," had improved on his earlier designs and produced units that could circulate, cool, and dehumidify the air. Air-conditioning became familiar in government buildings, banks, offices, and movie theaters. With the development of efficient window units in the early 1950s, residential sales grew tremendously. Finally, during the early 1970s, heat pumps with reverse cycles for heating or air-conditioning made climate control a technological possibility for Americans.[25]

Religious institutions adopted air-conditioning more in line with their congregation's domestic settings than their occupational ones. The cost of installation and maintenance, particularly of central heating and air-conditioning, provided a deterrent for many. Likewise, pride in one's stamina and ability to withstand the temperature without flinching, coupled with resignation over the regional climate, initially slowed their acceptance. By the mid-1950s, however, several Wilmington churches, including First Presbyterian, First Baptist, St. Paul's Lutheran, and Fifth Avenue Methodist, had installed air-conditioning in their sanctuaries. Once in place, most parishioners could not imagine worshipping without "heat and air," and soon climate control became as much a fact of religious life as it was of commercial or residential life in the South.

War often transforms the home front as much as the battlefront. Certainly the domestic implications of World War II were extensive in the Cape Fear region, especially for Wilmington, Fayetteville, and their environs. Southeastern North Carolina was both a battleground and a training ground during the war. German submarines patrolled in its waters, and more Allied shipping and German U-boats were sunk off its coast than anywhere else in the Western Hemisphere. German prisoners of war were interned in camps in Wilmington, and local tradition claims that a German submarine surfaced and fired on the Ethyl-Dow Chemical Company operation in Kure Beach on July 24, 1943.[26]

Of the 15 million Americans who served in the armed forces, more than 2 million trained in North Carolina, most of them in bases in the southeastern part of the state. For example, Camp David and Camp Lejeune, just north in Onslow County; Fort Bragg, outside of Fayetteville in Cumberland County; the Coast Guard station at Southport in Brunswick County; and the U.S. Army Air Force base at Bluethenthal Field in Wilmington all trained or stationed military personnel. The massive civilian defense industry in Wilmington centered on the North Carolina Shipbuilding Company and was augmented by the Atlantic Coast Line Railroad. The docks built Liberty ships, producing 243 before their shutdown in 1946. The railroad provided the transportation backbone in the South Atlantic for personnel, cargo, and war materials. The influx of service personnel, military families, shipyard workers, friends and relatives of draftees, and other visitors skyrocketed Wilmington's population and strained public services and housing. Individuals rented out available rooms, and housing projects such as Lake Forest, Hillcrest, Maffitt Village, and Greenfield Terrace were constructed. Wilmington became a wartime boomtown the likes of which had not been seen since the heyday of the blockade runners.[27]

Churches and synagogues in the Port City responded to these challenges as best they could. New congregations emerged in the neighborhoods near the shipyards and railroads, while existing ones throughout the city received an influx of visitors with diverse denominational backgrounds. First Baptist, St. James Episcopal, St. Mary Roman Catholic, First Presbyterian, Church of the Covenant, Trinity Methodist, Fifth Avenue Methodist, Temple of Israel, B'nai Israel, St. Stephen African Methodist Episcopal, and St. Paul's Lutheran provided shelter, cots and blankets, refreshments, and other services for soldiers on weekend leaves, for the fourteen United Service Organizations (USO) centers in New Hanover County, and for others in need. Likewise, the practice of inviting visiting military personnel home for a meal after Sabbath services became a familiar expression of religious etiquette and southern hospitality.[28]

Fayetteville experienced many of the same social transformations as Wilmington, though without the same degree of economic revitalization. Defense officials and congressional leaders expanded the size and facilities of Fort Bragg. From 1940 to its wartime peak, the population of the fort increased from 5,400 to 159,000. Housing, social services, and public transportation in nearby Fayetteville were again insufficient for this human tidal wave. Churches, the Red Cross, the USO, and other agencies tried to help, but the scale of the challenge was daunting. Racial tensions never lay too far below the surface and sometimes erupted in incidents both in North Carolina and elsewhere in the nation.[29]

Scholars have demonstrated the impact of the war on the subsequent struggles of blacks and women for increased political and social equality. The development of both the civil rights movement and the feminist movement is much more complex than simply the experience of serving in the army or working in the industrial sector. Nevertheless, serving one's country either at home or abroad provided both an experiential and a rhetorical claim for increased rights for blacks and women in subsequent decades.[30]

Wilmington experienced the turbulence of the 1960s and 1970s, as did other cities in the South and throughout America. Racial segregation was a reality in Wilmington, as were efforts to replace it with guarantees of political equality and social justice. In Wilmington there were forces for reform in the courts, in community organizations, and on the streets. Hubert Eaton, a local black physician, successfully brought lawsuits that helped end segregation of the medical staffs at hospitals, the local public schools, and previously all-white institutions such as the Wilmington YMCA. The Reverend Edward Kirton of St. Mark's Episcopal Church, the Reverend B. H. Baskerville of Chestnut Street Presbyterian Church, and the Reverend J. Ray Butler of Ebenezer Baptist Church were active leaders in the black community. In December 1965 the desegregated Wilmington Ministerial Association elected Kirton as its president. He also served on the New Hanover Human Relations Commission.[31]

Popular protest movements, symbolized by the rioting in response to the Reverend Martin Luther King Jr.'s assassination on

April 4, 1968, and culminating in the violence and convictions of the so-called Wilmington Ten, dramatized the involvement of local churches in these issues. King had been scheduled to speak in Wilmington on April 4, 1968; however, he changed his itinerary in order to remain in Memphis and support the ongoing strike of sanitation workers there. Although a group of two hundred black students from Williston High School peacefully marched in memory of King, rioting soon broke out in Wilmington, as it did elsewhere in the nation. The mayor declared a state of emergency, and more than a thousand National Guard troops were ordered to Wilmington to maintain order.[32]

Issues of racial discrimination, police harassment, and social injustice remained alive within the black community. In the early weeks of 1971, in the context of public school integration, tensions mounted and fights broke out between black and white students attending New Hanover and John T. Hoggard high schools. On January 28 one hundred students met at Gregory Congregational Church to discuss plans for a boycott of classes. Gregory's white pastor, the Reverend Eugene Templeton, welcomed the students and supported their efforts to bring about change. On February 1 the Reverend Ben Chavis, a community organizer associated with the North Carolina–Virginia Commission for Racial Justice, an agency of the United Church of Christ, arrived in Wilmington. Over the next two weeks black and white students boycotted classes and gathered inside Gregory Congregational Church; several businesses and Southside Baptist Church suffered damage from firebombs; and violence, including white vigilantism, escalated. Both black and white citizens died during the rioting. On February 7 the mayor declared a curfew as seventy-five members of the North Carolina Highway Patrol and six hundred National Guardsmen patrolled Wilmington's streets.[33]

By Valentine's Day, civic calm if not brotherly love had settled on Wilmington, and the troops had departed—but not before photographs of rifle-toting National Guardsmen deployed on Wilmington streets and cordoning off Gregory Congregational Church had circulated worldwide. Gunshots had been fired at the church, and both Templeton and Chavis had received threats. Many Wilmingtonians, both black and white, recalled the events of 1898. Chavis not only helped organize the student protest but also assisted in the local formation of the First African Congregation of the Church of the Black Messiah. Affiliated with the Reverend Albert Cleague of Detroit, this group met on Castle Street. Chavis also gained notoriety as one of the Wilmington Ten, the eight high school students and two adults convicted on charges rising out of the riots and sentenced to prison for more than twenty years. Eventually their sentences were reduced, and in 1980 a federal appeals court overturned their convictions.[34]

Chavis went on to serve as executive director of the National Association for the Advancement of Colored People (NAACP), and Wilmingtonians again faced their legacy and experience of racial division. Some congregations tried to reach out, holding common services and social events, such as those between Gregory Congregational and the Unitarian Universalist Fellowship or between Pearsall Memorial Presbyterian Church and Chestnut Street Presbyterian Church. Nevertheless, for most Wilmingtonians, as King once observed, "the most segregated hour of Christian America is eleven o'clock on Sunday morning."[35]

During the second half of the nineteenth century, the first wave of the American feminist movement featured religious groups, including the Women's Christian Temperance Union, as well as political ones, such as the National American Woman Suffrage Association. After the passage in 1920 of the Nineteenth Amendment giving women the right to vote, the reemergent feminist movement of the 1960s pursued an expanded agenda. Building on Title VII of the 1964 Civil Rights Act, which banned discrimination in employment on the basis of race, color, religion, national origin, and sex, as well as Title IX of the 1972 Educational Amendment Act, which prohibited sex discrimination in institutions of higher education receiving federal assistance, feminists struggled to end sexual prejudice in all areas of public life.[36]

Within the life of twentieth-century American churches and synagogues, questions of female lay leadership, access to seminary education, and ordination to pastoral positions proved controversial. Women continued to manipulate and sometimes subvert the traditional gender prescriptions and their powerful conventions regarding women's status and place. But their demands to have their gifts for ministry recognized, to be placed in positions of lay leadership, and to be ordained to the ministry stepped outside this familiar framework of docile usefulness.

Working to achieve full discipleship within religious institutions paralleled the earlier struggle for full citizenship within the civic life of the nation. Could women have a voice and vote in church meetings? Could women serve on the vestry, the session, the parish council? Could they be ordained as clergy to preach and lead worship? Could they be admitted to all programs in seminaries? Arguments to restrict such opportunities along gender lines once again invoked biblical texts and historic experience.

Congregationalists, with their decentralized polity, had ordained a woman in 1853. Roughly a hundred years later, in 1956, the General Conference of the Methodist Church cut through the tangle of previous legislation and granted full ecclesiastical equality to Methodist women. In the same year the Presbyterian Church in the United States of America (Northern) accepted female ordination, and in 1964 its Southern counterpart followed suit. In the 1970s the Evangelical Lutheran Church in America and the Protestant Episcopal Church in the United States allowed women to be ordained as ministers. In 1972 Reform Judaism ordained its first female rabbi, and in 1985 Conservative Judaism did likewise. Some denominations, including Roman Catholics, the Eastern Orthodox, and the Mormons, continued to refuse to ordain women as pastors. In June 2000 the Southern Baptist Convention voted that the office of pastor should be restricted to males. Nevertheless, the convention stated that previously ordained women could remain in their positions.[37]

Trends in Wilmington followed national patterns. By 2000 women had served as pastors, co-pastors, or associate pastors in a number of denominations, including Disciples of Christ, Episcopal, Lutheran, Methodist, Metropolitan Community, Moravian, Pentecostal, Presbyterian, and Unitarian congregations. Their tenures could be isolated and frustrating, however, as they faced denominational inertia and cultural skepticism. As one scholar noted, winning ordination and full gender equality within the religious world was a process, not an event, and it would likely remain conflicted for some time.[38]

The fourth major social force that shaped contemporary religion in the Cape Fear region concerned changes in immigration policy and the effects of broader demographic trends. In 1924 Congress passed legislation that reduced the total number of immigrants and set up a nationality-based quota system using population figures from the 1890 census. This legislation, which was designed to discriminate against the more recent immigrants from eastern and southern Europe, as well as to tighten the exclusion of all Asian immigrants, remained the nation's basic immigration law until 1965. The Immigration and Nationality Act of 1965, however, eliminated the national origin quotas and established a preference system based on skills needed in the United States and on family reunification. The results, though probably unintended by the legislation's supporters, have been striking. In the 1950s Europeans accounted for over half of all immigrants; by the 1980s this number had dropped to just over 10 percent. During the same period, legal immigration by persons from Latin America and Asia grew dramatically. Latin Americans accounted for a fifth of all immigrants in the 1950s; by the 1980s that proportion had increased to over a third. Similarly, Asian immigrants rose from 6 percent in 1950 to nearly half of all immigrants by the 1980s.[39]

Comparison of the federal census figures from 1950 and 2000 for the Cape Fear region shows similar trends (see the accompanying table). The figures from the two censuses are not absolutely comparable, because the 1950 census reflects foreign-born persons older than twenty-one years of age, and the 2000 census simply in-

Foreign-Born Population in the Cape Fear Region, 1950 and 2000				
	1950		2000	
County	Number	Percentage	Number	Percentage
Brunswick	19,238	0.001	73,143	2.9
New Hanover	63,272	0.011	160,307	3.2
Pender	18,423	0.005	41,082	3.6
Bladen	29,703	0.001	32,278	2.3
Duplin	41,074	0.001	49,063	11.3
Columbus	50,621	0.002	54,749	1.4
Robeson	87,769	0.001	123,339	4.2
Sampson	49,780	0.001	60,161	7.1
Cumberland	96,006	0.008	302,963	5.3
Statewide	4,061,929	0.003	8,049,313	5.3

dicates foreign-born persons. Nevertheless, comparison of the two sets of numbers demonstrates the significant percentage increase in foreign-born individuals in the Cape Fear region during the intervening fifty years.

Other immigrants to southeastern North Carolina in the last quarter of the twentieth century were those who relocated or retired to the area. Economic growth in the region during this era caused many people to move because of job transfers or in pursuit of new occupations. Likewise, retirees from other regions of the country, particularly the Northeast, added to the demographic swelling. Popularly known as "snowbirds" for their seasonal retreat or year-round retirement to the coastal communities of the Cape Fear, these individuals added further variety to the area and its religious institutions. Bumper stickers stating "I Don't Care How You Did It Back North" suggested some of the tensions that locals and newly relocated individuals faced, but more often than not, the contributions of these internal immigrants were appreciated. The fact that Americans from elsewhere moved to the South not only attested to economic opportunity but also verified the widespread adoption of air-conditioning, which eased the region's sultry reputation and allowed local developers and chambers of commerce to highlight other more positive features.

Immigrants, whether foreign-born or internal, thus contributed to the religious makeup of the Cape Fear and added to many of its congregations. One set of statistics demonstrates this latter point. Between 1980 and 1990, while the population of Brunswick County increased 42 percent and that of New Hanover grew 16.2 percent, Brunswick's Roman Catholic population surged 270 percent, and that of New Hanover rose 102 percent. Such growth posed challenges for the region's religious institutions and helped shape their agenda for the future.[40]

Technology, the domestic impact of World War II, the civil rights and feminist movements, and immigration patterns were all long-term factors shaping Cape Fear religion in the last two-thirds of the twentieth century. In the first half of that century, two specific events occurred that helped determine the religious identity of Wilmington's downtown area. In 1925 fire destroyed the First Presbyterian Church, and in 1947 a blaze gutted Grace Methodist Church. Both these churches were familiar anchors in the downtown community, and both congregations considered moving to suburban locations. But in the end, they remained at their same spots and reaffirmed their commitment to the downtown core of Wilmington.

The Presbyterians commissioned Hobart Upjohn to design their new church, and the result was a building that subsequently served as a landmark in the skyline of the Port City. Grandson of Richard Upjohn, the English architect who had championed the Gothic Revival style in America in the mid-nineteenth century, Hobart Upjohn was a nationally known church architect. His previous projects in Wilmington were the 1924 Parish Hall at St. James Episcopal and the 1912 Episcopal Church of the Good Shepherd. Upjohn's other North Carolina projects included a new Chapel of the Cross in Chapel Hill, Temple Emanuel and First Presbyterian in Greensboro, and the library at North Carolina State University.[41]

Upjohn's design for First Presbyterian, Wilmington, felicitously incorporated three complementary styles: French Neo-Gothic for

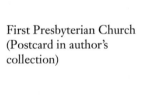

First Presbyterian Church
(Postcard in author's
collection)

the sanctuary, Norman Gothic in the chapel, and a half-timbered and stucco Tudor style for the education building. The exterior of the sanctuary included a massive tower topped by a spire that was visible for miles. The interior linked verticality and luminescence in a restrained but powerful architectural statement. Beneath a high vaulted ceiling, the long nave contained a center aisle and two side aisles. The orientation propelled the worshipper forward toward the lectern and raised pulpit on either side of the communion table. Here, word and sacrament were the focus of the service, enriched by the 1928 Ernest M. Skinner organ with its thirty-six ranks of pipes. German woodcutters carved the delicate reredos in the chancel capped by figures of John Calvin and John Knox. Stunning stained glass filled the sanctuary with light. George Owen Bonawit of New York City crafted the chancel's rose window, as well as the depictions of the twelve apostles in the chapel. These pieces were installed in 1928, the same year that the buildings were completed and dedicated. From 1954 through 1986 the distinguished Willet Stained Glass Studios of Philadelphia designed the other windows. The nave is fronted by the simplicity of the rose window and flanked by the magnificent depiction of biblical motifs in the clerestory, side aisle, and narthex windows. In the western facade a depiction of the triumphant Christ faces congregants as they exit.[42]

The building committee of Grace Methodist Church commissioned Harold E. Wagoner to design a Gothic replacement for their 1890 Romanesque Revival church. Wagoner had worked for the Methodist Bureau of Architecture before branching out on his own. Prominent in the field of Protestant church architecture, his Philadelphia-based firm designed more than five hundred religious buildings. Wagoner's sturdy stone design was augmented by beautiful stained glass windows also constructed by the Willet Studios of Philadelphia. This new church reopened on Christmas Eve 1950.[43]

While First Presbyterian and Grace Methodist continued in their downtown locations, other groups left. Three congregations, each with long experience in Wilmington, relocated to suburbia. As noted in the last chapter, Wilmington's first suburbs emerged in the early years of the twentieth century. They offered many advantages, and some congregations made the move. For example, in 1953 St. John Episcopal Church left its original site, where it had been built a century earlier, for a new Gothic-style home in the Forest Hills suburbs. Immanuel Presbyterian Church started in 1865 as a mission outreach in the southern area of the city. By 1891 it had grown in members, and the Boys' Brigade, a program for teenaged boys, met there as well. In 1922 the congregation built a handsome Neo-Federal church with tall columns, monumental portico, and pediment and capped with a steeple and spire. However, on September 1, 1967, the congregation was dissolved. Its members temporarily met for services at other Presbyterian churches, but by 1970 most of Immanuel's membership had joined the Windemere Presbyterian Church on the northeast edge of town. Finally, Southside Baptist Church, which had been founded in 1894, moved in 1972 to the southern outskirts of the city.[44]

In all three cases, members of these historic downtown churches voiced concerns about nighttime safety, changes in residential patterns, and deterioration of Wilmington's downtown core. Counterpoised to these perceived problems was the allure of the suburb, with its room for growth, parking lots, and recreational activities. The nexus between residential location and congregational identity had been strained in Wilmington for some time. By the 1960s and 1970s, urban renewal projects reconfigured city centers. Meanwhile, the attraction of suburban neighborhoods, the emergence of shopping malls outside the city core, and the widespread availability of automobiles, which made access to all this possible, established suburban patterns in Wilmington that paralleled those in Charlotte, Raleigh, and throughout the nation.

As population increased, further residential and commercial developments distinct from the downtown occurred. In the aftermath of the successful launch of the Carolina Place, Carolina Heights, and Winoca Terrace neighborhoods, real estate developers undertook new projects. With these new homes came new churches. A short distance east of the Winoca Terrace residences, though still sited on the Market Street axis, was Pearsall Memorial Presbyterian Church. Constructed in 1914 in a style that quoted elements of both English Gothic and Romanesque Revival, this church was a memorial to Rachel H. Pearsall, wife of Oscar Pearsall. Another congregation in the Winoca Terrace precinct was Temple Baptist. In 1923 the Baptists bought the Classical Revival building previously used by the Christian Science congregation before their move to Carolina Heights. In March 1952 this building burned, and the congregation rebuilt in a new location, this time in a Neo-Federal style.[45]

As the Market Street axis filled in, new suburbs expanded out toward the east and south. The road to Wrightsville Beach had once been paved with discarded oyster shells, but by the twentieth century it provided the path for trolley lines and later automobile routes. The Winter Park suburb grew up adjacent to this thoroughfare, and it soon supported three churches.

Begun as a Baptist mission Sunday school, Winter Park Baptist's original 1911 building was replaced in 1926. By 1956, as the congregation continued to grow, a remodeling of the sanctuary occurred, continuing the Classical form of the earlier building. The Classical Revival also shaped Winter Park Presbyterian Church, which likewise started as a Sunday school mission. It was formally organized as a congregation in 1913, and the first church was dedicated in March 1916. In January 1939 fire gutted this building, which had featured Ionic columns supporting a pedimented portico and topped with a cupola. Another building, in the same style and on the same location, emerged within ten months. Finally, the Winter Park Methodist Episcopal Church, South, organized in 1914, changed its name in 1916 to Wesley Memorial Methodist Church. Its first church was a simple brick building, but the widening of an adjacent street in 1956 necessitated a new structure. Designed in an English Gothic style, this house of worship hosted its first services by June of that year.[46]

Expansion east also included Airlie Gardens and Wrightsville Beach. Two distinctive churches were located in the Airlie area. Mount Lebanon Chapel was the oldest church still standing in 2000 in New Hanover County. Completed in 1835 on land donated by Dr. Thomas Wright to St. James Episcopal Church, Mount Lebanon Chapel served families who left Wilmington during the summer months to escape the heat. Rather than travel back to town along the shell-topped corduroy road, the Wrights built this mission chapel under the moss-draped cedar trees that provided the inspiration for the chapel's name. Another Episcopal church, St. Andrew's On-the-Sound, grew out of Mount Lebanon's congregation. Dedicated in 1924 and designed by Leslie Boney Sr., this was the only Spanish Colonial Mission–style church in the area. With characteristic red tile roofs, scalloped gable ends, and broad, unbroken exterior sur-

St. Andrew's On-the-Sound Episcopal Church (Photo by author)

faces of rough cement stucco, this architectural style was popular in California, Florida, and elsewhere during the 1920s.[47]

Wrightsville Beach is located on a narrow barrier island roughly ten miles east of Wilmington. For many years its only visitors were fishermen and others taking food from the Atlantic Ocean. The Carolina Yacht Club constructed the first substantial building in 1853, but it was not until 1888 that the Wilmington Seacoast Railroad provided transportation across the channel to the island. Eventually, the beachfront hosted residences, the Oceanic Hotel, and the Lumina Pavilion. With commercialization came more and more people. In 1970 the town's population was 1,593; in 2000 there were an additional 1,000 full-time residents, along with the summer influx of vacationers.[48]

Four congregations emerged to serve the island's residents and visitors. The Diocese of Raleigh purchased land for a Roman Catholic church in 1895 so that Catholics from Wilmington and elsewhere could attend services at the beach. Begun as a mission of St. Mary Catholic Church in Wilmington, the parishioners worshipped in a small frame house known as the Church of Our Lady Star of the Sea. Although priests from St. Mary initially officiated at services, in 1938 the diocese assigned the church a resident priest. In October 1944 a new brick building was dedicated, and the parish was renamed the Church of St. Therese the Little Flower. In 1976 another Catholic church, St. Mark, was established on the mainland as an outgrowth of St. Therese Parish. Its initial three hundred family members grew to more than two thousand families by 2000, by which time a spacious new sanctuary had been constructed in a modern style, with stained glass produced by a Trappist monastery and semicircular seating so that parishioners and the altar were visible to all. In 1907 the rector of St. James Episcopal and the pastor of First Presbyterian recognized that many of their parishioners moved to the beach for the summer. These two men collaborated on weekly summer worship and Sunday school meetings that would serve members of both congregations. In 1952 this church, known as the Little Chapel on the Boardwalk, affiliated with the Presbyterian denomination. The previous year, a new house of worship had been constructed using the plans of Charles H. Boney for a contemporary church design, one of the first in southeastern North Carolina. The edifice was embellished by stained glass windows from the Henry Willet Studios and murals by Claude Howell, a Wilmington artist whose work won national acclaim.[49]

St. Mark Roman Catholic Church (Postcard in author's collection)

Baptists and Methodists were also present at the beach. In 1947 Methodists began meeting in a youth center that was a summer ministry of other churches. In March 1954 the congregation of Wrightsville Methodist Church broke ground for a building, and on December 5, 1954, the first worship service in the new church took place. That same year, Wrightsville Beach Baptists dedicated their church. Begun as an outreach of Seagate Baptist Church, this congregation experienced growth at the end of the twentieth century, as did other denominations on the island.[50]

Dramatic suburban expansion took place south of the city. Sunset Park, for example, was a planned development first begun in 1912 but stalled by the Depression of the 1930s. Sunset Park's proximity to North Carolina shipbuilding facilities made it ideal as housing for shipyard and railroad workers beginning in the 1940s. Nearby Greenfield Lake offered recreational activities, and the subdivision's Colonial Revival and California Bungalow housing styles provided comfortable residences. Responding to the wartime civilian and military growth, Baptists and Methodists organized churches. Begun in a tent in 1942, Sunset Park Baptist Church completed a Neo-Federal style building in 1951. Sunset Park Methodist Church began holding services in February 1943. By October a new Colonial Revival sanctuary had been completed. With the closure of the shipyards in the aftermath of the war and the departure of the Atlantic Coast Line Railroad headquarters (with its thirty-five hundred employees) to Florida in 1960, several churches lost members. The boom and bust of economic growth and retrenchment was a national experience paralleled in Wilmington. Many congregations tried to hang on in the face of decaying facilities and dwindling memberships. Some made it, but others did not. In 1998 the Sunset Park Methodist congregation of 125 closed their church, with its seating for nearly 700, and merged with Grace United Methodist Church.[51]

Although the Sunset suburb suffered reverses, three other areas of the city experienced steady growth. The spoke of Oleander Drive, extending out from the city toward the east, contained several suburban churches. The Disciples of Christ Church in the Forest Hills neighborhood anchored one end; Oleander Methodist and the Seagate Community Chapel marked the boulevard's other terminus. The First Christian Church (Disciples of Christ) organized a congregation in Wilmington in 1907. The Disciples of Christ is a denomination founded in 1809 by Thomas and Alexander Campbell, men who hoped to heal the divisions within Christianity by restoring what they considered to be the essence of New Testament Christianity. In 1963, fifty years after its initial organization, the congregation purchased a lot on Oleander Drive and dedicated a new church. This structure, designed by the Wilmington architect Charles H. Boney, provided a lofty sanctuary in a contemporary design. For some observers, the angular A-frame of the building was a reminder of the stylistic vocabulary used by the German expressionist architects, such as Fritz Höger in his Hamburg office building, the Chilehaus; alternatively, it was reminiscent of the U.S. Air Force Academy Chapel, with its pointed verticality recalling traditional Gothic design but without the bulk of the original. Other observers simply saw symbolic hands extending in prayer in the structure's exterior lines. Whatever its provenance, the building made a striking statement of contemporary design in Wilmington's ecclesiastical inventory.[52]

Located on opposite sides of Oleander Drive, Oleander Methodist Church and Seagate Community Chapel both served the Seagate neighborhood. The Seagate Community Chapel was or-

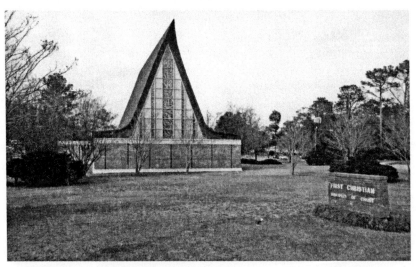

Disciples of Christ Church (Photo by author)

ganized in 1947 and completed a new brick building with a large steeple in 1958. The Oleander Methodist Church grew out of the Seagate Methodist Church. In 1957 Oleander Methodist dedicated a new house of worship and absorbed the older Seagate Methodist congregation.[53]

The Pine Valley subdivision, ringed by Shipyard Boulevard and College Road, is an almost stereotypical example of the bedroom communities that grew up in the South in the 1960s. One-story ranch-style brick homes are sited on curving streets named for Confederate military leaders. A private country club with golf and tennis facilities nests in the middle of the development. In 1956 Presbyterians erected the Cape Fear Presbyterian Church on Shipyard Boulevard. Designed by the local architectural firm of Ballard, McKim, and Sawyer, the sanctuary is striking for its parabolic shape and separated spire. Farther up the same road, three other churches rest together. In July 1961 a Baptist congregation opened its first sanctuary. As its membership grew, Pine Valley Baptist Church built a new contemporary sanctuary in 1975. In November 1961 Pine Valley United Methodist Church constructed its first building. Paralleling their Baptist neighbor's growth, the Methodists erected a new house of worship in 1974. Unlike other Wilmington churches, the Methodists' building exhibited tentlike panels that, in their sculpted and interlocked finish, reminded one of the geodesic domes popularized by R. Buckminster Fuller. Finally, the Pine Valley Church of God, affiliated with the Church of God (Cleveland, Tennessee), was a Holiness congregation. First organized in Wilmington in 1929, this congregation completed its Pine Valley structure in 1971.[54]

On the College Road perimeter, a number of congregations relocated, and new congregations planted themselves. Although Lutherans had been represented by the St. Paul's and St. Matthew's congregations since the nineteenth century, in 1966 another group, Messiah Lutheran Church, Missouri Synod, began to meet. Gathering first in a home and then in a storefront, the congregation purchased land on College Road in 1970 and completed their sanctuary that year. This simple building was renovated but proved too small for the congregation. In 1999 a handsome new sanctuary was finished. Not far from the Lutherans, the congregation of Pine Valley Church of Christ built. Organized in the 1930s, this congregation moved to the Pine Valley site in 1976; its sister congregation, the Central Church of Christ, also began in 1976.[55]

Farther south along College Road, Moravian and Adventist congregations were formed. Although the Moravians' roots in North Carolina extend back to the 1750s and the founding of the Wachovia settlement (present-day Winston-Salem), Moravian extension into eastern North Carolina was slow. In 1974 Lewis Swaim, director of the Southern Province's Board of Homeland Missions, visited those Moravians living in Wilmington and its environs. Subsequently, regular meetings took place in private homes until 1978, when Swaim became the organizing pastor for Covenant Moravian Church in Wilmington. By December of the following year a temporary sanctuary had been erected, followed in 1982 by the dedication of a sturdy new sanctuary in a contemporary design. Moravian traditions such as Advent stars, Moravian cookies and candle tea, and Christmas Love feasts were introduced into Wilmington's religious life by this congregation. Beyond these folkways, in 2000 this congregation was the largest Moravian church east of Raleigh and the only one in the Cape Fear. Another noteworthy aspect of Covenant's history was the installation of the Reverend Carol Foltz as the interim pastor of the church in 1989. When she was installed as the regular pastor in 1990, she was the first woman to be the full-time pastor of a Moravian church in the Southern Province.[56]

The United Advent Christian Church grew out of a 1970 merger of two other Wilmington Adventist congregations. Although there were other autonomous Adventist groups, such as the Seventh-Day Adventists, in southeastern North Carolina, this congregation was affiliated with the Advent Christian General Conference of America, with headquarters in Charlotte, North Carolina. The terms of the merger included provisions for a new church, and in 1974 the building dedication took place.[57]

In the opposite direction on College Road, just north of the Pine Valley subdivision, other congregations built. The first meetinghouse of the Church of Jesus Christ of Latter-day Saints, popularly known as the Mormons, was completed in 1918. As early as 1911 members held meetings in their homes. Even earlier, in 1900, a debate on the Mormon faith between Mormon leaders and two Wilmington Protestant pastors took place before a crowd of three hundred eager listeners in Hampstead. A second meetinghouse was begun at Market and Borden streets in 1930 but was not dedicated until 1950. Construction of the meetinghouse located on College Road began in October 1964 and was completed in 1967. This building reflected the Standard Plan design employed by the Church Building Committee and encompassed the chapel, classrooms, cultural hall, and offices. Images of Mormons range from nineteenth-century polygamists to clean-cut twentieth-century missionaries, but this denomination is America's largest homegrown religion. Founded by its martyr-prophet Joseph Smith and led to Utah by Brigham Young, the Mormon religion claimed 11 million members worldwide in 2000. That same year in Wilmington, two congregations (called wards) incorporating the Mormon population from the city and the surrounding area assembled separately at the College Road meetinghouse.[58]

Although several prominent Baptist congregations were affiliated with the Southern Baptist Convention, Grace Baptist Church on College Road remained independent. Started in 1953 by Ray and Opal Norland, the church moved to one location on College Road in 1959 and then to another larger site on the same avenue in 1978. In 1969 the church started the Wilmington Christian Academy as a private school, eventually spanning kindergarten through twelfth grade. Pentecostal congregations were also present in the suburbs. Spring Valley Pentecostal Free Will Baptist Church, founded in Wilmington in 1900, moved several times before settling at its College Road location. Significantly, the Reverend Ruth Ketchum was the church's first female pastor in the early 1940s. The Pentecostals of Wilmington congregation likewise moved about before building on the western perimeter of Pine Valley by 2000. Finally, the New Harbour Foursquare Gospel Church, located farther out, belonged to the denomination founded in 1923 by Aimee Semple McPherson.[59]

Pentecostal-Holiness traditions, with their roots in the Azusa Street revivals of the early twentieth century, include speaking in tongues, a literal interpretation of the Bible, and an expressive style of worship. In addition to familiar organ and choir offerings, these worship services often feature drums, tambourines, and fast-paced songs. Many congregations are racially integrated, or at least would be considered so by prevailing southern standards. In the Cape Fear region the Pentecostals' houses of worship ranged from storefronts to substantial tabernacles with state-of-the-art technology. Thus, the Pentecostals and, in a larger sense, the revivalist tradition can be found in southeastern North Carolina. In 1965, for example, Billy Graham, the well-known evangelist, led a two-week revival in Wilmington. Coordinating with other churches in town, Graham's crusade staff held the event in the local high school gymnasium. When Graham returned to Wilmington thirty years later, he and his son, Franklin, invited the more than seven thousand persons filling the university coliseum to respond to his invitation for repentance. Although Graham is recognized for his effective use of technology, especially television, and his well-planned pre- and post-crusade organization, other revivalists continued the earlier tradition of setting up street-corner tents with little prior publicity and offering old-fashioned preaching and promises of healing, forgiveness, and salvation.[60]

Just as Billy Graham was familiar in the late twentieth century, Dwight L. Moody and Sam P. Jones were legends in revival circles in their own eras. In 1893, just six years before his death, Moody came to Wilmington, where, in front of crowds reportedly in the thousands, he led a weeklong series of meetings. In his nightly sermons he fervently called on his audience to repent and accept Jesus as their savior. In line with the growing fundamentalist movement of his day, Moody insisted on a literal interpretation of the Bible, including that Jonah had actually been swallowed by a whale and survived. Though he shied away from commentary on topical issues, Moody did commend the YMCA movement, with which he had worked, and stated that America needed a revitalization of family piety in which wives would once again obey their husbands.[61]

Three years before Moody's visit, Sam Jones—the man many called the "Moody of the South"—preached in Wilmington. Jones was a reformed alcoholic, and he made a reputation as a blunt, forceful speaker. During his Wilmington revival, which reportedly drew crowds of six thousand persons, Jones lived up to his reputation. After insisting that all in attendance contribute to the offering that was taken up in each service, Jones declared, "the gospel of Jesus ought to have heat and fire. God give us heat to burn out sin in Wilmington." Going on to denounce dancing, selling liquor, and drinking any form of alcohol, Jones bellowed, "the wages of sin is death . . . the virus of sin will kill your soul . . . it is only a question of time." In classic revivalist fashion he then closed with the invitation to renounce sin and accept Jesus, the "one remedy for a sinful soul."[62]

Moody and Jones were leaders among conservatives in the late-nineteenth-century Third Great Awakening. Their modernist opponents criticized them and other fundamentalists for their individualistic approach to problems, their avoidance of pressing racial and social injustice, and their appeal to the middle class. Ironically, some of these same charges were leveled at those suburban churches that developed in the mid-twentieth century. Decrying the "suburban captivity of the church," religious activists and ivory-towered scholars alike pointed to the isolation of suburban existence as these churches disengaged from the city center and focused their energies on membership growth. Insisting that the suburban church served to crystallize the social identity of middle-class residential groups, these critics saw much amiss in the seemingly successful story of suburban church expansion. Opportunities for outreach to an increasingly mobile population simply masked the exclusion of those who were financially unable to move to the suburbs. Coffee-hour hospitality really functioned to reinforce the social and economic homogeneity of the congregations, while attention to tee times on the golf course and positions in restaurant buffet lines kept sermons abbreviated and restrained efforts to help the needy and feed the hungry. Race continued to play a role; the suburban churches were overwhelmingly white, while the churches of the black community remained downtown. Thus, although not all these charges fit the Wilmington suburban experience, enough of them did to make at least some pastors and congregations aware of the criticisms that their location and development provoked.[63]

It is not surprising that as many white congregations relocated or began anew in the suburbs, the black religious community evolved too. The foundation of the black religious community continued to be provided by flagship congregations such as St. Stephen African Methodist Episcopal (AME), St. Luke AME Zion, First Baptist, Chestnut Street Presbyterian, St. Mark's Episcopal, and Gregory Congregational. Additional Baptist, AME, and AME Zion congregations sprang up by the mid-twentieth century. Central Baptist Church began in 1883 when the Reverend L. T. Christmas traveled to Wilmington to preach. After an 1887 fire destroyed this congregation's meetinghouse, they began construction on a Gothic Revival church with high pitched gables and arched stained glass windows. The origin of Ebenezer Missionary Baptist Church was an exodus out of First African Baptist in 1868. Initially meeting in a simple frame building, the congregation built a new sanctuary, designed by Wilmington craftsman James F. Post, in 1896. The congregation occupied a series of buildings until its last move in 1998. Shiloh Missionary Baptist Church began in 1870 when a group left Ebenezer Missionary Baptist. The 1914 Gothic Revival house of worship was destroyed by fire in 1955, and the congregation rebuilt.[64]

Three AME and two AME Zion congregations also began in this era. In 1980 Mount Olive AME Church celebrated its centennial anniversary. Initially meeting in the homes of its members, the congregation soon built a church. After that building burned in 1907, construction of a new house of worship started. Mount Zion AME began in 1870. By 1944, several buildings had served this congregation. The third AME congregation was St. Phillip, founded in 1921. The beginnings of St. Andrew AME Zion church date to home meetings in 1914, from which a congregation emerged. Similarly, Warner Temple AME Zion began in 1919. Maintaining their downtown locations, all these congregations explored opportunities for social ministries dealing with education, poverty, and health as supplements to their worship and pastoral programs.[65]

Independent religious groups were also present; some were formally affiliated with the Pentecostal-Holiness tradition, and others simply shared that tradition's emotional style of worship and acceptance of charismatic gifts. Although the New Covenant Holiness Church dated back to the start of the twentieth century, most of these groups arose since the 1960s. The Greater Love Chapel Church of God in Christ (1968), the Macedonia Fire Baptized Holiness Church of God in the Americas (1970), the Soul Saving Station (1977), and the Restoration Word of Faith Church (1998) are just a sampling of this tradition. Regardless of whether they adapted storefronts or built substantial edifices, these groups added to the twentieth-century variety of Wilmington's religious tapestry.[66]

One of the most fascinating examples of independent religious traditions in the region was the congregation of the United House of Prayer for All People and its founder, Bishop Charles M. ("Sweet Daddy") Grace. Born in the Cape Verde Islands in 1881, Grace im-

Soul Saving Station (Photo by author)

migrated to the United States around 1903. Taking the title of bishop, Grace established his first House of Prayer in West Wareham, Massachusetts, in 1924. Beginning the next year he started tent preaching but eventually organized Houses of Prayer from Florida to New York. Georgia and the Carolinas contained the greatest number of houses, and the one in Charlotte, North Carolina, was the largest single black church structure in the city in the 1960s. In 1947 the Charlotte celebration of the Twenty-first Grace Holy Convocation Week climaxed with twenty-five thousand people witnessing the Daddy Grace Parade; participants included the Grace Concert Band from Washington, D.C., Grace Flower Girls, Grace Queens, Grace Soul Hunters, Grace Armor Bearers, and assorted others. When Grace died in 1960, Elder Walter McCollough assumed leadership of the organization.[67]

As early as 1946 Bishop Grace built a tabernacle on Dawson Street in Wilmington. By the 1990s this structure had been replaced by a spacious, well-equipped house of worship. With flowing hair, two-inch fingernails, and a cutaway coat, Grace was a flamboyant presence whose personality stamped his organization. Although his headquarters were in Washington, D.C., Grace maintained a residence in Wilmington on South Seventh Street. In April 1952 Dr. Hubert Eaton, the civil rights activist, visited Grace at his home, seeking his support for Eaton's campaign for a seat on the local school board. Bishop Grace was eating lunch and invited Eaton to join him. Eaton likened the scene to a medieval banquet in which serving attendants surrounded Grace. "I marveled at the showmanship of this man," Eaton wrote, and other commentators both local and national agreed in this assessment.[68]

Though not exclusively African American denominations, both the Seventh-Day Adventists and the Jehovah's Witnesses have had a high percentage of black members in their Wilmington congregations. Dating from 1911, Ephesus Seventh-Day Adventist Church followed the custom of many black Adventist congregations by taking the name of the first of the seven churches listed in the book of Revelation. Constructed in 1956, its sanctuary was a familiar sight in its Castle Street neighborhood. In the 1930s members of the Jehovah's Witness faith met in one another's Wilmington homes. By 1970 two Kingdom Halls had been built, and several congregations had formed. Known for their door-to-door proselytizing and literature distribution, the Jehovah's Witnesses have remained active in Wilmington.[69]

Another dimension of Wilmington's black religious community in the late twentieth century was the growing presence of Islam. As noted in chapter 4, Muslims were part of the slave population in America, and the person of Omar Ibn Said documented their antebellum presence in the Cape Fear region.

Evidence for the existence of the Muslim faith in twentieth-century southeastern North Carolina is much easier to find. In the late 1950s and early 1960s individuals from Durham traveled to Wilmington and helped establish a fledgling congregation that met in private residences. In 1973 Abdul Rahman Shareef, born in Brooklyn, New York, but raised in Wilmington, converted to Islam. Shareef was initially influenced by Malcolm X, as were many other black Americans, and he served in the Fruit of Islam under the direction of Elijah Muhammad. In 1975, upon the death of Muhammad, his son and successor, Warith Deen Mohammed, returned to a more orthodox Islamic faith. Emphasizing the universal appeal of Islam as well as its Five Pillars—the declaration of faith, prayer, fasting, giving alms, and pilgrimage—W. D. Mohammed moved the center of American Islam closer to traditional Sunni patterns. By the early 1980s Shareef had assumed the position of imam, or leader, for a Wilmington congregation. The small group met in a storefront building on Castle Street and affiliated with W. D. Mohammed's Muslim American Society. As the congregation grew in the 1990s, it drew not only African Americans but also persons of Pakistani, Turkish, Jordanian, Lebanese, and Palestinian descent. Such a variety of nationalities was in line with broader trends that indicated that American Muslims attending services were 29 percent Indo-Pakistani, 29 percent African American, 21 percent Arab, and the remainder a number of other backgrounds.[70]

The Wilmington mosque, first called Masjid Mohammed and later renamed Tauheed Islamic Center to emphasize the unity of Allah, provided information about Islam through public events and lectures to the wider Wilmington community. Beyond that, in 1993 a Pakistani businessman opened the Halal Meat and Food Corporation in Bladenboro in rural Bladen County. Certified to prepare meat according to strict Muslim standards, this venture underscored the Muslim presence in the Cape Fear and the region's commercial ties with national and international markets.[71]

The visibility of Muslims in Wilmington by the year 2000 was further attested to in another congregation. Although W. D. Mohammed broke with his father's teachings in 1975, other black Muslims remained faithful to them. Revived in 1978 by minister Louis Farrakhan, the Nation of Islam retained Elijah Muhammad's beliefs in the racial basis of Islam and his own status as the final prophet. Such views differentiated the Nation of Islam from mainstream Muslims, just as the former organized itself separately. Developing a congregation and study group in Wilmington in the early 1990s, the Nation of Islam was also visible in the black community, with its well-dressed, bow-tied salesmen selling copies of *Muhammad Speaks* and preaching self-improvement and self-reliance. Significantly, in 2000 Farrakhan pledged to reconcile with his longtime rival Mohammed, although the Wilmington Muslim congregations remained separate.[72]

Parallel developments took place in Fayetteville's black community. In addition to numerous Missionary, Independent, and Southern Baptists as well as AME Zion churches, there were congregations such as the Deliverance Church of Jesus Christ Apostolic, the Door of Faith Church, the God Be Glorified Ministries, and the Glad Tidings Tabernacle Non Denominational Church. A score of Pentecostal-Holiness congregations, including the North Carolina headquarters of the Pentecostal-Holiness Church, resided in Fayetteville, as did half a dozen Jehovah's Witness congregations. The Islamic congregation Masjid Omar Ibn Sayyid commemorated the region's antebellum Muslim heritage and provided a home for its present-day adherents.

A striking variation on this theme of religion and race occurred in the Middle Cape Fear. The Waccamaw Siouans of Columbus County and the Lumbee Indians of Robeson County both attested to the continuing presence of Native Americans in the Cape Fear. Although some consider the ancestry of the Waccamaw Siouans conflicted, late-twentieth-century powwows, providing fellowship with kin and other Indians, served as markers for Indian identity among the Waccamaw. Tribal parades with carloads of dignitaries and other guests, dance contests with participants in full regalia, and plenty of home-cooked food were all part of the experience. These rituals extended back centuries, invoking the experiences of feasting and fellowship celebrated by prehistoric Native Americans along the Cape Fear River as discussed in chapter 1. As a means of reaffirming cultural identity, the powwow represented the paradox of introducing the new (technology, pan-tribal intermingling) while seeking to reinforce local practices and old traditions. The powwow dramatized the challenge for Native Americans of walking in two worlds—the Indian world and "the world of suits and ties."[73]

Another arena for mixing the new and the old was the practice of Native American Christianity. Scholars have convincingly shown a spectrum of relationships between Christianity and Native American religious traditions, from complete acceptance of Christianity by native peoples through syncretic blending of traditions to rejection of Christian practices and attempts to revitalize native ones. Though nominally a secular event, the Waccamaw powwow opened with a Christian prayer, and Christian hymns made up part of the singing program. Pricilla Jacobs, a leader in the tribe who eventually served as chief, was also a part-time preacher. Most Waccamaw Siouans worshipped at the local Baptist churches in the area. In this respect they mirrored many of their rural Columbus County neighbors. However, with a higher percentage of Native Americans in

2000 in Columbus County (3.1 percent) than in the state on average (1.2 percent), some church memberships had a Native American
majority and thus the potential for a Native Christianity acknowledging contemporary Indian values and struggles.[74]

Adjacent Robeson County had an even larger native population
(38 percent in 2000), composed largely of Lumbee Indians. Dif-
fering accounts trace the Lumbees back to Walter Raleigh's Lost
Colony of 1587, to eastern Siouan peoples, or to an amalgamation
of tribes from the geographical area. Given different names over the
years, in 1953 the tribe adopted the designation Lumbee Indians of
North Carolina, in honor of the Lumber River that flows through
Robeson County. Episodes such as the Lowrie War of 1864–1874
and the routing of the Ku Klux Klan in 1958 demonstrated the
tribe's involvement in the larger issues of the region. Similarly,
Lumbee participation in the "Year of the Native American" in conjunction with North Carolina's four hundredth anniversary signaled
their recognition as part of North Carolina's native population. It
also reminded North Carolinians of the triracial (white, black, red)
experience in many areas of the state and the South.[75]

Baptists and Methodists were the largest denominations in Lum-
beeland, although there were also Presbyterian, Lutheran, Episcopalian, Roman Catholic, Holiness, and Mormon congregations. In
1880 Lumbee Baptists organized a congregation at Burnt Swamp,
which later evolved into the Burnt Swamp Association; by 1973
this circuit included six thousand members in forty-two churches.
Methodists also date their beginnings in this area to the late nineteenth century. In 1900 a schism occurred within the local Methodist churches. The Reverend Henry Lowry led a group of Lumbees
out of the Methodist Church to form an all-Indian conference that
took the name Holiness Methodist Church of the Lumber River.
The Reverend William Luther Moore assumed leadership of the
remaining churches in the United Methodist Church. Lowry and
his descendants led the Holiness Methodists for sixty-two years, and
by 1974 their organization had roughly sixteen hundred members in
seven churches.[76]

Prospect United Methodist Church, founded by 1870, served
a large congregation (six hundred in 1975) of Native Americans. In
1975 there were eighteen hundred Lumbee members in the United
Methodist Church and nine churches in addition to Prospect in the

area. Other institutional developments took place as well. In the late 1960s the United Methodist Church began the Robeson County Church and Community Center under the direction of the Reverend Robert L. Mangum. By the 1990s the Native American Larger Parish Ministry and the Southeastern Jurisdictional Association for Native American Ministries had been organized. Seven Lumbees had been ordained as Methodist clergy, and images of the pipe and the sacred circle had been incorporated into the cross and flame of Methodist iconography in local Lumbee churches.[77]

The hybridity evident in Native Christianity can also be seen in contexts where Christianity met Asian religions. In the aftermath of the war in Southeast Asia and the Immigration and Nationality Act of 1965, Fayetteville became one of the most ethnically diverse cities in North Carolina. The International Folk Festival celebrated this reality and included Koreans, Vietnamese, Filipinos, Okinawans, and other participants. The 2,653 Asians counted in Fayetteville's 2000 census represented the largest concentration of Asians in North Carolina outside of the Piedmont. Churches, such as the Korean Baptist Church, the Korean Central Baptist Church, the Fayetteville Korean United Methodist Church, the Korean Presbyterian Church (Presbyterian Church USA), and the Church of Korea Bethel (Presbyterian Church in America), as well as the Chinese Baptist Mission, mirrored mainstream Protestant denominational fractures as much as missionary development among Asian Americans. Beyond that, singing hymns, reciting prayers, listening to sermons, and fellowshipping at meals in the cadences and languages of the old country led to the emergence of other creole combinations.[78]

In Wilmington a related but divergent pattern emerged. For example, Chinese-language worship services began at Pine Valley Baptist Church in 1996, and Chinese Bible study took place at Calvary Baptist Church. Korean Baptists had their own congregation, and Korean Presbyterians began worshipping separately at Winter Park Presbyterian Church in February 1999; in February 2003 they moved into their own church facility. Asian Christianity, particularly of the Protestant variety, was well represented in the Port City.[79]

Wilmington and the Lower Cape Fear also contained a number of congregations of adherents to historic Asian religions. The phrase *Asian religions* is a term of convenience that lumps together a variety of ethnic groups as well as complex religious traditions. Chinese, Japanese, Indians, Koreans, Filipinos, Laotians, Thais, Cambodians, and Vietnamese made up the 682 Asians captured in Wilmington's 2000 census. And although it would be wrong to assume that all immigrants are members of religious organizations, religion has played an important role in immigrant communities in the past as a source of moral support and cultural identity. Consequently, Hinduism and representatives of major schools of Buddhism are both present in the Lower Cape Fear.

In October 1994 Wilmington had its first India Festival, hosted by the city's Indian community of roughly fifty families. Expressing the diversity of the Indian culture, the festival offered exhibits of crafts, demonstrations of traditional dances, and samples of Indian cuisine. Many of these families had come to Wilmington since 1973 and found employment in medicine, communications, computer technology, and other professions. The closest Hindu temple is more than a hundred miles away in Raleigh, but this poses no insuperable obstacles, as families can have shrines in their own homes. Life-cycle rites around birth, puberty, and death and seasonal rituals such as Navaratri, Holi, and the New Year play important roles in Hindu religious life. So too does the discipline of individual meditation technique. Divali, the celebration of good over evil, is associated with the goddess Lakshmi and is another widely recognized occasion. In the sacred geography of India, rivers are important, and the Ganges is the archetype. The confluence of more than one river, such as the juncture of the Ganges, Yamuna, and Sarasvati rivers, is especially significant. Appreciation for that sacred geography can even extend to recognition of the union of the two branches of the Cape Fear River at Wilmington. And since it is believed that the Ganges extends to all the rivers of the world, the Cape Fear River is auspicious as well.[80]

The Buddhist experience in Wilmington and the Cape Fear provides a microcosm of the many issues confronting contemporary American Buddhism. Buddhism is divided into three major forms—Mahayana, Theravada, and Vajrayana—and a 2000 survey found examples of all three among the thirty-three Buddhist temples and centers located in North Carolina. Although Jack Kerouac sketched part of *Dharma Bums* (1959) at his Rocky Mount, North Carolina, home and meditated outdoors while sitting between two pine trees, the growth of national and North Carolina Buddhism took place mainly from the late 1960s onward.[81]

As a university town, Wilmington has been home to many informal study groups and workshops. The Wilmington Zen Group was one example. Begun in 2000, the group met weekly to practice *zazen* (sitting meditation) interspersed with periods of *kinhin* (walking meditation). The Wilmington community maintained close ties with the Chapel Hill Zen Center, whose abbess, Taitaku Pat Phelan Sensei, led workshops for the Port City association. Zen is part of the Mahayana tradition, as is the Nichiren Buddhist movement. Named for a thirteenth-century Japanese Buddhist reformer, Nichiren organized in America in the 1960s and is known for its chanting of the Lotus Sutra. In 1991 the movement divided between the Nichiren Soshu Temple, led by priests, and Soka Gakkai International–USA, which is a lay movement. Both Fayetteville and Wilmington had Sokka Gakkai chapters.[82]

Formal prostrations and meditation were part of the twice-weekly services of the Cape Fear Tibetan Buddhism Study Group established in 2000. Tibetan Buddhism belongs to the Vajrayana school and is familiar in contemporary American culture through the person of the Dalai Lama, Tibet's political and spiritual leader, and various celebrities who have taken up the cause of Tibetan freedom from Chinese occupation. The recitation of mantras and the construction of mandalas are part of Tibetan practice, as is the study of religious texts.[83]

The Zen, Sokka Gakkai, and Tibetan Buddhist groups met in private homes or rented storefront space. Their local congregations were predominantly non-Asian converts augmented by sympathizers and what one scholar called "nightstand Buddhists," for their unaffiliated and eclectic interests. The relative invisibility of these congregations enabled religious options without cultural confrontation with the larger society. Their spiritual and spatial neighbors may be ignorant of their presence, and their longevity in their present form, like other such informal organizations, may be limited.[84]

The Theravada experience presents a very different situation. In June 1988 twenty-seven acres of land in Bolivia, North Carolina, a town in Brunswick County just south of Wilmington, were incorporated for a Theravada Thai temple, Wat Carolina Buddhajakra Vanaram. Scholars estimate that one-half to three-quarters of a million ethnic Asian Theravada Buddhists lived in the United States in 1990. The first Theravada temple was constructed in 1966, but most of the roughly 150 temples in the United States in existence in 1990 were begun after 1970. In 2000 the Wat Carolina temple was still the only Theravada temple between Washington, D.C., and Atlanta.[85]

This temple displayed many of the characteristics of its Theravada Thai heritage. The three monks sent from Thailand to Wat Carolina were members of the Dhammayuttika monastic lineage, an order closely tied to the monarchy in Thailand. Mongkut, who upon assuming the royal throne became Rama IV (1851–1868), and his son Chulalongkorn, Rama V (1868–1910), initiated reforms of the Thai Theravada monastic community, including more serious study of scripture, an emphasis on meditation, and renewed monastic discipline. The Dhammayuttika order incorporated these changes. Monks are prohibited from contact with women, and their personal possessions include only their robes, a food bowl, a razor for shaving, and a sewing needle for the repair of clothes. The abbot of Wat Carolina, Phrakru Buddamonpricha, was born in Thailand in 1940. After serving as an elementary school teacher for several years, he began his training as a Theravada monk. His daily routine at Wat Carolina began around 6:00 A.M. with chanting and meditation. He took his one daily meal at 11:00; the food was prepared by the lay community, for active lay support of monks has always characterized Thai Buddhism. Upon the conclusion of the meal, the abbot thanked and blessed those who had prepared his food and then spent the remainder of the day studying, meditating, and performing chores.[86]

Sounthone Hemvong, the abbot's brother and a resident of Wilmington since 1976, purchased and donated the land for the monastery. On a visit to North Carolina in 1986, Phrakru Buddamonpricha was struck by the serenity and natural beauty of the site and its suitability for a facility to serve the Buddhist population. He submitted a proposal for the temple and received authorization from Thailand. At the groundbreaking ceremony on July 2, 1989, the Most Venerable Chao Khun Phra Yanavarodom, secretary-general of the Dhammayuttika order, presided. He presented a gift of three wooden pillars, symbolic of the foundation of the building, from Somdej Phra Nyanasamvara Somdej Phrasangharaja, the supreme patriarch of Thailand and the principal sponsor and honorary chairman of the Wat Carolina building program.[87]

In 2000 a small farmhouse located on the property still contained the monk's sleeping and eating space as well as an altar. The 10,700-square-foot multipurpose complex that was begun in 1989 was just part of a larger building program. One section of the finished building housed a meditation area adjacent to an altar decorated with statues of the Buddha, arrangements of lotus flowers, tiers of candles, and containers of incense sticks. Wat Carolina embodied many of the ideals of Buddhist monastic architecture. The monastery lay outside the city but was not completely isolated. The surrounding site was full of trees and had a good supply of water. This retreat (*Vanaram* means "forest retreat" in Thai) could accommodate both resident monks and lay visitors and served as an educational center as well as a worship space. The structure was built in a traditional Thai architectural style; resting on heavy pilings, it was topped with telescoping red tile roofs and finished with sharply peeked gables and flared cornices. With its contrastive pale yellow exterior walls, the structure provided a sharp break with its surrounding built environment.[88]

Wat Carolina Buddhajakra Vanaram (Photo by author)

The rhythms of ritual life at Wat Carolina followed the lunar calendar but ranged from daily monastic prayer and meditation through weekly services to annual celebrations. Four yearly festivals shape the Theravada liturgical calendar. Songkhran is the lunar New Year, and Visakha Pucha commemorates three episodes in the life of the Buddha. Kathin and Loi Kratong mark the end of the rainy season in Thailand and the confinement of the monks. Finally, Magha Pucha remembers an assembly of the Buddha and 1,250 of his disciples. In these events, which were attended by as many as 500 persons from all over the eastern seaboard as well as the Cape Fear, social function joined religious purposes. Reunion of friends and families, enjoyment of ethnic cuisines, and development of new relationships would match any Baptist congregation's homecoming. Similarly, experiencing purification, listening to sermons ("dharma talks"), and making offerings signified the spiritual efforts undertaken by the laity.[89]

The annual rites of the liturgical calendar of Wat Carolina illustrate many of the concerns facing contemporary American Buddhism. Adaptations to the American religious context pose some of these issues. For example, both annual events and weekly services take place on Sunday, in line with the Christian day of rest that allows American Buddhists freedom from work as well. Moreover, whereas the Theravada tradition is markedly hierarchical, with laypersons supportive of but always subservient to the monastic orders, the traditional power of the laity in American religious history has begun to seep into Buddhist experience. Thus, in the face of nonexistent or inadequate patronage from the patriarchy or state agency back home, American Buddhists have undertaken their own lay-led fund-raising efforts. They have begun to form boards of trustees and to seek legal advice concerning incorporation and achievement of tax-exempt status. Finally, whatever its position in the old country, Buddhism in America operates within a voluntaristic context. Such circumstances can result in what one scholar called "parallel congregations," with one group of ethnic Asian cradle Buddhists and another group of Euro-American converts coexisting separately within the same congregation. At Wat Carolina this has not occurred. The ethnic cradle Buddhists outnumber the converts, but English translations are always provided for those portions of the services conducted or written in Thai.[90]

Beyond these issues of institutional formation and sociological identity, the challenge of cultural encounters also loomed. Whereas the Zen and Sokka Gakkai groups were nearly invisible, the Theravada presence in the middle of the Bible Belt was architecturally and ritually unmistakable. In August 1988 the next-door neighbors of Wat Carolina at Antioch Baptist Church were wary. Unfamiliar with the doctrines or practices of Buddhism and mindful of the popular media's fascination with so-called cults, these Brunswick Baptists were skeptical, if not frightened, by the approach of this unknown body. By July of the next year, however, fears had abated, and southern hospitality provided a foundation for religious pluralism. At the groundbreaking ceremony in July 1989, the mayor of the town of Bolivia and representatives of several churches were in attendance, beaming their approval. Similarly, the pastor of Antioch Baptist Church noted that there had been few problems, and he advocated the Christian value of loving the area's new neighbor.[91]

This American experience of Asian religions was significant in a number of ways. Unlike the earlier nineteenth-century interest in Asia, this late-twentieth-century episode was not confined to intellectuals but included white-collar and working-class Americans and reached into literature, art, and popular culture. Beyond that, this turn to the East was part of a broader restructuring of American religion occurring in the decades after World War II.

Wilmington, like the nation, witnessed a dazzling proliferation of religious institutions. For example, the Wilmington City Directory of 1942 listed 53 religious organizations, while the Wilmington Yellow Pages of 2000 included 325. The character of postwar America matched this explosion of religious options. The postwar population, but especially the so-called baby-boom generation born between 1946 and 1964, was less hesitant than some older generations to switch denominations. Prizing the perception of compatibility in social and economic status and lifestyle fit, as well as reflecting the increased occupational and geographical mobility that characterized their lives, the boomers visited, shopped around, tried out, explored, and experienced denominations as well as congregations. Inherited religious identity had much less purchase, especially among Protestants.[92]

Beyond fluidity in affiliation, a related shift was the development of the "third disestablishment." Whereas the first disestablishment of the 1790s had legally separated church and state in America, and the second disestablishment of the 1890s had challenged Protestant dominance in American culture due to the influx of immigrants, the third disestablishment of the 1990s, with its roots in the so-cial revolutions of the 1960s and 1970s, weakened the very connec-tions—custodial, literary, and existential—between Christianity and American culture. In 1959 *Time* magazine ran a cover story on Prot-estant theologian Paul Tillich. In the 1990s, if a national magazine advertised an upcoming cover story about the Madonna, chances are that most readers would anticipate something on the pop star rather than the mother of Jesus.[93]

Religious individualism and personal choice of religious op-tions, never more than dormant in America's spiritual heritage, have powerfully reemerged. In this context, U.S. religious institutions, including those in the Cape Fear, have pondered how they might increase, in a widely used and telling business phrase, their mar-ket share of this religious population. Previous strategies of warm hospitality, ample parking, and top-notch child care augmented programming targeted to the baby boomers. Some congregations tried holding worship services on Saturday evening as well as Sun-day morning. Many congregations experimented with new styles of worship, incorporating the latest technology into so-called contem-porary worship services in an attempt to retain members, attract switchers, and capture returners.[94]

Begun in 1996 in the southern part of New Hanover County, Harbor United Methodist Church, for example, emphasized music in its worship. The early service employed traditional styles, but the 11:00 A.M. Sunday service featured contemporary Christian and crossover tunes played by a band and accompanied by a praise choir. Liturgical dance could also be found at Harbor Methodist as well as at its older spiritual cousin, the Episcopal Church of the Servant. Organized in the 1970s in what was then a northern precinct of the city, the sanctuary floor of Church of the Servant contained a laby-rinth walk, based on the one built in Chartres Cathedral. Encourag-ing any who trod this path to do so with an open mind and an open heart, this congregation offered a historically familiar but locally fresh option to religious believers.[95]

Another type of new appeal was the development of Spanish-language services for the culturally diverse but linguistically consolidated Latino population in the region. This Latino sector derived from several different countries, and by 2000 four Fayetteville congregations were actively at work: Capilla Cristo Redentor Assembly of God, Primera Iglesia Bautista Hispana, Igleslia Ni Cristo Church of Christ, and Iglesia De Dios Pentecostal. In Wilmington the Templo Adoracion y Alabanza assisted the Spanish-speaking community. So too did Primera Iglesia Bautista, begun in 1983 by the Reverend Agustine Lara. Beyond worship, this congregation worked with migrant laborers in Pender County. Social services such as a health clinic were also part of the ministry to Latinos carried out at St. Mary Roman Catholic Church. It first offered Spanish Masses in 1988; special feast days, such as that for Our Lady of Guadalupe, were also celebrated as Latinos grew in number and recognition.[96]

Three other factors—reduction of interfaith barriers, culture wars causing religious realignment, and the development of seeker spirituality—help explain the changing structures and dynamics of contemporary religious life in the Cape Fear region. One legacy of organizational developments such as the ecumenical movement has been an erosion of the view that denominational loyalty mattered and that denominational differences were important. For instance, national polls in the 1970s and 1980s indicated that generally most Protestants viewed other Protestant groups favorably. These positive feelings extended to cooperation in social service projects such as Habitat for Humanity, which built houses, or Wilmington Interfaith Hospitality, which provided short-term shelter for homeless families. It also motivated cooperative worship services, such as the annual Thanksgiving Day service celebrated together by St. James Episcopal and First Presbyterian. Beyond that, beginning in 2000, Episcopalians and the Evangelical Lutheran Church in America were in full communion with each other, meaning that although the denominations remained separate, pastors from either group could serve congregations and lead worship in either church. Finally, campus ministries supported by coalitions of Protestant denominations and their congregations existed at many college campuses, including the University of North Carolina at Wilmington, the University of North Carolina at Pembroke, and Fayetteville State University.[97]

Other barriers seemed less immutable than previously. By 1983, 77 percent of Americans approved of marriages between Protestants and Catholics or between Jews and Christians. Moreover, with the Roman Catholic population growing in the Lower Cape Fear, anecdotal evidence suggested that cooperative efforts in disaster relief; informal contacts among priests, pastors, and rabbis; and congregants' occasional visits to services of faiths other than their own also occurred.[98]

"Culture wars" was the term one scholar gave to the increasingly polarized tendencies within contemporary American cultural life. This divide between liberals and conservatives pertained to issues of moral authority and thus extended inexorably into America's religious orbit. The upshot of this cultural conflict was realignment in many denominations. Sometimes this took place through secession, as one side or the other voluntarily left. Other times it occurred through appointment or election of one side's slate and the subsequent purge of the other side's members. In any case, specific issues such as abortion, ordination of women, and gay rights became markers in these increasingly strident clashes occurring within denominations. In Wilmington, Baptists, Episcopalians, Presbyterians, Roman Catholics, and Lutherans witnessed these dynamics. Interestingly, in some cases these particular issues seemed to be at the forefront of discussion; in other cases, a general concern about the perceived drift of American society provided the animus for debate.[99]

For example, by 1990 some Baptists in the South had become disenchanted with what they called the fundamentalist resurgence within the Southern Baptist Convention. In response, in August 1990 the National Cooperative Baptist Fellowship was organized as a moderate alternative to the Southern Baptist Convention, and by 1993 North Carolinians had formed a state branch. By 2000 some 130 churches had joined the Cooperative Baptist Fellowship in North Carolina, including First Baptist and Winter Park Baptist in Wilmington and Snyder Memorial Baptist in Fayetteville.[100]

In the case of the Baptists it was the moderates and progressives who left, but in the example of the Episcopalians and Presbyterians, it was the conservatives who broke away and formed new options. Although the Charismatic Episcopal Church and the Anglican Church in America would deny that they were historically new, both were recent additions in their present forms to the Cape Fear region. During the colonial era, the Church of England was the established church in North Carolina. With the organization of the

Protestant Episcopal Church and the Diocese of North Carolina by the 1790s, the Anglican Church in North Carolina seemed fated to become a historical footnote. In its Affirmation of 1977, however, the Anglican Church of America stated that the Anglican Church of Canada and the Protestant Episcopal Church in the United States of America had both departed from orthodox Christian traditions. Therefore, with backing from the Anglican archbishops in Rwanda and Singapore, these Anglicans declared the United States to be a mission territory ripe for their renewed orthodox efforts. To this end, some forty churches, including All Saints Parish in Wilmington, were formed as congregations in the Anglican Church of America. The Charismatic Episcopal Church, drawing on Pentecostal, Anglican, and Eastern Orthodox traditions, began in 1992. Representing the Charismatic Episcopal Church in Wilmington since 1995, the Church of St. Peter the Fisherman combines charismatic and liturgical elements in its services. Although women are a visible part of these Anglican and Charismatic Episcopal congregations, they may not be ordained to the deaconate or to the priesthood in either group.[101]

Presbyterian newcomers to Wilmington in 2000 had a choice of groups. If they were white, they might not attend the African American Chestnut Street Presbyterian Church or the Korean Presbyterian Church. Nevertheless, they could still choose from other Presbyterian congregations belonging to the Presbyterian Church USA (PCUSA), the Presbyterian Church in America (PCA), the Evangelical Presbyterian Church (EPC), or the Associate Reformed Presbyterian Church (ARP). The PCUSA is the mainline national denomination, in reaction to which these other groups formed their contemporary identities. The fundamentalist-modernist controversy of the 1920s shaped the disposition of these other Presbyterians, encouraging them in their come-outer stance, with its desire for well-defined boundaries against the perceived relativism of modern culture, as well as in their strident militancy, with its confidence in their ability to define truth in all its purity.

The PCA was organized in December 1973 as Presbyterians nationally, but also those in the Presbyterian Church in the United States (Southern), began to ordain women. Claiming the 1645 Westminster Confession of Faith and its catechisms as its doctrinal standards, the PCA opposed what it considered to be the theological liberalism of the mainline denomination and explicitly forbade the ordination of women to church offices. Trinity Reformed Presbyterian Church, begun in the late 1970s, was the Wilmington representative of this denomination, which claimed over a thousand congregations in the United States in 2000.[102]

Presbyterians in the Masonboro section of Wilmington met in a Sunday school mission chapel of First Presbyterian Church beginning in 1919. In 1945 this small colonial-style chapel became Myrtle Grove Presbyterian Church, a congregation in the southern Presbyterian Church. Its ministers were educated at Bob Jones University, Gordon-Conwell Seminary, and Oral Roberts University. In 1982, with the congregation numbering more than a thousand, a new house of worship was finished for the Myrtle Grove congregation, and the old building was sold to the Federal Point Pentecostal Church.[103]

By the 1980s the Myrtle Grove congregation, particularly under the leadership of its senior pastor, the Reverend Horace Hilton, had developed a charismatic identity, with exuberant praise-style worship and regular testimonies about the gifts of the Holy Spirit. In 1983 the northern and southern Presbyterian churches reunited, and in 1989 the Myrtle Grove congregation sought dismissal from the PCUSA in order to join the EPC. Differences in worship styles between the local PCUSA and Myrtle Grove, though noticeable, were not the major stumbling block. Instead, issues of social ethics again provided the boundaries for congregational identity. Whereas the PCUSA ordained women as deacons, elders, and clergy, the EPC left such decisions concerning female deacons and elders to the local congregations and those concerning female clergy to the local presbyteries. Such a policy enshrined local option, but in so doing, it functionally ensured that few women would be able to buck male predominance in the religious traditions of the South and elsewhere in the nation. On the hot-button issues of homosexuality and abortion, however, there was no room for local determination. The EPC taught that homosexual practice was sinful and that the church opposed abortion and must do everything it could to provide alternatives.[104]

Although the ARP denomination could trace its roots back to Scotland in the early 1700s, it fit well within this conservative realignment of the Presbyterian denomination. Located on the northern outskirts of town, Wilmington's ARP congregation, Emmanuel Presbyterian Church, likewise forbade the ordination of women, opposed abortion in all cases, and considered homosexual practice a sin against God.[105]

For many Roman Catholics, the Second Vatican Council (1962–1965) was a liberating experience, opening the church to engagement with the world, affirming the wider Christian body, and inviting increased participation of the laity in the Mass through the use of vernacular language and other liturgical reforms. But these changes were not universally accepted by Catholics in America and elsewhere in the world. While churches such as Sacred Heart in Whiteville, Sacred Heart in Southport, and Immaculate Conception in Carolina Beach were enlarged to accommodate the burgeoning Catholic population, a different outreach occurred in the former site of a downtown restaurant. After his retirement from Immaculate Conception in Carolina Beach in 1993, Father Ernest Beck organized St. Anthony's Chapel and offered the Mass in Latin using the older Tridentine rite. In this Mass, which used Latin instead of English, the priest faced the altar rather than the congregation, and Gregorian chants rather than more current styles of music were utilized. For the roughly fifty people who attended these services, the Second Vatican Council's revisions had drained the Mass of its beauty and mystery. Estimates suggest that in the early 1990s approximately one hundred Catholic bishops in America allowed some form of Latin Masses in their dioceses, while another 150 chapels, like St. Anthony's, existed without diocesan approval. In 1997 Beck died and the chapel closed. In 2003 a representative of the Society of Saint Pius X traveled to Wilmington to offer again the Latin Mass. Hoping that this would become at least an annual event, the Reverend Kenneth Novak stated, "We're not watered down like the other churches. . . . The church does not change for society."[106]

Resisting change and upholding orthodox standards were also the maxims of the Missouri Synod in the Lutheran Church. Several Lutheran organizations began to ordain females in the 1970s; however, the Lutheran Church–Missouri Synod (LCMS) steadfastly refused to sanction these practices. Consequently, when the Reverend Rachel Connelly began Water of Life Lutheran Church (Evangelical Lutheran Church in America) in 2000, even though it was only a few miles down the road from Messiah Lutheran Church (LCMS), the two congregations were worlds apart: Connelly led Water of Life, Messiah opposed female ordination; Water of Life encouraged casualness and less structure, Messiah was more formal and traditional; Water of Life downplayed hierarchy, Messiah employed it theologically and liturgically. Here then, in the polarization over theological, liturgical, and social issues taking place within American Christianity and the opportunities such divisions spawn, one can see another source for the proliferation of religious organizations in contemporary America.[107]

Choice of personal religious style and the individualism that it engendered were even more visible in that congeries of impulses, dispositions, and affiliations known as seeker spirituality. Emblematic of those who would identify themselves as spiritual but not religious, this attitude privileges experience over institutions, inquiry over structure, and individual expression over habitual custom.

Such an attitude, particularly as it has been expressed by the demographic bulge represented by the baby boomers, has supported a smorgasbord of spiritual offerings in the religious marketplace of America and of the Cape Fear. Many of these organizations claim a nondenominational identity, though culturally they are firmly Christian. The Salvation Army, for instance, began in England in the mid-1860s by declaring war on sin and poverty and organizing itself along military lines. The Wilmington congregation, founded in 1887, continued to hold weekly services, manage a thrift store and shelter, and collect donations at Christmas. During worship the brass band played and the congregation sang praise-style hymns while the pastors admonished their listeners to forsake sin and follow God's laws.[108]

Music and moralism were featured in other nondenominational churches. The Spirit of Truth Apostolic and Prophetic Ministries, begun in 1986; the Judah House of Praise Ministries, organized in 1997; the Upper Room Praise and Worship Center, founded in 1999 in the building that formerly housed Sunset Park Methodist Church; and the Believers Destiny Church, sharing space with a Christian social club for youth, all fit in this niche.[109]

Three other Wilmington congregations demonstrated the eclectic nature of seeker congregations. The Rock of Wilmington, founded in 1988 by its husband and wife co-pastors, proclaimed that it was "spirit-filled, multi-racial, and non-denominational."

The two-hour worship services included preaching by the pastors and expressions of "our deepest passion and devotion to the Father through music, dance, and drama." With its slogan, "You never knew church could be like this," the Rock sought to break with past images of stodgy suburban respectability and racial exclusiveness. The congregation projected an image of joyful openness and uplift built on a solid foundation. It was just what the seekers were after, or so they hoped.[110]

Whereas the Rock was part of a network of nineteen similar organizations across the United States, the Coastal Community Vineyard could claim fellowship with more than five hundred other Vineyard congregations worldwide. After a decade of evangelical work, first in the Yorba Linda, California, Friends Church and then at the Charles E. Fuller Institute of Evangelism and Church Growth and at the Calvary Chapel of Yorba Linda, John Wimber joined the Vineyard movement in 1988 and became head of the group and its successor, the Association of Vineyard Churches. In 1991 the Reverend Steven Mattis left Myrtle Grove Presbyterian Church and founded the Coastal Community Vineyard congregation in Wilmington. Emphasizing an expressive and nontraditional style of worship in which speaking in tongues, prophesying, and teaching figured prominently, Coastal Community Vineyard drew many of its members from the baby-boom generation.[111]

Port City Community Church was inspired by the Willow Creek megachurch in South Barrington, Illinois. In 1996 Mike Ashcraft, a youth minister in Wilmington, attended a Church Leadership Conference at Willow Creek Community Church. In October 1999 he started the Port City Community Church, and in 2000 it met in a middle-school gymnasium for Sunday worship. Like the Rock and the Vineyard, its members were young and its worship lively and informal; soliloquies and staged presentations might substitute for a traditional sermon, and contemporary music replaced Bach, Beethoven, and Mozart. Holding to the final authority of scripture in all matters of faith and practice, Port City announced that it sought to help its members in their individual walks with God.[112]

If ecstatic religious experience, a casual worship atmosphere, and flowing testimonies of past problems and new accomplishments characterized some groups, other Cape Fear seekers followed a more serene path. The Baha'i faith emphasizes the oneness of religions and the oneness of humanity. Consequently, the Baha'is teach that each of the major world religions reflects divine revelations and that Baha'i's original teacher, Bahá'u'lláh, is included on a list with Moses, Christ, Krishna, Muhammad, and Buddha. Combating racism was another characteristic of the Baha'i community. During the 1920s Louis G. Gregory, a Fisk University graduate and Howard University–trained lawyer, visited Wilmington to talk about the Baha'i faith. Gregory had already served on the national Baha'i coordinating committee, and his teachings deeply impressed Frederick Sadgwar and his daughter, Felice. They, as well as other members of the Sadgwar family, embraced Baha'i. Felice and her sister, Mabel, willed their residence to the Wilmington Baha'is, and it served as a center for devotions and the study of Baha'i scriptures. Significantly, the appeal of Baha'i, especially its emphasis on racial harmony, was not confined to Wilmington. Fayetteville first had a Baha'i assembly in 1971, which reestablished itself in 1981.[113]

Historically, Sufism grew up in eighth-century Islam as a reform movement emphasizing asceticism, meditation, and the wearing of simple cloaks of wool (in Arabic, *suf*). In the United States, Hazrat Inayat Khan founded the Sufi Order in the West in 1910. Hazrat's teachings, particularly as they were further promulgated by his son, Vilayat Inayat Khan, emphasized harmony, meditation with music and dance, and the unity of all beings. Hazrat stressed the universality of his teachings and thus distanced himself from historical Islam. Vilayat, whose mother was Ora Ray Baker, cousin of Mary Baker Eddy, witnessed a rejuvenation of the Sufi order during the 1960s and 1970s as part of the American counterculture's interest in Asian religions. The Sufi Order of Wilmington emphasized meditation in times of spiritual growth, drawing on Hazrat's teachings and other world scriptures for its two dozen members.[114]

Inclusiveness and meditation also characterized two spiritual relatives, Unity Christ Church and the Coastal Carolina Religious Science Center. Emma Curtis Hopkins studied with Mary Baker Eddy until they had a falling out in 1885. Hopkins went on to become one of the organizational leaders of the New Thought movement in fin de siècle America. One of Hopkins's early students, Myrtle Fillmore, founded the Unity School of Christianity; and one of her later students, Ernest Homes, organized the Church of Religious Science. Following Fillmore's lead, the Unity Church and its Wilmington congregation taught equal access by all to a loving, personal, and beneficent God and the use of meditation as a way to align oneself positively with the spirit of Christ. At the Wilmington Religious Science Center, developing one's own spiritual awareness and understanding rather than identifying with the inherited teachings of a tradition were the goals. Drawing on any useful sources in philosophy, religion, or science, Religious Science seeks practical applications to life's spiritual quandaries.[115]

Five other spiritual alternatives in the Cape Fear—Society of Friends, Unitarians, Messianic Judaism, Metropolitan Community Church, and Covenant of Cape Fear Pagans—all shared a complex relationship to traditional Christianity, while at the same time signifying the further spread of seeker spirituality in the area. The Society of Friends, or Quakers, can be traced back in the Cape Fear to the colonial era. In the 1960s and 1970s the Friends experienced a renewal as their testimony of social justice and their affection for quiet simplicity attracted many of the disaffected in society. If the Quakers' belief in the Inner Light and silent worship put them outside the universe of much of Christianity, the Unitarian Universalists' denial of the divinity of Jesus and their affirmation of unlimited salvation placed them even further outside orthodoxy. Unitarianism had a stronghold in New England in the early nineteenth century, symbolized by the ministry of William Ellery Channing and the cliché that Unitarians believed in the Fatherhood of God, the Brotherhood of Man, and the Neighborhood of Boston. Universalism also found New England congenial, and in 1961 the Unitarian Universalist Association was organized, with its headquarters on Beacon Hill in Boston.[116]

As nineteenth-century Unitarians were assembling in Boston, Universalists were gathering in the Cape Fear. On June 2, 1827, delegates from Universalist societies in New Hanover, Sampson, and Duplin counties met in Kenansville to establish the Southern Convention of Universalists. A year earlier, the Reverend Jacob Frieze had arrived in Wilmington and established a small society. At the Kenansville meeting the society appointed Frieze corresponding secretary and its delegate to the New England and New York Conventions of Universalists. Although the Kenansville group later disbanded, its descendants founded the Red Hill Universalist Church in Sampson County in 1884.[117]

Wilmington's Unitarian territory was also left fallow until the mid-1800s. Boston Unitarians sent Amy Bradley, a schoolteacher, to establish a public school in Reconstruction Wilmington in 1866. Bradley's efforts in education were noteworthy, though she did nothing to advance the Unitarian cause in the Port City. A century later, in May 1968, Unitarians in Wilmington began to meet again, and in 1969 they purchased an old residence in downtown Wilmington for fellowship meetings. By 1983 this group, dedicated to the search for truth and understanding in a religion without creeds, opened a new house of worship.[118]

Messianic Judaism believes that Yeshua (Jesus) was the Messiah promised in the Jewish scriptures and that he will return again. This belief differentiates Messianic Judaism from traditional Judaism, which still awaits the coming of the Messiah and regards Jesus as merely a prophet. Messianic Jews pattern their practices after the example of first-century Jews: observance of the Sabbath and traditional Jewish holidays, circumcision, readings from the Torah, and kosher diets. Additionally, however, they read from the New Testament gospels and epistles. Begun in the 1990s, Wilmington's Beit Hallel Messianic Synagogue was affiliated with the International Alliance of Messianic Congregations and Synagogues, a group that started under the auspices of the Messianic Jewish Alliance of America, begun in 1915. Beit Hallel would not accept converted members but required that each member have a Jewish parent or grandparent. Disavowing the proselytizing style of groups such as Jews for Jesus, Beit Hallel considered itself part of the fulfillment of Judaism, although that identity was disputed by traditional Jews and often misunderstood by Christians as well.[119]

In 1968 Troy Perry, a former Pentecostal minister, began the Universal Fellowship of Metropolitan Community Churches as a ministry to homosexuals, bisexuals, and transsexuals and their heterosexual supporters. Recognizing the widespread condemnation of homosexuality in traditional Christian churches, the Metropolitan Community Church sought to be a safe and sustaining environment for gay, lesbian, bisexual, and transgendered Christians. St. Jude Metropolitan Community Church started in Wilmington in 1992 in the building that formerly housed a Primitive Baptist congregation on Castle Street. Actively working with HIV and AIDS patients, St. Jude's typical Sunday morning congregation of eighty worshippers also provided counseling, resources for the Cape Fear Gay Youth Group, and spiritual direction for its members and others.[120]

Neo-paganism is an umbrella term for a wide range of beliefs and practices. It includes such groups as the Aquarian Tabernacle Church, the Church of Pan, the Ossirian Temple Assembly, the Church of All Worlds, and Wicca. Wicca, which has its own set of subgroups, was probably the best-known example of the neo-pagan craft in America at the end of the twentieth century. Persecution of witches was a mainstay of European Christianity from the Middle Ages through the early 1700s, and the Salem witch trial episode is known by most Americans. In 1954, after the 1951 revocation of the last law in England against witchcraft, Gerald Gardiner published *Witchcraft Today*. Gardiner described Wicca as a survival of witchcraft practices from medieval times, portraying it as the Celtic worship of the Great Goddess. Raymond and Rosemary Buckland studied with Gardiner in 1963 and shortly thereafter, upon their move to New York City, introduced Gardinerian Wicca to America.[121]

Because there is no canonical scripture in neo-paganism, and because the specific historical relation between many neo-pagan rituals and preexisting religious traditions is much debated, neo-paganism has been a particularly fluid movement. In general, however, three themes are characteristic: recognition of a polytheistic assembly of goddesses and gods, with a heavy emphasis on the feminine principle in divinity; the ethics of cosmic payback, or what you put into the world comes back; and the use of magic as a coercive power that is available for benevolent purposes, though some would also claim its use for malevolent goals. The liturgical calendar of many neo-pagan groups celebrates the winter and summer solstices, the vernal and autumnal equinoxes, May Day, Halloween, and the lunar cycles. On such occasions, casting sacred circles, using symbols to represent earth, fire, water, and air as well as the four cardinal directions; invoking the goddesses and gods; sharing food and drink; and recounting sacred stories constitute the ritual activities.[122]

Due to personal criticism and public animosity, many neo-pagan practitioners have followed their craft surreptitiously. But Gavin and Yvonne Frost, who lived in New Bern, North Carolina, in the 1980s, publicly defended their brand of Wicca and occasionally came to Wilmington. Cape Fear Wiccans met privately until April 2001, when they organized the Covenant of Cape Fear Pagans. Assembling "to learn, to discuss our path in an openminded and respectful manner," the organizers anticipated opportunities to "meet for picnics, barbcue, etc." This organizational drive continued, and in 2004 the Cape Fear Pagans met at the Wilmington Unitarian church to provide fairy ring classes for their children, an effort one leader described as "kind of like Sunday school or Vacation Bible School."[123]

As the Wiccans gathered for their barbecues and their circle meetings, they joined a long and varied list of recent religious arrivals in the Cape Fear. Amidst this dizzying roster of spiritual entrepreneurs, ranging from Baha'is to Unitarians, from Charismatic Episcopalians to Tridentine Catholics, from groups numbering two dozen to two hundred, one complex trait stood out: a therapeutic temperament built on a matrix of small groups.

Religion has often functioned to quench the intellectual, emotional, and social needs of its adherents. Nevertheless, in Christianity, for example, individual desires and demands were always described as subordinate to recognition of God's work in the world through Jesus Christ. Such a theological affirmation matched the sociological insight that commitments to such belief systems led one out of the self and into the world. By contrast, the emphasis in seeker spirituality has been to privilege the needs of ordinary persons and to promise them access to God or a higher power as a source of personal transformation. With its focus on interior lives, on the search for personal fulfillment in religious traditions that were often personally unfamiliar, this journey theology, as one scholar called it, expressed itself in the potpourri of spiritual groups found in contemporary America. In a twenty-fifth anniversary speech, a Wilmington Unitarian minister canvassed the reasons for the membership's attendance: curiosity, nostalgia for old friends, hope for solace, a desire for intellectual challenge, and the need to explore beliefs in a supportive setting. Less analytically, other groups stated that they wished to assist each member in his or her individual walk with God or in finding his or her own spiritual path. Again, this emphasis on meeting personal needs is not new in American religious history, although the extent to which the question "Are my spiritual needs being met?" now circulated in America's culture was significant.[124]

In such an ideologically fluid and institutionally fragmented situation, the impulse to pick and choose what is personally attractive in religion and the marketing of faith through small groups also characterized the seeker experience. Existing inside or alongside religious organizations, the small-group movement provided decentralized, face-to-face familiarity with like-minded seekers. Whether it was Alcoholics Anonymous, Overeaters Anonymous, Debtors Anonymous, or a score of other groups, seeker congregations, and traditional ones as well, have been carving up their schedules, assigning rooms, and appealing to members and outsiders alike. Here again, small groups, like individual searches for the holy, are not new in American religious culture. Scripture study groups, youth fellowship meetings, and men's and women's organizations have been part of the Jewish and Christian religious scene for a long time. Nevertheless, small-group organization has shifted front and center, and under the auspices of seeker organizations, small groups have emerged as a principal focus for their organization and development, as exemplified by the congregations of Port City Community Church and Coastal Community Vineyard Fellowship. Other Wilmington churches have developed outreach ministries for prison inmates and homeless people and medical clinics out of small groups as well. Although feeding the hungry, clothing the naked, and visiting inmates are arguably extensions of ministry into the social world, some observers still charge that the therapeutic focus on personal needs, personal experience, and personal insights never left.[125]

A portrait of religion in Wilmington by the 1990s would reflect the age of Aquarius, the era of the evangelical, and the generation of the baby boomers. No longer a melting pot, it now appeared more like a salad bowl, with an emphasis on individual identity and distinct contributions. What could hold it all together—the confines of the bowl, the traditions of the dressing, or simply the presentation of the salad itself—remained a question for the twenty-first century.

Conclusion

In April 1760 the Reverend John McDowell described the Cape Fear region as "inhabited by many sorts of people, of various nations and different opinions, customs, and manners." McDowell's statement regarding the present could also serve as a prophecy of the Cape Fear's future. At the end of the twentieth century the threads of Wilmington's religious life extended to Bodh Gaya and Benares, Jerusalem and Mecca, Rome and Geneva, Moscow and Constantinople, Cahokia, Salt Lake City, Mount Athos, Westminster Abbey, and Ife in Yorubaland. Worship services took place in locales spanning the sensual banquet of sights, sounds, and smells in a Greek Orthodox church through the almost Cistercian austerity of a clapboard country church to the informal assemblies around coffee and cookies of covenant fellowships in domestic residences. And if buildings varied in their interior capacities, their exterior architectural lineages stretched through history to quote the Federal style of St. Martin's-in-the Field, the Classicism of the Parthenon, the Gothic elements from Chartres Cathedral, and even the open-plan modernism of Ludwig Mies van der Rohe.[1]

Religious pluralism, meaning not simply the tolerance of religious outsiders but also their participation in forming and implementing the agenda of society, is the object of much contemporary commentary. Who counts as an "outsider" is always relative to time and place, as this volume has shown. In any case, that Baptists and Buddhists could thrive together in Brunswick County, that the black pastor of St. Mark's Episcopal Church could serve as the president of the New Hanover Human Relations Commission, or that a Wilmington rabbi could be active in the New Hanover Ministerial Association is indicative of a new religious pluralism developing in the Cape Fear.

Wilmington's place on the map of contemporary southern religious life is instructive. Clearly, if "southern religion" means having mostly Baptists and Methodists and maybe a few Presbyterians thrown in for predestinarian spice, then Wilmington's myriad religious population is striking and perhaps, for a city of its size, exceptional. As scholars examine the assortment within southern Protestantism, the variety within southern evangelicalism, and even the complexity of the contemporary religious life in a metropolis such as Atlanta, the religious diversity of the Cape Fear region is notable not only for its current reality but also, as McDowell indicated, for its historical precedent and continuing presence. Regional identity provides a matrix for understanding important aspects of American religious history. Pacific Slope, Upper Midwest, New England, and Great Basin are all areas, along with the South, that combine regional and religious attributes. Recognition of subregions, such as the Cape Fear, is important in mapping this new geography of American religion.

While academic scholars, newspaper editors, and everyday folks debate the prospects of a pluralistic culture in America—some condemning it, and others praising it—it is clear that the genie of religious diversity is already out of the bottle, even in the South. Economically, the South is involved in the broad processes of globalization, not only in financial centers such as Charlotte or Atlanta but also in places such as Wilmington. The post–Civil War shipping of cotton and other materials by Alexander Sprunt and his son, James, directly from Wilmington to Europe was multiplied in the late twentieth century by the Port of Wilmington's exports to Europe, Africa, South America, Asia, and the Mediterranean. Similarly, Wilmingtonians could purchase imports from these locales in venues ranging from boutique shops to franchise conglomerates. And just as Wilmington was part of an international economic network, so too did it display connections to the major religious traditions of the world. Thus, the blending of enduring traditions, such as Protestant evangelicalism, with emerging patterns, such as religious diversity, is the hallmark of the religious experience of the Cape

Fear. Stitching together this "coat of many colors" has become the emblematic challenge of the present; in the Cape Fear region, it is also the legacy of the past.

Notes

1. The Cape Fear and Its Indians

1. Lawrence C. Wroth, *The Voyages of Giovanni da Verrazzano, 1524–1528* (New Haven, Conn.: Yale University Press, 1970), 133.

2. See ibid., 74–79, 133–34; Samuel Eliot Morison, *The European Discovery of America: The Northern Voyages A.D. 500–1600* (New York: Oxford University Press, 1971), 288–89.

3. Morison, *European Discovery*, 332.

4. Paul E. Hoffman, *A New Andalucia and a Way to the Orient: The American Southeast during the Sixteenth Century* (Baton Rouge: Louisiana State University Press, 1990), 3, 14, 41–47, 50–58.

5. Ibid., 66–76; Morison, *European Discovery*, 332–34; Paul E. Hoffman, "Lucas Vazquez de Ayllón's Discovery and Colony," in *The Forgotten Centuries: Indians and Europeans in the American South, 1521–1704*, ed. Charles Hudson and Carmen Chaves Tesser (Athens: University of Georgia Press, 1994), 36–49.

6. Eugene Lyon, *The Enterprise of Florida: Pedro Menéndez de Avilés and the Spanish Conquest of 1565–1568* (Gainesville: University Presses of Florida, 1976); Hoffman, *A New Andalucia*, 318–19; Morison, *European Discovery*, 332–33.

7. J. Leitch Wright Jr., "William Hilton's Voyage to Carolina in 1662," *Essex Institute Historical Collections* 105 (April 1969): 96–102.

8. William Hilton, "A Relation of a Discovery, 1664," in *Narratives of Early Carolina, 1650–1708*, ed. Alexander S. Salley Jr. (New York: Charles Scribner's Sons, 1911), 45–53.

9. Hoffman, *A New Andalucia*, 53; William P. Cumming, *The Southeast in Early Maps*, 3rd rev. ed. (Chapel Hill: University of North Carolina Press, 1998), 106–7.

10. Cumming, *Southeast in Early Maps*, 157–58, 163, 174–75.

11. Wroth, *Voyages of Verrazzano*, 82–83; Ernest Hatch Wilkins, "Arcadia in America," *Proceedings of the American Philosophical Society* 101 (February 15, 1957): 4–30.

12. Wright, "Hilton's Voyage," 100–101; Hilton, "Relation of a Discovery," 47.

13. Cumming, *Southeast in Early Maps*, 133–35; Patrick Wolfe, "Imperialism and History," *American Historical Review* 102 (April 1997): 417–18; Hugh Honor, *The New Golden Land: European Images of America from the Discoveries to the Present Time* (New York: Pantheon Books, 1975); Karen Ordahl Kupperman, ed., *America in European Consciousness, 1493–1750* (Chapel Hill: University of North Carolina Press, 1995); J. B. Harley, *The New Nature of Maps: Essays in the History of Cartography*, ed. Paul Laxton (Baltimore: Johns Hopkins University Press, 2001); Karen Ordahl Kupperman, *Indians and English: Facing Off in Early America* (Ithaca, N.Y.: Cornell University Press, 2000), 41–76.

14. Jeannette D. Black, ed., *The Blathwayt Atlas*, 2 vols. (Providence, R.I.: Brown University Press, 1970–1975), 2:125–33; Cumming, *Southeast in Early Maps*, 169.

15. Hilton, "Relation of a Discovery," 58–59.

16. William P. Cumming, *Captain James Wimble, His Maps, and the Colonial Cartography of the North Carolina Coast* (Raleigh, N.C.: Department of Archives and History, 1969).

17. John R. Swanton, *The Indians of the Southeastern United States* (Washington, D.C.: Smithsonian Institution Press, 1946), 11–12; J. Leitch Wright Jr., *The Only Land They Knew: The Tragic Story of the American Indians in the Old South* (New York: Free Press, 1981), 23–24; James Mooney, *The Siouan Tribes of the East* (Washington, D.C.: Government Printing Office, 1894), 65–67.

18. For an overview of the archaeology of North Carolina, see H. Trawick Ward and R. P. Stephen Davis Jr., *Time before History: The Archaeology of North Carolina* (Chapel Hill: University of North Carolina Press, 1999).

19. Ibid., 32–36; Thomas C. Loftfield, *Excavations at 31ON33, a Late Woodland Seasonal Village* (Wilmington: Marine Science Fund, University of North Carolina at Wilmington, 1979), 4; Mark Wilde-Ramsing, "Archaeological Survey and Testing on Prehistoric Shell Midden Sites in New Hanover County, North Carolina" (master's thesis, Catholic University of America, 1984), 2; Albert C. Goodyear III et al., "The Earliest South Carolinians," in *Studies in South Carolina Archaeology*, ed. Albert C. Goodyear III and Glen T. Hanson (Columbia: University of South Carolina Press, 1989), 23.

20. Ward and Davis, *Time before History*, 2; Wilde-Ramsing, "Archaeological Survey," 13; Margaret S. Smith and Emily H. Wilson, *North Carolina Women: Making History* (Chapel Hill: University of North Carolina Press, 1999), 4–10; Cheryl P. Claassen, "Gender, Shellfishing, and the Shell Mound Archaic," in *Engendering Archaeology: Women and Prehistory*, ed., Joan M. Gero and Margaret W. Conkey (Oxford: Basil Blackwell, 1991), 276–300.

21. Ward and Davis, *Time before History*, 55–57; Stanley South, *An Archaeological Survey of Southeastern North Carolina*, Institute of Archaeology and Anthropology Notebook 8 (Columbia: University of South Carolina Press, 1976), 3.

22. Ward and Davis, *Time before History*, 3; Julia E. Hammett, "Ethnohistory of Aboriginal Landscapes in the Southeastern United States," *Southern*

Indian Studies 41 (1992): 11–15; Bruce D. Smith, *Rivers of Change: Essays on Early Agriculture in Eastern North America* (Washington, D.C.: Smithsonian Institution Press, 1992); Smith and Wilson, *North Carolina Women*, 5; Patty Jo Watson and Mary C. Kennedy, "The Development of Horticulture in the Eastern Woodlands of North America: Women's Role," in Gero and Conkey, *Engendering Archaeology*, 255–75.

23. Ward and Davis, *Time before History*, 194; Richard E. Lonsdale, *Atlas of North Carolina* (Chapel Hill: University of North Carolina Press, 1967), 34.

24. William E. Myers, "Indian Trails of the Southeast," in *42nd Annual Report* (Washington, D.C.: Bureau of American Ethnology, 1928); Lonsdale, *Atlas of North Carolina*, 39.

25. Roy Parker Jr., *Cumberland County: A Brief History* (Raleigh, N.C.: Department of Archives and History, 1990), 3; Wilde-Ramsing, "Archaeological Survey," 11.

26. Wilde-Ramsing, "Archaeological Survey," 81–97.

27. Ibid., 99–118.

28. Loftfield, *Late Seasonal Village*; Thomas C. Loftfield and David C. Jones, "Late Woodland Architecture on the Coast of North Carolina: Structural Meaning and Environmental Adaptation," *Southeastern Archaeology* 14 (Winter 1995): 120–35; Hilton, "Relation of a Discovery," 46, 50.

29. Rudolf Otto, *The Idea of the Holy*, trans. John W. Harvey (New York: Oxford University Press, 1958).

30. Joachim Wach, *Sociology of Religion* (Chicago: University of Chicago Press, 1944), 55–56.

31. Catherine Bell, *Ritual: Perspectives and Dimensions* (New York: Oxford University Press, 1997), 191.

32. For a description of Piedmont Siouan ritual, see H. Trawick Ward and R. P. Stephen Davis Jr., *Indian Communities on the North Carolina Piedmont, AD 1000 to 1700*, Monograph 2 (Chapel Hill: Research Laboratories of Anthropology, University of North Carolina, 1993), 410–11.

33. John R. Swanton, "Aboriginal Culture of the Southeast," in *42nd Annual Report* (Washington, D.C.: Bureau of American Ethnology, 1928), 698.

34. Thomas C. Loftfield, "Ossuary Interments and Algonquian Expansion on the North Carolina Coast," *Southeastern Archaeology* 9 (Winter 1990): 116; Ward and Davis, *Time before History*, 216–18.

35. Ward and Davis, *Time before History*, 206–7.

36. David I. Bushnell Jr., *Native Cemeteries and Forms of Burial East of the Mississippi*, Bulletin 71 (Washington, D.C.: Bureau of American Ethnology, 1920), 135; H. Trawick Ward and Jack H. Wilson Jr., "Archaeological Excavations at the Cold Morning Site," *Southern Indian Studies* 32 (October 1980): 5–40; Joffre Coe et al., *Archaeological and Paleo-Osteological Investigations at the Cold Morning Site, New Hanover County, North Carolina* (Chapel Hill: Research Laboratories of Anthropology, University of North Carolina, 1982); Loftfield, "Ossuary Interments," 117–18; Ward and Davis, *Time before History*, 222–23.

37. Howard A. MacCord, "The McLean Mound, Cumberland County, North Carolina," *Southern Indian Studies* 18 (October 1966): 3–45.

38. Mircea Eliade, *A History of Religious Ideas*, 3 vols. (Chicago: University of Chicago Press, 1978–1985), 1:9; Charles Hudson, *The Southeastern Indians* (Knoxville: University of Tennessee Press, 1976), 54–55; Ivar Paulson, "Zur Phänomenologie des Schamanismus," *Zeitschrift für Religions- und Geistesgeschichte* 15 (1964): 121–41; A. Irving Hallowell, "Bear Ceremonialism in the Northern Hemisphere," *American Anthropologist* 28 (January–March 1926): 135–63; Waldemar Jochelson, *The Koryak*, Memoirs of the American Museum of Natural History (New York: American Museum of Natural History, 1905), 91–93.

39. Joseph R. Caldwell, "The Archeology of Eastern Georgia and South Carolina," in *Archaeology of Eastern United States*, ed., James B. Griffin (Chicago: University of Chicago Press, 1952), 317; Michael B. Trinkely, "An Archaeological Overview of the South Carolina Woodland Period: It's the Same Old Riddle," in Goodyear and Hanson, *Studies in South Carolina Archaeology*, 83–84; Ward and Davis, *Time before History*, 112–15; Elizabeth I. Monahan, "Bioarchaeological Analysis of the Mortuary Practices at the Broad Reach Site (31CR218), Coastal North Carolina," *Southern Indian Studies* 44 (1995): 59.

40. John Lawson, *A New Voyage to Carolina*, ed. Hugh T. Lefler (Chapel Hill: University of North Carolina Press, 1967), 98; William Merrill, "The Beloved Tree: *Ilex vomitoria* among Indians of the Southeast and Adjacent Regions," in *Black Drink: A Native American Tea*, ed. Charles M. Hudson (Athens: University of Georgia Press, 1979), 40, 53–56, 72–74.

41. Hudson, *Southeastern Indians*, 320–21.

42. Ibid., 121.

43. Ibid., 336.

44. MacCord, "McLean Mound," 21–25, 43; Hudson, *Southeastern Indians*, 54.

45. MacCord, "McLean Mound," 34–35; Stanley South, "Exploratory Excavation of the MacFayden Mound, Brunswick County," *Southern Indian Studies* 18 (October 1966): 60; Thomas E. Emerson, *Cahokia and the Archaeology of Power* (Tuscaloosa: University of Alabama Press, 1997), 212–18; Hudson, *Southeastern Indians*, 120–83, 376–400.

46. Lawson, *New Voyage*, 175; Joseph C. Winter, "From Earth Mother to Snake Woman: The Role of Tobacco in the Evolution of Native American Religious Organizations," in *Tobacco Use by Native North Americans: Sacred Smoke and Silent Killer*, ed. Joseph C. Winter (Norman: University of Oklahoma Press, 2000), 265–304; Hudson, *Southeastern Indians*, 353–55.

47. Jordan Paper, *Offering Smoke: The Sacred Pipe and Native American Religion* (Moscow: University of Idaho Press, 1988), 5–7, 36–39; Joffre Lanning Coe, *Town Creek Indian Mound* (Chapel Hill: University of North Carolina Press, 1995), 221.

48. Wright, "Hilton's Voyage," 100–101.

49. Hilton, "Relation of a Discovery," 46–48; Hammett, "Ethnohistory of Aboriginal Landscapes," 36–37.

50. Hilton, "Relation of a Discovery," 49–52.

51. James Mooney, *The Aboriginal Population of America North of Mexico*

(Washington, D.C.: Smithsonian Institution, 1928), 6; Chapman J. Milling, *Red Carolinians* (Columbia: University of South Carolina Press, 1969), 222; Hugh Meredith, *An Account of the Cape Fear Country*, ed., Earl G. Swem (Perth Amboy, N.J.: Charles F. Heartman, 1922), 28.

52. Ward and Davis, *Time before History*, 231, 257; Lawson, *New Voyage*, 232.

53. Lawrence Lee, *Indian Wars in North Carolina, 1663–1763* (Raleigh, N.C.: Carolina Charter Tercentenary Commission, 1963), 77; John Barnwell, "Letters of ___," *South Carolina Historical and Genealogical Magazine* 9 (January 1908): 30–31.

54. Lawrence Lee, *The Lower Cape Fear in Colonial Days* (Chapel Hill: University of North Carolina Press, 1965), 80–83; Meredith, *Account of the Cape Fear*, 28.

2. Tensions in the Colonial Era

1. For the text of the royal charter, see William L. Saunders, ed., *The Colonial Records of North Carolina*, 10 vols. (Raleigh, N.C.: P. M. Hale, 1886–1890), 1:20–23.

2. Ibid., 22, 32–33.

3. Robert Horne, "A Brief Description of the Province of North Carolina, 1666," in *Narratives of Early Carolina, 1650–1708*, ed. Alexander S. Salley Jr. (New York: Charles Scribner's Sons, 1911), 66–73; Saunders, *Colonial Records*, 1:72–73.

4. Saunders, *Colonial Records*, 1:90, 93, 160. For a full discussion of the dissolution of Charles Town, see Lawrence Lee, *The Lower Cape Fear in Colonial Days* (Chapel Hill: University of North Carolina Press, 1965), 43–53.

5. For a review of the South Carolina developments, see Lee, *Lower Cape Fear*, 96–99; Walter Edgar, *South Carolina: A History* (Columbia: University of South Carolina Press, 1998), 138–39; Robert M. Weir, *Colonial South Carolina: A History* (Millwood, N.Y.: KTO Press, 1983), 143–45. On Maurice Moore, see Lawrence F. London, "Maurice Moore," in *Dictionary of North Carolina Biography*, 6 vols., ed. William S. Powell (Chapel Hill: University of North Carolina Press, 1979–1996), 4:303–4.

6. Lee, *Lower Cape Fear*, 94.

7. Saunders, *Colonial Records*, 3:261, 454; Lawrence Lee, *The History of Brunswick County, North Carolina* (Charlotte, N.C.: Heritage Press, 1980), 32–33; Hugh Meredith, *An Account of the Cape Fear Country*, ed. Earl G. Swem (Perth Amboy, N.J.: Charles F. Heartman, 1922), 15.

8. Walter Clark, ed., *The State Records of North Carolina*, 16 vols. (numbered 11–26) (Winston and Goldsboro, 1895–1906), 23:6–10.

9. Saunders, *Colonial Records*, 1:600, 2:126.

10. Charles B. Hirsch, "The Experience of the S.P.G. in Eighteenth Century North Carolina" (Ph.D. diss., Indiana University, 1953), 15–28; Robert J. Cain, ed., *The Church of England in North Carolina: Documents, 1699–1741* (Raleigh, N.C.: Division of Archives and History, 1999), 97–102.

11. Alfred W. Newcombe, "The Appointment and Instruction of S.P.G. Missionaries," *Church History* 5 (1936): 340–58.

12. Cain, *Church of England*, 39–42.

13. Clark, *State Records*, 22:733; Saunders, *Colonial Records*, 1:572.

14. George Stevenson, "John Urmston," in Powell, *Dictionary of North Carolina Biography*, 6:77–81; Saunders, *Colonial Records*, 1:763–64; Cain, *Church of England*, 180, 245–46.

15. Cain, *Church of England*, 223; Stevenson, "John Urmston," 78–80.

16. Charles R. Holloman, "John Blacknall, in Powell, *Dictionary of North Carolina Biography*, 1:167–68.

17. Cain, *Church of England*, 313; Gertrude S. Carraway and W. Keats Sparrow, "John LaPierre," in Powell, *Dictionary of North Carolina Biography*, 4:20–21.

18. Edgar, *South Carolina*, 85, 124–25; Lillian Fordham Wood, "The Reverend John LaPierre," *Historical Magazine of the Protestant Episcopal Church* 90 (1971): 407–30.

19. Saunders, *Colonial Records*, 3:530.

20. Claiborne T. Smith Jr., "Richard Marsden," in Powell, *Dictionary of North Carolina Biography*, 4:219–20; Fleming H. James, "Richard Marsden, Wayward Clergyman," *William and Mary Quarterly* 11 (1954): 578–91; Cain, *Church of England*, 343.

21. Smith, "Richard Marsden," 219–20; Saunders, *Colonial Records*, 4:11–14; Cain, *Church of England*, 383, 408.

22. Saunders, *Colonial Records*, 3:32–47, 110–13.

23. There is often confusion over the date of the founding of Wilmington due to the change in calendars in the 1700s. Under the new-style Gregorian calendar, the date was February 1740; under the old-style Julian calendar, used in Britain and its colonies until 1752, the date was February 1739. In 1989 the city of Wilmington celebrated its 250th anniversary, and I based my dates on that celebration. For a discussion of the founding of Wilmington, see Lee, *Lower Cape Fear*, 120–25; Alan D. Watson, *Wilmington, North Carolina, to 1861* (Jefferson, N.C.: McFarland and Company, 2003), 8–16; Clark, *State Records*, 23:133–35.

24. Lee, *Lower Cape Fear*, 123–24; Clark, *State Records*, 23:133–35.

25. Clark, *State Records*, 23:239–43; Lee, *History of Brunswick County*, 45–46.

26. See A. Roger Ekirch, *"Poor Carolina": Politics and Society in Colonial North Carolina, 1729–1776* (Chapel Hill: University of North Carolina Press, 1981), 33–34.

27. Ibid., 11–13, 20–23, 33–38; Lee, *Lower Cape Fear*, 127–29; Alan D. Watson, *Wilmington: Port of North Carolina* (Columbia: University of South Carolina Press, 1992), 10–12.

28. Nina Moore Tiffany, ed., *Letters of James Murray, Loyalist* (Boston: n.p., 1901), 24–25.

29. Saunders, *Colonial Records*, 4:607, 755.

30. Clark, *State Records*, 25:391–92; Saunders, *Colonial Records*, 5:158–59, 6:235.

31. Clark, *State Records*, 23:535–37; Saunders, *Colonial Records*, 7:515, 789; Stanley A. South, *Colonial Brunswick, 1726–1776* (Raleigh, N.C.: Department of Archives and History, 1960), 40–44; N. C. Curtis, "St. Philip's Church, Brunswick County, N.C. Text and Measured Drawings," *Architectural Record* 47 (1920): 181–87; Catherine W. Bishir, *North Carolina Architecture* (Chapel Hill: University of North Carolina Press, 1990), 41.

32. Alexander M. Walker, ed., *New Hanover County Court Minutes*, 4 vols. (Bethesda, N.C.: Alexander M. Walker, 1958–1960), 1:56–57, 92; 2:28.

33. Donald R. Lennon, "The Development of Town Government in Colonial North Carolina," in *Of Tar Heel Towns, Shipbuilders, Reconstructionists, and Alliancemen: Papers in North Carolina History*, ed. Joseph F. Steelman (Greenville, N.C.: East Carolina University Publications, 1981), 6–8; Saunders, *Colonial Records*, 5:158; Peter DuBois to Samuel Johnston Jr., February 8, 1757, Hayes Papers, Southern Historical Collection, University of North Carolina at Chapel Hill.

34. Clark, *State Records*, 25:243–44, 391–92.

35. Leora H. McEachern, *History of St. James Parish, 1729–1979* (Wilmington, N.C.: n.p., 1985), 3–7; Preservation Society of Charleston, *The Churches of Charleston and the Lowcountry* (Columbia: University of South Carolina Press, 1994), 22–23.

36. Clark, *State Records*, 25:244, 257–63.

37. George Whitefield, *George Whitefield's Journals* (Edinburgh: Banner of Truth Trust, 1989), 380.

38. Tiffany, *Letters of James Murray*, 20; Donald R. Lennon and Ida Brooks Kellam, eds., *The Wilmington Town Book, 1743–1778* (Raleigh, N.C.: Division of Archives and History, 1973), 6, 24–25, 29–30, 38, 120; Kemp P. Battle, *Letters and Documents Relating to the Early History of the Lower Cape Fear* (Chapel Hill: University [of North Carolina], 1903), 11–12, 14; Elizabeth F. McKoy, *Wilmington Block by Block: From 1733 On* (Wilmington, N.C.: Edwards and Broughton, 1967), 129–30; Walker, *New Hanover County Court Minutes*, 1:13, 2:3

39. Edward G. Hartmann, *Americans from Wales* (New York: Octagon Books, 1983), 44, 50; *Records of the Welsh Tract Baptist Meeting, Pencader Hundred, New Castle County, Delaware*, Papers of the Historical Society of Delaware (Wilmington, Del.: Historical Society of Delaware, 1904), 3; W. T. Skinner, *History of the Pencader Presbyterian Church* (Wilmington, Del.: John M. Rogers Press, 1899), 35.

40. Hartmann, *Americans from Wales*, 51; Meredith, *Account of the Cape Fear*, 21, 27–28; *Cape Fear Mercury*, January 13, November 22, 1773.

41. Saunders, *Colonial Records*, 4:72–73; Hugh T. Lefler and William S. Powell, *Colonial North Carolina: A History* (New York: Charles Scribner's Sons, 1973), 93–94, 96; Nicholas Canny, "Early Modern Ireland, 1500–1700," in *The Oxford History of Ireland*, ed. R. F. Foster (Oxford: Oxford University Press, 1989), 113–15; Celeste Ray, *Highland Heritage: Scottish Americans in the American South* (Chapel Hill: University of North Carolina Press, 2001), 220, n. 1.

42. Saunders, *Colonial Records*, 4:212–15, 687; 5:104; Tiffany, *Letters of James Murray*, 34–35, 81.

43. Lefler and Powell, *Colonial North Carolina*, 59–65; Alan D. Watson, *A History of New Bern and Craven County* (New Bern, N.C.: Tryon Palace Commission, 1987), 41–42, 48; James I. Martin Sr., "The Palatine Settlements of 1710–1800," *Footnotes: Occasional Papers of the Duplin County Historical Society* 53 (1994): 1–4.

44. Jennifer F. Martin, *Along the Banks of the Old Northeast: The Historical and Architectural Development of Duplin County, North Carolina* (Rose Hill, N.C.: Duplin County Historical Foundation, 1999), 2, 4–5; William H. Foote, *Sketches of North Carolina*, 2nd ed. (Dunn, N.C.: Reprint Company, 1912), 158–59.

45. Foote, *Sketches*, 159–60, 172–77.

46. Faison W. McGowen and Pearl C. McGowen, eds., *Flashes of Duplin's History and Government* (Kenansville, N.C.: n.p., 1971), 76.

47. Ibid., 75; Saunders, *Colonial Records*, 6:1020, 1040; 7:273–74.

48. Saunders, *Colonial Records*, 7:457, 8:13–14; McGowen and McGowen, *Flashes*, 75.

49. Saunders, *Colonial Records*, 8:14, 63–64; 9:306–7; McGowen and McGowen, *Flashes*, 75.

50. Duane Meyer, *The Highland Scots of North Carolina, 1732–1776* (Chapel Hill: University of North Carolina Press, 1961), 72–75; David Dobson, *Scottish Emigration to Colonial America, 1607–1785* (Athens: University of Georgia Press, 1994), 110–11.

51. A. I. B. Stewart, "The North Carolina Settlement of 1739," in *Colorful Heritage Documented*, ed. Victor E. Clark Jr. and Louise D. Curry (Dallas, N.C.: Argyll Printing Center, 1989), 140–48 (Stewart's article originally appeared in *Scottish Genealogist* 32 [March 1985]: 7–12); Saunders, *Colonial Records*, 4:489–90.

52. Meyer, *Highland Scots*, 15, 30–53; quotation 15–16.

53. Alexander Murdoch, "A Scottish Document Concerning Emigration to North Carolina in 1772," *North Carolina Historical Review* 67 (1990): 449. Further evidence can be seen in the letters of Alexander and Hector McAllister in the Alexander McAllister Papers, Southern Historical Collection, University of North Carolina at Chapel Hill.

54. See A. R. Newsome, ed., *Records of Emigrants from England and Scotland to North Carolina, 1774–1775* (Raleigh, N.C.: Division of Archives and History, 1989), 17–29, for the accounts cited.

55. Saunders, *Colonial Records*, 7:543–44; 8:526; 9:259, 364; Meyer, *Highland Scots*, 63–64, 85; William Caudle, "The Highland Scots in the Cape Fear Region" (Cape Fear Museum, Wilmington, N.C., November 5, 1999).

56. Roy Parker Jr., *Cumberland County: A Brief History* (Raleigh, N.C.: Division of Archives and History, 1990), 10–12.

57. Minutes of Presbytery of Inveraray, February 27, 1739, in Clark and Curry, *Colorful Heritage Documented*, 151–53; quotation 152.

58. See the letter of Dugal McTavish et al.; the minutes of the Presbytery of Inveraray, April 3 and 24, 1739; and the minutes of the Scottish Society for the Propagation of Christian Knowledge, June 7, 1739, all in Clark and Curry, *Colorful Heritage Documented*, 153–55.

59. See the minutes of the Scottish Society for the Propagation of Christian Knowledge, March 19, 1741, January 7, 1742; the minutes of the Presbytery of Inveraray, June 16, 1741, November 3, 1741; the minutes of the Presbytery of Kintyre, January 14, 1748; and the 1748 petition to the Synod of Argyll, all in Clark and Curry, *Colorful Heritage Documented*, 157–63.

60. Foote, *Sketches*, 171; Douglas F. Kelly, *Carolina Scots* (Dillon, S.C.: 1739 Publications, 1998), 41.

61. Foote, *Sketches*, 131–32; Whitefield, *Journals*, 352–53.

62. Foote, *Sketches*, 132–34.

63. Ibid., 135; Meyer, *Highland Scots*, 116; Saunders, *Colonial Records*, 10:577.

64. Saunders, *Colonial Records*, 6:236.

65. Ibid., 3:110.

66. Clark, *State Records*, 23:3.

67. Saunders, *Colonial Records*, 3:111; Clark, *State Records*, 23:173–75.

68. Walker, *New Hanover County Court Minutes*, 1:2, 22, 25–26, 77; 3:13, 32; Donna J. Spindel, *Crime and Society in North Carolina, 1663–1776* (Baton Rouge: Louisiana State University Press, 1989), 63, 105.

69. Saunders, *Colonial Records*, 4:549.

70. Hugh T. Lefler, "The Anglican Church in North Carolina: The Proprietary Period," in *The Episcopal Church in North Carolina, 1701–1959*, ed. Lawrence F. London and Sarah M. Lemmon (Raleigh: Episcopal Diocese of North Carolina, 1987), 5, 10; Hugh T. Lefler, "The Anglican Church in North Carolina: The Royal Period," in ibid., 22–25. See also Marvin L. Michael Kay, "The Payment of Provincial and Local Taxes in North Carolina, 1748–1771," *William and Mary Quarterly* 26 (1969): 218–40; Alan D. Watson, "The Anglican Parish in Royal North Carolina, 1729–1775," *Historical Magazine of the Protestant Episcopal Church* 48 (1979): 303–19.

71. Clark, *State Records*, 23:601–7, 660–62; Lefler, "Anglican Church: Royal Period," 23.

72. Saunders, *Colonial Records*, 3:110; Clark, *State Records*, 25:153; Joseph B. Cheshire, "The Church in the Province of North Carolina," in *Sketches of Church History in North Carolina*, ed. Joseph B. Cheshire (Wilmington, N.C.: Wm. L. DeRosset, 1892), 59.

73. Saunders, *Colonial Records*, 7:43.

74. Ibid., 6:265, 729–30; 7:164.

75. M. A. Huggins, *A History of North Carolina Baptists, 1727–1932* (Raleigh: Baptist State Convention of North Carolina, 1967), 40; Saunders, *Colonial Records*, 6:1040, 8:15.

76. Clark, *State Records*, 23:11, 559.

77. Saunders, *Colonial Records*, 2:212, 7:103; Clark, *State Records*, 23:158–60; Stephen Beauregard Weeks, *Church and State in North Carolina* (Baltimore: Johns Hopkins Press, 1893), 43.

78. Clark, *State Records*, 23:672–74, 826; Weeks, *Church and State*, 42–45.

79. Saunders, *Colonial Records*, 3:110–11; Meyer, *Highland Scots*, 114–15.

80. Saunders, *Colonial Records*, 4:755, 5:1137, 6:5, 7:137–38, 9:239; Wayne

S. Arnold, "Early Presbyterianism in the Lower Cape Fear," *Lower Cape Fear Historical Society Bulletin* 17 (1974): 3.

81. Clark, *State Records*, 23:244–45, 519, 787–88, 941.

82. See Paul Conkin, "The Church Establishment in North Carolina, 1765–1776," *North Carolina Historical Review* 32 (1955): 1–30; Gloria B. Baker, "Dissenters in Colonial North Carolina" (Ph.D. diss., University of North Carolina at Chapel Hill, 1970), 48; Lefler, "Anglican Church: Royal Period," 24–26.

83. For Urmston's comment, see Saunders, *Colonial Records*, 1:769; for exchanges between royal governors and legislatures, see ibid., 3:564; 5:234, 1095; for exchanges between clergy and vestries, see ibid., 2:126–27; 3:392, 529–30; 4:606–7; 6:552–58; for discussion of the reluctance of the British government to appoint a bishop in the American colonies, see Frederick V. Mills Sr., *Bishops by Ballot* (New York: Oxford University Press, 1978), 25–61.

3. Religious Liberty and Denominational Expansion

1. For a discussion of the resistance in North Carolina and the other colonies, see Walter H. Conser Jr. et al., eds., *Resistance, Politics, and the American Struggle for Independence, 1765–1775* (Boulder, Colo.: Lynne Rienner, 1986).

2. Mark A. DeWolfe Howe, ed., "Journal of Josiah Qunicy, Junior, 1773," *Massachusetts Historical Society Proceedings* 49 (1916): 460; Evangeline Walker Andrews, ed., *Journal of a Lady of Quality* (New Haven, Conn.: Yale University Press, 1923), 193; Duane Meyer, *The Highland Scots of North Carolina, 1732–1776* (Chapel Hill: University of North Carolina Press, 1961), 156–60.

3. Douglass Adair and John A. Schutz, eds., *Peter Oliver's Origin and Progress of the American Rebellion* (Stanford, Calif.: Stanford University Press, 1961), 63; Hugh T. Lefler, "The Anglican Church in North Carolina: The Royal Period," in *The Episcopal Church in North Carolina, 1701–1959*, ed. Lawrence F. London and Sarah M. Lemmon (Raleigh: Episcopal Diocese of North Carolina, 1987), 51–52, 56–57.

4. Elkanah Watson, *Men and Times of the Revolution or Memoirs of Elkanah Watson*, ed. Winslow C. Watson (New York: Dana and Company, 1856), 50; Walter Clark, ed., *The State Records of North Carolina*, 16 vols. (numbered 11–26) (Winston and Goldsboro, 1895–1906), 15:445; Johann D. Schoepf, *Travels in the Confederation, 1783–1784*, 2 vols., ed. Alfred J. Morrison (1911; New York: Burt Franklin, 1968), 2:145; Francis Asbury, *Journals and Letters of Francis Asbury*, 3 vols., ed. Elmer T. Clark et al. (Nashville: Abingdon Press, 1958), 2:425.

5. Robert Brent Drane, "Historical Notes, 1843," in *One Hundredth Anniversary Commemorating the Building of St. James Church, Wilmington, North Carolina*, ed. William L. DeRosset (Wilmington, N.C.: William L. DeRosset, 1939); Alan D. Watson, *Wilmington, North Carolina to 1861* (Jefferson, N.C.: McFarland and Company, 2003), 90–93.

6. Henry G. Connor and Joseph B. Cheshire Jr., eds., *The Constitution of the State of North Carolina, Annotated* (Raleigh, N.C.: Broughton, 1911), xviii–xx.

7. Robert L. Ganyard, *The Emergence of North Carolina's Revolutionary State Government* (Raleigh, N.C.: Division of Archives and History, 1978), 71.

8. Earle H. Ketcham, "The Sources of the North Carolina Constitution of 1776," *North Carolina Historical Review* 6 (1929): 223; John L. Cheney, ed., *North Carolina Government, 1589–1979* (Raleigh, N.C.: Department of the Secretary of State, 1981), 810.

9. Cheney, *North Carolina Government*, 814; Clark, *State Records*, 23:997.

10. Cheney, *North Carolina Government*, 814; William L. Saunders, ed., *The Colonial Records of North Carolina*, 10 vols. (Raleigh, N.C.: P. M. Hale, 1886–1890), 10:870d; Samuel A. Ashe, *History of North Carolina*, 2 vols. (Greensboro, N.C.: Charles Van Noppen, 1908), 1:565; William H. Foote, *Sketches of North Carolina* (New York: Robert Carter, 1846), 240.

11. Cheney, *North Carolina Government*, 814; Gary R. Govert, "Something There Is That Doesn't Love a Wall: Reflections on the History of North Carolina's Religious Test for Public Office," *North Carolina Law Review* 64 (1986): 1074–79; John V. Orth, *The North Carolina State Constitution* (Chapel Hill: University of North Carolina Press, 1995), 4.

12. Connor and Cheshire, *Constitution of North Carolina*, xxii–xxiii; Ganyard, *Emergence of Revolutionary State Government*, 81–83; Thomas J. Curry, *The First Freedoms: Church and State in America to the Passage of the First Amendment* (New York: Oxford University Press, 1986), 150–92.

13. Jonathan Elliot, ed., *The Debates in the Several State Conventions on the Adoption of the Federal Constitution*, 5 vols. (1888; New York: Burt Franklin, 1968), 4:190–200; quotations 192, 199.

14. Sidney Mead, *The Lively Experiment* (New York: Harper and Row, 1963), 103. For a more recent analysis, see Russell E. Richey and Robert B. Mullin, eds., *Reimagining Denominationalism* (New York: Oxford University Press, 1994).

15. Artemus Boies to "Dear Brother," April 7, 1819, Miscellaneous Letters, Southern Historical Collection, University of North Carolina at Chapel Hill; James Sprunt, *Chronicles of the Cape Fear River, 1660–1916* (1916; Wilmington, N.C.: Broadfoot Publishing, 1992), 163.

16. *Seventy-fifth Anniversary Memorial of the First Presbyterian Church, Wilmington, N. C.* (Richmond, N.C.: Whittet and Shepperson, 1893), 9; Wayne S. Arnold, "Early Presbyterianism in the Lower Cape Fear," *Lower Cape Fear Historical Society Bulletin* 17 (1943): 4.

17. Raleigh Register, November 12, 1819; *Seventy-fifth Anniversary Memorial of First Presbyterian Church*, 10.

18. William H. Pierson Jr., *American Buildings and Their Architects*, 2 vols. (1970; New York: Oxford University Press, 1986), 1:68–71, 94–105; Leland M. Roth, *American Architecture: A History* (Boulder, Colo.: Westview Press, 2001), 69.

19. Roth, *American Architecture*, 70; Pierson, *American Buildings*, 1:131–40; Terry Friedman, *James Gibbs* (New Haven, Conn.: Yale University Press, 1984).

20. Roth, *American Architecture*, 91–95; Asher Benjamin, *The American Builder's Companion* (1806; New York: Dover Publishers, 1968).

21. H. W. Janson and Anthony F. Janson, *History of Art: The Western Tradition*, rev. 6th ed. (Upper Saddle River, N.J.: Pearson and Prentice Hall, 2004), 682–84, 690–91, 727–31; Nikolaus Pevsner, *An Outline of European Architecture* (1943; Harmondsworth: Penguin Books, 1963), 350–51, 376–84; Diana Walsh Pasulka, "The Aesthetics of Nostalgia: The Return of the Real in Postmodern Christian Discourse" (Ph.D. diss., Syracuse University, 2003).

22. "Old First Presbyterian Church," *Ballou's Pictorial Drawing Room Companion*, September 26, 1857; description of church interior in *North Carolina Presbyterian*, July 2, 1873, Historical Files, First Presbyterian Church, Wilmington, N.C.

23. Ernest Trice Thompson, *Presbyterians in the South*, 3 vols. (Richmond, Va.: John Knox Press, 1963–1973), 1:216.

24. Ibid., 216–19; Julius Melton, *Presbyterian Worship in America: Changing Patterns since 1787* (Richmond, Va.: John Knox Press, 1967), 12.

25. Thompson, *Presbyterians in the South*, 1:216, 219–21; Melton, *Presbyterian Worship*, 23–25.

26. Thompson, *Presbyterians in the South*, 1:226–27.

27. Leigh Eric Schmidt, *Holy Fairs: Scottish Communion and American Revivals in the Early Modern Period* (Princeton, N.J.: Princeton University Press, 1989), 57.

28. Ibid., 156–57; Thompson, *Presbyterians in the South*, 1:228–29.

29. Frederick E. Maser and Howard T. Maag, eds., *The Journal of Joseph Pilmore, Methodist Itinerant* (Philadelphia: Message Publishing Company, 1969), 175–76, 189–90; Frederick A. Norwood, *The Story of American Methodism* (Nashville: Abingdon Press, 1974), 65.

30. *Minutes of the Methodist Conferences, 1773–1813* (1813; Swainsboro, Ga.: Magnolia Press, 1983), 44, 46, 53.

31. Frederick E. Maser and George Singleton, "Further Branches of Methodism Are Founded," in *The History of American Methodism*, 3 vols., ed. Emory Stevens Bucke (New York: Abingdon Press, 1964), 1:617–22; Larry E. Tise, "North Carolina Methodism from the Revolution to the War of 1812," in *Methodism Alive in North Carolina*, ed. O. Kelly Ingram (Durham, N.C.: Duke Divinity School, 1976), 37; Margaret Martin, *Methodism or Christianity in Earnest* (Nashville: E. Stevenson, 1854), 35–37; A. M. Chreitzberg, "Early Methodism in Wilmington, N. C.," Historical Society of the North Carolina Conference, Methodist Episcopal Church, South (Durham, N.C.: n.p., 1897), 8–9; Thomas A. Smoot, "Early Methodism on the Lower Cape Fear," *Historical Papers of the North Carolina Conference Historical Society* (Durham, N.C.: n.p., 1925), 14–16.

32. Chreitzberg, "Early Methodism," 9; Smoot, "Early Methodism," 16; W. L. Grissom, *History of Methodism in North Carolina* (Nashville: Methodist Episcopal Church, South Publishing House, 1905), 223.

33. Russell E. Richey, *Early American Methodism* (Bloomington: Indiana University Press, 1991), 59–60; John B. Boles, ed., *Masters and Slaves in the House of the Lord: Race and Religion in the American South, 1740–1870* (Lexington: University Press of Kentucky, 1988); *Minutes of the Methodist Conferences,*

240, 558; William M. Wightman, ed., *Life of William Capers* (Nashville: Southern Methodist Publishing House, 1859), 164.

34. *Minutes of the Methodist Conferences*, 25–26; Sylvia R. Frey and Betty Wood, *Come Shouting to Zion: African American Protestantism in the American South and British Caribbean to 1830* (Chapel Hill: University of North Carolina Press, 1998), 153, 156–57; Cynthia L. Lyerly, *Methodism and the Southern Mind, 1770–1810* (New York: Oxford University Press, 1998), 60–62.

35. Thomas O. Summers, ed., *Autobiography of the Rev. Joseph Travis, A. M.* (Nashville: E. Stevenson, 1856), 65. On the importance of the spoken word in early Methodism, see Donald G. Mathews, "Evangelical America—The Methodist Ideology," in *Perspectives on American Methodism: Interpretive Essays*, ed. Russell E. Richey et al. (Nashville: Abingdon Press, 1993), 19–20.

36. John H. Wigger, *Taking Heaven by Storm: Methodism and the Rise of Popular Christianity in America* (New York: Oxford University Press, 1998), 104; Wightman, *Life of William Capers*, 164–65, 202; Donald G. Mathews, "North Carolina Methodists in the Nineteenth Century: Church and Society," in Ingram, *Methodism Alive in North Carolina*, 60.

37. Mathews, "Evangelical America—The Methodist Ideology," 20.

38. Wightman, *Life of William Capers*, 53–54.

39. Asbury, *Journals*, 2:425; *Wilmington Gazette*, May 29, 1804; Karen B. Westerfield Tucker, *American Methodist Worship* (New York: Oxford University Press, 2001), 74–81.

40. Wightman, *Life of William Capers*, 92, 123, 136, 163, 178–79; *Minutes of the Methodist Conferences*, 26, 46.

41. Catherine A. Brekus, "Female Evangelism in the Early Methodist Movement, 1784–1845," in *Methodism and the Shaping of American Culture*, ed. Nathan O. Hatch and John H. Wigger (Nashville: Abingdon Press, 2001), 136–45; Catherine A. Brekus, *Strangers and Pilgrims: Female Preaching in America, 1774–1845* (Chapel Hill: University of North Carolina Press, 1998); Jean Miller Schmidt, *Grace Sufficient: A History of Women in American Methodism, 1760–1939* (Nashville: Abingdon Press, 1999), 51–66.

42. Wightman, *Life of William Capers*, 167; *Amazing Grace: Two Hundred Years of Methodism* (Wilmington, N.C.: Grace United Methodist Church, 1985), 15–16.

43. See the essays by Nathan O. Hatch, David Hempton, and William R. Sutton in Hatch and Wigger, *Methodism and the Shaping of American Culture*, as well as A. Gregory Schneider, *The Way of the Cross Leads Home: The Domestication of American Methodism* (Bloomington: Indiana University Press, 1993).

44. Richard Bushman, *The Refinement of America: Persons, Houses, Cities* (New York: Alfred A. Knopf, 1992), xii–xvii.

45. For a discussion of the Greek Revival style, see Talbot Hamlin, *Greek Revival Architecture in America* (New York: Oxford University Press, 1944); Pierson, *American Buildings*, 1:417–60; Roth, *American Architecture*, 151–56, 169–70; W. Barksdale Maynard, *Architecture in the United States, 1800–1850* (New Haven, Conn.: Yale University Press, 2002), 219–60.

46. George Tucker, "On Architecture," *Portfolio* 4 (1814): 560; Town is quoted in Maynard, *Architecture in the United States*, 255.

47. Catherine W. Bishir, *North Carolina Architecture* (Chapel Hill: University of North Carolina Press, 1990), 96; Janet K. Seapker, "Wood Works: The Architectural Creations and Personal Histories of John Coffin and Robert Barclay Wood," *Lower Cape Fear Historical Society Bulletin* 39 (1994); Asbury, *Journals*, 2:494. For the ward divisions of the city, see *Amazing Grace*, 14.

48. Norwood, *Story of American Methodism*, 206; Donald G. Mathews, *Slavery and Methodism: A Chapter in American Morality, 1780–1845* (Princeton, N.J.: Princeton University Press, 1965). Catherine Brekus argues that by the 1840s the Methodist quest for respectability had silenced and constrained the previously wide-ranging experience of Methodist women as well. See Brekus, "Female Evangelism," 165–70.

49. Summers, *Autobiography of Joseph Travis*, 101–02; Wightman, *Life of William Capers*, 124–28; Grissom, *History of Methodism in North Carolina*, 235–37; John A. Oates, *The Story of Fayetteville and the Upper Cape Fear* (Fayetteville, N.C.: n.p., 1950), 495; *Minutes of the Methodist Conferences*, 552.

50. Sarah M. Lemmon, "The Decline of the Church, 1776–1816," in London and Lemmon, *The Episcopal Church in North Carolina*, 72.

51. Ibid., 85, 88; Leora H. McEachern, *History of St. James Parish, 1729–1979* (Wilmington, N.C.: n.p., 1985), 53; Susan Taylor Block, *Temple of Our Fathers: St James Church, 1729–2004* (Wilmington, N.C.: Artspeaks, 2004), 35–39.

52. Mortimer DeMott, "Sojourn in Wilmington and the Lower Cape Fear, 1837," *Lower Cape Fear Historical Society Bulletin* 22 (1979), 4; McEachern, *History of St. James*, 8.

53. Kenneth Clark, *The Gothic Revival* (London: John Murray, 1962), 95; John Burchard and Albert Bush-Brown, *The Architecture of America: A Social and Cultural History* (Boston: Little Brown, 1961), 49; Phoebe B. Stanton, *The Gothic Revival and American Church Architecture* (Baltimore: Johns Hopkins Press, 1968), xviii–xxii; James Early, *Romanticism and American Architecture* (New York: A. S. Barnes, 1965), 85; Susan B. Matheson, "Making a Point: Gothic Revival Architecture in America," in Susan B. Matheson and Derek D. Churchill, *Modern Gothic: The Revival of Medieval Art* (New Haven, Conn.: Yale University Art Gallery, 2000), 36–69. Drane's remarks are from the *Wilmington Advertiser*, April 5, 1839.

54. Pierson, *American Buildings*, 2:129–44; quotation by Town, 132.

55. For a discussion of the career of Thomas U. Walter, see William S. Rusk, "Thomas U. Walter and his Works," *Americana Illustrated* 33 (1939): 151–79; Robert B. Ennis, "Thomas U. Walter," in *Macmillan Encyclopedia of Architects*, 4 vols., ed. Adolf K. Placzek (New York: Collier Macmillan, 1982), 4:365–70; Susan B. Wojcik, "Thomas U. Walter and Iron in the United States Capitol: An Alliance of Architecture, Engineering, and Industry" (Ph.D. diss., University of Delaware, 1999).

56. Catherine W. Bishir et al., eds., *Architects and Builders in North Carolina: A History of the Practice of Building* (Chapel Hill: University of North Carolina Press, 1990), 168–76; Seapker, "Wood Works."

57. "Diary of the Right Rev. John England," *Records of the American Catholic Historical Society of Philadelphia* 6 (1895): 45–46.

58. Ibid., 46, 186–87.

59. Ibid., 47.

60. Ibid., 46, 47. On "republican Catholicism," see Jay Dolan, *In Search of an American Catholicism* (New York: Oxford University Press, 2002), 35–36. For a discussion of the constitution and England's opposition to pew rentals, see Peter Guilday, *The Life and Times of John England*, 2 vols. (New York: American Press, 1927), 1:346–47, 365–79. On the trustee controversy in general, see Patrick W. Carey, *People, Priests, and Prelates: Ecclesiastical Democracy and the Tensions of Trusteeism* (Notre Dame, Ind.: University of Notre Dame Press, 1987).

61. Dolan, *In Search of an American Catholicism*, 38.

62. Ibid., 40; Jay Dolan, *The American Catholic Experience* (Garden City, N.Y.: Doubleday, 1985), 208–13; Ann Taves, *The Household of Faith: Roman Catholic Devotions in Mid-Nineteenth Century America* (Notre Dame, Ind.: University of Notre Dame Press, 1986).

63. John Gilmary Shea, *A History of the Catholic Church within the Limits of the United States*, 4 vols. (1886–1892; New York: Arno Press, 1978), 4:90–98; Gerald P. Fogerty, *American Catholic Biblical Scholarship* (New York: Harper and Row, 1989), 16.

64. Stephen C. Worsley, "Catholicism in Antebellum North Carolina," *North Carolina Historical Review* 60 (1983): 406, 411; Joseph E. Waters Sheppard, "A Brief History of the Church of St. Thomas the Apostle" (unpublished manuscript); *St. Thomas the Apostle Catholic Church* (Wilmington, N.C.: St. Thomas the Apostle Catholic Church, 1947), 2–3.

65. Seapker, "Wood Works."

66. M. A. Huggins, *A History of North Carolina Baptists, 1727–1932* (Raleigh: Baptist State Convention of North Carolina, 1967), 40; Saunders, *Colonial Records*, 6:59, 730.

67. William G. McLoughlin, *New England Dissent, 1630–1833: The Baptists and the Separation of Church and State*, 2 vols. (Cambridge, Mass.: Harvard University Press, 1971), 1:329–477; Huggins, *History of North Carolina Baptists*, 50–52, 71; G. W. Paschal, "Morgan Edwards' Materials towards a History of the Baptists in the Province of North Carolina," *North Carolina Historical Review* 7 (1930): 392; David Benedict, *A General History of the Baptist Denomination in America and Other Parts of the World* (New York: Lewis Colby and Co., 1848), 683–84; David T. Morgan Jr., "The Great Awakening in North Carolina, 1740–1775: The Baptist Phase," *North Carolina Historical Review* 45 (1968): 264–83; John Sparks, *The Roots of Appalachian Christianity: The Life and Legacy of Elder Shubal Stearns* (Lexington: University Press of Kentucky, 2001).

68. Saunders, *Colonial Records*, 7:164; Benedict, *General History of the Baptist Denomination*, 684.

69. Separate Baptists in Virginia shared many similarities with those in North Carolina; see Rhys Isaac, *The Transformation of Virginia, 1740–1790* (1982; New York: Norton, 1988), 163–72.

70. J. Marcus Kester, *Historical Sketch of First Baptist Church, Wilmington N. C., 1808–1933* (Wilmington, N.C.: First Baptist Church, 1933), 15; Huggins, *History of North Carolina Baptists*, 75–77, 106, 122.

71. Kester, *Historical Sketch*, 16–17; Huggins, *History of North Carolina Baptists*, 123–24.

4. Bonds of Association

1. Alexis de Tocqueville, *Democracy in America*, 2 vols., ed. Phillips Bradley (New York: Vintage Books, 1945), 1:319, 2:114; Philip Schaff, *America*, ed. Perry Miller (Cambridge, Mass.: Harvard University Press, 1961), 6–7.

2. J. Marcus Kester, *Historical Sketch of First Baptist Church, Wilmington N. C., 1808–1933* (Wilmington, N.C.: First Baptist Church, 1933), 18–19; John R. Dail, *A History of Wilmington Presbytery* (Burgaw, N.C.: Southern Printing Company, 1984), 20; *North Carolina Conference Historical Directory* (Raleigh: North Carolina Conference on Archives and History, 1984), 87; M. A. Huggins, *A History of North Carolina Baptists, 1727–1932* (Raleigh: Baptist State Convention of North Carolina, 1967), 124.

3. Francis Asbury, *Journals and Letters of Francis Asbury*, 3 vols., ed. Elmer T. Clark et al. (Nashville: Abingdon Press, 1958), 3:186, 325; *North Carolina Conference Historical Directory*, 10–11; *Seventh Census of the United States: 1850* (Washington, D.C.: Robert Armstrong, 1853), 326; Bill Reaves, *Southport (Smithville): A Chronology*, 2nd ed., 4 vols. (Wilmington, N.C.: Broadfoot Publishing, 1985), 1:37, 39; Walter G. Curtis, *Reminiscences of Wilmington and Smithville-Southport, 1848–1900*, 2nd ed. (Southport, N.C.: Herald Job Office, 1999), 9.

4. Huggins, *History of North Carolina Baptists*, 400–434; David Benedict, *A General History of the Baptist Denomination in America and Other Parts of the World* (New York: L. Colby and Co., 1848), 688–90; C. E. Crawford, *A History of Bladen County, North Carolina* (Elizabethtown, N.C.: Bladen County Historical Society, 1987), 16; Ann Little, ed., *Columbus County, North Carolina: Recollections and Records* (Whiteville, N.C.: County Commissioners, 1980), 64, 152, 214, 269.

5. Catherine W. Bishir and Michael T. Southern, *A Guide to the Historic Architecture of Eastern North Carolina* (Chapel Hill: University of North Carolina Press, 1996), 420–22; *Carver's Creek Church and Gravestones* (Elizabethtown, N.C.: Bladen County Bicentennial Commission, 1976), 1–2; *North Carolina Conference Historical Directory*, 24, 35, 98, 103–4.

6. Bishir and Southern, *Guide to Historic Architecture*, 420, 422; Crawford, *History of Bladen County*, 22–23; Dail, *History of Wilmington Presbytery*, 20; Little, *Columbus County*, 66; Catherine W. Bishir, *North Carolina Architecture* (Chapel Hill: University of North Carolina Press, 1990), 188–89; Historical Files, Centre Presbyterian Church, Maxton, N.C.

7. "Brief History of the Black River Presbyterian Church," Historical Files, Black River Presbyterian Church, Ivanhoe, N.C.

8. John A. Oates, *The Story of Fayetteville and the Upper Cape Fear* (Fayette-

ville, N.C.: n.p., 1950), 200; Roy Parker Jr., *Cumberland County: A Brief History* (Raleigh, N.C.: Division of Archives and History, 1990), 28, 53–59; Bishir and Southern, *Guide to Historic Architecture*, 405–6.

9. *North Carolina Journal* and *Carolina Observer,* united edition, May 29, 1831; Oates, *Story of Fayetteville*, 208–11; Harriet Rankin, *History of First Presbyterian Church, Fayetteville, N.C.* (Fayetteville, N.C.: First Presbyterian Church, 1928), 18; Bishir and Southern, *Guide to Historic Architecture*, 399–400; *Carolina Observer,* August 7, 1832.

10. *North Carolina Conference Historical Directory*, 28–29; Oates, *Story of Fayetteville*, 495; Bishir and Southern, *Guide to Historic Architecture*, 404; *Fayetteville Observer,* June 23, 1835; C. Franklin Grill, *Methodism in the Upper Cape Fear Valley* (Nashville: Parthenon Press, 1966); James M. Lamb, "Sketches of the History of Methodism in Fayetteville," *Historical Papers of the North Carolina Conference Historical Society* (Durham, N.C.: n.p., 1901), 34–49.

11. Oates, *Story of Fayetteville*, 500–503; Bishir and Southern, *Guide to Historic Architecture*, 406; Parker, *Cumberland County*, 47; Huggins, *History of North Carolina Baptists*, 420, 424–25, 432.

12. Oates, *Story of Fayetteville*, 507–8; Henry S. Lewis, "The Formation of the Diocese of North Carolina," in *The Episcopal Church in North Carolina, 1701–1959*, ed. Lawrence F. London and Sarah H. Lemmon (Raleigh: Episcopal Diocese of North Carolina, 1987), 149; *Carolina Observer,* July 8, 1832; Catherine W. Bishir et al., *Architects and Builders in North Carolina: A History of the Practice of Building* (Chapel Hill: University of North Carolina Press, 1990), 164.

13. Stephen C. Worsley, "Catholicism in Antebellum North Carolina," *North Carolina Historical Review* 60 (1983): 401–2; "Diary of the Right Rev. John England," *Records of the American Catholic Historical Society of Philadelphia* 6 (1895): 186.

14. Worsley, "Catholicism in Antebellum North Carolina," 411–12; Oates, *Story of Fayetteville*, 498–499; *Seventh Census of the United States: 1850*, 326–30.

15. *Wilmington Chronicle*, April 6, 1842, June 2, 1847; David Bennett, *The Altar Call: Its Origin and Present Usage* (Lanham, Md.: University Press of America, 2000), 97; Charles Grandison Finney, *Lectures on Revivals of Religion*, ed. William G. McLoughlin (Cambridge, Mass.: Harvard University Press, 1960), 176.

16. Minutes of the First Baptist Church, Wilmington, February 1845; Historical Files, First Presbyterian Church, Wilmington, N.C.

17. Guion G. Johnson, *Antebellum North Carolina* (Chapel Hill: University of North Carolina Press, 1937), 416; *First Report of the Board of Managers of the Fayetteville Auxiliary Bible Society* (Fayetteville, N.C.: Bowell and Black, 1817); *Constitution of the Bible Society of Wilmington, North Carolina* (Wilmington, N.C.: n.p., 1819); *Wilmington Chronicle*, March 2, 1842; *Wilmington Journal*, February 23, 1853. See also the discussion of the American Bible Society in Peter J. Wosh, *Spreading the Word: The Bible Business in Nineteenth-Century America* (Ithaca, N.Y.: Cornell University Press, 1994), and Paul C. Gutjahr, *An American Bible: A History of the Good Book in the United States, 1777–1880* (Stanford, Calif.: Stanford University Press, 1999).

18. Artemus Boies to "Dear Brother," April 7, 1819, Miscellaneous Letters, Southern Historical Collection, University of North Carolina at Chapel Hill; minutes of First Baptist Church, Wilmington, May 1844.

19. Finney, *Lectures on Revivals*, 47.

20. Daniel J. Whitener, *Prohibition in North Carolina, 1715–1945* (Chapel Hill: University of North Carolina Press, 1946), 24; *Wilmington Journal*, December 22, 1848; *Wilmington Chronicle*, March 26, 1851; Johnson, *Antebellum North Carolina*, 454–58.

21. *Wilmington Chronicle*, December 11, 1844; *Appeal of the Seamen's Friends Society of the Port of Wilmington* (Wilmington, N.C.: n.p., 1853).

22. Thomas Hunt, *Life and Thoughts of Thomas P. Hunt* (Wilkes-Barre, Pa.: Robert Baur, 1901), 87.

23. John Lawson, *A New Voyage to Carolina*, ed. Hugh T. Lefler (Chapel Hill: University of North Carolina Press, 1967), 91.

24. Barbara Welter, "The Cult of True Womanhood, 1820–1860," *American Quarterly* 18 (1966): 151–74; Susan H. Lindley, *You Have Stept out of Your Place* (Louisville, Ky.: Westminster John Knox Press, 1996), 48–58; Cynthia Kierner, *Beyond the Household: Women's Place in the Early South* (Ithaca, N.Y.: Cornell University Press, 1998), 181–87.

25. *Wilmington Chronicle*, December 11, 1844; Kierner, *Beyond the Household*, 193; Johnson, *Antebellum North Carolina*, 266, 425; Lewis, "Formation of the Diocese," 162.

26. *Seventy-fifth Anniversary Memorial of the First Presbyterian Church, Wilmington, N.C.* (Richmond, N.C.: Whittet and Shepperson, 1893), 11; Lewis, "Formation of the Diocese," 162; Leora H. McEachern, *History of St. James Parish, 1729–1979* (Wilmington, N.C.: n.p., 1985), 41.

27. Johnson, *Antebellum North Carolina*, 419–22; Lewis, "Formation of the Diocese," 162; *Amazing Grace: Two Hundred Years of Methodism* (Wilmington, N.C.: Grace United Methodist Church, 1985), 16; *Seventy-fifth Anniversary Memorial of the First Presbyterian Church*, 47, 49; minutes of the First Baptist Church, Wilmington, February 1839.

28. Kierner, *Beyond the Household*, 184–88.

29. Mark C. Carnes, *Secret Ritual and Manhood in Victorian America* (New Haven, Conn.: Yale University Press, 1989), 25–27.

30. Ibid.; *Wilmington Chronicle*, March 18, 1842; Alan D. Watson, *Wilmington, North Carolina to 1861* (Jefferson, N.C.: McFarland Publishers, 2003), 144; James Sprunt, *Chronicles of the Cape Fear River, 1660–1916* (Wilmington, N.C.: Broadfoot Publishing, 1992), 171.

31. Carnes, *Secret Ritual*, 22; Watson, *Wilmington*, 44; William S. Powell, *The North Carolina Gazetteer* (Chapel Hill: University of North Carolina Press, 1968), 315.

32. Donald R. Lennon, "Cornelius Harnett, Jr.," in *Dictionary of North Carolina Biography*, 6 vols., ed. William S. Powell (Chapel Hill: University of North Carolina Press, 1979–1996), 3:37; Steven C. Bullock, *Revolutionary Brotherhood: Freemasonry and the Transformation of the American Social Order, 1730–1840* (Chapel Hill: University of North Carolina Press, 1996), 26, 228–29, 232–34.

33. John Livingstone, "History of St. John's Lodge, no. 1, A.F. & A.M.," *Nocalore* 1 (1931): 139; Tony Wrenn, *Wilmington, North Carolina: An Architectural and Historical Portrait* (Charlottesville: University Press of Virginia, 1984), 200–201, 236–38; Parker, *Cumberland County*, 36–37; Bishir and Southern, *Guide to Historic Architecture*, 411.

34. *Wilmington Chronicle*, December 28, 1842; Bullock, *Revolutionary Brotherhood*, 277–79.

35. Carnes, *Secret Ritual*, 31, 72; *Wilmington Chronicle*, January 3, 1844; *Wilmington Journal*, January 3, 1846.

36. Carnes, *Secret Ritual*, 31, 62, 72.

37. *Seventh Census of the United States: 1850*, 307–8.

38. John Hope Franklin, *The Free Negro in North Carolina, 1790–1860* (1943; New York: W. W. Norton, 1971), 120, 157.

39. See the discussion and map of eighteenth-century plantations on the Lower Cape Fear River in Alfred M. Waddell, *History of New Hanover County and the Lower Cape Fear Region, 1723–1800* (Wilmington, N.C.: n.p., 1909), 38–72; Henry J. MacMillian, "Colonial Plantations of the Lower Cape Fear," *Lower Cape Fear Historical Society Bulletin* 12 (1969): 1–6. For further discussion of rice cultivation and slavery, see James M. Clifton, "Golden Grains of White: Rice Planting on the Lower Cape Fear," *North Carolina Historical Review* 50 (1973): 365–93; William Dusinberre, *Them Dark Days: Slavery in the American Rice Swamps* (New York: Oxford University Press, 1996).

40. Thomas H. Jones, *The Experience of Thomas H. Jones Who Was a Slave* (New Bedford, Mass.: E. Anthony, 1871), 8–9; William H. Robinson, *From Log Cabin to the Pulpit or Fifteen Years in Slavery* (Eau Claire, Wis.: James Tifft, 1913), 56; William Henry Singleton, *Recollections of My Slavery Days* (Raleigh, N.C.: Division of Archives and History, 1999), 44.

41. Jones, *Experience*, 32; Evangeline Walker Andrews, ed., *Journal of a Lady of Quality* (New Haven, Conn.: Yale University Press, 1923), 176–77; Catherine W. Bishir, "Black Builders in Antebellum North Carolina," *North Carolina Historical Review* 61 (1984): 423–61; William B. Gould, *Diary of a Contraband* (Stanford, Calif.: Stanford University Press, 2002), 37.

42. William L. Saunders, ed., *The Colonial Records of North Carolina*, 10 vols. (Raleigh, N.C.: P. M. Hale, 1886–1890), 4:14; 7:515; 2:332–33.

43. Jones, *Experience*, 23. See also the discussion in Larry Tise, *Proslavery: A History of the Defense of Slavery in America, 1701–1840* (Athens: University of Georgia Press, 1987), and Stephen R. Haynes, *Noah's Curse: The Biblical Justification of American Slavery* (New York: Oxford University Press, 2002).

44. John D. Bellamy, *Memoirs of an Octogenarian* (Charlotte, N.C.: Observer Printing House, 1942), 16.

45. George Rawick, ed., *The American Slave*, 19 vols. (Westport, Conn.: Greenwood Press, 1972), 14:67, 23; 15:40, 346; Bellamy, *Memoirs*, 16; see also Milton C. Sernett, *Black Religion and American Evangelicalism: White Protestants, Plantation Missions, and the Flowering of Negro Christianity, 1787–1865* (Metuchen, N.J.: Scarecrow Press, 1975), 97.

46. Rawick, *American Slave*, 14:69; Jones, *Experience*, 15–16; Franklin, *Free*

Negro, 168; Janet D. Cornelius, *Slave Missions and the Black Church in the Antebellum South* (Columbia: University of South Carolina, 1999), 128–31.

47. Robinson, *From Log Cabin,* 56, 78–79.

48. Bellamy, *Memoirs,* 16; Robinson, *From Log Cabin,* 60, 79; Rawick, *American Slave,* 14:83.

49. Rawick, *American Slave,* 15:3; Asbury, *Journals,* 2:380; Rufus Bunnell, untitled manuscript, 1858, Manuscript and Archives Department, Yale University Library, New Haven, Conn.; Philo Tower, *Slavery Unmasked* (1856; New York: Negro Universities Press, 1969), 79.

50. Marshall D. Haywood, *Lives of the Bishops of North Carolina* (Raleigh, N.C.: Alfred Williams, 1910), 101–2; Richard Rankin, *Ambivalent Churchmen and Evangelical Churchwomen* (Columbia: University of South Carolina, 1993), 143–44; *Seventy-fifth Anniversary Memorial of the First Presbyterian Church,* 13–14.

51. Worsley, "Catholics in Antebellum North Carolina," 407; minutes of the First Baptist Church, Wilmington, January 1845, May 1845.

52. Robinson, *From Log Cabin,* 12–13, 118; Austin Bearse, *Reminiscences of Fugitive Slave Law Days in Boston* (1880; New York: Arno Press, 1969), 34–37. For a discussion of the Underground Railroad, see Larry Gara, *The Liberty Line: The Legacy of the Underground Railroad* (Lexington: University Press of Kentucky, 1996).

53. Robinson, *From Log Cabin,* 29–30, 72; Alan D. Watson, "Impulse toward Independence: Resistance and Rebellion among North Carolina Slaves, 1750–1775," *Journal of Negro History* 63 (1978): 322; Jeffrey J. Crow, "Slave Rebelliousness and Social Conflict in North Carolina, 1775 to 1802," *William and Mary Quarterly* 37 (1980): 87–88; Marvin L. M. Kay and Lorin L. Cary, *Slavery in North Carolina, 1748–1775* (Chapel Hill: University of North Carolina Press, 1995), 125–30. For a general discussion of runaways, see John Hope Franklin and Loren Schweninger, *Runaway Slaves: Rebels on the Plantation* (New York: Oxford University Press, 1999).

54. Alexander M. Walker, ed., *New Hanover County Court Minutes,* 4 vols. (Bethesda, N.C.: Alexander M. Walker, 1958–1960), 1:80; Crow, "Slave Rebelliousness," 93–94; James H. Brewer, "An Account of Negro Slavery in the Cape Fear Region Prior to 1860," (Ph.D. diss., University of Pittsburgh, 1949), 72; Andrews, *Lady of Quality,* 199–200.

55. Freddie L. Parker, *Running for Freedom: Slave Runaways in North Carolina, 1775–1840* (New York: Garland, 1993), 39.

56. Peter P. Hinks, *To Awaken My Afflicted Brethren: David Walker and the Problem of Antebellum Slave Resistance* (University Park: Pennsylvania State University Press, 1997), 11, 39, 108. For the text of the pamphlet, see Peter P. Hinks, ed., *David Walker's Appeal to the Coloured Citizens of the World* (University Park: Pennsylvania State University Press, 2000).

57. Hinks, *To Awaken,* 137–39; Derris Lea Raper, "The Effects of David Walker's *Appeal* and Nat Turner's Insurrection on North Carolina" (master's thesis, University of North Carolina at Chapel Hill, 1969), 32–41; Franklin, *Free Negro,* 66–70. Hinks provides the text of the McRee letter in *David Walker's Appeal,* 104–6.

58. See the entries in the diary of Moses Ashley Curtis for September 9–23, 1831, in the Moses Ashley Curtis Papers, Southern Historical Collection, University of North Carolina at Chapel Hill, and Charles E. Morris, "Panic and Reprisal: Reaction in North Carolina to the Nat Turner Insurrection, 1831," *North Carolina Historical Review* 62 (1985): 40–44.

59. Parker, *Running for Freedom*, 35–37; Walker, *New Hanover County Court Minutes*, 1:69.

60. Franklin, *Free Negro*, 71–72.

61. Kay and Cary, *Slavery in North Carolina*, 178; Michael A. Gomez, *Exchanging Our Country Marks: The Transformation of African Identities in the Colonial and Antebellum South* (Chapel Hill: University of North Carolina Press, 1998), 246.

62. Kay and Cary, *Slavery in North Carolina*, 173–78.

63. Elizabeth A. Fenn, "A Perfect Equality Seemed to Reign: Slave Society and Jonkonnu," *North Carolina Historical Review* 65 (1988): 127–53; Kay and Cary, *Slavery in North Carolina*, 183–86.

64. John C. Inscoe, "Carolina Slave Names: An Index to Acculturation," *Journal of Southern History* 49 (1983): 532, 539; Kay and Cary, *Slavery in North Carolina*, 138–43; Robinson, *From Log Cabin*, 152; Gomez, *Exchanging Our Country Marks*, 274–77; Albert J. Raboteau, *Slave Religion: The "Invisible Institution" in the Antebellum South* (New York: Oxford University Press, 1978), 228–31.

65. Sylviane A. Diouf, *Servants of Allah: African Muslims Enslaved in the Americas* (New York: New York University Press, 1998), 4, 46–48. See also the discussion in Allan D. Austin, *African Muslims in Antebellum America: Transatlantic Stories and Spiritual Struggles* (New York: Routledge, 1997); Richard B. Turner, *Islam in the African-American Experience* (Bloomington: Indiana University Press, 1997); and Gomez, *Exchanging Our Country Marks*, 59–87.

66. Allan D. Austin, *African Muslims in Antebellum America: A Sourcebook* (New York: Garland, 1984), 445–54, 464–68.

67. Austin, *African Muslims: Transatlantic Stories*, 128–56; Diouf, *Servants of Allah*, 76.

68. Diouf, *Servants of Allah*, 49–70. Matthew Grier's statement is reproduced in Austin, *African Muslims: Sourcebook*, 482. For Ibn Said's writings, see Austin, *African Muslims: Sourcebook*, 464, 466, and *African Muslims: Transatlantic Stories*, 137, 144.

69. *Biblical Recorder*, April 8, 1858.

70. Sandra Sizer, "Politics and Apolitical Religion: The Great Urban Revivals of the Late Nineteenth Century," *Church History* 48 (1979): 89; Kathryn T. Long, *The Revival of 1858* (New York: Oxford University Press, 1998), 8.

71. Prichard is quoted in *Wilmington Journal*, March 26, 1858; Deems is quoted in *Wilmington Journal*, April 9, 1858.

72. *North Carolina Standard* (Raleigh), March 24 and 31, 1858; *Raleigh Register*, March 31, 1858. For a discussion of the counterpart revival taking place in Great Britain, see Richard Carwardine, *Transatlantic Revivalism: Popular Evangelicalism in Britain and America, 1790–1865* (Westport, Conn.: Greenwood Press, 1978), 159–97.

73. Grier is quoted in *Seventy-fifth Anniversary Memorial of First Presbyterian Church*, 31–35; see also Historical Files, First Presbyterian Church, Wilmington.

74. Leonard I. Sweet, "'A Nation Born Again': The Union Prayer Meeting Revival and Cultural Revitalization," in *In the Great Tradition: Essays on Pluralism, Voluntarism, and Revivalism*, ed. Joseph D. Ban and Paul R. Dekar (Valley Forge, Pa.: Judson Press, 1982), 195.

5. Mystic Chords of Memory

1. Ruth Little, *Sticks and Stones: Three Centuries of North Carolina Gravemarkers* (Chapel Hill: University of North Carolina Press, 1998), 35–36.

2. Ibid., 32, 45–49.

3. Ibid., 49, 54–57, 62–63.

4. David Schuyler, *The New Urban Landscape* (Baltimore: Johns Hopkins University Press, 1986), 39–40; David C. Sloane, *The Last Great Necessity: Cemeteries in American History* (Baltimore: Johns Hopkins University Press, 1991), 28, 34–39.

5. Elizabeth F. McKoy, *Early Wilmington Block by Block* (Wilmington, N.C.: Edwards and Broughton, 1967), 129–30.

6. *Wilmington Advertiser*, February 4, 1841; *Wilmington Chronicle*, August 23, 1844.

7. *A Tribute to Oakdale, 1852–1991* (Wilmington, N.C.: Oakdale Cemetery Co., 1991), 1–2; Sloane, *Last Necessity*, 49–50.

8. Sloane, *Last Necessity*, 44–46.

9. Ibid., 56; Tony Wrenn, *Wilmington, North Carolina: An Architectural and Historical Portrait* (Charlottesville: University Press of Virginia, 1984), 294; James J. Farrell, *Inventing the American Way of Death, 1830–1920* (Philadelphia: Temple University Press, 1980), 110–11.

10. Schuyler, *New Urban Landscape*, 50; *Wilmington Morning Star*, April 21 and May 16, 1878.

11. *Wilmington Morning Star*, January 14, 1869.

12. *Tribute to Oakdale*, 4; Sloane, *Last Necessity*, 73.

13. Sloane, *Last Necessity*, 77–78; Little, *Sticks and Stones*, 179–86, 200–215.

14. Little, *Sticks and Stones*, 214–15.

15. Jo Ann Corrigan, "Yellow Fever: Scourge of the South," in *Disease and Distinctiveness in the American South*, ed. Todd L. Savitt and James H. Young (Knoxville: University of Tennessee Press, 1988), 55–78; Margaret Humphreys, *Yellow Fever and the South* (New Brunswick, N.J.: Rutgers University Press, 1992); William O. McMillan, M.D., and Donna Flake, "A Visit from Kate and Yellow Jack" (presented at the American Osler Society annual meeting, Charleston, S.C., April 18, 2001).

16. Thucydides, *The Complete Writings* (New York: Random House, 1934), 113; John D. Bellamy, *Memoirs of an Octogenarian* (Charlotte, N.C.: Observer Printing House, 1942), 27; *Wilmington Morning Star*, October 14, 1870.

17. J. B. Purcell, *Wilmington in Health and Disease* (Wilmington, N.C.: Journal Printer, 1867), 18–24; *Wilmington Journal*, March 30, 1863; Leora H.

McEachern and Isabel M. Williams, "The Prevailing Epidemic—1862," *Lower Cape Fear Historical Society Bulletin* 11 (1967): 1–20.

18. William S. Powell, *North Carolina through Four Centuries* (Chapel Hill: University of North Carolina Press, 1989), 356, 361; Chris E. Fonvielle Jr., *The Wilmington Campaign* (Campbell, Calif.: Savas Publishing Company, 1997); Rod Gragg, *Confederate Goliath: The Battle of Fort Fisher* (Baton Rouge: Louisiana State University Press, 1991); Richard E. Wood, "Port Town at War: Wilmington, North Carolina, 1860–1865" (Ph.D. diss., Florida State University, 1976); Henry Judson Beeker, "Wilmington during the Civil War" (master's thesis, Duke University, 1941); A Late Confederate Officer, "Wilmington during the Blockade," *Harper's New Monthly Magazine* 196 (1866): 497–503; *New York Tribune*, March 8, 1865.

19. *Seventy-fifth Anniversary Memorial of the First Presbyterian Church, Wilmington, N.C.* (Richmond, N.C.: Whitter and Shepperson, 1893), 16–17; *Church Messenger*, July 7, 1881; *Journal of the Fiftieth Annual Convention of the Protestant Episcopal Church in the State of North Carolina* (1866), 14; J. D. Hufham, *Memoir of Rev. John L. Prichard* (Raleigh, N.C.: Hufham and Hughes, 1867), 119; Lawrence F. Brewster, "Alfred Augustin Watson: Episcopal Clergyman of the New South," in *Studies in the History of the New South, 1875–1922*, ed., Loren K. Campion et al. (Greenville, N.C.: East Carolina College, 1966), 1–23; Gotthardt D. Bernheim, *The First Twenty Years of St. Paul's Evangelical Lutheran Church* (Wilmington, N.C.: Hall Publishers, 1879), 33.

20. Wrenn, *Wilmington*, 295–98.

21. John J. Winberry, "'Lest We Forget': The Confederate Monument and the Southern Townscape," *Southeastern Geographer* 23 (1983): 107–21; Charles R. Wilson, *Baptized in Blood: The Religion of the Lost Cause, 1865–1920* (Athens: University of Georgia Press, 1980); Gaines M. Foster, *Ghosts of the Confederacy: Defeat, the Lost Cause, and the Emergence of the New South 1865 to 1913* (New York: Oxford University Press, 1987); Karen L. Cox, *Dixie's Daughters: The United Daughters of the Confederacy and the Preservation of Confederate Culture* (Gainesville: University Press of Florida, 2003).

22. *Wilmington Morning Star*, May 10, 1871, May 2, 1982.

23. Buck Yearns, "George Davis," in *Dictionary of North Carolina Biography*, 6 vols., ed. William S. Powell (Chapel Hill: University of North Carolina Press, 1979–1996), 2:32–33.

24. Wrenn, *Wilmington*, 85–86, 203–4, 295; Wilson, *Baptized in Blood*, 58–78; Catherine W. Bishir, "Landmarks of Power: Building a Southern Past in Raleigh and Wilmington, North Carolina, 1885–1915," in *Where These Memories Grow: History, Memory, and Southern Identity*, ed. W. Fitzhugh Brundage (Chapel Hill: University of North Carolina Press, 2000), 139–68.

25. Wrenn, *Wilmington*, 304–8.

26. Joseph K. Barnes, ed., *The Medical and Surgical History of the War of the Rebellion 1861–1865* (1870), reprinted as *The Medical and Surgical History of the Civil War*, 10 vols. (Wilmington, N.C.: Broadfoot Publishing, 1991), 5:332; Wrenn, *Wilmington*, 314–15.

27. Wrenn, *Wilmington*, 308–12.

28. *Wilmington Morning Star,* November 6, 1994, March 2, 1999.

29. *Wilmington Morning Star,* January 30, 1869, January 21, 1896.

30. Farrell, *Inventing the American Way of Death,* 115–20.

31. Sloane, *Last Necessity,* 160–65, 175, 183–84.

32. *Wilmington Morning Star,* February 2, 1988, January 11, 2001.

33. Albert J. Raboteau, "African-Americans, Exodus, and the American Israel," in *African-American Christianity,* ed. Paul E. Johnson (Berkeley: University of California Press, 1994), 13. For a general discussion of religious reconstruction, see Clarence E. Walker, *A Rock in a Weary Land: The African Methodist Episcopal Church during the Civil War and Reconstruction* (Baton Rouge: Louisiana State University Press, 1982); Katherine L. Dvorak, *An African-American Exodus: The Segregation of the Southern Churches* (Brooklyn, N.Y.: Carlson Publishing, 1991); Stephen Ward Angell, *Bishop Henry McNeal Turner and African-American Religion in the South* (Knoxville: University of Tennessee Press, 1992); Reginald F. Hildebrand, *The Times Were Strange and Stirring* (Durham, N.C.: Duke University Press, 1995); Daniel W. Stowell, *Rebuilding Zion: The Religious Reconstruction of the South, 1863–1877* (New York: Oxford University Press, 1998).

34. L. S. Burkhead, "History of the Difficulties of the Pastorate of the Front Street Methodist Church, Wilmington, N.C., for the year 1865," in *Historical Papers of Trinity College,* ser. 8 (Durham, N.C.: Trinity College Historical Society, 1909), 41–44.

35. Burkhead, "Difficulties," 66; Edwin S. Redkey, ed., *A Grand Army of Black Men* (New York: Cambridge University Press, 1992), 169; Frenise A. Logan, *The Negro in North Carolina, 1876–1894* (Chapel Hill: University of North Carolina Press, 1964), 165.

36. Burkhead, "Difficulties," 98–99; Bill Reaves, *Strength through Struggle* (Wilmington, N.C.: New Hanover County Library, 1998), 103; Charles S. Smith, *A History of the African Methodist Episcopal Church* (Philadelphia: Book Concern of the AME Church, 1922), 513.

37. Reaves, *Strength through Struggle,* 103.

38. Wrenn, *Wilmington,* 136–39; Catherine W. Bishir, *North Carolina Architecture* (Chapel Hill: University of North Carolina Press, 1990), 320–21; Edward F. Turberg, *A Survey of Black Historical Sites in Wilmington, New Hanover County, North Carolina* (Wilmington, N.C.: City of Wilmington, 1983); Reaves, *Strength through Struggle,* 103.

39. *Church Messenger,* July 14, 1881.

40. *Church Messenger,* July 21, 1881; Crummel H. McDonald and Lee A. Shelton, "History of St. Mark's Church," in *100th Anniversary, St. Mark's Episcopal Church* (Wilmington, N.C.: St. Mark's Church, 1969), 1.

41. John L. Bell Jr., "Protestant Churches and the Negro in North Carolina during Reconstruction" (master's thesis, University of North Carolina at Chapel Hill, 1961), 111; *Church Messenger,* July 21, 1881.

42. McDonald and Shelton, "History of St. Mark," 8; Cynthia Zaitzevsky, *The Architecture of William Ralph Emerson, 1833–1917* (Cambridge: Fogg Art Museum, 1969).

43. Wrenn, *Wilmington*, 152–55.

44. Morris G. Seigler, *History of St. Andrews-Covenant Presbyterian Church, Wilmington N.C.* (Wilmington, N.C.: St. Andrews-Covenant Presbyterian Church, 1967), 4; Wrenn, *Wilmington*, 179–80.

45. *Sessional Records of the First Colored Presbyterian Church of Wilmington, North Carolina*, April 21, 1867; *First Annual Report of the General Assembly Committee on Freedmen* (Pittsburgh: James McMillan, 1866), 11.

46. *First Annual Report on Freedmen*, 14; John L. Bell Jr., "The Presbyterian Church and the Negro in North Carolina during Reconstruction," *North Carolina Historical Review* 40 (1963): 30; Andrew E. Murray, *Presbyterians and the Negro—A History* (Philadelphia: Presbyterian Historical Society, 1966), 177–80.

47. Murray, *Presbyterians and the Negro*, 174.

48. Kathleen Clark, "Celebrating Freedom: Emancipation Day Celebrations and African American Memory in the Early Reconstruction South," in Brundage, *Where These Memories Grow*, 107–32; Geneviève Fabre, "African-American Commemorative Celebrations in the Nineteenth Century," in *History and Memory in African-American Culture*, ed. Geneviève Fabre and Robert O'Meally (New York: Oxford University Press, 1994), 72–91.

49. *History of First Baptist Church* (Wilmington, N.C.: First Baptist Church, 1979), 1; John L. Bell Jr., "Baptists and the Negro in North Carolina during Reconstruction," *North Carolina Historical Review* 42 (1965): 401.

50. *Historical Sketch of St. Luke A.M.E. Zion Church* (Wilmington, N.C.: St. Luke AME Zion Church, 1945); Charles Heatwole, "A Geography of the African Methodist Episcopal Zion Church," *Southeastern Geographer* 26 (1986): 1–11; Sandy Martin, *For God and Race: The Religious and Political Leadership of AMEZ Bishop James Walker Hood* (Columbia: University of South Carolina Press, 1999), 59–60.

51. Reaves, *Strength through Struggle*, 18–23; Martin, *For God and Race*, 121–23; Catherine W. Bishir and Michael T. Southern, *A Guide to the Historic Architecture of Eastern North Carolina* (Chapel Hill: University of North Carolina Press, 1996), 256.

52. Evelyn B. Higginbotham, *Righteous Discontent: The Women's Movement in the Black Baptist Church, 1880–1920* (Cambridge, Mass.: Harvard University Press, 1993), 185–229.

53. Maxine D. Jones, "'A Glorious Work': The American Missionary Association and Black North Carolinians, 1863–1880" (Ph.D. diss., Florida State University, 1982), 52; Joe M. Richardson, *Christian Reconstruction: The American Missionary Association and Southern Blacks, 1861–1890* (Athens: University of Georgia Press, 1986), 65.

54. Wrenn, *Wilmington*, 264–65; *Gregory Congregational United Church of Christ 125th Anniversary Commemorative Book* (Wilmington, N.C.: Gregory Congregational Church, 1995).

55. Horace James, *Annual Report of the Superintendent of Negro Affairs in North Carolina, 1864* (Boston: Brown and Co. Publishers, 1865), 61; Jones, "Glorious Work," 62; Redkey, *Grand Army*, 170; Committee from the New

Hanover Retired School Personnel, *History of Education in New Hanover County, 1800–1980* (Wilmington, N.C.: n.p., 1981), 10; Roberta Sue Alexander, *North Carolina Faces the Freedmen* (Durham, N.C.: Duke University Press, 1985), 161; Sally G. McMillen, *To Raise up the South: Sunday Schools in Black and White Churches, 1865–1915* (Baton Rouge: Louisiana State University Press, 2002).

56. Redkey, *Grand Army*, 170; E. Franklin Frazier, *The Negro Church in America* (New York: Schocken Books, 1974), 50; Jeffrey J. Crow et al., *A History of African Americans in North Carolina* (Raleigh, N.C.: Division of Archives and History, 1992), 83–93.

57. Delta Sigma Theta Sorority, *Legacies Untold: Histories of Black Churches in the Greater Duplin County Area* (Duplin County: Delta Sigma Theta Chapter, 2002), 12–15, 19–20, 68–69.

58. Ibid., 100–102, 114–15; Jennifer F. Martin, *Along the Banks of the Old Northeast: The Historical and Architectural Development of Duplin County, North Carolina* (Rose Hill, N.C.: Duplin County Historical Foundation, 1999), 19.

59. Martin, *For God and Race*, 60–62; Weeks Parker, *Fayetteville, North Carolina: A Pictorial History* (Norfolk, Va.: Donning Company, 1984), 75; Bishir, *North Carolina Architecture*, 315–16; Roy Parker Jr., *Cumberland County: A Brief History* (Raleigh, N.C.: Division of Archives and History, 1990), 95.

60. Jones, "Glorious Work," 201–2; Parker, *Cumberland County*, 84–85.

61. Bell, "Baptists and the Negro in North Carolina," 407–8; William J. Walls, *The African Methodist Episcopal Zion Church* (Charlotte, N.C.: AME Zion Publishing House, 1974), 188; Bell, "Protestant Churches and the Negro in North Carolina," 92; Bell, "Presbyterian Churches and the Negro in North Carolina," 30; Jones, "Glorious Work," 155.

62. Rachel Wischnitzer, *Synagogue Architecture in the United States: History and Interpretation* (Philadelphia: Jewish Publication Society of America, 1955), 11.

63. Ibid., 13–14, 19, 22; Alexander M. Walker, ed., *New Hanover County Court Minutes*, 4 vols. (Bethesda, N.C.: Alexander M. Walker, 1958–1960), 1:6, 13; Kimberly Sims, "Wilmington Jewry, 1800–1914" (unpublished manuscript, 1999), 3–6; Emily Bingham, *Mordecai: An Early American Family* (New York: Hill and Wang, 2003).

64. Leonard Dinnerstein and Mary D. Palsson, eds., *Jews in the South* (Baton Rouge: Louisiana State University Press, 1973), 25; Sims, "Wilmington Jewry," 8–10.

65. McKoy, *Early Wilmington Block by Block*, 115.

66. Jon Henry Gerdes, "The Early Jews of Wilmington," *Lower Cape Fear Historical Society Bulletin* 28 (1984): 4; Sims, "Wilmington Jewry," 11–12.

67. Martin Weitz, ed., *Bibilog* (Wilmington, N.C.: Temple of Israel, 1976), 12–14; Beverly Tetterton et al., eds., *History of the Temple of Israel, Wilmington, North Carolina, 1876–2001* (Wilmington, N.C.: Temple of Israel, 2001), 41–42; *Wilmington Morning Star*, October 1, 1867.

68. Leon A. Jick, *The Americanization of the Synagogue, 1820–1870* (Hanover, N.H.: University Press of New England, 1976), 81, 86; *Wilmington Morning Star*, November 26, 1872.

69. Tetterton et al., *History of the Temple of Israel*, 10, 32–34.

70. Miles Danby, *Moorish Style* (London: Phaidon Press, 1995), 188–96.

71. H. A. Meek, *The Synagogue* (London: Phaidon Press, 1995), 188–96; Danby, *Moorish Style*, 178–87; Wischnitzer, *Synagogue Architecture*, 69.

72. Meek, *Synagogue*, 194; Danby, *Moorish Style*, 190; Wischnitzer, *Synagogue Architecture*, 67–68, 70–85.

73. Danby, *Moorish Style*, 34–36.

74. Wrenn, *Wilmington*, 117–19; *Wilmington Morning Star*, May 13, 1876; James Sprunt, *Chronicles of the Cape Fear River, 1660–1916* (1916; Wilmington, N.C.: Broadfoot Publishing, 1992), 644; Harold N. Cooledge Jr., *Samuel Sloan: Architect of Philadelphia, 1815–1884* (Philadelphia: University of Pennsylvania Press, 1986), 67–71, 207, 229.

75. *Wilmington Morning Star*, October 23, 1989; Samuel Mendelsohn Papers, Special Collections, University of North Carolina at Wilmington.

76. Mendelsohn, "Inaugural Address," Mendelsohn Papers.

77. Tetterton et al., *History of the Temple of Israel*, 12–17, 25; *Wilmington Morning Star*, October 1, 1922.

78. Gerald Sorin, *A Time for Building: The Third Immigration, 1880–1920* (Baltimore: Johns Hopkins University Press, 1992), 32–33.

79. David J. Goldberg, "An Historical Community Study of Wilmington Jewry, 1738–1925" (unpublished manuscript, 1976), 36; Barbara F. Waxman et al., eds., *The First Hundred Years: A History of B'nai Israel Synagogue, 1898–1998* (Wilmington, N.C.: B'nai Israel Synagogue, 1998), 10.

80. Waxman et al., *History of B'nai Israel Synagogue*, 10–11; Wischnitzer, *Synagogue Architecture*, 41.

81. Leonard Rogoff, "The History of Jews in North Carolina" (Cape Fear Museum, January 21, 2001); *Wilmington Morning Star*, December 31, 1985, July 24, 1997, 30 September 30, 1998.

82. Waxman et al., *History of B'nai Israel Synagogue*, 19–20.

83. Ibid., 16–19, 22; interview with William Kingoff, April 1, 2004. On the broader patterns of Jewish life in the suburbs, see Jonathan D. Sarna, *American Judaism: A History* (New Haven, Conn.: Yale University Press, 2004), 282–93.

84. Eli N. Evans, *The Lonely Days Were Sundays* (Jackson: University Press of Mississippi, 1993); Eli N. Evans, *The Provincials: A Personal History of Jews in the South* (New York: Free Press, 1997); Tetterton et al., *History of the Temple of Israel*, 17; Waxman et al., *History of B'nai Israel Synagogue*, 22, 35; Leonard Dinnerstein, *Antisemitism in America* (New York: Oxford University Press, 1994), 175–96.

85. *Wilmington Morning Star*, August 13, 1995; *Newsweek*, August 21, 2001.

86. *Africo-American Presbyterian*, August 19, 1897.

87. *Wilmington Messenger*, November 8, 1898; George Rountree, "Memorandum of My Personal Recollection of the Election of 1898," Henry G. Connor Papers, Southern Historical Collection, University of North Carolina at Chapel Hill; *Wilmington Messenger*, October 25, 1898.

88. H. Leon Prather Sr., *We Have Taken a City: Wilmington Racial Massacre*

and Coup of 1898 (Wilmington, N.C.: NU Enterprises, 1998), 68–80. See also the essays in David S. Cecelski and Timothy B. Tyson, eds., *Democracy Betrayed: The Wilmington Race Riot of 1898 and Its Legacy* (Chapel Hill: University of North Carolina Press, 1998).

89. *Wilmington Messenger,* November 11, 1898; Prather, *We Have Taken a City,* 136–39.

90. B. F. Keith to Marion Butler, November 17, 1898, Marion Butler Papers, Southern Historical Collection, University of North Carolina at Chapel Hill; *Caucasian,* November 17, 1898; Prather, *We Have Taken a City,* 133–34.

91. Prather, *We Have Taken a City,* 96–98, 142; J. Allen Kirk, *A Statement of Facts Concerning the Bloody Riot in Wilmington, N.C.* (Wilmington, N.C.: J. Allen Kirk, 1898), 11–13; *News and Observer* (Raleigh), November 15, 1898; *Wilmington Messenger,* November 12, 1898.

92. *News and Observer,* November 15, 1898; *Wilmington Morning Star,* November 15, 1898; *Wilmington Messenger,* November 13, 1898.

93. *Wilmington Messenger,* October 25, 1898; *The Centennial Record* (Wilmington, N.C.: 1898 Centennial Foundation, 1998); Melton A. McLaurin, "Commemorating Wilmington's Racial Violence of 1898: From Individual to Collective Memory," *Southern Cultures* 6 (2000): 35–57.

6. Religion and the New South

1. *Wilmington: The Metropolis and Port of North Carolina* (Wilmington, N.C.: Chamber of Commerce, 1912), 1, 5; *Souvenir of Wilmington, N.C.* (Wilmington, N.C.: C. Yates, 1915).

2. *Wilmington: The Metropolis,* 17.

3. See "The Population Analyzed," Thomas Fanning Wood Papers, Special Collections, University of North Carolina at Wilmington.

4. J. Marcus Kester, *Historical Sketch of First Baptist Church in Wilmington N.C., 1808–1933* (Wilmington, N.C.: First Baptist Church, 1933), 21–25; James D. Hufham, *Memoir of Rev. John L. Prichard* (Raleigh, N.C.: Hufham and Hughes, 1867), 124; Tony P. Wrenn, *Wilmington, North Carolina: An Architectural and Historical Portrait* (Charlottesville: University Press of Virginia, 1984), 209–12.

5. *Seventy-fifth Anniversary Memorial of the First Presbyterian Church, Wilmington N.C.* (Richmond, N.C.: Whittet and Shepperson, 1893), 16; Wrenn, *Wilmington,* 92.

6. See Harold N. Cooledge Jr., *Samuel Sloan, Architect of Philadelphia, 1815–1884* (Philadelphia: University of Pennsylvania Press, 1986), and Catherine W. Bishir, *North Carolina Architecture* (Chapel Hill: University of North Carolina Press, 1990), 339–41.

7. Hufham, *Memoir of Prichard,* 121; Gotthardt D. Bernheim, *The First Twenty Years of St. Paul's Evangelical Lutheran Church* (Wilmington, N.C.: S. G. Hall, 1879), 11–12.

8. Bernheim, *First Twenty Years,* 11–15.

9. Ibid., 17–19, 27–28.

10. Ibid., 19–26, 34–43; Wrenn, *Wilmington*, 217–19.

11. *The Windows of St. Paul's* (Wilmington, N.C.: St. Paul's Church, 1989), 3–4; Gilbert L. Weeder and Ann Hewlett Hutteman, "Frank Ellsworth Weeder," *Stained Glass* 92 (1997): 130–36.

12. Virginia C. Raguin, *Glory in Glass: Stained Glass in the United States* (New York: American Bible Society, 1999), 1–3, 41.

13. Ibid., 79–80; *Windows of St. Paul's*, 3–4.

14. Raguin, *Glory in Glass*, 143–57; *Windows of St. Paul's*, 3–4.

15. Bernheim, *First Twenty Years*, 54; *Wilmington Morning Star*, April 11, 1871.

16. Bernheim, *First Twenty Years*, 52–53.

17. See "St. Matthew's Evangelical Church, Wilmington, North Carolina, 1892–1992" (typescript, 1992); Earl K. Bodie, *Historical Sketch of St. Matthew's Evangelical Lutheran Church, Wilmington, N.C.* (Wilmington, N.C.: St. Matthew's Evangelical Lutheran Church, 1933), 3–10; Raymond M. Bost and Jeff L. Norris, *All One Body: The Story of the North Carolina Lutheran Synod, 1803–1933* (Salisbury: North Carolina Synod, 1994), 196.

18. *Amazing Grace: Two Hundred Years of Methodism* (Wilmington, N.C.: Grace United Methodist Church, 1985), 19–25.

19. Ibid., 25–28; Leland M. Roth, *American Architecture: A History* (Boulder, Colo.: Westview Press, 2001), 181–83, 252–60.

20. "A Brief History of Fifth Avenue United Methodist Church" (typescript, n.d.); Wrenn, *Wilmington*, 149–50.

21. Wrenn, *Wilmington*, 149–50; Kenneth E. Rowe, "Redesigning Methodist Churches: Auditorium-Style Sanctuaries and Akron-Plan Sunday Schools in Romanesque Costume, 1875–1925," in *Connectionalism: Ecclesiology, Mission, and Identity*, ed. Russell E. Richey et al. (Nashville: Abingdon Press, 1997), 122–23; Roth, *American Architecture*, 216–26.

22. Wrenn, *Wilmington*, 149–50.

23. Rowe, "Redesigning Methodist Churches," 119–23; Jeanne Halgren Kilde, *When Church Became Theatre: The Transformation of Evangelical Architecture and Worship in Nineteenth-Century America* (New York: Oxford University Press, 2002).

24. *Directory of Fifth St. M. E. Church, South* (Wilmington, N.C.: Messenger Steam Power Presses, 1888), 6–8.

25. Rowe, "Redesigning Methodist Churches," 123–28.

26. Ibid., 127.

27. Ibid., 131; Karen B. Westerfield Tucker, *American Methodist Worship* (New York: Oxford University Press, 2001), 246–48.

28. Sterling Seagrave, *The Soong Dynasty* (New York: Harper and Row, 1985), 16–27.

29. Ibid., 28–39, 46, 59–62.

30. Ibid., 54, 68, 84, 96, 135–37, 189, 265–69, 416; *Wilmington Morning Star*, October 12, 2002.

31. Caroline D. Flanner, "The Reverend Augustus Foster Lyde (1813–1834)," *Lower Cape Fear Historical Society Bulletin* 4 (1961).

32. See the excellent study by Lawrence D. Kessler, *The Jiangyin Mission Station: An American Missionary Community in China, 1895–1951* (Chapel Hill: University of North Carolina Press, 1996); for biographical details on the Worths, see 20, 29–30.

33. Ibid., 2, 11–18, 31–38.

34. Ibid., 48, 131–33.

35. Ibid., 157–61; quotation 2. For a parallel conclusion on the efficacy of one group of nineteenth-century domestic missionaries, see William G. McLoughlin, *Cherokees and Missionaries, 1789–1839* (New Haven, Conn.: Yale University Press, 1984).

36. Kessler, *Jiangyin Mission Station*, 30–36, 146–152.

37. Ibid., 37–40, 133–39.

38. Ibid., 137, 153.

39. For an anecdotal reminiscence about David Herring, see the volume by his daughter, Susan Herring Jeffries, *Papa Wore No Halo* (Winston-Salem, N.C.: John Blair, 1963). For a photograph of the Worths, see Kessler, *Jiangyin Mission Station*, 32.

40. Kessler, *Jiangyin Mission Station*, 141; Jeffries, *Papa Wore No Halo*, 171; Lawrence D. Kessler, *North Carolina's "China Connection," 1840–1949* (Raleigh: North Carolina China Council, 1981).

41. D. F. Grant, "Thomas Frederick Price," in *Dictionary of North Carolina Biography*, 6 vols., ed. William S. Powell (Chapel Hill: University of North Carolina Press, 1979–1996), 5:145; John C. Murrett, *Tar Heel Apostle: Thomas Frederick Price* (New York: Longmans, 1944); Robert E. Sheridan, *The Founders of Maryknoll* (Maryknoll, N.Y.: Maryknoll Fathers, 1980); Angelyn Dries, *The Missionary Movement in American Catholic History* (Maryknoll, N.Y.: Orbis, 1998); *Wilmington Morning Star*, December 25, 1995.

42. John Tracy Ellis, *The Life of James Cardinal Gibbons*, 2 vols. (Milwaukee: Bruce Publishers, 1952); William F. Powers, *Tar Heel Catholics: A History of Catholicism in North Carolina* (Lanham, Md.: University Press of America, 2003), 467 n. 21.

43. Louis Garaventa, "Bishop James Gibbons and the Growth of the Roman Catholic Church in North Carolina, 1868–1872" (master's thesis, University of North Carolina at Chapel Hill, 1973), 21; James Gibbons, *Reminiscences of Catholicity in North Carolina* (Baltimore: n.p., 1891), 2–4.

44. Garaventa, "Bishop James Gibbons," 50–56; "Sisters of Mercy," in *Cape Fear Deanery 175th Anniversary* (Wilmington, N.C.: Diocese of Raleigh, 1997).

45. Charles H. Bowman Jr., "Dr. John Carr Monk: Sampson County's Latter Day 'Cornelius,'" *North Carolina Historical Review* 50 (January 1975): 60–64; Gibbons, *Reminiscences*, 9.

46. Powers, *Tar Heel Catholics*, 163–66; Gibbons, *Reminiscences*, 10–12; Bowman, "Monk," 64–69.

47. Powers, *Tar Heel Catholics*, 276; *Twenty-fifth Anniversary of St. Mary's Pro-Cathedral* (Wilmington, N.C.: St. Mary's Pro-Cathedral, 1937).

48. George R. Collins, "The Transfer of Thin Masonry Vaulting from Spain

to America," *Journal of the Society of Architectural Historians* 27 (1968):176–83; *Twenty-fifth Anniversary of St. Mary;* Wrenn, *Wilmington,* 145–46.

49. Collins, "Transfer of Thin Masonry," 191–200.

50. Powers, *Tar Heel Catholics,* 272–79; Cyprian Davis, *The History of Black Catholics in the United States* (New York: Crossroad, 1993), 205–6.

51. Powers, *Tar Heel Catholics,* 211–13, 277–78; James J. Kenneally, *The History of American Catholic Women* (New York: Crossroad, 1990), 55–56; Stephen J. Ochs, *Desegregating the Altar: The Josephites and the Struggle for Black Priests, 1871–1960* (Baton Rouge: Louisiana State University Press, 1990).

52. Powers, *Tar Heel Catholics,* 237–43; Jon W. Anderson and William B. Friend, eds., *The Culture of Bible Belt Catholics* (New York: Paulist Press, 1995).

53. *Wilmington Morning Star,* November 18, 1902.

54. Mrs. Frances E. Slattery, "The Catholic Woman in Modern Times," quoted in Rosemary Ruether and Rosemary Keller, eds., *Women and Religion in America,* 3 vols. (New York: Harper and Row, 1986), 3:188–90.

55. *St. Thomas the Apostle Catholic Church, 1847–1947* (Wilmington, N.C.: St. Thomas the Apostle Church, 1947), 11; *75th Jubilee, St. Mary Church, Wilmington, North Carolina, 1912–1987* (Wilmington, N.C.: St. Mary Church, 1987).

56. Susan Hill Lindley, *You Have Stept out of Your Place: A History of Women and Religion in America* (Louisville, Ky.: Westminster John Knox Press, 1996), 197–98.

57. Steven C. Bullock, *Revolutionary Brotherhood* (Chapel Hill: University of North Carolinas Press, 1996), 46; Bill Reaves, *Strength through Struggle* (Wilmington, N.C.: New Hanover County Library, 1998), 22; *St. Mary 75th Jubilee.*

58. *Wilmington Morning Star,* June 30, 1886; G. W. Steevens, *The Land of the Dollar* (New York: Dodd Mead and Co., 1897), 98. For a discussion of the social impact of electrification, see David E. Nye, *Electrifying America: Social Meanings of a New Technology* (Cambridge, Mass.: MIT Press, 1990).

59. *Calvary Baptist Church* (typescript, 1992); Morris Siegler, *History of St. Andrews-Covenant Presbyterian Church* (Wilmington, N.C.: St. Andrews-Covenant Presbyterian Church, 1967), 8–10.

60. Stephen D. Maguire, "Tidewater Power Company," *Trolley Sparks* 81 (1948): 4, 7; Michael J. Dunn III, "Age of the Trolley Cars," *State* 37 (1969): 8–10; *Wilmington Morning Star,* April 19, 1939; Kenneth T. Jackson, *Crabgrass Frontier: The Suburbanization of the United States* (New York: Oxford University Press, 1985), 103–15.

61. Margaret Supplee Smith, "The American Idyll in North Carolina's First Suburbs: Landscape and Architecture," in *Early Twentieth-Century Suburbs in North Carolina,* ed. Catherine W. Bishir and Lawrence S. Earley (Raleigh, N.C.: Division of Archives and History, 1985), 21; David R. Goldfield, "North Carolina's Early Twentieth-Century Suburbs and the Urbanizing South," in ibid., 14. See also Blaine A. Brownell and David R. Goldfield, eds., *The City in Southern History* (Port Washington, N.Y.: Kennikat Press, 1977),

and Lawrence H. Larsen, *The Rise of the Urban South* (Lexington: University Press of Kentucky, 1985).

62. William H. Wilson, *The City Beautiful Movement* (Baltimore: Johns Hopkins University Press, 1989); Goldfield, "Early Twentieth-Century Suburbs," 10–15.

63. S. Carol Gunter, *Carolina Heights* (Wilmington, N.C.: Planning Department of the City of Wilmington, 1982), 3–5, 53–56.

64. Ibid., 56–59.

65. Ibid., 59–66.

66. Ibid., 66.

67. Robert Peel, *Mary Baker Eddy: The Years of Discovery* (New York: Holt, Rinehart and Winston, 1966), 69–72; Gillian Gill, *Mary Baker Eddy* (Reading, Pa.: Perseus Books, 1998), 60–63.

68. Stephen Gottschalk, *The Emergence of Christian Science in American Religious Life* (Berkeley: University of California Press, 1973), 46–97.

69. Sydney E. Ahlstrom, *A Religious History of the American People* (New Haven, Conn.: Yale University Press, 1972), 1019.

70. Gunter, *Carolina Heights*, 59; Thomas J. Schlereth, "A High-Victorian Gothicist as Beaux-Arts Classicist: The Architectural Odyssey of Solon Spencer Beman," *Studies in Medievalism* 3 (1990): 144; Paul E. Ivey, *Prayers in Stone: Christian Science Architecture in the United States, 1894–1930* (Urbana: University of Illinois Press, 1999), 139–44.

71. Gunter, *Carolina Heights*, 70–73.

72. Harriet O. Jeffries, "Brief History of Saint Paul's Church" (typescript, 1978), 2; *Wilmington Morning Star,* July 14, 1912; Wrenn, *Wilmington*, 279–80.

73. Siegler, *History of St. Andrews-Covenant*, 36–42, 47–48; Wrenn, *Wilmington*, 277–78.

74. Betty Sue Westbrook, "History of Trinity United Methodist Church, Wilmington, North Carolina, 1889–1991" (typescript, 1991), 1–4; James Sprunt, *Chronicles of the Cape Fear* (1916; Wilmington, N.C.: Broadfoot Publishing, 1992), 396–406.

75. *Wilmington Morning Star*, June 22, 2002; Siegler, *History of St. Andrews-Covenant*, 47; Kester, *Historical Sketch of First Baptist*, 33.

7. Pluralism in the Port City and Beyond

1. Hugh MacRae, *Bringing Immigrants to the South* (New York: North Carolina Society of New York, 1908), 3; Robert W. Vincent, "Successful Immigrants in the South, *World's Work* 17 (1908): 10908–11; George Byrne, "Hugh MacRae's Practical Application of Common Sense in Colonization," *Manufacturers Record* 61 (1912): 49–53.

2. MacRae, *Bringing Immigrants*, 8–9; *Wilmington Messenger,* December 13, 1905; *Pender Chronicle*, February 28, 1996.

3. *Cape Fear Deanery 175th Anniversary* (Wilmington, N.C.: Diocese of Raleigh, 1997); Donald F. Staib, ed., *Diocese of Raleigh: Histories 1982* (Raleigh, N.C.: Diocese of Raleigh, 1982), 11–12.

4. Nestor J. Boruch, "In Observance of the 50th Anniversary of Sts. Peter and Paul Russian Orthodox Church" (typescript, 1982); *Wilmington Morning Star,* January 15, 1996.

5. Tamara Talbot Rice, *A Concise History of Russian Art* (New York: Praeger, 1963), 18; Boruch, *In Observance of the 50th Anniversary.* For further discussion of the Russian background, see George Heard Hamilton, *The Art and Architecture of Russia* (Harmondsworth: Penguin, 1975), 1–67; Catherine Evtuhov, David Goldfrank, Lindsey Hughes, and Richard Stites, *A History of Russia: Peoples, Legends, Events, Forces* (Boston: Houghton Mifflin, 2004), 50–53.

6. For a discussion of Russian Orthodoxy in America, see Thomas E. Fitzgerald, *The Orthodox Church* (Westport, Conn.: Praeger, 1998).

7. Staib, *Diocese of Raleigh,* 20–21; *Wilmington Morning Star,* July 27, 1997.

8. Militiades E. Efthimiou and George A. Christopoulos, eds., *History of the Greek Orthodox Church in America* (New York: Greek Orthodox Archdiocese of North and South America, 1984), 1–10.

9. Ibid., 1–36; Fitzgerald, *Orthodox Church,* 37–41, 53–62, 87–89; *Wilmington Morning Star,* September 22, 1996, August 20, 1999.

10. *Wilmington Morning Star,* November 21, 1910, March 22, 1913, March 21, 1932.

11. *Wilmington Morning Star,* January 19, 1911, April 9, 1911, January 20, 1917.

12. *St. Nicholas Greek Orthodox Church, 50th Anniversary, 1945–1995, Wilmington, North Carolina* (Wilmington, N.C.: St. Nicholas Greek Orthodox Church, 1995), 20–23; *Wilmington Morning Star,* October 8, 1988, September 10, 1993, March 24, 2001, October 10, 2003; Elizabeth H. Prodromou, "Religious Pluralism in Twenty-first-Century America: Problematizing the Implications for Orthodox Christianity," *Journal of the American Academy of Religion* 72 (2004): 733–57.

13. Historical Files, Sts. Constantine and Helen Greek Orthodox Church, Fayetteville, N.C.

14. Morris G. Siegler, *History of St. Andrews-Covenant Presbyterian Church* (Wilmington, N.C.: St. Andrews-Covenant Presbyterian Church, 1967), 17–19.

15. Anne Little, ed., *Columbus County, North Carolina: Recollections and Records* (Whiteville, N.C.: County Commissioners, 1980), 352.

16. Frederick C. Luebke, *Bonds of Loyalty: German Americans and World War I* (De Kalb: Northern Illinois University Press, 1974); Parish Register IV, 1907–1950, Historical Files, St. Paul's Evangelical Lutheran Church, Wilmington, N.C.

17. Little, *Columbus County,* 355–58; Staib, *Diocese of Raleigh,* 84–85; *Cape Fear Deanery 175th Anniversary.*

18. John F. Corey, "The Colonization and Contributions of Emigrants Brought to Southeastern North Carolina by Hugh MacRae" (master's thesis, Appalachian State Teachers College, 1957), 76.

19. Susan Taylor Block, "Van Eeden," *Lower Cape Fear Historical Society Bulletin* 40 (1995): 2–72.

20. *Wilmington Morning Star,* March 24, 1934, April 6, 1999, August 24, 1940.

21. *Wilmington Morning Star,* November 29, 1917, August 12, 1914, March 24, 1934; Jon A. Peterson, "The Impact of Sanitary Reform upon American Urban Planning, 1840–1890," *Journal of Social History* 13 (1979): 83–104.

22. William Jackson Greene, "Silent Holocaust: The Influenza Epidemic of 1918–19 and Its Effects on Wilmington, North Carolina," *Lower Cape Fear Historical Society Bulletin* 36 (1991): 1–7; David L. Cockrell, "'A Blessing in Disguise': The Influenza Pandemic of 1918 and North Carolina's Medical and Public Health Communities," *North Carolina Historical Review* 63 (1996): 309–27.

23. Joel A. Tarr, "Urban Pollution—Many Long Years Ago," *American Heritage* 22 (1971): 65–69, 106; Stephen D. Maguire, "Tidewater Power Company," *Trolley Sparks* 81 (1948): 7; *Wilmington Morning Star,* April 19, 1939.

24. *Wilmington Morning Star,* June 16, 1969; William F. Powers, *Tar Heel Catholics: A History of Catholicism in North Carolina* (Lanham, Md.: University Press of America, 2003), 48–52, 88.

25. Raymond Arsenault, "The End of the Long Hot Summer: The Air Conditioner and Southern Culture," *Journal of Southern History* 50 (1984): 597–628.

26. Everard H. Smith, "Wartime Wilmington: An Overview," *Lower Cape Fear Historical Society Bulletin* 43 (1999): 1; Wilbur D. Jones Jr., *A Sentimental Journey: Memoirs of a Wartime Boomtown* (Shippensburg, Pa.: White Mane Books, 2002), 127–42, 51–54.

27. Smith, "Wartime Wilmington," 3–4; Jones, *Sentimental Journey,* 55–65, 94–95.

28. Smith, "Wartime Wilmington," 4, 6; Jones, *Sentimental Journey,* 90, 161, 181.

29. Catherine Lutz, *Homefront: A Military City and the American Twentieth Century* (Boston: Beacon Press, 2001), 45–86.

30. Ibid., 59–61, 73.

31. See Hubert A. Eaton, *Every Man Should Try* (Wilmington, N.C.: Bonaparte Press, 1984), and Marjorie Megivern, *Human Relations—20 Years of Struggles, 1963–1983: A History of the New Hanover Human Relations Commission* (Wilmington, N.C.: New Hanover Human Relations Commission, 1984).

32. *Wilmington Morning Star,* April 8 and 11, 1968.

33. *Wilmington Morning Star,* February 4, 5, 11, and 14, 1971.

34. *Wilmington Morning Star,* February 18, 1996; John L. Godwin, *Black Wilmington and the North Carolina Way: Portrait of a Community in the Era of Civil Rights Protest* (Lanham, Md.: University Press of America, 2000), 242.

35. *Wilmington Morning Star,* October 12, 1997; James M. Washington, ed., *Testament of Hope: The Essential Writings of Martin Luther King, Jr.* (San Francisco: HarperSanFrancisco, 1991), 479.

36. See Kathleen C. Berkeley, *The Women's Liberation Movement in America* (Westport, Conn.: Greenwood Press, 1999).

37. Barbara Brown Zikmund, "Winning Ordination for Women in Main-

stream Protestant Churches," and Ann D. Braude, "Jewish Women in the Twentieth Century: Building a Life in America," in *Women and Religion in America*, 3 vols., ed. Rosemary Radford Ruether and Rosemary Skinner Keller (New York: Harper and Row, 1981–1986), 3:339–48 and 137–40; Susan Hill Lindley, *You Have Stept out of Your Place: A History of Women and Religion in America* (Louisville, Ky.: Westminster John Knox Press, 1996), 308–21.

38. Zikmund, "Winning Ordination," 348.

39. See Roger Daniels, *Coming to America* (New York: HarperCollins, 1990), 282–83, 328, 338–44.

40. *Wilmington Morning Star*, November 20, 1993, October 17, 1995, June 26, 1997.

41. Tony Wrenn, *Wilmington, North Carolina: An Architectural and Historical Portrait* (Charlottesville: University Press of Virginia, 1984), 92–93; "Obituary: Hobart Brown Upjohn," *Architectural Record* 106 (1949): 158.

42. Wrenn, *Wilmington*, 93–94; *Let There Be Light* (Wilmington, N.C.: First Presbyterian Church, 1990).

43. Wrenn, *Wilmington*, 171–73; *Amazing Grace: Two Hundred Years of Methodism* (Wilmington, N.C.: Grace United Methodist Church, 1985), 37.

44. *St. John's Episcopal Church* (Wilmington, N.C.: St. John's Episcopal Church, n.d.); *Wilmington Morning Star*, June 29, 1947; Historical Files, Windemere Presbyterian Church, Wilmington, N.C.; *A Historical Sketch of Southside Baptist Church, Wilmington, North Carolina, 1894–1994* (Wilmington, N.C.: Southside Baptist Church, 1994).

45. *Wilmington Morning Star*, August 5, 1956, September 30, 1998; Historical Files, Pearsall Memorial Presbyterian Church, Wilmington, N.C.

46. Raymond H. Taylor, *A History of Winter Park Baptist Church, 1913–1988* (Wilmington, N.C.: Jackson and Bell Printers, 1988); Historical Files, Winter Park Baptist Church, Wesley Memorial United Methodist Church, Wilmington, N.C.

47. Susan Taylor Block, "A History of Mt. Lebanon Chapel," *Lower Cape Fear Historical Society Bulletin* 42 (1998): 1–8; Historical Files, St. Andrews On-the-Sound Episcopal Church, Wilmington, N.C.; David Gebhard, "The Spanish Colonial Revival in Southern California 1895–1930," *Journal of the Society of Architectural Historians* 26 (1967): 131–47.

48. See Rupert Benson and Helen Benson, *Historical Narrative of Wrightsville Beach, North Carolina, 1841–1972* (Wilmington, N.C.: Carolina Printing Company, 1972); Greg Watkins, *Wrightsville Beach: A Pictorial History* (Wrightsville Beach, N.C.: Wrightsville Beach Publishing Company, 1997).

49. Historical Files, St. Therese Roman Catholic Church, Wrightsville Beach, N.C.; Helen W. McCarl and Huw Christopher, *What God Hath Wrought: A History of the Little Chapel on the Boardwalk* (Wilmington, N.C.: Little Chapel on the Boardwalk, 1992); *Wilmington Morning Star*, January 18, 2003; Historical Files, St. Mark Roman Catholic Church, Wilmington, N.C.

50. *Wilmington Morning Star*, November 17, 1984, July 21, 2001.

51. Edward F. Turberg, *Sunset Park Neighborhood Architectural Survey* (Wilmington, N.C.: Historic Wilmington Foundation, 1996); Annette H.

Davis, *Forty Fruitful Years, 1942–1982: A History of Sunset Park Baptist Church* (Wilmington, N.C.: Sunset Park Baptist Church, 1982); Historical Files, Sunset Park Baptist Church, Wilmington, N.C.; *Wilmington Morning Star,* June 21 and 22, 1998.

52. Historical Files, First Christian Church, Wilmington, N.C.; letter from Charles H. Boney to author, October 18, 2004; David Watkin, *A History of Western Architecture* (New York: Barnes and Noble, 1996), 515–16.

53. Historical Files, Seagate Community Chapel, Oleander United Methodist Church, Wilmington, N.C.

54. Historical Files, Cape Fear Presbyterian Church, Pine Valley Baptist Church, Pine Valley United Methodist Church, Pine Valley Church of God, Wilmington, N.C.

55. Historical Files, Messiah Lutheran Church, Missouri Synod; Pine Valley Church of Christ, Wilmington, N.C.; *Wilmington Morning Star,* April 20, 2002.

56. Interview with the Reverend Jon Peterson, November 14, 2003; Historical Files, Covenant Moravian Church; C. Daniel Crews and Richard W. Starbuck, *With Courage for the Future: The Story of the Moravian Church, Southern Province* (Winston-Salem, N.C.: Moravian Church in America, Southern Province, 2002), 724–25.

57. Historical Files, United Advent Christian Church, Wilmington, N.C.; *Wilmington Morning Star,* December 21, 2002.

58. Historical Files, Church of Jesus Christ of Latter-day Saints, Wilmington, N.C.; interview with Elder Rodney Earle, May 12, 1993; *Wilmington Dispatch,* April 9, 1900; Richard W. Jackson, *Places of Worship: 150 Years of Latter-day Saint Architecture* (Provo, Utah: Brigham Young University Press, 2003), 261–66, 276.

59. Historical Files, Grace Baptist Church, Wilmington, N.C.; *Wilmington Morning Star,* September 14, 2002; Historical Files, The Pentecostals of Wilmington, Wilmington, N.C.

60. *Wilmington Morning Star,* September 2, 1965, May 15 and 17, 1995, May 10, 1998.

61. *Wilmington Morning Star,* March 7 and 12–25, 1893; James F. Findlay Jr., *Dwight L. Moody, American Evangelist: 1837–1899* (Chicago: University of Chicago Press, 1969); William G. McLoughlin, *Modern Revivalism: Charles Grandison Finney to Billy Graham* (New York: Ronald Press, 1959), 166–281.

62. *Wilmington Morning Star,* September 30, 1890; McLoughlin, *Modern Revivalism,* 282–329.

63. See the classic statement of this critique by Gibson Winter, *The Suburban Captivity of the Churches* (New York: Macmillan, 1962).

64. *Wilmington Morning Star,* August 27, 1994, November 4, 2000; *History of the First Baptist Church* (Wilmington, N.C.: First Baptist Church, 1979), 1; Wrenn, *Wilmington,* 164.

65. Historical Files, Mount Olive African Methodist Episcopal Church, Wilmington, N.C.; *Wilmington Morning Star,* August 26, 1996, January 5, 2002; *Wilmington Journal,* April 18, 1996.

66. *Wilmington Morning Star,* June 27, 1994, September 14, 2000, July 28, 2001, January 12 and 19, 2002.

67. John O. Hodges, "Charles Manuel 'Sweet Daddy' Grace," in *20th Century Shapers of American Popular Religion,* ed. Charles Lippy (New York: Greenwood, 1989), 170–79; *Charlotte Observer,* September 8, 1947.

68. *Wilmington Morning Star,* May 22, 1946; Eaton, *Every Man Should Try,* 124.

69. Interview with Dr. Richard Laws, April 27, 1998.

70. Interview with Imam Abdul Shareef, April 17, 1998; Yvonne Y. Haddad, "Make Room for the Muslims," in *Religious Diversity and American Religious History,* ed. Walter H. Conser Jr. and Sumner B. Twiss (Athens: University of Georgia Press, 1997), 218. See also Yvonne Y. Haddad, ed., *The Muslims of America* (New York: Oxford University Press, 1991), and Jane I. Smith, *Islam in America* (New York: Columbia University Press, 1999).

71. *Wilmington Morning Star,* June 16, 1993.

72. *Wilmington Morning Star,* February 28, 2000, February 21, 2004. See also Edward E. Curtis IV, *Islam in Black America* (Albany: State University of New York Press, 2002); Richard Brent Turner, *Islam in the African-American Experience* (Bloomington: Indiana University Press, 1997); Aminah Beverly McCloud, *African American Islam* (New York: Routledge, 1995).

73. See Patricia B. Lerch, *Waccamaw Legacy: Contemporary Indians Fight for Survival* (Tuscaloosa: University of Alabama Press, 2004), 117–42; quotation 126.

74. On the spectrum of Native Christianities, see William G. McLoughlin, *The Cherokees and Christianity, 1794–1870* (Athens: University of Georgia Press, 1994), and Christopher Vecsey, "A Century of Lakota Sioux Catholicism at Pine Ridge," in Conser and Twiss, *Religious Diversity,* 262–96.

75. For a discussion of Lumbee history, see Adolph L. Dial and David K. Eliades, *The Only Land I Know: A History of the Lumbee Indians* (San Francisco: Indian Historian Press, 1975); W. McKee Evans, *To Die Game: The Story of the Lowry Band, Guerillas of Reconstruction* (Baton Rouge: Louisiana State University Press, 1971); Karen I. Blu, *The Lumbee Problem: The Making of an American Indian People* (New York: Cambridge University Press, 1980).

76. Dial and Eliades, *Only Land,* 106–10.

77. Ibid., 109–10; Michael Smith and Jane Smith, *The Lumbee Methodists* (Raleigh: North Carolina Methodist Conference, 1990).

78. Lutz, *Homefront,* 77.

79. Telephone interview with the Reverend Abraham Ho, October 26, 2004; Historical Files, Calvary Baptist Church, Korean Baptist Church, Wilmington, N.C.; telephone interview with Mrs. Myung Jang, March 12, 2003.

80. *Wilmington Morning Star,* October 21, 1994; interview with Dr. R. G. Bhat, October 23, 1994. On Hinduism, see C. J. Fuller, *The Camphor Flame: Popular Hinduism and Society in India* (Princeton, N.J.: Princeton University Press, 1990), and Diana L. Eck, *Banaras: City of Light* (New York: Columbia University Press, 1999), 211–15. For a discussion of Hinduism in America, see Diana L. Eck, *A New Religious America* (San Francisco: HarperSanFrancisco, 2001), 80–141.

81. For a discussion of American Buddhism, see Thomas A. Tweed, "Asian Religions in the United States: Reflections on an Emerging Subfield," in Conser and Twiss, *Religious Diversity*, 189–217; Charles S. Prebish and Kenneth K. Tanaka, eds., *The Faces of Buddhism in America* (Berkeley: University of California Press, 1998); Duncan R. Williams and Christopher S. Queen, eds., *American Buddhism* (Richmond, England: Curzon Press, 1999); Charles S. Prebish, *Luminous Passage: The Practice and Study of Buddhism in America* (Berkeley: University of California Press, 1999); Richard Hughes Seager, *Buddhism in America* (New York: Columbia University Press, 1999). For A discussion of Jack Kerouac's North Carolina connection, see Alex Albright, "Satori in Rocky Mount," in *The Coastal Plains: Writings on the Cultures of Eastern North Carolina*, ed. Leslie H. Garner Jr. and Arthur Mann Kaye (Rocky Mount: North Carolina Wesleyan College Press, 1989), 81–93.

82. Historical Files, Wilmington Zen Group, Wilmington, N.C.; *Wilmington Morning Star*, September 7, 1993, December 8, 2001; Seager, *Buddhism in America*, 70–89.

83. Thomas A. Tweed, *Buddhism and Barbecue: A Guide to Buddhist Temples in North Carolina* (Chapel Hill: Buddhism in North Carolina Project, 2001), 16; Seager, *Buddhism in America*, 113–35.

84. Tweed, "Asian Religions in the United States," 205.

85. Paul David Numrich, *Old Wisdom in the New World: Americanization in Two Immigrant Theravada Buddhist Temples* (Knoxville: University of Tennessee Press, 1996), xvii–xxi.

86. See Donald K. Swearer, "Buddhism in Southeast Asia," in *Encyclopedia of Religion*, 16 vols., ed. Mircea Eliade (New York: Macmillan, 1995), 1:394–97; *Wilmington Morning Star*, October 20, 1990.

87. Program for groundbreaking ceremony, Wat Carolina Buddhajakra Vanaram, Bolivia, N.C., July 2, 1989; *Wilmington Morning Star*, July 3, 1989.

88. Michael Willis, "Monastic Architecture," in *Buddhism: The Illustrated Guide*, ed. Kevin Trainor (New York: Oxford University Press, 2004), 100–103.

89. See the schedules for Visakha Pucha Day (June 6, 1993), Kathin and Loi Kratong (October 18, 1992, October 23, 1994), Magha Pucha Day (March 7, 1993, February 28, 1999), in Historical Files, Wat Carolina Buddhajakra Vanaram, Bolivia, N.C.; *Wilmington Morning Star*, October 22, 1989, April 15, 2000.

90. Numrich, *Old Wisdom in the New World*, 63–65, 140–44.

91. *Wilmington Morning Star*, August 20, 1988; *Brunswick Beacon*, July 6, 1989; *Myrtle Beach Sun News*, July 3, 1989.

92. Robert Wuthnow, *The Restructuring of American Religion* (Princeton, N.J.: Princeton University Press, 1988), 88–91; Wade Clark Roof and William McKinney, *American Mainline Religion* (New Brunswick, N.J.: Rutgers University Press, 1987), 162–81.

93. Phillip E. Hammond, *Religion and Personal Autonomy: The Third Disestablishment in America* (Columbia: University of South Carolina Press, 1992), 167–77; Wade Clark Roof, *Spiritual Marketplace: Baby Boomers and the Remaking of American Religion* (Princeton, N.J.: Princeton University Press, 1999), 150–52.

94. *Wilmington Morning Star*, August 26, 1999.

95. *Wilmington Morning Star*, November 20, 2000, December 14, 2002, March 16, 2002. For an insightful discussion of the development of the contemporary Christian music industry, see Stephen A. Marini, *Sacred Song in America: Religion, Music, and Popular Culture* (Urbana: University of Illinois Press, 2003), 296–319. David W. Stowe reflects on the dynamics of the crossover phenomenon in American sacred music in his volume *How Sweet the Sound: Music in the Spiritual Lives of Americans* (Cambridge, Mass.: Harvard University Press, 2004), 2–9.

96. *Wilmington Morning Star*, September 7, 2003, December 19, 2004.

97. Wuthnow, *Restructuring American Religion*, 91; *Wilmington Morning Star*, February 22, 1997.

98. Wuthnow, *Restructuring American Religion*, 93–96.

99. See James Davison Hunter, *Culture Wars: The Struggle to Define America* (New York: Basic Books, 1991).

100. Stephen Pressley, *A Decade of New Beginnings: CBFNC and the First Ten Years* (Winston-Salem, N.C.: CBFNC, 2004).

101. *Wilmington Morning Star*, October 6, 2001, August 27, 2002, September 22, 2001.

102. Historical Files, Trinity Reformed Presbyterian Church, Wilmington, N.C.; *Wilmington Morning Star*, November 9, 2002.

103. Charlene Thomas, *The History of Myrtle Grove Presbyterian Church, 1945–1995* (Wilmington, N.C.: Myrtle Grove Presbyterian Church, 1995); *Wilmington Morning Star*, May 25, 1969.

104. Historical Files, Myrtle Grove Presbyterian Church, Wilmington, N.C.

105. Randall Balmer and John R. Fitzmier, *The Presbyterians* (Westport, Conn.: Praeger, 1994), 107–8; Historical Files, Emmanuel Presbyterian Church, Wilmington, N.C.

106. *Wilmington Morning Star*, February 12, 1994, May 12, 1996, June 28 and 30, 2003; Mary Jo Weaver and R. Scott Appleby, eds., *Being Right: Conservative Catholics in America* (Bloomington: Indiana University Press, 1995).

107. Lindley, *You Have Stept out of Your Place*, 366–68; *Wilmington Morning Star*, November 17, 2001; Historical Files, Messiah Lutheran Church LCMS, Wilmington, N.C.

108. *Wilmington Morning Star*, August 24, 2002.

109. *Wilmington Morning Star*, November 3, 2001, May 4, 2002, May 25, 2002, October 19, 2002.

110. *Wilmington Morning Star*, July 27, 2002.

111. Historical Files, Coastal Community Vineyard, Wilmington, N.C.; Donald Miller, *Reinventing American Protestantism: Christianity in the New Millennium* (Berkeley: University of California Press, 1997); Mark A. Shibley, *Resurgent Evangelicalism in the United States: Mapping Cultural Changes since 1970* (Columbia: University of South Carolina Press, 1996), 83–110.

112. Historical Files, Port City Community Church, Wilmington, N.C. For further discussion of the megachurch phenomenon, see Anne C. Loveland

and Otis B. Wheeler, *From Meetinghouse to Megachurch: A Material and Cultural History* (Columbia: University of Missouri Press, 2003).

113. Robert H. Stockman, "The American Baha'i Community in the Nineties," in *America's Alternative Religions*, ed. Timothy Miller (Albany: State University of New York Press, 1995), 243–48; Bill Reaves, *Strength through Struggle* (Wilmington, N.C.: New Hanover County Library, 1998), 456–59; *Wilmington Morning Star*, May 5, 2001, February 26, 2002, February 21, 2004.

114. Gisela Webb, "Sufism in America," in Miller, *America's Alternative Religions*, 249–58; *Wilmington Morning Star*, February 16, 2002.

115. Gail Harley, "New Thought and the Harmonial Family," in Miller, *America's Alternative Religions*, 325–30; James R. Lewis, *Peculiar Prophets: A Biographical Dictionary of New Religions* (St. Paul: Paragon House, 1999), 89–90, 118–19; *Wilmington Morning Star*, February 23, 2002, June 22, 2002.

116. *Wilmington Morning Star*, October 27, 2001; Thomas D. Hamm, *The Quakers in America* (New York: Columbia University Press, 2003).

117. "A New Universalist Convention," *Universalist Magazine*, July 14, 1827, 2–3; Anne Russell and Marjorie Megivern, *North Carolina Portraits of Faith* (Norfolk, Va.: Donning Company, 1986), 130–31.

118. Diane Cashman, *Headstrong: The Biography of Amy Morris Bradley, 1823–1904* (Wilmington, N.C.: Broadfoot Publishing, 1990); Historical Files, Unitarian-Universalist Fellowship, Wilmington, N.C.; *Wilmington Morning Star*, November 24, 2001.

119. *Wilmington Morning Star*, November 16, 2003; Historical Files, Beit Hallel Messianic Synagogue, Wilmington, N.C.

120. *Wilmington Morning Star*, November 12, 1994, August 15, 1998, April 21, 2001. See also Melissa M. Wilcox, *Coming out in Christianity: Religion, Identity, and Community* (Bloomington: Indiana University Press, 2003).

121. Lewis, *Peculiar Prophets*, 43–44, 101–2.

122. Carol Matthews, "Neo-Paganism and Witchcraft," in Miller, *America's Alternative Religions*, 339–45; Margot Adler, *Drawing Down the Moon*, rev. ed. (New York: Arkana Publishers, 1986).

123. Lewis, *Peculiar Prophets*, 98–100; Adler, *Drawing Down the Moon*, 127; *Wilmington Morning Star*, October 2, 2004.

124. Roof, *Spiritual Marketplace*, 82–110; "Past, Present, and Future: The Next 25 Years" (typescript, September 12, 1993), in Historical Files, Unitarian-Universalist Fellowship, Wilmington, N.C.

125. Robert Wuthnow, ed., *I Come Away Stronger: How Small Groups Are Shaping American Religion* (Grand Rapids, Mich.: Eerdmans Publishing Company, 1994).

Conclusion

1. William L. Saunders, ed., *The Colonial Records of North Carolina*, 10 vols. (Raleigh, N.C.: P. M. Hale, 1886–1890), 6:236. For an insightful analysis of the issues surrounding pluralism, see William R. Hutchison, *Religious Pluralism in America* (New Haven, Conn.: Yale University Press, 2003).

Selected Bibliography

Manuscripts

Butler, Marion. Papers. Southern Historical Collection. University of North Carolina at Chapel Hill.

Curtis, Moses Ashley. Papers. Southern Historical Collection. University of North Carolina at Chapel Hill.

Goldberg, David J. "An Historical Community Study of Wilmington Jewry, 1738–1925." North Carolina Room. New Hanover County Public Library. Wilmington, N.C.

Hayes Collection. Southern Historical Collection. University of North Carolina at Chapel Hill.

McAllister, Alexander. Papers. Southern Historical Collection. University of North Carolina at Chapel Hill.

Mendelsohn, Samuel. Papers. Special Collections. University of North Carolina at Wilmington.

Miscellaneous Letters [Collection]. Southern Historical Collection. University of North Carolina at Chapel Hill.

Rountree, George. "Memorandum of My Personal Recollection of the Election of 1898." Henry G. Connor Papers. Southern Historical Collection. University of North Carolina at Chapel Hill.

Sheppard, Joseph E. Waters. "A Brief History of the Church of St. Thomas the Apostle." North Carolina Room. New Hanover County Public Library. Wilmington, N.C.

Sims, Kimberly. "Wilmington Jewry, 1800–1914." North Carolina Room. New Hanover County Public Library. Wilmington, N.C.

Wood, Thomas Fanning. Papers. Special Collections. University of North Carolina at Wilmington.

Newspapers

Africo-American Presbyterian
Ballou's Pictorial Drawing Room Companion

Biblical Recorder
Brunswick Beacon
Cape Fear Mercury
Carolina Observer
Charlotte Observer
Church Messenger
Fayetteville Observer
Myrtle Beach Sun News
News and Observer (Raleigh)
New York Tribune
North Carolina Journal
North Carolina Presbyterian
North Carolina Standard
Presbyterian Standard
Raleigh Register
Wilmington Advertiser
Wilmington Chronicle
Wilmington Gazette
Wilmington Journal
Wilmington Messenger
Wilmington Morning Star

Published Materials

Adair, Douglass, and John A. Schutz, eds. *Peter Oliver's Origin and Progress of the American Revolution*. Stanford, Calif.: Stanford University Press, 1961.

Adler, Margot. *Drawing Down the Moon*. Rev. ed. New York: Arkana Publishers, 1986.

Ahlstrom, Sydney E. *A Religious History of the American People*. New Haven, Conn.: Yale University Press, 1972.

Albright, Alex. "Satori in Rocky Mount." In *The Coastal Plains: Writings on the Cultures of Eastern North Carolina*, edited by Leslie H. Garner Jr. and Arthur Mann Keye, 81–93. Rocky Mount: North Carolina Wesleyan College Press, 1989.

Alexander, Roberta Sue. *North Carolina Faces the Freedmen*. Durham, N.C.: Duke University Press, 1985.

Amazing Grace: Two Hundred Years of Methodism. Wilmington, N.C.: Grace United Methodist Church, 1985.

Anderson, Jon W., and William B. Friend, eds. *The Culture of Bible Belt Catholics*. New York: Paulist Press, 1995.

Andrews, Evangeline Walker, ed. *Journal of a Lady of Quality*. New Haven, Conn.: Yale University Press, 1923.

Angell, Stephen Ward. *Bishop Henry McNeal Turner and African-American Religion in the South*. Knoxville: University of Tennessee Press, 1992.

Appeal of the Seamen's Friends Society of the Port of Wilmington. Wilmington, N.C.: n.p., 1853.

Arnold, Wayne S. "Early Presbyterianism in the Lower Cape Fear." *Lower Cape Fear Historical Society Bulletin* 17 (1974): 1–6.

Arsenault, Raymond. "The End of the Long Hot Summer: The Air Conditioner and Southern Culture." *Journal of Southern History* 50 (1984): 597–628.

Asbury, Francis. *Journals and Letters of Francis Asbury.* Edited by Elmer T. Clark. 3 vols. Nashville: Abingdon Press, 1958.

Ashe, Samuel A. *History of North Carolina.* 2 vols. Greensboro, N.C.: Charles Van Noppen, 1908.

Austin, Allan D. *African Muslims in Antebellum America: A Sourcebook.* New York: Garland Publishers, 1984.

———. *African Muslims in Antebellum America: Transatlantic Stories and Spiritual Struggles.* New York: Routledge, 1997.

Balmer, Randall, and John R. Fitzmier. *The Presbyterians.* Westport, Conn.: Praeger, 1994.

Barnes, Joseph K., ed. *The Medical and Surgical History of the War of the Rebellion, 1861–1875.* Reprinted as *The Medical and Surgical History of the Civil War.* 10 vols. Wilmington, N.C.: Broadfoot Publishing, 1991.

Barnwell, John. "Letters of ___." *South Carolina Historical and Genealogical Magazine* 9 (1908): 28–54.

Battle, Kemp P. *Letters and Documents Relating to the Early History of the Lower Cape Fear.* Chapel Hill: University [of North Carolina], 1903.

Bearse, Austin. *Reminiscences of Fugitive Slave Law Days in Boston.* New York: Arno Press, 1969. Original ed. 1880.

Bell, Catherine. *Ritual: Perspectives and Dimensions.* New York: Oxford University Press, 1997.

Bell, John L. Jr. "Baptists and the Negro in North Carolina during Reconstruction." *North Carolina Historical Review* 42 (1965): 391–409.

———. "The Presbyterian Church and the Negro in North Carolina during Reconstruction." *North Carolina Historical Review* 40 (1963): 15–36.

Bellamy, John D. *Memoirs of an Octogenarian.* Charlotte, N.C.: Observer Printing House, 1942.

Benedict, David. *A General History of the Baptist Denomination in America and Other Parts of the World.* New York: Lewis Colby and Co., 1848.

Benjamin, Asher. *The American Builder's Companion.* New York: Dover Publishers, 1968. Original ed. 1806.

Bennett, David. *The Altar Call: Its Origins and Present Usage.* Lanham, Md.: University Press of America, 2000.

Benson, Rupert, and Helen Benson. *Historical Narrative of Wrightsville Beach, North Carolina, 1841–1972.* Wilmington, N.C.: Carolina Printing Company, 1972.

Berkeley, Kathleen C. *The Women's Liberation Movement in America.* Westport, Conn.: Greenwood Press, 1999.

Bernheim, Gotthardt. *The First Twenty Years of St. Paul's Evangelical Lutheran Church.* Wilmington, N.C.: Hall Publishers, 1879.

Bingham, Emily. *Mordecai: An Early American Family.* New York: Hill and Wang, 2003.

Bishir, Catherine W. "Landmarks of Power: Building a Southern Past in Raleigh and Wilmington, North Carolina, 1885–1915." In Brundage, ed., *Where These Memories Grow*, 139–68.

———. *North Carolina Architecture*. Chapel Hill: University of North Carolina Press, 1990.

Bishir, Catherine W., and Michael T. Southern. *A Guide to the Historic Architecture of Eastern North Carolina*. Chapel Hill: University of North Carolina Press, 1996.

Bishir, Catherine W., and Lawrence C. Early, eds. *Early Twentieth-Century Suburbs in North Carolina*. Raleigh, N.C.: Department of Cultural Resources, 1985.

Bishir, Catherine W., et al., eds. *Architects and Builders in North Carolina: A History of the Practice of Building*. Chapel Hill: University of North Carolina Press, 1990.

Black, Jeannette D., ed. *The Blathwayt Atlas*. 2 vols. Providence, R.I.: Brown University Press, 1970–1975.

Block, Susan Taylor. "A History of Mt. Lebanon Chapel." *Lower Cape Fear Historical Society Bulletin* 42 (1998): 1–8.

———. *Temple of Our Fathers: St. James Church, 1729–2004*. Wilmington, N.C.: Artspeak, 2004.

———. "Van Eeden." *Lower Cape Fear Historical Society Bulletin* 40 (1995): 2–72.

Blu, Karen I. *The Lumbee Problem: The Making of an Indian People*. New York: Cambridge University Press, 1980.

Bodie, Earl K. *Historical Sketch of St. Matthew's Evangelical Lutheran Church, Wilmington, N.C.* Wilmington, N.C.: St. Matthew's Evangelical Lutheran Church, 1933.

Boles, John B., ed. *Masters and Slaves in the House of the Lord: Race and Religion in the American South, 1740–1870*. Lexington: University Press of Kentucky, 1988.

Bost, Raymond M., and Jeff L. Norris. *All One Body: The Story of the North Carolina Lutheran Synod, 1803–1933*. Salisbury, N.C.: North Carolina Synod, 1994.

Bowman, Charles H. Jr. "Dr. John Carr Monk: Sampson County's Latter Day 'Cornelius.'" *North Carolina Historical Review* 50 (1975): 52–72.

Braude, Ann D. "Jewish Women in the Twentieth Century: Building a Life in America." In Ruether and Keller, eds., *Women and Religion in America*, 3:131–43.

Brekus, Catherine A. "Female Evangelism in the Early Methodist Movement, 1784–1845." In Hatch and Wigger, eds., *Methodism and the Shaping of American Culture*, 135–73.

———. *Strangers and Pilgrims: Female Preaching in America, 1774–1845*. Chapel Hill: University of North Carolina Press, 1998.

Brewster, Lawrence F. "Alfred Augustine Watson: Episcopal Clergyman of the New South." In Campion et al., eds. *Studies in the History of the New South*, 1–23.

Brownell, Blaine A., and David R. Goldfield, eds. *The City in Southern History.* Port Washington, N.Y.: Kennikat Press, 1977.

Brundage, W. Fitzhugh, ed. *Where These Memories Grow: History, Meaning, and Southern Identity.* Chapel Hill: University of North Carolina Press, 2000.

Bucke, Emory Stevens, ed. *The History of American Methodism.* 3 vols. New York: Abingdon Press, 1964.

Bullock, Steven C. *Revolutionary Brotherhood: Freemasonry and the Transformation of the American Social Order, 1730–1840.* Chapel Hill: University of North Carolina Press, 1996.

Burchard, John, and Albert Bush-Brown. *The Architecture of America: A Social and Cultural History.* Boston: Little Brown, 1961.

Burkhead, L. S. "History of the Difficulties of the Pastorate of the Front Street Methodist Church, Wilmington, N.C. for the Year 1865." In *Historical Papers of Trinity College,* ser. 8. Durham, N.C.: Trinity College Historical Society, 1909.

Bushman, Richard. *The Refinement of America: Persons, Houses, Cities.* New York: Alfred A. Knopf, 1992.

Bushnell, David I. *Native Cemeteries and Forms of Burial East of the Mississippi.* Bulletin 71. Washington, D.C.: Bureau of American Ethnology, 1920.

Byrne, George. "Hugh MacRae's Practical Application of Common Sense in Colonization." *Manufacturers Record* 61 (1912): 49–53.

Cain, Robert J., ed. *The Church of England in North Carolina: Documents, 1699–1741.* Raleigh, N.C.: Division of Archives and History, 1999.

Caldwell, Joseph. "The Archaeology of Eastern Georgia and South Carolina." In Griffin, ed., *Archaeology of Eastern United States,* 312–21.

Campion, Loren K., et al., eds. *Studies in the History of the New South, 1875–1922.* Greenville, N.C.: East Carolina College, 1966.

Canny, Nicholas. "Early Modern Ireland, 1500–1700." In Foster, ed., *Oxford History of Ireland,* 88–133.

Cape Fear Deanery 175th Anniversary. Wilmington, N.C.: Diocese of Raleigh, 1997.

Carey, Patrick. *People, Priests, and Prelates: Ecclesiastical Democracy and the Tensions of Trusteeism.* Notre Dame, Ind.: University of Notre Dame Press, 1987.

Carnes, Mark C. *Secret Ritual and Manhood in Victorian America.* New Haven, Conn.: Yale University Press, 1989.

Carraway, Gertrude S., and W. Keats Sparrow. "John LaPierre." In Powell, ed., *Dictionary of North Carolina Biography,* 4:20–21.

Carver's Creek Church and Gravestones. Elizabethtown, N.C.: Bladen County Bicentennial Commission, 1976.

Carwardine, Richard. *Transatlantic Revivalism: Popular Evangelicalism in Britain and America, 1790–1865.* Westport, Conn.: Greenwood Press, 1978.

Cashman, Diane. *Headstrong: The Biography of Amy Morris Bradley, 1823–1904.* Wilmington, N.C.: Broadfoot Publishing, 1990.

Cecelski, David S., and Timothy B. Tyson, eds. *Democracy Betrayed: The Wilmington Race Riot of 1898 and Its Legacy.* Chapel Hill: University of North Carolina Press, 1998.

Cheney, John L., ed. *North Carolina Government, 1589–1979*. Raleigh, N.C.: Department of the Secretary of State, 1981.

Cheshire, Joseph B., ed. *Sketches of Church History in North Carolina*. Wilmington, N.C.: Wm. L. DeRosset, 1892.

Chreitzberg, A. M. "Early Methodism in Wilmington, N.C." *Historical Society of the North Carolina Conference, Methodist Episcopal Church, South*, 5–24. Durham, N.C.: n.p., 1897.

Clark, Kathleen. "Celebrating Freedom: Emancipation Day Celebrations and African American Memory in the Early Reconstruction South." In Brundage, ed., *Where These Memories Grow*, 107–32.

Clark, Kenneth. *The Gothic Revival*. London: John Murray, 1962.

Clark, Victor E. Jr., and Louise D. Curry, eds. *Colorful Heritage Documented*. Dallas, N.C.: Argyll Printing Center, 1989.

Clark, Walter E., ed. *The State Records of North Carolina*. 16 vols. (numbered 11–26). Winston and Goldsboro, 1895–1905.

Classen, Cheryl P. "Gender, Shellfishing, and the Shell Mound Archaic." In Gero and Conkey, eds., *Engendering Archaeology*, 276–300.

Clifton, James M. "Golden Grains of White: Rice Planting on the Lower Cape Fear." *North Carolina Historical Review* 50 (1973): 365–93.

Cockrell, David L. "'A Blessing in Disguise': The Influenza Pandemic of 1918 and North Carolina's Medical and Public Health Communities." *North Carolina Historical Review* 63 (1996): 309–27.

Coe, Joffre Lanning. *Town Creek Indian Mounds*. Chapel Hill: University of North Carolina Press, 1995.

Coe, Joffre, et al. *Archaeological and Paleo-Osteological Investigations at the Cold Morning Site, New Hanover County, North Carolina*. Chapel Hill: Research Laboratories of Anthropology, University of North Carolina, 1982.

Collins, George R. "The Transfer of Thin Masonry Vaulting from Spain to America." *Journal of the Society of Architectural Historians* 27 (1968): 176–201.

Committee from the New Hanover Retired School Personnel. *History of Education in New Hanover County, 1800–1980*. Wilmington, N.C.: n.p., 1981.

Conkin, Paul. "The Church Establishment in North Carolina, 1765–1776." *North Carolina Historical Review* 32 (1955): 1–30.

Connor, Henry G., and Joseph B. Cheshire, eds. *The Constitution of the State of North Carolina, Annotated*. Raleigh, N.C.: Broughton, 1911.

Conser, Walter H. Jr., and Sumner B. Twiss, eds. *Religious Diversity and American Religious History*. Athens: University of Georgia Press, 1997.

Conser, Walter H. Jr., et al., eds. *Resistance, Politics, and the American Struggle for Independence, 1765–1775*. Boulder, Colo.: Lynne Rienner, 1986.

Constitution of the Bible Society of Wilmington. Wilmington, N.C.: n.p., 1819.

Cooledge, Harold N. Jr. *Samuel Sloan: Architect of Philadelphia, 1815–1884*. Philadelphia: University of Philadelphia, 1986.

Cornelius, Janet D. *Slave Missions and the Black Church in the Antebellum South*. Columbia: University of South Carolina Press, 1999.

Corrigan, Jo Ann. "Yellow Fever: Scourge of the South." In Savitt and Young, eds., *Disease and Distinctiveness in the American South*, 55–78.

Cox, Karen L. *Dixie's Daughters: The United Daughters of the Confederacy and the Preservation of Confederate Culture.* Gainesville: University Press of Florida, 2003.

Crawford, C. E. *A History of Bladen County, North Carolina.* Elizabethtown, N.C.: Bladen County Historical Society, 1987.

Crews, C. Daniel, and Richard W. Starbuck. *With Courage for the Future: The Story of the Moravian Church, Southern Province.* Winston-Salem, N.C.: Moravian Church in America, Southern Province, 2002.

Crow, Jeffrey J. "Slave Rebelliousness and Social Conflict in North Carolina, 1775 to 1802." *William and Mary Quarterly* 37 (1980): 79–102.

Crow, Jeffrey J., et al. *A History of African Americans in North Carolina.* Raleigh, N.C.: Division of Archives and History, 1992.

Cumming, William P. *Captain James Wimble, His Maps, and the Colonial Cartography of the North Carolina Coast.* Raleigh, N.C.: Department of Archives and History, 1969.

———. *The Southeast in Early Maps.* 3rd rev. ed. Chapel Hill: University of North Carolina Press, 1998.

Curry, Thomas J. *The First Freedoms: Church and State in America to the Passage of the First Amendment.* New York: Oxford University Press, 1986.

Curtis, N. C. "St. Philip's Church, Brunswick County, N.C. Text and Measured Drawings." *Architectural Record* 47 (1920): 181–87.

Curtis, Walter G. *Reminiscences of Wilmington and Smithville-Southport, 1848–1900.* 2nd ed. Southport, N.C.: Herald Job Office, 1999.

Dail, John R. *A History of Wilmington Presbytery.* Burgaw, N.C.: Southern Printing Company, 1984.

Danby, Miles. *Moorish Style.* London: Phaidon Press, 1995.

Daniel, Roger. *Coming to America.* New York: HarperCollins, 1990.

David, Annette H. *Forty Fruitful Years, 1942–1982: A History of Sunset Park Baptist Church.* Wilmington, N.C.: Sunset Park Baptist Church, 1982.

Davis, Cyprian. *The History of Black Catholics in the United States.* New York: Crossroad, 1993.

Delta Sigma Theta Sorority. *Legacies Untold: Histories of Black Church in the Greater Duplin County Area.* Duplin County, N.C. Delta Sigma Theta Chapter, 2002.

DeMott, Mortimer. "Sojourn in Wilmington and the Lower Cape Fear, 1837." *Lower Cape Fear Historical Society Bulletin* 22 (1979): 1–6.

DeRosset, William L., ed. *One Hundredth Anniversary Commemorating the Building of St. James Church in Wilmington, North Carolina.* Wilmington, N.C.: William L. DeRossett, 1939.

Dial, Adolph, and David K. Eliades. *The Only Land I Know: A History of the Lumbee Indians.* San Francisco: Indian Historian Press, 1975.

"Diary of the Right Rev. John England." *Records of the American Catholic Historical Society of Philadelphia* 6 (1895): 29–224.

Dinnerstein, Leonard. *Antisemitism in America.* New York: Oxford University Press, 1994.

Dinnerstein, Leonard, and Mary D. Palsson, eds. *Jews in the South.* Baton Rouge: Louisiana State University Press, 1973.

Diouf, Sylviane. *Servants of Allah: African Muslims Enslaved in the Americas.* New York: New York University Press, 1998.

Directory of Fifth St. M. E. Church South. Wilmington, N.C.: Messenger Steam Power Presses, 1888.

Dobson, David. *Scottish Emigration to Colonial America, 1607–1785.* Athens: University of Georgia Press, 1994.

Dolan, Jay. *In Search of an American Catholicism.* New York: Oxford University Press, 2002.

Drane, Robert Brent. "Historical Notes, 1843," In DeRosset, ed., *One Hundredth Anniversary of St. James Church.*

Dries, Angelyn. *The Missionary Movement in American Catholic History.* Maryknoll, N.Y.: Orbis, 1998.

Dunn, Michael J. III. "Age of the Trolley Cars." *State* 37 (1969): 8–10.

Dusinberre, William. *Them Dark Days: Slavery in the American Rice Swamps.* New York: Oxford University Press, 1996.

Dvorak, Katherine L. *An African-American Exodus: The Segregation of the Southern Churches.* Brooklyn, N.Y.: Carlson Publishing, 1991.

Early, James. *Romanticism and American Architecture.* New York: A. S. Brown, 1965.

Eaton, Hubert A. *Every Man Should Try.* Wilmington, N.C.: Bonaparte Press, 1984.

Eck, Diana L. *Banares: City of Light.* New York: Columbia University Press, 1999.

———. *A New Religious America.* San Francisco: HarperSanFrancisco, 2001.

Edgar, Walter. *South Carolina: A History.* Columbia: University of South Carolina Press, 1998.

Efthimiou, Militiades, and George A. Christopolous, eds. *History of the Greek Orthodox Church in America.* New York: Greek Orthodox Archdiocese of North and South America, 1984.

Ekrich, A. Roger. *"Poor Carolina": Politics and Society in Colonial North Carolina, 1729–1776.* Chapel Hill: University of North Carolina Press, 1981.

Eliade, Mircea. *A History of Religious Ideas.* 3 vols. Chicago: University of Chicago Press, 1978–1985.

Elliot, Jonathan, ed. *The Debates in the Several State Conventions on the Adoption of the Federal Constitution.* 5 vols. New York: Burt Franklin, 1888.

Ellis, John Tracy. *The Life of James Cardinal Gibbons.* 2 vols. Milwaukee: Bruce Publishers, 1952.

Emerson, Thomas E. *Cahokia and the Archaeology of Power.* Tuscaloosa: University of Alabama Press, 1997.

Ennis, Robert B. "Thomas U. Walter." In Placzek, ed. *Macmillan Encyclopedia of Architects,* 4:365–70.

Evans, Eli N. *The Lonely Days Were Sundays.* Jackson: University Press of Mississippi, 1993.

———. *The Provincials: A Personal History of Jews in the South.* New York: Free Press, 1997.

Evans, W. McKee. *To Die Game: The Story of the Lowry Band, Guerillas of Reconstruction.* Baton Rouge: Louisiana State University Press, 1971.

Evtuhov, Catherine, David Goldfrank, Lindsey Hughes, and Richard Stites. *A History of Russia: Peoples, Legends, Events, Forces*. Boston: Houghton Mifflin, 2004.

Fabre, Geneviève. "African-American Commemorative Celebrations in the Nineteenth Century." In Fabre and O'Meally, eds., *History and Memory*, 72–91.

Fabre, Geneviève, and Robert O'Meally, eds. *History and Memory in African-American Culture*. New York: Oxford University Press, 1994.

Farrell, James T. *Inventing the American Way of Death, 1830–1920*. Philadelphia: Temple University Press, 1980.

Fenn, Elizabeth A. "A Perfect Equality Seemed to Reign: Slave Society and Jonkonnu." *North Carolina Historical Review* 65 (1988): 127–53.

Findlay, James F. Jr. *Dwight L. Moody, American Evangelist: 1837–1899*. Chicago: University of Chicago Press, 1969.

Finney, Charles Grandison. *Lectures on Revivals of Religion*. Edited by William G. McLoughlin. Cambridge, Mass.: Harvard University Press, 1960.

First Annual Report of the General Assembly Committee on Freedmen. Pittsburgh: James McMillan, 1866.

First Report of the Board of Managers of the Fayetteville Auxiliary Bible Society. Fayetteville, N.C.: Bowell and Black, 1817.

Fitzgerald, Thomas E. *The Orthodox Church*. Westport, Conn.: Praeger, 1998.

Flanner, Caroline. "The Reverend Augustus Foster Lyde (1813–1834)." *Lower Cape Fear Historical Society Bulletin* 4 (1961).

Fogerty, Gerald P. *American Catholic Biblical Scholarship*. New York: Harper and Row, 1989.

Fonvielle, Chris E. Jr. *The Wilmington Campaign*. Campbell, Calif.: Savas Publishing Company, 1997.

Foote, William H. *Sketches of North Carolina*. 2nd ed. Dunn, N.C.: Reprint Company, 1912. Original ed. 1846.

Foster, Gaines M. *Ghosts of the Confederacy: Defeat, the Lost Cause, and the Emergence of the New South, 1865 to 1913*. New York: Oxford University Press, 1987.

Foster, R. F., ed. *The Oxford History of Ireland*. Oxford: Oxford University Press, 1989.

Franklin, John Hope. *The Free Negro in North Carolina, 1790–1860*. New York: W. W. Norton, 1971. Original ed. 1943.

Franklin, John Hope, and Loren Schweninger. *Runaway Slaves: Rebels on the Plantation*. New York: Oxford University Press, 1999.

Frazier, E. Franklin. *The Negro Church in America*. New York: Schocken Books, 1974.

Frey, Sylvia R., and Betty Wood. *Come Shouting to Zion: African American Protestantism in the American South and British Caribbean to 1830*. Chapel Hill: University of North Carolina Press, 1998.

Friedman, Terry. *James Gibbs*. New Haven, Conn.: Yale University Press, 1984.

Fuller, C. J. *The Camphor Flame: Popular Hinduism and Society in India.* Princeton, N.J.: Princeton University Press, 1990.

Ganyard, Robert L. *The Emergence of North Carolina's Revolutionary State Government.* Raleigh, N.C.: Division of Archives and History, 1978.

Gara, Larry. *The Liberty Line: The Legacy of the Underground Railroad.* Lexington: University Press of Kentucky, 1996.

Gebhard, David. "The Spanish Colonial Revival in Southern California, 1895–1930." *Journal of the Society of Architectural Historians* 26 (1967): 131–47.

Gerdes, Jon Henry. "The Early Jews of Wilmington." *Lower Cape Fear Historical Society Bulletin* 28 (1984): 1–5.

Gero, Joan M., and Margaret W. Conkey, eds. *Engendering Archaeology: Women and Prehistory.* Oxford: Basil Blackwell, 1991.

Gibbons, James. *Reminiscences of Catholicity in North Carolina.* Baltimore: n.p., 1891.

Gill, Gillian. *Mary Baker Eddy.* Reading, Pa.: Perseus Books, 1998.

Godwin, John L. *Black Wilmington and the North Carolina Way: Portrait of a Community in the Era of Civil Rights Protest.* Lanham, Md.: University Press of America, 2000.

Goldfield, David R. "North Carolina's Early Twentieth-Century Suburbs and the Urbanizing South." In Bishir and Early, eds., *Early Twentieth-Century Suburbs,* 9–19.

Gomez, Michael A. *Exchanging Our Country Marks: The Transformation of African Identities in the Colonial and Antebellum South.* Chapel Hill: University of North Carolina Press, 1998.

Goodyear, Albert C. III, et al. "The Earliest South Carolinians." In Goodyear and Hanson, eds., *Studies in South Carolina Archaeology,* 19–52.

Goodyear, Albert C. III, and Glen T. Hanson, eds. *Studies in South Carolina Archaeology.* Columbia: University of South Carolina Press, 1989.

Gottschalk, Stephen. *The Emergence of Christian Science in American Religious Life.* Berkeley: University of California Press, 1973.

Gould, William B. *Diary of a Contraband.* Stanford, Calif.: Stanford University Press, 2002.

Govert, Gary R. "Something There Is That Doesn't Love a Wall: Reflections on the History of North Carolina's Religious Test for Public Office." *North Carolina Law Review* 64 (1986): 1071–98.

Gragg, Rod. *Confederate Goliath: The Battle of Fort Fisher.* Baton Rouge: Louisiana State University Press, 1991.

Grant, D. F. "Thomas Frederick Price." In Powell, ed., *Dictionary of North Carolina Biography,* 5:145.

Greene, William Jackson. "Silent Holocaust: The Influenza Epidemic of 1918–1919 and Its Effects on Wilmington, North Carolina." *Lower Cape Fear Historical Society Bulletin* 36 (1991): 1–7.

Gregory Congregational United Church of Christ 125th Anniversary Commemorative Book. Wilmington, N.C.: Gregory Congregational United Church of Christ, 1995.

Griffin, James B., ed. *Archaeology of Eastern United States*. Chicago: University of Chicago Press, 1952.

Grill, C. Franklin. *Methodism in the Upper Cape Fear Valley*. Nashville: Parthenon Press, 1966.

Grissom, W. L. *History of Methodism in North Carolina*. Nashville: Methodist Episcopal Church, South Publishing House, 1905.

Guilday, Peter. *The Life and Times of John England*. 2 vols. New York: Arno Press, 1927.

Gunter, S. Carol. *Carolina Heights*. Wilmington, N.C.: Planning Department of the City of Wilmington, 1982.

Gutjahr, Paul. *An American Bible: A History of the Good Book in the United States, 1777–1880*. Stanford, Calif.: Stanford University Press, 1999.

Haddad, Yvonne Y. "Make Room for the Muslims." In Conser and Twiss, eds., *Religious Diversity and American Religious History*, 218–61.

———, ed. *The Muslims of America*. New York: Oxford University Press, 1991.

Hallowell, Irving A. "Bear Ceremonialism in the North Hemisphere." *American Anthropologist* 28 (1926): 135–63.

Hamilton, George Heard. *The Art and Architecture of Russia*. Harmondsworth: Penguin, 1975.

Hamlin, Talbot. *Greek Revival Architecture in America*. New York: Oxford University Press, 1944.

Hamm, Thomas D. *The Quakers in America*. New York: Columbia University Press, 2003.

Hammett, Julia. "Ethnohistory of Aboriginal Landscapes in the Southeastern United States." *Southern Indian Studies* 41 (1992): 1–50.

Hammond, Phillip E. *Religion and Personal Autonomy: The Third Disestablishment in America*. Columbia: University of South Carolina, 1992.

Harley, Gail. "New Thought and the Harmonial Family." In Miller, ed., *America's Alternative Religions*, 325–30.

Harley, J. B. *The New Nature of Maps: Essays in the History of Cartography*. Edited by Paul Laxton. Baltimore: Johns Hopkins University Press, 2001.

Hartmann, Edward G. *Americans From Wales*. New York: Octagon Books, 1983.

Hatch, Nathan O., and John H. Wigger, eds. *Methodism and the Shaping of American Culture*. Nashville: Abingdon, 2001.

Haynes, Stephen R. *Noah's Curse: The Biblical Justification of American Slavery*. New York: Oxford University Press, 2002.

Haywood, Marshall D. *Lives of the Bishops of North Carolina*. Raleigh, N.C.: Alfred Williams, 1910.

Heatwole, Charles. "A Geography of the African Methodist Episcopal Zion Church." *Southeastern Geographer* 26 (1986): 1–11.

Higginbotham, Evelyn B. *Righteous Discontent: The Women's Movement in the Black Baptist Church, 1880–1920*. Cambridge, Mass.: Harvard University Press, 1993.

Hildebrand, Reginald F. *The Times Were Strange and Stirring*. Durham, N.C.: Duke University Press, 1995.

Hilton, William. "A Relation of a Discovery, 1664." In Salley, ed., *Narratives of Early Carolina*, 37–61.

Hinks, Peter P. *To Awaken My Afflicted Brethren: David Walker and the Problem of Antebellum Slave Resistance*. University Park: Pennsylvania State University Press, 1997.

———, ed. *David Walker's Appeal to the Colored Citizens of the World*. University Park: Pennsylvania State University Press, 2000.

Historical Sketch of St. Luke A.M.E. Zion Church. Wilmington, N.C.: St. Luke AME Zion Church, 1945.

A Historical Sketch of Southside Baptist Church, Wilmington, North Carolina, 1894–1994. Wilmington, N.C.: Southside Baptist Church, 1994.

History of the First Baptist Church. Wilmington, N.C.: First Baptist Church, 1979.

Hodges, John O. "Charles Manuel 'Sweet Daddy' Grace." In Lippy, ed., *20th Century Shapers of American Popular Religion*, 170–79.

Hoffman, Paul E. "Lucas Vazquez de Ayllón's Discovery and Colony." In Hudson and Tesser, eds., *Forgotten Centuries*, 36–49.

———. *A New Andalucia and a Way to the Orient: The American Southeast during the Sixteenth Century*. Baton Rouge: Louisiana State University Press, 1990.

Holloman, Charles R. "John Blacknall." In Powell, ed., *Dictionary of North Carolina Biography*, 1:167–68.

Honor, Hugh. *The New Golden Land: European Images of America from the Discoveries to the Present Time*. New York: Pantheon Books, 1975.

Horne, Robert. "A Brief Description of the Province of North Carolina, 1666." In Salley, ed., *Narratives of Early Carolina*, 65–73.

Howe, Mark De Wolfe. "Journal of Josiah Quincy, Junior, 1773." *Massachusetts Historical Society Proceedings* 49 (1916): 424–81.

Hudson, Charles. *The Southeastern Indians*. Knoxville: University of Tennessee Press, 1976.

———, ed. *The Black Drink: A Native American Tea*. Athens: University of Georgia Press, 1979.

Hudson, Charles, and Carmen Chaves Tesser, eds. *The Forgotten Centuries: Indians and Europeans in the American South, 1521–1704*. Athens: University of Georgia Press, 1994.

Hufham, J. D. *Memoir of Rev. John L. Prichard*. Raleigh, N.C.: Hufham and Hughes, 1867.

Huggins, M. A. *A History of North Carolina Baptists, 1727–1932*. Raleigh: Baptist State Convention of North Carolina, 1967.

Humphreys, Margaret. *Yellow Fever and the South*. New Brunswick, N.J.: Rutgers University Press, 1992.

Hunt, Thomas. *Life and Thoughts of Thomas P. Hunt*. Wilkes-Barre, Pa.: Robert Baur, 1901.

Hunter, James Davison. *Culture Wars: The Struggle to Define America*. New York: Basic Books, 1991.

Hutchison, William R. *Religious Pluralism in America*. New Haven, Conn.: Yale University Press, 2003.

Ingram, O. Kelly, ed. *Methodism Alive in North Carolina*. Durham, N.C.: Duke Divinity School, 1976,

Inscoe, John C. "Carolina Slave Names: An Index to Acculturation." *Journal of Southern History* 49 (1983): 527–53.

Isaac, Rhys. *The Transformation of Virginia, 1740–1790*. New York: Norton, 1988. Original ed. 1982.

Ivey, Paul E. *Prayers in Stone: Christian Science Architecture in the United States, 1894–1930*. Urbana: University of Illinois Press, 1999.

Jackson, Kenneth T. *Crabgrass Frontier: The Suburbanization of the United States*. New York: Oxford University Press, 1985.

Jackson, Richard W. *Places of Worship: 150 Years of Latter-day Saint Architecture*. Provo, Utah: Brigham Young University Press, 2003.

James, Fleming H. "Richard Marsden, Wayward Clergyman." *William and Mary Quarterly* 11 (1954): 578–91.

James, Horace. *Annual Report of the Superintendent of Negro Affairs in North Carolina, 1864*. Boston: Brown and Co., 1865.

Janson, H. W., and Anthony F. Janson. *History of Art: The Western Tradition*. Rev. 6th ed. Upper Saddle River, N.J.: Pearson and Prentice Hall, 2004.

Jeffries, Susan Herring. *Papa Wore No Halo*. Winston-Salem, N.C.: John Blair, 1963.

Jick, Leon A. *The Americanization of the Synagogue, 1820–1870*. Hanover, N.H.: University Press of New England, 1976.

Jochelson, Waldemar. *The Koryak*. Memoirs of the American Museum of Natural History. New York: American Museum of Natural History, 1905.

Johnson, Guion G. *Antebellum North Carolina*. Chapel Hill: University of North Carolina Press, 1937.

Johnson, Paul E., ed. *African-American Christianity*. Berkeley: University of California Press, 1994.

Jones, Thomas H. *The Experience of Thomas H. Jones Who Was a Slave*. New Bedford, Mass.: E. Anthony, 1871.

Jones, Wilbur D. Jr. *A Sentimental Journey: Memoirs of a Wartime Boomtown*. Shippensburg, Pa.: White Mane Books, 2002.

Kay, Marvin L. Michael. "The Payment of Provincial and Local Taxes in North Carolina, 1748–1771." *William and Mary Quarterly* 26 (1969): 218–40.

Kay, Marvin L. M., and Lorin L. Cary. *Slavery in North Carolina, 1748–1775*. Chapel Hill: University of North Carolina Press, 1995.

Kelly, Douglas F. *Carolina Scots*. Dillon, S.C.: 1739 Publications, 1998.

Kenneally, James T. *The History of American Catholic Women*. New York: Crossroad, 1990.

Kessler, Lawrence D. *The Jiangyin Mission Station: An American Missionary Community in China, 1895–1951*. Chapel Hill: University of North Carolina Press, 1996.

———. *North Carolina's "China Connection," 1840–1949*. Raleigh: North Carolina China Council, 1981.

Kester, J. Marcus. *Historical Sketch of First Baptist Church, Wilmington N.C. 1808–1933*. Wilmington, N.C.: First Baptist Church, 1933.

Ketcham, Earle H. "The Sources of the North Carolina Constitution of 1776." *North Carolina Historical Review* 6 (1929): 215–36.

Kierner, Cynthia. *Beyond the Household: Women's Place in the Early South.* Ithaca, N.Y.: Cornell University Press, 1998.

Kilde, Jeanne Halgren. *When Church Became Theatre: The Transformation of Evangelical Architecture and Worship in Nineteenth-Century America.* New York: Oxford University Press, 2002.

Kirk, J. Allen. *A Statement of Facts Concerning the Bloody Riot in Wilmington, N.C.* Wilmington, N.C.: J. Allen Kirk, 1898.

Kupperman, Karen Ordahl. *Indians and English: Facing Off in Early America.* Ithaca, N.Y.: Cornell University Press, 2000.

———, ed. *America in European Consciousness, 1493–1750.* Chapel Hill: University of North Carolina Press, 1995.

Lamb, James M. "Sketches of the History of Methodism in Fayetteville." In *Historical Papers of the North Carolina Conference Historical Society,* 34–49. Durham, N.C.: n.p., 1901.

Larsen, Lawrence H. *The Rise of the Urban South.* Lexington: University Press of Kentucky, 1985.

A Late Confederate Officer. "Wilmington during the Blockade." *Harper's Monthly Magazine* 196 (1866): 497–503

Lawson, John. *A New Voyage to Carolina.* Edited by Hugh T. Lefler. Chapel Hill: University of North Carolina Press, 1967.

Lee, Lawrence. *The History of Brunswick County, North Carolina.* Charlotte, N.C.: Heritage Press, 1980.

———. *Indian Wars in North Carolina, 1663–1763.* Raleigh, N.C.: Carolina Charter Tercentenary Commission, 1963.

———. *The Lower Cape Fear in Colonial Days.* Chapel Hill: University of North Carolina Press, 1965.

Lefler, Hugh T. "The Anglican Church in North Carolina: The Proprietary Period." In London and Lemmon, eds., *The Episcopal Church in North Carolina,* 1–19.

———. "The Anglican Church in North Carolina: The Royal Period." In London and Lemmon, eds., *The Episcopal Church in North Carolina,* 22–58.

Lefler, Hugh T., and William S. Powell. *Colonial North Carolina: A History.* New York: Charles Scribner's Sons, 1973.

Lemmon, Sarah M. "The Decline of the Church, 1776–1816." In London and Lemmon, eds., *The Episcopal Church in North Carolina,* 61–93.

Lennon, Donald R. "The Development of Town Government in Colonial North Carolina." In Steelman, ed., *Of Tar Heel Towns,* 1–25.

Lennon, Donald R., and Ida Brooks Kellam, eds. *The Wilmington Town Book: 1743–1778.* Raleigh, N.C.: Division of Archives and History, 1973.

Lerch, Patricia B. *Waccamaw Legacy: Contemporary Indians Fight for Survival.* Tuscaloosa: University of Alabama Press, 2004.

Let There Be Light. Wilmington, N.C.: First Presbyterian Church, 1990.

Lewis, Henry S. "The Formation of the Diocese of North Carolina." In London and Lemmon, eds., *The Episcopal Church in North Carolina,* 94–170.

Lewis, James R. *Peculiar Prophets: A Biographical Dictionary of New Religions.* St. Paul: Paragon House, 1999.

Lindley, Susan H. *You Have Stept out of Your Place.* Louisville, Ky.: Westminster John Knox Press, 1996.

Lippy, Charles, ed. *20th Century Shapers of American Popular Religion.* New York: Greenwood, 1989.

Little, Ann, ed. *Columbus County, North Carolina: Recollections and Records.* Whiteville, N.C.: County Commissioners, 1980.

Little, Ruth. *Sticks and Stones: Three Centuries of North Carolina Gravemarkers.* Chapel Hill: University of North Carolina Press, 1998.

Livingstone, John. "History of St. John's Lodge, no. 1, A.F. & A.M." *Nocalore* 1 (1931): 135–50.

Loftfield, Thomas. *Excavations at 310N33, a Late Woodland Seasonal Village.* Wilmington: Marine Science Fund, University of North Carolina at Wilmington, 1979.

———. "Ossuary Interments and Algonquian Expansion on the North Carolina Coast." *Southeastern Archaeology* (1990): 116–23.

Loftfield, Thomas, and David C. Jones. "Late Woodland Architecture on the Coast of North Carolina: Structural Meaning and Environmental Adaptation." *Southeastern Archaeology* 14 (1995): 120–35.

Logan, Frenise A. *The Negro in North Carolina, 1876–1894.* Chapel Hill: University of North Carolina Press, 1964.

London, Lawrence F. "Maurice Moore." In Powell, ed., *Dictionary of North Carolina Biography,* 4:303–4.

London, Lawrence F., and Sarah M. Lemmon, eds. *The Episcopal Church in North Carolina, 1701–1959.* Raleigh: Episcopal Diocese of North Carolina, 1987.

Long, Kathryn L. *The Revival of 1858.* New York: Oxford University Press, 1998.

Lonsdale, Richard E. *Atlas Of North Carolina.* Chapel Hill: University of North Carolina Press, 1967.

Loveland, Anne C., and Otis B. Wheeler. *From Meetinghouse to Megachurch: A Material and Cultural History.* Columbia: University of Missouri Press, 2003.

Luebke, Frederick C. *Bonds of Loyalty: German Americans and World War I.* De Kalb: Northern Illinois University Press, 1974.

Lutz, Catherine. *Homefront: A Military City and the American Twentieth Century.* Boston: Beacon Press, 2001.

Lyerly, Cynthia. *Methodism and the Southern Mind, 1770–1810.* New York: Oxford University Press, 1998.

Lyon, Eugene. *The Enterprise of Florida: Pedro Menéndez de Avilés and the Spanish Conquest of 1565–1568.* Gainesville: University Presses of Florida, 1976.

MacCord, Howard A. "The McLean Mound, Cumberland County, North Carolina." *Southern Indian Studies* 18 (1966): 3–45.

MacMillian, Henry J. "Colonial Plantations of the Lower Cape Fear." *Lower Cape Fear Historical Society Bulletin* 12 (1969): 1–6.

MacRae, Hugh. *Bringing Immigrants to the South.* New York: North Carolina Society of New York, 1908.

Maguire, Stephen D. "Tidewater Power Company." *Trolley Sparks* 81 (1948): 4, 7.

Marini, Stephen A. *Sacred Song in America: Religion, Music, and Popular Culture.* Urbana: University of Illinois Press, 2003.

Martin, James I. Sr. "The Palatine Settlements of 1710–1800." Occasional Papers of the Duplin County Historical Society. *Footnotes* 53 (1994): 1–4.

Martin, Jennifer F. *Along the Banks of the Old Northeast: The Historical and Architectural Development of Duplin County, North Carolina.* Rose Hill, N.C.: Duplin County Historical Foundation, 1999.

Martin, Sandy. *For God and Race: The Religious and Political Leadership of AMEZ Bishop James Walker Hood.* Columbia: University of South Carolina, 1999.

Maser, Frederick E., and Howard T. Maag, eds. *The Journal of Joseph Pilmore, Methodist Itinerant.* Philadelphia: Message Publishing Company, 1969.

Maser, Frederick, and George Singleton. "Further Branches of Methodism Are Founded." In Bucke, ed., *History of American Methodism,* 1:601–35.

Matheson, Susan B., and Derek Churchill. *Modern Gothic: The Revival of Medieval Art.* New Haven, Conn.: Yale University Art Gallery, 2000.

Mathews, Donald G. "Evangelical America—The Methodist Ideology." In Richey, ed., *Perspectives on American Methodism,* 17–30.

———. "North Carolina Methodists in the Nineteenth Century." In Ingram, ed., *Methodism Alive in North Carolina,* 59–74.

———. *Slavery and Methodism: A Chapter in American Morality, 1780–1845.* Princeton, N.J.: Princeton University Press, 1965.

Matthews, Carol. "Neo-Paganism and Witchcraft." In Miller, ed., *America's Alternative Religions,* 339–45.

Maynard, W. Barksdale. *Architecture in the United States, 1800–1850.* New Haven, Conn.: Yale University Press, 2002.

McCarl, Helen W., and Huw Christopher. *What God Hath Wrought: A History of the Little Chapel on the Boardwalk.* Wilmington, N.C.: Little Chapel on the Boardwalk, 1992.

McCloud, Aminah Beverly. *African American Islam.* New York: Routledge, 1995.

McDonald, Crummel H., and Lee A. Shelton. "History of St. Mark's Church." In *100th Anniversary, St. Mark's Episcopal Church.* Wilmington, N.C.: St. Mark's Episcopal Church, 1969.

McEachern, Leora H. *History of St. James Parish, 1729–1979.* Wilmington, N.C.: n.p., 1985.

McEachern, Leora H., and Isabel M Williams. "The Prevailing Epidemic— 1862." *Lower Cape Fear Historical Society Bulletin* 11 (1967): 1–20.

McGowan, Faison W., and Pearl C. McGowan, eds. *Flashes of Duplin's History and Government.* Kenansville, N.C.: n.p., 1971.

McKoy, Elizabeth F. *Wilmington Block by Block: From 1733 On.* Wilmington, N.C.: Edwards and Broughton, 1967.

McLaurin, Melton A. "Commemorating Wilmington's Racial Violence of

1898: From Individual to Collective Memory." *Southern Cultures* 6 (2000): 35–57.

McLoughlin, William G. *The Cherokees and Christianity, 1794–1870.* Athens: University of Georgia Press, 1994.

———. *Cherokees and Missionaries, 1789–1839.* New Haven, Conn.: Yale University Press, 1984.

———. *Modern Revivalism: Charles Grandison Finney to Billy Graham.* New York: Ronald Press, 1959.

———. *New England Dissent, 1630–1833: The Baptists and the Separation of Church and State.* 2 vols. Cambridge, Mass.: Harvard University Press, 1971.

McMillen, Sally G. *To Raise up the South: Sunday Schools in Black and White Churches, 1865–1915.* Baton Rouge: Louisiana State University Press, 2002.

Mead, Sidney. *The Lively Experiment.* New York: Harper and Row, 1963.

Meek, H. A. *The Synagogue.* London: Phaidon Press, 1995.

Megivern, Marjorie. *Human Relations—20 Years of Struggles, 1963–1983: A History of the New Hanover Human Relations Commission.* Wilmington, N.C.: New Hanover Human Relations Commission, 1984.

Melton, Julius. *Presbyterian Worship in America: Changing Patterns since 1787.* Richmond, Va.: John Knox Press, 1967.

Meredith, Hugh. *An Account of the Cape Fear Country.* Edited by Earl G. Swem. Perth Amboy, N.J.: Charles F. Heartman, 1922.

Merrill, William. "The Beloved Tree: *Ilex vomitoria* among Indians of the Southeast and Adjacent Regions." In Hudson, ed., *Black Drink,* 40–82.

Meyer, Duane. *The Highland Scots of North Carolina, 1732–1776.* Chapel Hill: University of North Carolina Press, 1961.

Miller, Donald. *Reinventing American Protestantism: Christianity in the New Millennium.* Berkeley: University of California Press, 1997.

Miller, Timothy, ed. *America's Alternative Religions.* Albany: State University of New York Press, 1995.

Milling, Chapman J. *Red Carolinians.* Columbia: University of South Carolina Press, 1969.

Mills, Frederick V. Sr. *Bishops by Ballot.* New York: Oxford University Press, 1978.

Minutes of the Methodist Conferences, 1773–1813. Swainsboro, Ga.: Magnolia Press, 1983. Original ed. 1813.

Minutes of the Presbytery of Inverary. In Clark and Curry, eds., *Colorful Heritage Documented,* 151–55.

Minutes of the Scottish Society for the Propagation of Christian Knowledge. In Clark and Curry, eds., *Colorful Heritage Documented,* 153–63.

Monahan, Elizabeth I. "Bioarchaeological Analysis of the Mortuary Practices at the Broad Reach Site (31CR218), Coastal North Carolina." *Southern Indian Studies* 44 (1995): 37–69.

Mooney, James. *The Aboriginal Population of America North of Mexico.* Washington, D.C.: Smithsonian Institution, 1928.

————. *The Siouan Tribes of the East.* Washington, D.C.: Government Printing Office, 1894.

Morgan, David T. Jr. "The Great Awakening in North Carolina: 1740–1775: The Baptist Phase." *North Carolina Historical Review* 45 (1968): 264–83.

Morison, Samuel Eliot. *The European Discovery of America: The Northern Voyages A.D. 500–1600.* New York: Oxford University Press, 1971.

Morris, Charles E. "Panic and Reprisal: Reaction in North Carolina to the Nat Turner Insurrection, 1831." *North Carolina Historical Review* 62 (1985): 29–52.

Murdoch, Alexander. "A Scottish Document Concerning Emigration to North Carolina in 1772." *North Carolina Historical Review* 67 (1990): 438–49.

Murray, Andrew E. *Presbyterians and the Negro—A History.* Philadelphia: Presbyterian Historical Society, 1966.

Murrett, John C. *Tar Heel Apostle: Thomas Frederick Price.* New York: Longmans, 1944.

Myers, William E. "Indian Trails of the Southeast." In *42nd Annual Report.* Washington, D.C.: Bureau of American Ethnology, 1928.

Newcombe, Alfred W. "The Appointment and Instruction of S.P.G. Missionaries." *Church History* (1936): 340–58.

Newsome, A. R., ed. *Records of Emigrants from England and Scotland to North Carolina, 1774–1775.* Raleigh, N.C.: Division of Archives and History, 1989.

North Carolina Conference Historical Directory. Raleigh: North Carolina Conference on Archives and History, 1984.

Norwood, Frederick A. *The Story of American Methodism.* Nashville: Abingdon Press, 1974.

Numrich, Paul David. *Old Wisdom in the New World: Americanization in Two Immigrant Theravada Buddhist Temples.* Knoxville: University of Tennessee Press, 1996.

Nye, David E. *Electrifying America: Social Meanings of a New Technology.* Cambridge, Mass.: MIT Press, 1990.

Oates, John A. *The Story of Fayetteville and the Upper Cape Fear.* Fayetteville, N.C.: n.p., 1950.

"Obituary: Hobart Brown Upjohn." *Architectural Record* 106 (1949): 158.

Ochs, Stephen J. *Desegregating the Altar: The Josephites and the Struggle for Black Priests, 1871–1960.* Baton Rouge: Louisiana State University Press, 1990.

Orth, John V. *The North Carolina State Constitution.* Chapel Hill: University of North Carolina Press, 1995.

Otto, Rudolf. *The Idea of the Holy.* Translated by John W. Harvey. New York: Oxford University Press, 1958.

Paper, Jordan. *Offering Smoke: The Sacred Pipe and Native American Religion.* Moscow: University of Idaho Press, 1988.

Parker, Freddie L. *Running for Freedom: Slave Runaways in North Carolina, 1775–1840.* New York: Garland, 1993.

Parker, Roy Jr. *Cumberland County: A Brief History.* Raleigh, N.C.: Department of Archives and History, 1990.

Parker, Weeks. *Fayetteville, North Carolina: A Pictorial History.* Norfolk, Va.: Donning Company, 1984.

Paschal, G. W. "Morgan Edwards' Materials towards a History of the Baptists in the Province of North Carolina." *North Carolina Historical Review* 7 (1930): 365–99.

Paulson, Ivar. "Zur Phänomenolgie des Schmanismus." *Zeitschrift für Religionsund Geistesgeschichte* 15 (1964): 121–41.

Peel, Robert. *Mary Baker Eddy: The Years of Discovery.* New York: Holt Rinehart and Winston, 1966.

Peterson, Jon A. "The Impact of Sanitary Reform upon American Urban Planning, 1840–1890." *Journal of Social History* 13 (1979): 83–104.

Pevsner, Nickolaus. *An Outline of European Architecture.* Harmondsworth: Penguin Books, 1963.

Pierson, William H. Jr. *American Buildings and Their Architects.* 2 vols. New York: Oxford University Press, 1970.

Placzek, Adolf K., ed. *Macmillan Encyclopedia of Architects.* 4 vols. New York: Collier Macmillan, 1982.

Powell, William S. *The North Carolina Gazetteer.* Chapel Hill: University of North Carolina Press, 1968.

———. *North Carolina through Four Centuries.* Chapel Hill: University of North Carolina Press, 1989.

———, ed. *Dictionary of North Carolina Biography.* 6 vols. Chapel Hill: University of North Carolina Press, 1979–1996.

Powers, William F. *Tar Heel Catholics: A History of Catholicism in North Carolina.* Lanham, Md.: University Press of America, 2003.

Prather, H. Leon Sr. *We Have Taken a City: Wilmington Racial Massacre and Coup of 1898.* Wilmington, N.C.: NU Enterprises, 1998.

Presbish, Charles S. *The Luminous Passage: The Practice and Study of Buddhism in America.* Berkeley: University of California, 1999.

Prebish, Charles S., and Kenneth K. Tanaka, eds. *The Faces of Buddhism in America.* Berkeley: University of California Press, 1998.

Preservation Society of Charleston. *The Churches of Charleston and the Lowcountry.* Columbia: University of South Carolina Press, 1994.

Pressley, Stephen. *A Decade of New Beginnings: CBFNC and the First Ten Years.* Winston-Salem, N.C.: CBFNC, 2004.

Prodromou, Elizabeth H. "Religious Pluralism in Twenty-first-Century America: Problematizing the Implications for Orthodox Christianity." *Journal of the American Academy of Religion* 72 (2004): 733–57.

Purcell, J. B. *Wilmington in Health and Disease.* Wilmington, N.C.: Journal Printer, 1867.

Raboteau, Albert J. "African-Americans, Exodus, and the American Israel." In Johnson, ed., *African-American Christianity,* 1–17.

———. *Slave Religion: The "Invisible Institution" in the Antebellum South.* New York: Oxford University Press, 1978.

Raguin, Virginia C. *Glory in Glass: Stained Glass in the United States.* New York: American Bible Society, 1999.

Rankin, Harriet. *History of First Presbyterian Church, Fayetteville, N.C.* Fayetteville, N.C.: First Presbyterian Church, 1928.

Rankin, Richard. *Ambivalent Churchmen and Evangelical Churchwomen.* Columbia: University of South Carolina Press, 1993.

Rawick, George, ed. *The American Slave.* 19 vols. Westport, Conn.: Greenwood Press, 1972.

Ray, Celeste. *Highland Heritage: Scottish Americans in the American South.* Chapel Hill: University of North Carolina Press, 2001.

Reaves, Bill. *Southport (Smithville): A Chronology.* 2nd ed. 4 vols. Wilmington, N.C.: Broadfoot Publishing, 1985.

———. *Strength through Struggle.* Wilmington, N.C.: New Hanover County Library, 1998.

Records of the Welsh Tract Baptist Meeting, Pencader Hundred, New Castle County, Delaware. Papers of the Historical Society of Delaware. Wilmington, Del.: Historical Society of Delaware, 1904.

Redkey, Edwin S., ed. *A Grand Army of Black Men.* New York: Cambridge University Press, 1992.

Rice, Tamara Talbot. *A Concise History of Russian Art.* New York: Praeger, 1963.

Richardson, Joe M. *Christian Reconstruction: The American Missionary Association and Southern Blacks, 1861–1890.* Athens: University of Georgia Press, 1986.

Richey, Russell E. *Early American Methodism.* Bloomington: Indiana University Press, 1991.

Richey, Russell E., and Robert B. Mullins, eds. *Reimagining Denominationalism.* New York: Oxford University Press, 1994.

Richey, Russell E., et al., eds. *Connectionalism, Ecclesiology, Mission, and Identity.* Nashville: Abingdon Press, 1997.

Richey, Russell E., et al., eds. *Perspectives on American Methodism: Interpretive Essays.* Nashville: Abingdon Press, 1993.

Robinson, William H. *From Log Cabin to the Pulpit or Fifteen Years in Slavery.* Eau Claire, Wis.: James Tifft, 1913.

Roof, Wade Clark. *Spiritual Marketplace: Baby Boomers and the Remaking of American Religion.* Princeton, N.J.: Princeton University Press, 1999.

Roof, Wade Clark, and William McKinney. *American Mainline Religion.* New Brunswick, N.J.: Rutgers University Press, 1987.

Roth, Leland. *American Architecture: A History.* Boulder, Colo.: Westview Press, 2001.

Rowe, Kenneth E. "Redesigning Methodist Churches: Auditorium-Style Sanctuaries and Akron-Plan Sunday Schools in Romanesque Costume, 1875–1925." In Richey et al., eds., *Connectionalism,* 117–34.

Ruether, Rosemary R., and Rosemary S. Keller, eds. *Women and Religion in America.* 3 vols. New York: Harper and Row, 1986.

Rusk, William S. "Thomas U. Walter and His Works." *Americana Illustrated* 33 (1939): 151–79.

Russell, Anne, and Marjorie Megivern. *North Carolina Portraits of Faith.* Norfolk, Va.: Donning Company, 1986.

St. John's Episcopal Church. Wilmington, N.C.: St. John Episcopal Church, n.d.

St. Nicholas Greek Orthodox Church, 50th Anniversary, 1945–1995, Wilmington, North Carolina. Wilmington, N.C.: St. Nicholas Greek Orthodox Church, 1995.

St. Thomas the Apostle Catholic Church. Wilmington, N.C.: St. Thomas the Apostle Catholic Church, 1947.

Salley, Alexander S. Jr., ed. *Narratives of Early Carolina, 1650–1708*. New York: Charles Scribner's Sons, 1911.

Sarna, Jonathan D. *American Judaism: A History*. New Haven, Conn.: Yale University Press, 2004.

Saunders, William L., ed. *The Colonial Records of North Carolina*. 10 vols. Raleigh, N.C.: P. M. Hale, 1886–1890.

Savitt, Todd L., and James H. Young, eds. *Disease and Distinctiveness in the American South*. Knoxville: University of Tennessee Press, 1988.

Schaff, Philip. *America*. Edited by Perry Miller. Cambridge, Mass.: Harvard University Press, 1961.

Schlereth, Thomas J. "A High Victorian Gothicist as Beaux-Arts Classicist: The Architectural Odyssey of Solon Spencer Beman." *Studies in Medievalism* 3 (1990): 129–52.

Schmidt, Jean Miller. *Grace Sufficient: A History of Women in American Methodism, 1760–1939*. Nashville: Abingdon Press, 1999.

Schmidt, Leigh Eric. *Holy Fairs: Scottish Communion and American Revivals in the Early Modern Period*. Princeton, N.J.: Princeton University Press, 1989.

Schneider, A. Gregory. *The Way of the Cross Leads Home: The Domestication of American Methodism*. Bloomington: Indiana University Press, 1993.

Schoepf, Johann. *Travels in the Confederation, 1783–1784*. Edited by Alfred J. Morrison. 2 vols. New York: Burt Franklin, 1911.

Schuyler, David. *The New Urban Landscape*. Baltimore: Johns Hopkins University Press, 1986.

Seager, Richard Hughes. *Buddhism in America*. New York: Columbia University Press, 1999.

Seagrave, Sterling. *The Soong Dynasty*. New York: Harper and Row, 1985.

Seapker, Janet K. "Wood Works: The Architectural Creations and Personal Histories of John Coffin and Robert Barclay Wood." *Lower Cape Fear Historical Society Bulletin* 39 (1994).

Seigler, Morris G. *History of St. Andrews-Covenant Presbyterian Church, Wilmington, N.C.* Wilmington, N.C.: St. Andrews-Covenant Presbyterian Church, 1967.

Sernett, Milton C. *Black Religion and American Evangelicalism: White Protestants, Plantation Missions, and the Flowering of Negro Christianity, 1787–1865*. Metuchen, N.J.: Scarecrow Press, 1975.

Seventy-fifth Anniversary Memorial of the First Presbyterian Church, Wilmington, N.C. Richmond, N.C.: Whittet and Shepperson, 1893.

75th Jubilee, St. Mary Church, Wilmington, North Carolina, 1912–1987. Wilmington, N.C.: St. Mary Church, 1987.

Shea, John Gilmary. *A History of the Catholic Church within the Limits of the United States*. 4 vols. New York: Arno Press, 1978. Original ed. 1886–1892.

Sheridan, Robert E. *The Founders of Maryknoll*. Maryknoll, N.Y.: Maryknoll Fathers, 1980.

Shibley, Mark A. *Resurgent Evangelicalism in the United States: Mapping Cultural Changes since 1970*. Columbia: University of South Carolina Press, 1996.

Singleton, William Henry. *Recollections of My Slavery Days*. Raleigh, N.C.: Division of Archives and History, 1999.

Sizer, Sandra. "Politics and Apolitical Religion: The Great Urban Revivals of the Late Nineteenth Century." *Church History* 48 (1979): 81–98.

Skinner, W. T. *History of the Pencader Presbyterian Church*. Wilmington, Del.: John M. Rogers Press, 1899.

Slattery, Francis E. "The Catholic Woman in Modern Times." In Ruether and Keller, eds., *Women and Religion*, 3:187–91.

Sloane, David C. *The Last Great Necessity: Cemeteries in American History*. Baltimore: Johns Hopkins University Press, 1991.

Smith, Bruce D. *Rivers of Change: Essays on Early Agriculture in Eastern North America*. Washington, D.C.: Smithsonian Institution Press, 1992.

Smith, Charles S. *A History of the African Methodist Episcopal Church*. Philadelphia: Book Concern of the AME Church, 1922.

Smith, Claiborne Jr. "Richard Marsden." In Powell, ed., *Dictionary of North Carolina Biography*, 4:219–20.

Smith, Everard H. "Wartime Wilmington: An Overview." *Lower Cape Fear Historical Society Bulletin* 43 (1999): 1–7.

Smith, Jane I. *Islam In America*. New York: Columbia University Press, 1999.

Smith, Margaret Supplee. "The American Idyll in North Carolina's First Suburbs: Landscape and Architecture." In Bishir and Early, eds., *Early Twentieth-Century Suburbs*, 21–28.

Smith, Margaret S., and Emily H. Wilson. *North Carolina Women: Making History*. Chapel Hill: University of North Carolina Press, 1999.

Smith, Michael, and Jane Smith. *The Lumbee Methodists*. Raleigh: North Carolina Methodist Conference, 1990.

Smoot, Thomas A. "Early Methodism on the Lower Cape Fear." In *Historical Papers of the North Carolina Conference Historical Society*. Durham, N.C.: n.p., 1925.

Sorin, Gerald. *A Time for Building: The Third Immigration, 1880–1920*. Baltimore: Johns Hopkins University Press, 1992.

South, Stanley A. *An Archaeological Survey of Southeastern North Carolina*. Institute of Archaeology and Anthropology, Notebook 8. Columbia: University of South Carolina Press, 1976.

———. *Colonial Brunswick, 1726–1776*. Raleigh, N.C.: Department of Archives and History, 1960.

———. "Exploratory Excavation of the MacFayden Mound, Brunswick County." *Southern Indian Studies* 18 (1966): 59–61.

Souvenir of Wilmington, N.C. Wilmington, N.C.: C. Yates, 1915.

Sparks, John. *The Roots of Appalachian Christianity: The Life and Legacy of Elder Shubal Stearns*. Lexington: University Press of Kentucky, 2001.

Spindel, Donna J. *Crime and Society in North Carolina, 1663–1776*. Baton Rouge: Louisiana State University Press, 1989.

Sprunt, James. *Chronicles of the Cape Fear River, 1660–1916*. Wilmington, N.C.: Broadfoot Publishing, 1992. Original ed. 1916.

Staib, Donald F., ed. *Diocese of Raleigh: Histories 1982*. Raleigh, N.C.: Diocese of Raleigh, 1982.

Stanton, Phoebe B. *The Gothic Revival and American Church Architecture*. Baltimore: Johns Hopkins University Press, 1968.

Steelman, Joseph F., ed. *Of Tar Heel Towns, Shipbuilders, Reconstructionists, and Alliancemen*. Greenville, N.C.: East Carolina University Publications, 1981.

Steevens, G. W. *The Land of the Dollar*. New York: Dodd Mead and Co., 1897.

Stevens, George. "John Urmston." In Powell, ed., *Dictionary of North Carolina Biography*, 6: 77–81.

Stewart, A. J. B. "The North Carolina Settlement of 1739." In Clark and Curry, eds., *Colorful Heritage Documented*, 140–48.

Stockman, Robert H. "The American Baha'i Community in the Nineties." In Miller, ed., *America's Alternative Religions*, 243–48.

Stowe, David W. *How Sweet the Sound: Music in the Spiritual Lives of Americans*. Cambridge, Mass.: Harvard University Press, 2004.

Stowell, Daniel W. *Rebuilding Zion: The Religious Reconstruction of the South, 1863–1877*. New York: Oxford University Press, 1998.

Summers, Thomas O., ed. *Autobiography of the Rev. Joseph Travis, A.M.* Nashville: E. Stevenson, 1856.

Swanton, John R. "Aboriginal Culture of the Southeast." In *42nd Annual Report*. Washington, D.C.: Bureau of American Ethnology, 1928.

———. *The Indians of the Southeastern United States*. Washington, D.C.: Smithsonian Institution Press, 1946.

Sweet, Leonard I. "'A Nation Born Again': The Union Prayer Meeting Revival and Cultural Revitalization." In *In the Great Tradition: Essays on Pluralism, Voluntarism, and Revivalism*, edited by Joseph D. Ban and Paul R. Dekar, 193–221. Valley Forge, Pa.: Judson Press, 1982.

Tarr, Joel A. "Urban Pollution—Many Long Years Ago." *American Heritage* 22 (1971): 65–69.

Taves, Ann. *The Household of Faith: Roman Catholic Devotions in Mid-Century America*. Notre Dame, Ind.: University of Notre Dame, 1986.

Taylor, Raymond H. *A History of Winter Park Baptist Church, 1913–1988*. Wilmington, N.C.: Jackson and Bell, 1988.

Tetterton, Beverly, et al., eds. *History of the Temple of Israel, Wilmington, North Carolina, 1876–2001*. Wilmington, N.C.: Temple of Israel, 2001.

Thomas, Charlene. *The History of Myrtle Grove Presbyterian Church, 1945–1995*. Wilmington, B.C.: Myrtle Grove Presbyterian Church, 1995.

Thompson, Ernest Trice. *Presbyterians in the South*. 3 vols. Richmond, Va.: John Knox Press, 1963–1973.

Thucydides. *The Complete Writings.* New York: Random House, 1934.

Tiffany, Nina Moore, ed. *Letters of James Murray, Loyalist.* Boston: n.p., 1901.

Tise, Larry E. "North Carolina Methodism from the Revolution to the War of 1812." In Ingram, ed., *Methodism Alive in North Carolina,* 33–48.

———. *Proslavery: A History of the Defense of Slavery in America, 1701–1840.* Athens: University of Georgia Press, 1987.

Tocqueville, Alexis de. *Democracy in America.* 2 vols. Edited by Phillips Bradley. New York: Vintage Books, 1945.

Tower, Philo. *Slavery Unmasked.* New York: Negro Universities Press, 1969. Original ed. 1856.

Trainor, Kevin, ed. *Buddhism: The Illustrated Guide.* New York: Oxford University Press, 2004.

A Tribute to Oakdale, 1852–1991. Wilmington, N.C.: Oakdale Cemetery Company, 1991.

Trinkley, Michael B. "An Archaeological Overview of the South Carolina Woodland Period: It's the Same Old Riddle." In Goodyear and Hanson, eds., *Studies in South Carolina Archaeology,* 73–89.

Tucker, Karen B. Westerfield. *American Methodist Worship.* New York: Oxford University Press, 2001.

Turberg, Edward F. *Sunset Park Neighborhood Architectural Survey.* Wilmington, N.C.: Historic Wilmington Foundation, 1996.

———. *A Survey of Black Historical Sites in Wilmington, New Hanover County, North Carolina.* Wilmington, N.C.: City of Wilmington, 1983.

Turner, Richard B. *Islam in the African-American Experience.* Bloomington: Indiana University Press, 1997.

Tweed, Thomas A. "Asian Religions in the United States: Reflections on an Emerging Subfield." In Conser and Twiss, eds., *Religious Diversity and American Religious History,* 189–217.

———. *Buddhism and Barbeque: A Guide to Buddhist Temples in North Carolina.* Chapel Hill: Buddhism in North Carolina Project, 2001.

Twenty-fifth Anniversary of St. Mary's Pro-Cathedral. Wilmington, N.C.: St. Mary Pro-Cathedral, 1937.

Vecsey, Christopher. "A Century of Lakota Sioux Catholicism at Pine Ridge." In Conser and Twiss, eds., *Religious Diversity and American Religious History,* 262–95.

Vincent, Robert W. "Successful Immigrants in the South." *World's Work* 17 (1908): 10908–11.

Wach, Joachim. *Sociology of Religion.* Chicago: University of Chicago Press, 1944.

Waddell, Alfred W. *History of New Hanover County and the Lower Cape Fear Region, 1723–1800.* Wilmington, N.C.: n.p., 1909.

Walker, Alexander M., ed. *New Hanover County Court Minutes.* 4 vols. Bethesda, N.C.: Alexander M. Walker, 1958–1960.

Walker, Clarence E. *A Rock in a Weary Land: The African Methodist Episcopal Church during the Civil War and Reconstruction.* Baton Rouge: Louisiana State University Press, 1982.

Walls, William J. *The African Methodist Episcopal Zion Church*. Charlotte, N.C.: AME Zion Publishing House, 1974.

Ward, H. Trawick, and R. P. Stephen Davis Jr. *Indian Communities on the North Carolina Piedmont, A.D. 1000 to 1700*. Monograph 2. Chapel Hill: Research Laboratories of Anthropology, University of North Carolina, 1993.

———. *Time before History: The Archaeology of North Carolina*. Chapel Hill: University of North Carolina Press, 1999.

Ward, H. Trawick, and Jack H. Wilson Jr. "Archaeological Excavation at the Cold Morning Site." *Southern Indian Studies* 32 (1980): 5–40.

Washington, James M., ed. *Testament of Hope: The Essential Writings of Martin Luther King, Jr.* San Francisco: HarperSanFrancisco, 1991.

Watkin, David. *A History of Western Architecture*. New York: Barnes and Noble, 1996.

Watkins, Greg. *Wrightsville Beach: A Pictorial History*. Wrightsville Beach, N.C.: Wrightsville Beach Publishing Company, 1997.

Watson, Alan D. "The Anglican Parish in Royal North Carolina, 1729–1775." *Historical Magazine of the Protestant Episcopal Church* 48 (1979): 303–19.

———. *A History of New Bern and Craven County*. New Bern, N.C.: Tryon Palace Commission, 1987.

———. "Impulse toward Independence: Resistance and Rebellion among North Carolina Slaves, 1730–1775." *Journal of Negro History* 63 (1978): 317–27.

———. *Wilmington, North Carolina, to 1861*. Jefferson, N.C.: McFarland and Company, 2003.

———. *Wilmington: Port of North Carolina*. Columbia: University of South Carolina Press, 1992.

Watson, Elkanah. *Men and Times of the Revolution or Memoirs of Elkanah Watson*. New York: Dana and Company, 1856.

Watson, Patty Jo, and Mary C. Kennedy. "The Development of Horticulture in the Eastern Woodlands of North America: Women's Role." In Gero and Conkey, eds., *Engendering Archaeology*, 255–75.

Waxman, Barbara, et al., eds. *The First Hundred Years: A History of B'nai Israel Synagogue, 1898–1998*. Wilmington, N.C.: B'nai Israel Synagogue, 1998.

Weaver, Mary Jo, and R. Scott Appleby, eds. *Being Right: Conservative Catholics in America*. Bloomington: Indiana University Press, 1995.

Webb, Gisela. "Sufism in America." In Miller, ed., *America's Alternative Religions*, 249–58.

Weeder, Gilbert L., and Ann Hewlett Hutteman. "Frank Ellsworth Weeder." *Stained Glass* 92 (1997): 130–36.

Weeks, Stephen Beauregard. *Church and State in North Carolina*. Baltimore: Johns Hopkins Press, 1893.

Weir, Robert M. *Colonial South Carolina: A History*. Millwood, N.Y.: KTO Press, 1983.

Weitz, Martin, ed. *Bibilog*. Wilmington, N.C.: Temple of Israel, 1976.

Welter, Barbara. "The Cult of True Womanhood, 1820–1860." *American Quarterly* 18 (1966): 151–74.

Whitefield, George. *George Whitefield's Journals*. Edinburgh: Banner of Truth Trust, 1989.

Whitener, Daniel J. *Prohibition in North Carolina, 1715–1945*. Chapel Hill: University of North Carolina Press, 1946.

Wigger, John H. *Taking Heaven by Storm: Methodism and the Rise of Popular Christianity in America*. New York: Oxford University Press, 1998.

Wightman, William M., ed. *Life of William Capers*. Nashville: Southern Methodist Publishing House, 1859.

Wilcox, Melissa M. *Coming out in Christianity: Religion, Identity, and Community*. Bloomington: Indiana University Press, 2003.

Wilkins, Ernest Hatch. "Arcadia in America." *Proceedings of the American Philosophical Society* 101 (1957): 4–30.

Williams, Duncan R, and Christopher S. Queens, eds., *American Buddhism*. Richmond, England: Curzon, 1999.

Willis, Michael. "Monastic Architecture." In Trainor, ed., *Buddhism*, 100–103.

Wilmington: The Metropolis and Port of North Carolina. Wilmington, N.C.: Chamber of Commerce, 1912.

Wilson, Charles R. *Baptized in Blood: The Religion of the Lost Cause, 1865–1920*. Athens: University of Georgia Press, 1980.

Wilson, William H. *The City Beautiful Movement*. Baltimore: Johns Hopkins University Press, 1989.

Winberry, John J. "'Lest We Forget': The Confederate Monument and the Southern Townscape." *Southeastern Geographer* 23 (1983): 107–21.

The Windows of St. Paul's. Wilmington, N.C.: St. Paul's Church, 1989.

Winter, Gibson. *The Suburban Captivity of the Churches*. New York: Macmillan, 1962.

Winter, Joseph C. "From Earth Mother to Snake Woman: The Role of Tobacco in the Evolution of Native American Religious Organizations." In Winter, ed., *Tobacco Use by Native Americans*, 265–304.

———, ed. *Tobacco Use by Native North Americans: Sacred Smoke and Silent Killer*. Norman: University of Oklahoma Press, 2000.

Wischnitzer, Rachael. *Synagogue Architecture in the United States: History and Interpretation*. Philadelphia: Jewish Publication Society of America, 1955.

Wolfe, Patrick. "Imperialism and History." *American Historical Review* 102 (1997): 388–420.

Wood, Lillian Fordham. "The Reverend John LaPierre." *Historical Magazine of the Protestant Episcopal Church* 90 (1971): 407–30.

Worsely, Stephen C. "Catholicism in Antebellum North Carolina." *North Carolina Historical Review* 60 (1983): 399–430.

Wosh, Peter J. *Spreading the Word: The Bible Business in Nineteenth-Century America*. Ithaca, N.Y.: Cornell University Press, 1994.

Wrenn, Tony. *Wilmington, North Carolina: An Architectural and Historical Portrait*. Charlottesville: University Press of Virginia, 1984.

Wright, J. Leitch Jr. *The Only Land They Knew: The Tragic Story of the American Indians of the Old South*. New York: Free Press, 1981.

———. "William Hilton's Voyage to Carolina in 1662." *Essex Institute Historical Collections* 105 (1969): 96–102.

Wroth, Lawrence C. *The Voyages of Giovanni da Verrazzano, 1524–1528.* New Haven, Conn.: Yale University Press, 1970.

Wuthnow, Robert. *The Restructuring of American Religion.* Princeton, N.J.: Princeton University Press, 1988.

———, ed. *I Come Away Stronger: How Small Groups Are Shaping American Religion.* Grand Rapids, Mich.: Eerdmans Publishing Co., 1994.

Yearns, Buck. "George Davis." In Powell, ed., *Dictionary of North Carolina Biography,* 2:32–33.

Zaitzevsky, Cynthia. *The Architecture of William Ralph Emerson, 1833–1917.* Cambridge: Fogg Art Museum, 1969.

Zikmund, Barbara Brown, "Winning Ordination for Women in Mainstream Protestant Churches." In Ruether and Keller, eds., *Women and Religion in America,* 3:339–48.

Theses, Dissertations, Lectures, and Typescripts

Baker, Gloria B. "Dissenters in Colonial North Carolina." Ph.D. diss., University of North Carolina at Chapel Hill, 1970.

Beeker, Henry Judson. "Wilmington during the Civil War." Master's thesis, Duke University, 1941.

Bell, John L. Jr. "Protestant Churches and the Negro in North Carolina during Reconstruction." Master's thesis, University of North Carolina at Chapel Hill, 1961.

Boruch, Nestor J. "In Observance of the 50th Anniversary of Sts. Peter and Paul Russian Orthodox Church." Typescript, 1982.

Brewer, James H. "Account of Negro Slavery in the Cape Fear Region Prior to 1860." Ph.D. diss., University of Pittsburgh, 1949.

"A Brief History of Fifth Avenue United Methodist Church." Typescript, n.d.

"Calvary Baptist Church." Typescript, 1992.

Caudle, William. "The Highland Scots in the Cape Fear Region." Cape Fear Museum, Wilmington, N.C., November 5, 1999.

Corey, John F. "The Colonization and Contributions of Emigrants Brought to Southeastern North Carolina by Hugh MacRae." Master's thesis, Appalachian State Teachers College, 1957.

Garaventa, Louis. "Bishop James Gibbons and the Growth of the Roman Catholic Church in North Carolina, 1868–1872." Master's thesis, University of North Carolina at Chapel Hill, 1973.

Hirsch, Charles B. "The Experience of the S.P.G. in Eighteenth Century North Carolina." Ph.D. diss., Indiana University, 1953.

Jeffries, Harriet O. "Brief History of Saint Paul's Church." Typescript, 1978.

Jones, Maxine D. "'A Glorious Work': The American Missionary Association and Black North Carolinians, 1863–1880." Ph.D. diss., Florida State University, 1982.

McMillan, William O., and Donna Flake. "A Visit from Kate and Yellow Jack." American Osler Society annul meeting, Charleston, S.C., April 18, 2001.

Pasulka, Diana Walsh. "The Aesthetics of Nostalgia: The Return of the Real in Postmodern Christian Discourse." Ph.D. diss., Syracuse University, 2003.

Raper, Derris Lea. "The Effects of David Walker's *Appeal* and Nat Turner's Insurrection on North Carolina." Master's thesis, University of North Carolina at Chapel Hill, 1969.

Rogoff, Leonard. "The History of Jews in North Carolina." Cape Fear Museum, Wilmington, N.C., January 21, 2001.

"St. Matthew's Evangelical Church, Wilmington, North Carolina, 1892–1992." Typescript, 1992.

Westbrook, Betty Sue. "History of Trinity United Methodist Church, Wilmington, North Carolina, 1881–1991." Typescript, 1991.

Wilde-Ramsing, Mark. "Archaeological Survey and Testing on Prehistoric Shell Midden Sites in New Hanover County, North Carolina." Master's thesis, Catholic University of America, 1984.

Wojcik, Susan B. "Thomas U. Walter and Iron in the United States Capitol: An Alliance of Architecture, Engineering, and Industry." Ph.D. diss., University of Delaware, 1999.

Wood, Richard E. "Port Town at War: Wilmington, North Carolina, 1860–1865." Ph.D. diss., Florida State University, 1976.

Index